Fighting Ships and Prisons

The publication of this book was
assisted by the Atkinson Fund

FIGHTING SHIPS AND PRISONS

The Mediterranean Galleys of France in the Age of Louis XIV

PAUL W. BAMFORD

with drawings by John W. Ekstrom

The University of Minnesota Press • Minneapolis

Published in Great Britain and India
by the Oxford University Press, London
and Delhi, and in Canada by the Copp Clark Publishing Co.
Limited, Toronto

Library of Congress Catalog Card Number: 72-92334

ISBN 0-8166-0655-2

Part of the sixth chapter, "Officers and the Crown," appeared
in modified form as "The Knights of Malta and the Kings of
France, 1665–1700," in *French Historical Studies*, 1964, 429–453.
A large part of the eighth chapter, "The Procurement of
Slaves," appeared in modified form as an essay entitled "Slaves
for the Galleys of France, 1665 to 1700," in John Parker's
festschrift for James Ford Bell, *Merchants and Scholars*
(Minneapolis: University of Minnesota Press, 1965), 171–191;
© 1965 by the University of Minnesota. An early version of parts
of the chapters "The Procurement of Slaves" and "Condemnations to the Oar" appeared in "The Procurement of Oarsmen
for French Galleys, 1660–1748," in *American Historical Review*,
October 1959, No. 1, 31–48. Scattered parts of the "Conclusions
and Reflections" were included in "The Barbary Pirates:
Victims and the Scourge of Christendom," James Ford Bell
Lecture, University of Minnesota, 1973.

To Polly, Stacey, Philip, and Tom

Preface

The history of French galleys has never before been the subject of a book in the English language. This is surprising, since the subject has drawn much attention and many writers in France. Perhaps the nearest approximation to a treatment in English is the memoir of Jean Marteilhe, a Huguenot condemned to the galleys for his faith, who not only survived but obtained his release and wrote about his experiences from exile in Amsterdam and London. Naturally enough, French Protestants have been particularly drawn to the subject of galleys. One of the best and most assiduous of the twentieth-century scholars in this Huguenot tradition was the late Gaston Tournier. His principal work is a monumental compendium of the names and biographical sketches of Protestant galériens, preceded by an essay on the galleys of France; those three volumes bring together the results of his earlier work and some of that by coreligionist predecessors.

Understandably, not all French historians have found this somber, partly sectarian subject of galley history to their taste. When mentioning the topic at all, some historians (and other writers as well) have treated galley history as a phase of technical or foreign naval history, as did Jurien de la Gravière. Some have approached it as an incidental phase of some biographical study, where the focus was naturally on the man — for example, Roncière's *Valbelle* and Jal's *Duquesne*. Galleys have been played down in general histories of the French navy, being considered to have had little importance as fighting ships and therefore to have been unimportant. This traditional but narrow conception of the nature of naval history, the gunsmoke approach, often fascinating in itself, has been broadened in this book.

Among the works by French historians treating the subject of galleys, several of the early ones (Laforet, Savine) drew heavily on the memoirs of Marteilhe, though of course both of them also made use of archival materials. In the early 1930's, Yvonne Bezard published a monograph dealing with the family of one of the intendants of the period, Michel Bégon; another intendant, Nicolas Arnoul, received treatment about that time in a careful study by Gaston Rambert. Then Paul Masson made a more general contribution, in the form of two long articles published in the *Annales de la Faculté des Lettres d'Aix* (1937); Masson already had detailed knowledge of the history of the city and region of Marseilles, its maritime commerce, and its role in early modern Mediterranean history — almost half of his book-length study concerned the galleys of the age of Louis XIV. In addition, a number of other significant articles and notes, old and recent, have been valuable in the preparation of the present work, but the bibliography lists only those actually cited in connection with the text. The bulk of the data for the present work were drawn from the manuscript holdings of the central archive of the ministry of marine at the Archives Nationales.

No period in the history of oar-driven craft is richer in documentation than the age of Louis XIV. By then the bureaucracy and paperwork of modern times had begun to create staggering quantities of correspondence and office files connected with government administration. Hundreds of volumes and cartons of papers relating to the history of galleys survive in official archives from the seventeenth and eighteenth centuries. They constitute an enormously rich source, carefully kept. But since it was also an age for which some family archives are rich, though not now open to public use, many particular phases of galley history including the roles of some distinguished officers remain obscure, and when treated can throw much more light on many phases of the subject.

Every historian has debts. Mine to archivists and librarians are very great. Many on the staffs of the Archives Nationales, Archives des Affaires Étrangères, and Bibliothèque Nationale have helped. The facilities and holdings of the Service Historique de la Marine were placed at my disposal, at the Bibliothèque Historique de la Marine, Bibliothèque du Service Hydrographique, Dépôt des Cartes et Plans and Musée de la Marine in Paris, and in the provinces, at the Archives of the IIIᵉ Région Maritime in Toulon. At Aix-en-Provence and Marseilles, help and the benefits of an "open door" policy were received in various archives and libraries, in the Archives Départementales du Bouches-du-Rhône, Archives Municipales, and the Archives de la Chambre de Commerce. In London, the staffs of the British Museum, the Public Record Office, and the University of London, Institute of Historical Research, and related facilities were most cooperative, as were the staff of the National Maritime Museum at Greenwich, and that of the (Royal) Malta Archives and Library, and at the (Royal) University of Malta. The Bibliothèque de la Société de l'Histoire du Protestantisme Français in Paris and the Library of the Huguenot Society of London were both used, as were the collections of the Royal Library in Copenhagen, the New York Public Library, the Firestone Library of Princeton University, and most of all of course, the libraries of The Ohio State University and the University of Minnesota.

Mention should also be made of the institutions whose cooperation made possible the preparation and shipment of a considerable number of volumes of documents from Toulon to Paris for use and filming in Paris: the VIᵉ Section of the École des Hautes Études, University of Paris, the Service Historique de la Marine, the Archives du IIIᵉ Region Maritime, the Archives Nationales, and the Graduate School of the University of Minnesota. Without their assistance, some of the documents at Toulon could not have been used in connection with this study.

Many individuals gave helpful counsel at various stages of the research and writing. I am grateful to all of them. But I want particularly to acknowledge the help, in the research, from Mlle Mireille Forget at Toulon, the late Olivier de Prat and his successor as conservateur of the navy papers at the Archives Nationales, Étienne Taillemite. In work with the manuscript, I had help from Professors Ragnhild Hatton, Georges A. Barrois, Halil Inalcik, Harold T. Parker, Thorsten Sellin, Mulford Sibley, and Martin Wolfe, all of whom read substantial parts of the manuscript and gave me the benefit of comment and criticism. Of course none of these helpful people is in any way responsible for the faults, though each one did share, in some degree, in making it a better book. A succession of graduate assistants and students have done that too, by helping to compile and interpret statistical evidence concerning slaves, men condemned to the galleys, and Knights of Malta; among these students: Ronald Abler, Robert C. Adams, Mary Dunlap, Thadd E. Hall, Gregory Weiler, and Gordon Mork.

The writer's research on this subject dates from 1955–56, and was inaugurated during tenure on an E. C. Howald Faculty Fellowship from The Ohio State University. In 1960–61 Guggenheim and Fulbright research fellowships permitted additional work in France, where the opportunity to work at the Centre Universitaire International made work both fruitful and pleasurable. Later, a sabbatical leave from teaching, a quarter of assigned research duty, a travel grant from the McMillan Fund of the University of Minnesota, and a "tightening of the belts" in the family made possible another year of work, part of it spent on Malta and in Paris. Finally, writing and revision were assisted by an academic year at the Institute for Advanced Study at Princeton, New Jersey. For all this help, and the encouragement and intellectual stimulation afforded by my patient wife and our children, I express appreciation.

P. W. B.

University of Minnesota
Minneapolis

Contents

Introduction   3

The Uses of Galleys   10

Limitations of the Oar   31

The Base at Marseilles   52

Building and Victualing the Galley Corps   68

Officers and the Crown   95

Chaplains, Lower Officers, and Freeman Crew   114

The Procurement of Slaves   138

Condemnations to the Oar   173

Life Aboard   200

Life Ashore   225

Releases and Escapes   250

The Transition to Prisons   272

Conclusions and Reflections   298

Glossary   319

Notes   327

Bibliography   353

Index   363

Fighting Ships and Prisons

Introduction

In some respects the Corps des Galères of Louis XIV was a cross-section of French society and governmental institutions of the period. All three Estates were represented on the galleys of France. Famous families of the high nobility willingly gave sons to serve in the Corps, even as junior officers and unpaid volunteers. Beside these aristocrats, and working with them, were the galley chaplains — followers of Vincent de Paul, members of the First Estate, and for the most part, priests of the Congrégation de la Mission. The collaboration of aristocratic officers and these chaplains provided the leadership, the Church-State command structure aboard the galleys. Beneath them were the noncommissioned officers and crewmen, who implemented their decisions. These subordinates were recruited from the unprivileged mass of the population. At the bottom of the galley hierarchy were the oarsmen, a miscellaneous lot of men including sailors, soldiers, farmers, peasants, urban workers, artisans, and tradesmen of all kinds — nearly all of them classified as conscripts, debtors, deserters, or criminals — set to forced labor along with some Protestants who had been condemned, essentially for religious reasons. And finally there were the slaves, most of them from Moslem lands, some of them renegades or pagans, and all of them infidels from the Christian point of view.

Louis XIV's Galley Corps was created during the years following 1665

3

as a tool of royal authority. As such, it bore the stamp of Louis' policies and aspirations, of his preoccupation with the implementation and extension of his power and control. In some ways the Corps symbolized the strengths and weaknesses of the Crown, mirroring the King's secular and spiritual concerns, commitments, and responsibilities.

As a branch of the armed forces, the Corps received attention and was responsive to Louis' will and hand, within certain limits. The difficulties encountered in developing and managing this tool were significant indicators of the operational effectiveness and limitations of royal authority. Naturally, vested interests and tradition tended to be defensive in the face of growing royal authority. Provincial and local interests and officials were still strong enough in Louis' day to obstruct the functioning of the King's power in many ways; at times they even prevented the achievement of specific objectives of royal policy, and often they entangled the Crown's representatives in complex problems and ties that effectively thwarted and leashed the "absolutism" of Louis XIV.

The phases of galley history in France having the most pervasive consequences were probably those associated with the relations of Church and King. Their harmonies and differences alike were reflected in the administration of the Corps. The King of France, the Gallican clergy, and the Pope had deep-seated, historic differences over the leadership, administration, and control of the Church in France, and over the methods to be employed in protecting and promoting Church-State authority and the Faith, to which they were collectively committed. They also had differences relating to foreign policy, particularly relations with "infidel" Ottoman and North African powers in the Mediterranean. French royal galleys were designed to promote royal purposes, and could be controlled as effectively as any institutional tool by the King. Thus, Louis used them to delineate the issues of French domestic and foreign affairs on which he and the Pope had significant differences amid their general agreement. Such delineation could be helpful to Louis in his relations both with certain of the Catholic powers and with the Gallican clergy of his realm.

The differences between King of France and Pope of Rome were most heavily underscored in galley history by the fact that the officers and commanders of French galleys were Knights of Malta, committed by vows of fidelity to the Grand Master of their Order and to their first

4

superior, the Pope. Serving more than one master was bound to be difficult at any time; for Knights of Malta, serving as galley officers, such
service involved grave problems when each of their masters claimed to
be the first and most deserving object of their loyalty, and expected to be
served accordingly.

The presence of Knights of Malta and of Catholic chaplains supervising temporal and spiritual life aboard French galleys gave a significant element of religious purpose, even of crusading commitment, to
the Galley Corps. Both Knights of Malta and chaplain-missionaries were
committed to the propagation of the Faith, and aboard French galleys
they had not far to seek for such work. The slaves employed at French
galley oars were, for the most part, prisoners of war taken in the perennial but sporadically intensified warfare between Christians and infidel
states in the Mediterranean. French galleys were or could seem to be
engines of religious enterprise serving the Church and Christendom in
the fashion of the galleys of the Order of St. John. French galleys —
built by the King of France, Eldest Son of the Church, commanded by
Knights of Malta and (spiritually) by missionaries, and propelled by
Moslem slaves and Protestant heretics — suggested that Louis XIV
was an active protector-propagator of the Faith. The convergence of
secular and spiritual purposes, of royal and Roman Catholic interests,
seemed, in some phases of galley affairs, to be harmonious or identical.
However, that was only one face of the facts.

The general history of French galleys is more than naval history,
more than the history of a notorious penal institution, and much more
than straightforward social history played out, at times dramatically,
in a Mediterranean setting. In many ways galley history mirrors that
of the monarchy itself, giving significant perspective on the underpin-
nings of the "age of baroque" in France, laying bare social and economic
foundations of the magnificence that Versailles is usually considered to
epitomize. If in galley history Louis XIV appears as the tyrant and the
bigot he has often been portrayed as having been, he also appears as
an able, willful, capricious, and calculating manipulator of men and
institutions, having an eye almost always steadily fixed on his interests
and those of France. Although self-interested and despotic, Louis thus
emerges in galley history as a distinguished — some would say a great —
Gallican Catholic prince, often a willing servant of the Church even

though religion, as such, was seldom if ever a prime mover in his general policies.

Louis XIV's aims for France diverged from those of the Gallican Church, just as they diverged in much greater degree, more sharply from those of Rome. Through the medium of his galleys, Louis did give some incidental aid, usually ostentatious and self-interested, to the religious warfare that the Papacy encouraged Christian aristocrats and kings to undertake against the infidels. Yet Louis, for his part, wanted an accommodation with the Moslem powers. He wanted treaties of peace with them wherever and whenever practicable, and alliances with them against certain Christian powers that both he and they considered enemies. Louis was perfectly willing, even anxious to have other states continue their crusading (*crusading* seems the proper term, since the maritime enterprises involved had religious as well as other purposes, and usually had hearty support from Rome). Louis especially encouraged warfare between the English and the Dutch on the one hand, and the infidels of North Africa on the other. Louis' was a complicated, but shrewdly self-interested policy.

Louis XIV found useful the fact that galleys epitomized the great Christian tradition of fighting for the Faith. In the seventeenth century, many mariners thought galleys were good for little else. Galleys, after all, were the chosen instruments of the Knights of Saint John, the professional soldiers of the Church, who used them in their defense of the Faith. Louis XIV modeled his galleys, his galley establishment, his methods in galley management, and his Galley Corps itself in some significant particulars after those of the Knights of St. John. Louis saw to it that many, sometimes a majority of his galleys were commanded by those same crusading Knights. He gave them preference over others even though he knew that Knights vowed to fight the infidels, the same infidels with whom he sought treaties of peace. He favored Knights knowing that their vows and his purposes were in significant respects antithetical, knowing that their commitments could prevent them from giving him the full measure of loyalty and obedience he desired.

From Louis' point of view, there was positive advantage in the fact that galleys were popularly identified with crusading. Such connotations added to their usefulness. The Catholic laity in France and many of the Gallican clergy in the realm looked on Louis' galleys as religious tools. In rural France, the news of the outside world most heard, and that considered by the curés especially worthy of repeating in the hamlets, villages, and towns, must have been reports of the exploits of the valorous Knights of Saint John. Their victories over the infidel were talked about and celebrated. Prayers were said for them. In hundreds of localities a scion of a local family had gone off to serve with them. Sometimes Knights were mourned, and the help of God was asked in the struggle to defend and propagate the Faith. In Marseilles, leaflets were sometimes printed about the victories of the galleys of the Knights, familiarly called the galleys of *La Religion*. Galleys themselves for generations had been associated, not exclusively but inextricably, with fighting for the Faith.

When Louis XIV built galleys, and put Knights of Saint John in command, and said he was determined to have more galleys than any other Mediterranean prince for use against "pirates" or "corsairs," and when his galleys campaigned against the Moslems, thereby "protecting" French traders and sailors from the infidel, he was, or seemed to be, demonstrating zeal for the protection of Christendom and the Faith; he seemed to be contributing in multiple ways to the crusading enterprises of the Knights of Saint John and the Church of Rome. If his contribution seemed much larger than it really was, Louis intended

Galley under Way

that it should. The campaigns of his Knights and his galleys helped to dissipate the general impression of Louis' wickedness, and to distract attention from his policy of seeking treaties of peace and alliance with infidels. The trappings of crusading cloaked his ties with infidels, and effectively obscured the fundamental nature of the clash between his peace policy and the Papacy's war policy vis-à-vis infidels. The impression that he had a regular commitment to crusading was created and sustained by the campaigns of his galleys, and it helped to fortify the support he had from the French clergy and Gallican Catholics generally. Thus, in Louis' hands galleys were simultaneously effective tools for coastal defense, tools for use against Catholic Spain, and highly effective tools of propaganda — influencing ecclesiastical and lay opinion in behalf of his interests and strengthening his authority both in his realm and in the Catholic world.

It mattered little that the fighting usefulness of French galleys had degenerated to little more than patrols and coastal defense against corsairs, and to merely occasional and limited utility for operations with the sailing fleet. The general populace and clergy could not have been aware that galleys were rapidly becoming ineffective for offensive operations, even against infidels. In most parts of France it could hardly be known that galleys almost always proved to be as much a liability as an asset in combined operations — particularly in the expeditions Louis sent from time to time to the near shores of North Africa to impose the peace he sought. The high-ranking noblemen who served as officers on Louis' galleys could not be expected to advertise the fact that almost all the combat capabilities of the galleys they commanded could be matched or exceeded by seventeenth-century sailing vessels.

Through the determination and design of the king, a fleet of nearly obsolete vessels of war was created and made larger than the fleet of any other Mediterranean prince. Louis spent tens of millions constructing galleys, mobilizing manpower, and maintaining the Corps, because that Corps made a valued contribution both as a limited-objective fighting force and as an ostentatious tool serving to increase his power and prestige in France and abroad, above all in the Mediterranean.

Galleys symbolized Louis' superiority. They helped assert the mastery Louis claimed to exercise in the Mediterranean. In his hands, galleys were instruments with multiple temporal and spiritual functions, domestic and foreign, political, economic, and religious. The very act of creating and maintaining such a fleet conferred on him a superiority that he could use in establishing and re-enforcing his leadership both in his own realm and among the Catholic galley powers — which were, after all, the only maritime powers Louis considered worthy and serious rivals in the Mediterranean. Although Louis led France to revolt against the crusading promoted by the Papacy, he was still a defender of the spiritual values of the Gallican Church, and of the Catholic system in France and in Europe. One wonders whether the Gallican quarrel of the seventeenth century did in fact end "with the undoubted victory of the spiritual over the temporal," as has been claimed by historians of the Church.

There is abundant evidence that Louis XIV was perfectly aware that hereditary monarchs derive authority and strength not only from the threat or direct use of force, but also from political and religious theory and tradition, from the approval and active collaboration of a multitude of institutions and individuals. The composite sources of a King's authority, he knew, can be elaborated by dissimulation, the shrewd use of pressure, guile, and duplicity. Louis excelled in the methodology of government and related arts. He particularly excelled in the "modern" arts of propaganda and public relations, the organized effort to influence opinion, directly and indirectly, by word and by deed. He derived strength even from the equivocal nature of his words and public acts. His "ambiguity" has led different men to very different conclusions about him. He followed, and sometimes wanted to appear to be following, two or more policies at once. These can be seen as different levels of policy, interpreted as concurrent actions serving different, sometimes unharmonious immediate aims, yet contributing to the same general long-term end — and Louis XIV's long-term aim was the increase of his own authority, prestige, and power in his realm and in Catholic Christendom. One of the principal concerns of this study is to explain how the Galley Corps, as a versatile tool of policy, gave service to the multiple levels and aims of the domestic and foreign policies of Louis XIV.

The Uses of Galleys

T he history of galleys includes little of the romance and adventure of the sea. Galleys are identified, instead, with slavery and forced labor, cruel punishments, and arbitrary authority. Modern literature and cinema are the latest of many circumstances that help associate the history of oar-driven craft with the sufferings of the men who worked their oars. The very word *galley* now conjures up a picture of men in chains, working in appalling circumstances; some of the worst horrors of life afloat are associated with galley history. Galleys are now notorious, whether French or Spanish, Maltese, Italian, Turkish, or North African. Their notoriety has been rooted deeply and spread in ways that made people feel and talk about the injustice and inhumanity connected with the galleys. Tens of thousands of families in France saw fathers, sons, and husbands or coreligionists and friends condemned to the oar and marched away in chains, never to be seen again by family and friends. People, even the ordinary subjects of kings, had feelings, strong attachments, and long memories. Some of their descendents have not forgotten the galleys, even now.

French galleys were given immense publicity in the seventeenth and eighteenth centuries by French Protestants and their friends. Protestant Europe exploded after 1680 with condemnations of Louis XIV's treatment of his Protestant subjects. In ending religious tolerance in France,

Louis sent thousands of Protestants to the galleys. Tens of thousands of others succeeded in escaping. Their influence can still be traced in the countries where they sought refuge, by the scattering of memorials, Huguenot historical societies, private archives, libraries, and museums, some of them dedicated to the men condemned to the galleys for their faith, found in Switzerland, Germany, England, the Netherlands, and America, as well as in France itself.[1]

Louis XIV added much to the heritage of bitterness from the era of the Counter Reformation, and worsened the reputation of French galleys. The decades that followed his reign (1643–1715) preserved and spread the opprobrium because galleys continued to be used as weapons and prisons in much of Mediterranean Europe and the Baltic, and still played a role in struggles over religious differences, still had a reputation for injustice and inhumanity. The eighteenth century did nothing to sweeten their popular history. "After the Bastille, the galleys were the greatest horror of the old regime." [2]

No one, sectarian writer or historian, could deny that oarsmen lived and worked in awful circumstances aboard French galleys in early modern times. The archives of the navy in France, and those of other navies, offer abundant proof that the notoriety of oar-driven craft is rooted in historical fact. But the archives also show, at least for France, that conditions differed radically over time, under various circumstances, for different kinds of oarsmen and for different individuals.

Most oarsmen on French galleys were treated relatively well in the period after 1660, ever better from the 1680's onward. There were exceptions. Men put to the oar in connection with religious differences were often given "exceptional" treatment. Thus, the treatment given to Protestants, reputed to have been severe, was in fact intended to be more rigorous than that accorded to other oarsmen, and became extremely rigorous after 1690. Renegades were also treated with exceptional rigor. The treatment of some other oarsmen, including Moslem infidels held as slaves, was often among the least rigorous of any given (except in the matter of releases). Naturally, many oarsmen had complaints and sometimes managed to make their circumstances known; friends, co-religionists, or other persons outside the galley service and even foreign governments could be led to intervene. The condition of infidel slaves in the French galley establishment was surprisingly well known to North African governments, but little known in Christian Europe. The condition of Christian, Roman Catholic, and Huguenot oarsmen was the focus of sympathy in Europe. The severities they suffered, especially the Huguenots' condition, was the principal basis for the notoriety of French galleys of the time, even though Protestants constituted but a small minority of French galley oarsmen.

The condition of oarsmen was not the only basis by which galleys could be judged. Until the seventeenth century, the reputation of oar-driven craft was high in the Mediterranean. Galleys had been used for both commerce and war for hundreds of years — by Phoenicians, Greeks, and Romans; by medieval city states, crusaders, and caliphates; by sultans and Christian princes and popes. The reasons for holding galleys in high esteem were as varied as the resources, policies, and purposes of the men and governments building and using them at different times.

Generally, esteem for the galley declined in the age of discovery, especially among the powers directly involved in the far-flung expansion of Europe, because oar-driven craft were clearly not suited for long oceanic voyages. European overseas expansion would seem to have doomed the galley to speedy extinction. Yet the galley still had regional utility, and continued to be used extensively in some European navies. Indeed, during the early period of overseas expansion, the use of oars actually increased in the Mediterranean. As late as 1571, Lepanto, the greatest Mediterranean sea battle of the time, was fought exclusively with oar-driven craft. Galleys also served outside the Mediterranean. For example, Venetian merchant galleys were still voyaging regularly along the Atlantic coasts of Europe in the fifteenth and earlier sixteenth centuries, touching at some of the very ports whence Portuguese and Spanish ships were fitting out for voyages to Brazil, India, and Central America. The galley was even found to have limited colonial utility: the Spaniards built some in the Caribbean and the Philippines to run down marauders. Oar-driven craft were included in the Spanish Armada. A century afterward, in the single year 1690, Louis XIV of France built fifteen galleys for use on the Atlantic seaboard, and the eighteenth century saw Peter the Great deploy galleys to great effect in the Baltic.

Thus, after the age of expansion was well advanced, and sailing ships had established their supremacy, some of the powers of Europe chose to continue building galleys in preference to the larger and more powerful sailing ships then coming into general use. The historian is bound to ask why, to try to understand what uses galleys continued to have, why they were favored more by some Mediterranean maritime powers than by others, and in particular, why Louis XIV decided to revive and develop the French galley fleet as late as the last four decades of the seventeenth century, and to make the French Corps des Galères the largest galley establishment in Europe.

Expense was perhaps the foremost consideration in the minds of the governors of smaller Mediterranean maritime states where defense was involved. Compared with sailing craft, galleys could be relatively inexpensively built and maintained. This feature did not enhance the appeal of galleys for a conspicuous consumer like Louis XIV (whatever the attitude of his parsimonious minister Colbert), but Louis was influenced by the action of his neighbors — particularly by the fact that the lesser princes and powers of the Mediterranean were disposed to continue to use oar-driven naval craft for their own defense.

The assertion that galleys were economical vessels of war may seem surprising, considering that the user of galleys had to buy the services of oarsmen and crewmen in large numbers, and also had to feed, clothe, and, following the custom at Mediterranean ports, even house the men the year round. The aggregate outlays for recruitment of men, purchase of slaves, and provision of food, clothing, and housing — not to mention salaries paid to crewmen, and the cost of building and maintaining the galleys themselves — seem certain to have boosted the cost of maintaining a half dozen galleys far above that of keeping a more sparsely manned large sailing craft. Even a third- or fourth-rate ship of the line and surely a frigate, laid up virtually unmanned in peacetime or most of the year (as they usually were), would not be a source of such great and continuing expense as half a dozen hungry galleys.

The cost of galleys could be high or low, depending on the nature and efficiency of management. Galleys could cost substantially less than sailing warships. Expenses were minimized if forced labor was exclusively employed at the oars, since oarsmen could then be kept busy at productive work the year round. If properly managed, oarsmen were confined and housed in the bagne or workhouse found in most major Mediterranean ports which kept galleys, traded in slaves, or kept a convict labor force (as did Leghorn, for example, and the French ports of Marseilles and Toulon). With good management (and the luck to have healthy oarsmen), the earnings from oarsmen's forced labor in the off-season could not only defray the cost of their own keep but also contribute to the maintenance of the galley itself. The maritime condottiere of the Mediterranean ports apparently found they could keep galleys and, with campaign successes, could make galleys pay.[3] The galleys maintained by Mediterranean princes and powers for defense could thus be largely or entirely self-sustaining as far as maintenance of crew and oarsmen was concerned, and could incidentally provide a labor force for use in commerce and industry during the seasons when galleys were in port. Such a forced labor establishment could have added value for the control of the local free laborers and others — not only for confining lawbreakers and other unruly men, but also capable of providing strikebreakers and occasional labor to keep wage levels "within reason."

Another consideration making galleys relatively less troublesome to build and maintain than sailing craft was the fact that there had been a significant shortage of ship timber and masting trees in the Mediterranean basin for many centuries.[4] This scarcity was uneven. Thus, the Ottomans, who could draw on timber-rich Black Sea sources, and the French, who could bring supplies down the Rhône from the interior of their realm, were insulated against the dearth. On the other hand, the Barbary States of North Africa as well as Venice and other Italian principalities suffered keenly from early and severe shortages. Construction of a large sailing vessel could require many times the quantity of timber that went into a galley, and timber of much larger dimensions. Large sailing warships, if used at all by early modern Mediterranean powers, were apt to be built abroad or largely with timber grown outside the Mediterranean basin. Comparatively early in the sixteenth century Venice relied on foreign builders to supply heavy sailing ships, and some smaller, impoverished Mediterranean naval powers had even more reason than the Venetian Republic to continue to use oar-driven craft.[5]

The smaller, poorer Mediterranean principalities and states must have found the quantity and expense of ordnance required for arming large sailing vessels prohibitive. Ordnance, particularly that of large caliber, was extremely costly. All ordnance placed on shipboard was in danger of being lost. Heavy guns might better be used in fortresses commanding the harbor or approaches to the city walls, than risked afloat. Each large sailing warship carried forty or more pieces of ordnance; the guns carried by a frigate or ship of the line, if used instead in harbor batteries, could make such fortifications so strong that floating enemies would keep away, and the guns needed for a ship of the line would arm a squadron of galleys. The astronomical costs of acquiring ordnance, added to the cost of building and maintaining the heavy ships themselves, put such ships beyond the reasonable reach of some small Mediterranean states, and made galleys an attractive alternative for many of them.[6]

This stress on cost should not suggest that galleys were built and used simply because they were cheap. Galleys had some positive operational advantages in the Mediterranean: They offered both flexibility and dependability of movement — being capable of great precision of navigation in skirting obstacles, and at times of turning both weather and topography to advantage. They were particularly favored by Mediterranean princes for inshore and amphibious operations in the narrow, rocky and island-strewn, or shallow waters of the Aegean, Adriatic, and Tyrrehenian seas. Variable tides and currents, coupled with the intermittent winds, squalls, and calms that characterize even the summer Mediterranean, involved serious handicaps for sailing vessels. Sighting an enemy, the commander of a galley could change course with minimum regard for wind and weather. He could quickly take good tactical position, choosing either to engage or, in the face of overwhelming strength, to seek some port or river refuge, regardless of the wind. In short, oar-driven craft were well adapted to dealing with some of the peculiar characteristics of sea warfare in the Mediterranean climate and geography.

Furthermore, galleys could be almost entirely manned by nonmaritime elements of the population: oarsmen, crewmen, and officers alike could be relatively inexperienced with the sea. French galley squadrons normally sailed and rowed within sight and easy reach of land. When heavy weather threatened, and even at nightfall, they often sought refuge in some coastal haven. Familiarity with coastal underwater features was obviously useful to commanders, but pilots and soundings could usually suffice. Knowledge of celestial navigation was unnecessary. However, the fighting success of the galley was apt to be decisively influenced by the courage and tactical judgment of her commander; her success could be determined by the ability and willingness of her fighting men to clamber aboard the enemy and fight hand to hand. Hence,

French galleys were often manned by infantry, and commanded by fighting men with military experience but only limited experience at sea. Intelligence, fighting skill, and courage were the essentials; seamanship and saltwater experience were useful but not required.

Sailing ships established their preponderance over galleys at an early date. The average galley was incapable of contending with any well-armed cannon carrier of medium or larger size, a fact made clear at Lepanto, if not before, by the effectiveness of the Venetian galleasses. But the simple galley, with its special virtues, played an important role in Mediterranean naval affairs for a century and a half after Lepanto. Sixteenth- and seventeenth-century sailing vessels could not be depended on to deal effectively with galleys — sailing ships almost never caught, captured, or even damaged galleys if the galley commander was disposed to get away. Understandably therefore, Mediterranean powers considered galleys to be dependable weapons for dealing with other oar-driven craft, and also for controlling smaller enemies under sail.

Considering the highly competitive nature of princely rivalries and international relations in that day (as now), it was clear that as long as any one power made extensive use of galleys, every rival state on the Mediterranean had to face the possibility of dealing with them. No significant state could allow another, least of all a rival, to employ a weapon without developing an effective counter-weapon of its own. Since there were many tactical and strategic circumstances in which galleys could deal effectively with other oar-driven craft, the mere possession of an active fleet of galleys by one major power could constitute a strong sanction for their construction and use by neighbors.

Spain was the galley power par excellence among Mediterranean Christian states of the mid-seventeenth century. The prestige of Spanish sea power was somewhat tarnished in northwestern Europe after the Armada, but her prestige as a galley power remained greater than that of any other Mediterranean state until France challenged and finally surpassed her late in the seventeenth century. "Galeras, galeras y mas galeras" was the method of His Most Catholic Majesty of Spain, and the French concluded that the galley was an instrument that France herself was obliged to develop, if she intended to contend seriously with the sea power and communications of Spain.[7]

Italian city states were equally committed to the use of oar-driven craft as instruments of policy. The Venetian Republic possessed a fleet based at various ports that was reported in the later seventeenth century to include several dozen galleys. Even such maritime powers as the Papacy and Genoa maintained squadrons of five or six galleys each. The Duke of Savoy, with only a few leagues of coast, had a pair of galleys, ordinarily stationed at Villefranche. Throughout the seventeeth century, the galley remained a major maritime weapon, and in the case of some of the lesser princes and powers, it was the only maritime weapon relied upon for keeping coastal marauders away.

There was always some maritime banditry in the Mediterranean, carried on without sanction or support from any legitimate authority. But banditry or piracy, as distinguished from privateering and naval activity, was relatively unimportant in the last third of the seventeenth century. More important and difficult to control were the privateers that almost every government around the Mediterranean, and many outside it, played some role in creating, supporting, and protecting.[8] The relations of governments and privateers were extremely varied; the purposes of governments in aiding or creating privateers were equally diverse. Some sought commercial advantage, or wanted a share of the booty that privateers could produce; others had political or religious purposes or some combination of such objectives. Sometimes, of course, the guerre de course became wholesale naval activity, as it was for the French in the 1690's and early eighteenth century. Whatever their motives, governments bore heavy collective responsibility for such activities. By directly or indirectly supporting maritime predators, they effectively transformed irregular privateering into a semipermanent struggle, a type of warfare in which all the peoples and powers of the early modern Mediterranean were inextricably, and in varying degrees and ways, involved.

The oar was employed in such warfare by both the predators and the police of the Mediterranean. Privateers naturally used any craft their circumstances made practicable. But without a secure and permanent base, privateers could not build, maintain, and operate full-fledged galleys although some did use galliots or demi-galleys (with oars as auxiliary motive power) . The well-equipped galley was usually found only in the hands of governments, large or small, Christian or Moslem, and was well suited to hunting down the usual run of privateers and pirates.

Thus, the merchants of the southern littoral of France saw the galley as the best defense for their shipping and trade. Naturally they preferred to have the King build galleys, and they continually urged him to do so or, in lieu of that, to grant concessions or financial aids to encourage private enterprise to do the same. When royal support was unavailable, as was usually the case early in the century, the merchants sought the collaboration of merchants from neighboring French ports to share costs. Between 1611 and 1616 merchants of Marseilles were forced to arm galleys on their own account, employing Jacques de Vincheguerre, a Knight of Malta, to campaign. His squadron and its operation cost 450,000 livres, of which the merchants of Marseilles paid three-fourths and those of other ports of Provence and Languedoc one-fourth.[9] In 1619, the Duke de Guise sought to put down corsair operations by the infidels with an armament, probably including galleys along with other craft, that his family later claimed cost him 300,000 livres.[10] Then in 1621 several ports along the southern coast of France, though not usually willing to cooperate on anything, did collaborate in paying for the protection of Vice Admiral Mantin's squadron of galleys. Thirty years later the municipal chamber of commerce at Marseilles again employed private galleys to secure the coasts, at a cost of 4,000 livres per month;[11] in 1653 the merchants of Marseilles were pleased to accept the use of the galley *La Reine*, offered by Anne, Queen Mother of France, and a few years later the chamber had occasion to indicate its satisfaction with the services performed by that galley in defending the coasts: "the mere shadow of a galley [coupled] with the belief that we can arm it quickly, will shield us from our enemies."[12] Not only princes and powers, but even tightfisted merchants saw the galley as a first line of defense.

During Cardinal Richelieu's regime as first minister to Louis XIII, many petitions were received at Court from southern merchants, especially from Marseilles, seeking help against corsairs and hostile neighboring states. Richelieu recognized that a strong navy offered the most formidable defense, and showed special solicitude for both galleys and vessels as elements of the fleet. Immediately after he came to power, he undertook the construction of new galleys. Richelieu used the galleys of the Order of Saint John as a model for the fleet he undertook to build, dispatching the Chevalier de Roches, captain of the galley *Cardinale*, to Malta to report in detail on the construction and maintenance of the Order's galleys.[13] As early as 1625 he expressed the hope that France could develop a large fleet of galleys. Richelieu had around him a number of men who strongly counselled building galleys, but few could have favored them more than the Chevalier de Razilly. In 1626 this Isaac de Razilly, then a commander in the Brittany squadron on the Atlantic seaboard, strongly seconded the pleas of the merchants of Marseilles and other southern ports, urging the construction of galleys either at Toulon or Marseilles for the defense of coasts and trade. The Bailiff de Forbin, subsequently Lieutenant-Général des Galères, was equally strong in his counsel that they be built. Cardinal Richelieu apparently harkened to such counsels, because he armed both vessels and galleys for the protection of French trade against attacks. A series of cruises against the corsairs organized by him between 1637 and 1641 effectively diminished the number of prizes they were taking.[14]

To campaign in defense of trade in the western Mediterranean was to crusade against the infidel. This is not to say that all the enemies of French commercial shipping in the Mediterranean were infidels — there were Spanish privateers, often based on Majorca, Sardinia, or Corsica, and a sprinkling of Moslem, renegade, or Christian predators entered the western Mediterranean from the Atlantic or Adriatic and Levantine waters. But most privateers in the western and central Mediterranean, with which French naval forces were ordinarily concerned in the seventeeth century, were based in North Africa. They were considered corsairs and pirates by the French and other Western European powers, although most such "pirates," whether Moslems or renegade Christians or others, campaigned under the flag of legitimate Moslem states. Whatever the variations in the overall composition of the enemies ready to pounce on French commercial shipping, there were always "infidels" among them, and at most times in the seventeenth century, persons classed by Christians as infidels were probably in the majority. Clearly, French expeditions sent against the predators of the western Mediterranean, though undertaken for political or economic reasons, were concurrently crusading enterprises.

In promoting such campaigns, Cardinal Richelieu conveniently combined service to the Crown, the merchant community, and the Church. Campaigns against infidel privateers were undertaken to defend French trading interests and to uphold the dignity of the Crown. But in addition to being a statesman and "Grand Master and Superintendant of Navigation," Richelieu was always an ecclesiastic: he never forsook his personal commitment to the Church or his habit, and he kept an architect of crusades as his confessor-counsellor. Interlocking motives and purposes must have underlain the special privileges, immunities, and exemptions that were accorded during Richelieu's ministry for the vast properties that the Order of Saint John of Malta held in France. The privileges given to the Order were described as "evidence of the particular affection" of the Crown for the Roman Catholic faith. Such concessions and advantages strengthened the Order and helped "to combat the infidel enemies of the Church."[15] Obviously, the Knights not only campaigned against the infidel, but also kept down many sorts of seaborne predators and some infidel commercial competitors that French shipping might otherwise have faced. In many important particulars, the great Cardinal in France synchronized the machinery of Church and State with the apparent intention and effect of benefiting both.

Cardinal Richelieu was most openly preoccupied, of course, with strengthening the Crown and with the enforcement of the King's will among his subjects. The long and costly campaigns at La Rochelle proved to the Cardinal and Louis XIII the weakness of France at sea, and the dangers and humiliations that such weakness could entrain. The King and Richelieu had to stoop to obtaining men and matériel from foreign princes and powers; sailing vessels or galleys were sent by the Order of Malta and the King of Spain and Portugal, and a fleet was also borrowed from the Dutch — all to put down the Huguenot insurrection. Such humiliation more than justified the effort to develop a royal navy in seventeenth-century France.

It is more characteristic of the "classic" Richelieu, the "Machiavellian" Cardinal who was "more statesman than ecclesiastic," to find him recommending French galleys as tools that could be employed effectively against His Most Catholic Majesty of Spain. Richelieu was very much aware of the King of Spain's reliance on galleys as instruments of Mediterranean policy. Spanish galleys were seen frequently off the southern coasts of France — they sometimes passed insultingly, openly contemptuous of the maritime weakness of the French. For Richelieu, the fighting qualities of the Spaniards and the power of Spain were not blurred or distorted, as they often seem to have been for Spain's religious enemies. He saw the King of Spain as a Mediterranean prince whose maritime superiority and threatening mien had been suffered overlong by kings of France. Spain depended heavily on galleys in the Mediterranean, and France needed them to deal with her.

In Richelieu's own experience, several maritime campaigns sent against Spain brought the French face to face with squadrons of Spanish galleys. Both vessels and galleys were of importance, as at Taragona (1641). But a special role for galleys was clearly indicated by the engagement that took place off Genoa in 1638 when fifteen French galleys were pitted against an equal number of Spanish. In that clear-cut duel, each commander was confident of victory. The Spanish commander, Don Roderigo de Velasco, boasted on the eve of the combat, "We'll take them like chickens," and vowed that he would either make himself worthy to be a grandee of Spain that day or die in the attempt. With 3,000 troops aboard, he had numerical superiority, but that fact was offset when French oarsmen were unchained in large numbers during the engagement and promised liberty if they fought with valor. For three hours the two fleets fought. There were countless acts of courage and fighting prowess on each side. Almost 6,000 men were drowned or killed in the slaughter, 4,000 of them Spanish and 2,000 French. The remnants of the Spanish squadron limped into Genoa after losing six galleys and leaving Don Velasco, mortally wounded, in enemy hands. The French counted only three galleys lost. They had the obvious claim to victory, if there was victory in such a bloody battle. Richelieu had reason to be gratified when he heard reports of the triumphal entry of the French galleys into Mediterranean ports, trailing captured Spanish galleys on towlines behind, with the banners of Spain drooping into the sea in defeat. Perhaps Pavia was partly revenged; *Te Deum*'s were sung in the principal churches for the victory. There may have been some bitterness among men who felt that such a battle represented useless intra-Catholic quarreling, a waste of Christian forces that weakened both Spain and France and strengthened mutual enemies; but the battle did demonstrate incontestably that galleys had great value, and were highly esteemed as fighting ships in the Mediterranean.[16]

Even without such a battle, Richelieu would have been persuaded that galleys were indispensable tools for France. They are strongly recommended in the *Testament politique* that bears his name, a document presumably prepared by him and the men around him for the education of the young Louis XIV. The *Testament* recommends both sailing ships and galleys, recognizing that sailing ships were needed to support French interests generally, and that galleys were needed for the Mediterranean. Describing galleys as "light vessels that make great speed by strength of oar in the calms so frequent in the Mediterranean,"[17] the *Testament* calls for a fleet of no fewer than thirty. Admittedly, such a force would not balance all the oar-driven forces of Spain and her allies, but it would suffice for France because her galleys could easily be maintained as a single fleet, operated from a base on the southern coast. French galleys would thus threaten the Spaniards, since Spanish forces and possessions were divided among two peninsulas and several island bases. The *Testament* intones that the Spanish "cannot assemble without passing before the ports and roadsteads of Provence";[18] the French could cut communications if they had galleys.

Richelieu's endorsement of the galley as a component of French sea power was itself enough to outweigh murmurs of dissent from increasing numbers of sailors with high seas experience who showed skepticism about the worth of galleys for combat. One might question whether counsels from Cardinal Richelieu could (or did) serve as long-term aims or were useful blueprints for Louis XIV's navy two or more decades after the Cardinal's death. Even though technological change was relatively gradual in that day, some significant modifications were taking place. Many circumstances, old and new, were limiting the operational utility and general attractiveness of galleys, whereas no changes of any importance were improving the fighting potential of oar-driven craft. But the youthful King Louis XIV and his counsellors obviously believed that galleys still had many forms of usefulness. For reasons already discussed, virtually every contemporary Mediterranean power employed oar-driven craft. France had to face Spain and the city states of North Africa in the Mediterranean, and galleys were useful against them both. Thus, to downgrade or abandon the use of galleys would have been a most unlikely course for Louis.

Early in the 1660's it became clear that the government of Louis XIV intended to develop a large galley establishment. The Chevalier de la Guette, a veteran Knight of Malta, was charged with the administration and development of a refurbished Mediterranean galley base. Instructions issued for him late in 1663 declared in no uncertain terms that Louis had resolved "to employ all possible means to re-establish the number, strength and reputation of his Corps des Galères." Those same instructions indicated that His Majesty believed that galleys were his "most important maritime force, [the force] that can have the greatest effect in war, and in peace [can] contribute most notably to the re-establishment of commerce inside and outside the realm by assuring liberty of navigation and [by] purging the Mediterranean Sea of all corsairs." [19] This may at first glance seem to be a remarkable appraisal of the galley. But some such high estimate must have been the basis of the high priority galleys were accorded in the crucial matter of defense expenditures — spending for galleys stood at more than 25 per cent of the entire expenditure for the navy in 1662, and over 50 per cent went for oardriven craft in 1663! [20]

In the tradition of Cardinal Richelieu, the young King dispatched missions to Malta, headed by Knights of the Order who were to determine how galleys could best be built and obtain men for them. Grand Master Nicolas Cotoner may have been pleased, at first, to learn that the young King of France was zealously pursuing objectives that seemed to parallel so closely the crusading purposes of his Order. Cotoner was first of all a Knight, and not a man to allow his Spanish origin to deter him from giving help to Louis, even though the navy Louis was building might well be used, at times, against Spain. Louis' emissary was allowed to buy some slaves that Louis said he needed. Word was also brought from France that Louis would welcome Cotoner's suggestions about "all the enterprises that could be undertaken" by Louis' vessels and galleys against the corsairs of Barbary, "either in raids to take slaves or as insults or attacks against their vessels or fortified ports and towns." [21] Louis also suggested a joint expedition of the galleys of the Order and those of France against the corsairs of North Africa. The project would divert forces from Crete, where the Order, the Papacy, and their allies were then hard pressed by the Ottoman; but Louis ignored the diversionary effect, and insisted. As a result, the "Gigery" (Djielli) expedition was undertaken in 1664 — with disastrous results, and the effect of weakening the Christian forces at Crete.

From the beginning of his direct rule, Louis' government showed apparent energy in developing the navy, especially his Galley Corps, although counsellors probably had more direct share in the process than young Louis. Perhaps Louis' famous "lack of interest in the affairs of the sea" was even then part of his disposition, but in the development of policies and tools of policy, Louis was responsible, and must be credited with both. He was obviously impatient, as young men tend to be;

he wanted immediate results, some action of éclat. In this context one can understand Colbert's "extreme impatience" to have a full report when the King's galleys captured a North African corsair in 1662. "If this capture is confirmed," said Colbert, "it will be a double advantage — we will have turcs to fortify our rowing force and even a small success could lead the King to take more interest in the navy." [22] The commitment of funds to the navy in the sixties was already great, but Colbert understandably felt that the King's enthusiasm could be further increased by reports of victories at sea.

However, the next few years, and indeed the whole decade, produced few of the outstanding victories that both the King and his counsellors sought. French galleys were conspicuously active in a distinctly secondary combat role; some strengths and many weaknesses were underscored. By 1670 French galleys were well-known tools. But knowing their limitations did not prevent Louis XIV from deciding to enlarge the Corps — first to thirty, later to forty, and finally to over fifty galleys in 1690. Neither combat capability nor tactical considerations could have justified such increases. Other impelling reasons must have underlain the sequence of decisions to increase the size of the fleet.

Galleys had unique qualities that appealed to the sensibilities of Louis XIV, and to officers that relished elaborate display. Galleys could be dashing and vigorous, compared with major units under sail. Colbert ordered small galleys to be built to scale at Versailles. He had French galleys, especially the flagships of the fleet, painted and decorated with fringes, flags, cloth of gold, fine cabinetwork, and sculpture by Pierre Puget. Colbert himself said he thought them splendid: "nothing," he said, "is so impressive to the eye, nothing so clearly bespeaks the King's magnificence." [23] Of course there were skeptics who claimed that the fringes and elaborate sculptures borne by some of Louis' vessels and galleys were highly undesirable — they were out of place, some said; others complained of the expense. For the flagships, Puget reportedly produced some splendid decorative pieces. The réales which bore the work were much admired.

The military characteristics of galleys probably had particular appeal to authorities in seventeenth-century France. Galley battles involved hand-to-hand combat — indeed, the fighting men were called by Colbert the infanterie des galères. Maneuvers and parades by galleys resembled those conducted by armies. Galleys were the most "obedient" and responsive of all seagoing craft. They quickly executed the commands of their officers, could perform precise and intricate evolutions under oars, and often participated in rituals and pageantry afloat. Galleys could move by force of oar into the wind or in the stillest calms, thanks to the disciplined muscle of men. Oar-driven craft must have appealed to military men and to aristocratic officers who liked the prerogatives of command and were accustomed to being obeyed and served.

Side View of Galley

Galleys had another useful function: every French galley was a prison, making the base at Marseilles a major penal institution. Seventeenth-century prisons were usually local establishments, sometimes maintained by municipalities or seigneurs. But the galleys were a royal, central prison for the whole realm. Hence, galley officers were always prison wardens as well as fighting men, a double role that did not debase, but on the contrary could at that time have enhanced, the value of the services performed by them for their king.

The methods used by galley officers in managing their prison–fighting ship commands they learned by experience in the Corps itself, and from fellow officers who were Knights and who had learned their profession systematically in the Order of Saint John at Malta or among the maritime condottiere. The three years each aspirant for the knighthood of Saint John served on the galleys of the Order (known as caravans) were intended as a training period, to inculcate knowledge of the command and management methods of the Order in all their essential details. Generation after generation of French aristocrats destined to serve as members of the Order, and as Knights and officers on galleys, served their apprenticeships at Malta. Just as the fighting methods of the Knights qualified their Order as a "school of naval warfare" for the principal Mediterranean Catholic powers, so their methods for holding and working forçats and slaves were seen and learned by men destined for service aboard galleys. It was to tap the resources of the Order that Richelieu and Louis XIV alike sent special missions to Malta. Until the European powers established their own naval academies, the Order of Saint John must have been the most important officer training school in Catholic Europe. The extent of the influence the Order exercised as a school of prison administration must also have been relatively large, for it had few, if any rivals in that field, in the old regime.

In their role as prison wardens, galley officers were involved with a wide range of problems connected with the organization and management of this forced-labor establishment. Compared to other penal institutions of the day, galleys offered advantages. The most notable and far-reaching differences stemmed from the fact that many officials in the Galley Corps had an interest in preserving the physical health of oarsmen. The reputation of officers, their own lives, and the lives of their crew could depend in combat on the well-being of their oarsmen. Under royal auspices, the intendant and the officers of the galleys, especially the noncommissioned ones, were defenders of many of the interests of the oarsmen. Administrators devised a wide range of regulations to keep the rowing force not only secure, but well fed and healthy. Whatever their many grievances, oarsmen did have defenders and could have higher expectations of serious solicitude than inmates of other prisons in that age.

To appreciate the "advantages" enjoyed by those sentenced to serve the oar, we need only recall that in the average prison of the time, prisoners had to pay for any services received, even being obliged in some jails to sell their clothing to pay avaricious jailors for the bread they ate and for the straw on which they lay. The customary phrases heard by prisoners, after they arrived in prison, were some equivalent of "pay or strip" — and those could be calamitous words for men without funds or friends. Few possessed the resources to pay for their own subsistence during a long imprisonment. At least in this respect, conditions on the galleys of the King of France were a distinct improvement. There, even men without funds — and this included most oarsmen — had assurance of reasonable subsistence, for food and clothing were furnished by the King. If conditions on the galleys were in some respects lamentable, they were preferable from the standpoint of able-bodied men to languishing in some cold, wet, filthy prison. Local prisons were not intended to keep men for long-term incarceration. Their inability to do so, and the cost of doing so, was at least part of the reason why the punitive code of the time was so severe. The conviction existed that men had to be punished with firmness if crime was to be deterred; but in view of the shortage of public funds, severe bodily punishment, publicly inflicted for the sake of example, apparently seemed to governors of society to be a cheap, effective alternative to prison. In this light, the galleys of Mediterranean societies were relatively mild forms of public chastisement and constraint, made notorious in France by the spectacle of chained convicts seen throughout the country trudging their way down to the galley base. The trek to Marseilles was apt to be the most severe phase of the punishment inflicted on men condemned to the galleys. By comparison, conditions at the galley base were usually mild.

French galleys normally went to sea only during the spring or summer of the year, for a campaign of two or three months at most; during the remainder of the year they were tied up in port (except for irregular forays near Marseilles to exercise or train their oarsmen), and the rowing force was employed ashore. The men worked in the naval arsenal, or at the commercial docks or shipyards, or in the city of Marseilles, not only as manual labor, but also as craftsmen and skilled artisans in the employ of merchants and manufacturers. With luck and a rugged physique, a man condemned to the oar might continue, at least on a part-time basis, to follow his trade or special skill. A man who came to the galleys without a trade could often learn a skill that could produce some income even while he was on the galleys. Such income was useful in supplementing rations, and even for such amenities as alcohol, tobacco, and other "luxuries" sold aboard the galleys by the crewmen themselves or with their permission. A trade learned in the galleys might provide a livelihood when (and if) a man was released. It is no exaggeration to say that the Galley Corps in France performed a useful function in providing training and work for many thousands of men. "Oblige men to work, and you certainly make them honest," was one of Voltaire's favorite prescriptions for the rehabilitation of offenders. That idea was generally implemented on French galleys. Insofar as constructive labor and vocational education could contribute to that end, the galleys could render valuable rehabilitative service.

A wide range of possible treatment could be received by a convict within the framework of the "system" of the royal galleys. Lenient and helpful experiences were the lot of some men; severe and terrible the servitude of others. Service aboard the galleys brought an early end to the lives of many — unruly or unlucky men, or men of firmly unorthodox religious persuasion. As already implied, the extreme severities suffered by the minority contributed much to the appalling reputation the Galley Corps acquired. On the other hand, condemnation to the galleys in France could be far less horrendous than the sufferings of the "galley slave" of cinema and novel. The "system of the galleys" in France was in some respects positively constructive. Rules and operating procedures that were humane even by twentieth-century standards were written into regulations for the galleys, especially from the 1680's onward. In many particulars the regulations were applied; in some cases, intentionally, they were not.

Galleys were useful not only to keep law and order in the State, but also to support political and religious orthodoxy and authority. The monarchy and the Gallican Church in France had significant common purposes in enforcing obedience, eliciting loyalty and belief, deepening the mystique of monarchy, and promoting the acceptance of one religion, the King's, the Catholic faith. Collaboration in those areas of mutual interest and concern was fruitful, and galleys played a significant role, serving both these authorities, concurrently, as fighting ships and prisons.

Considered as a group, men serving on the galleys were being held for having broken the law. Many of their offenses against the laws of the State were simultaneously breaches of moral, scriptural, or ecclesiastical codes. Hence, the chaplains on the galleys had, as one of their charges, to minister to more or less orthodox Catholic convicts who had transgressed the laws of King or Church or both. Thus, they had their own dual role, being chaplains in the service of the King and priests in the service of the Church. Their job was to guide men toward "the right road," as defined by Church and King.

This religiopolitical role of the Galley Corps was further underscored by the presence of thousands of Protestant forçats on the galleys after

The Uses of Galleys

1685. Here, too, the dual role of the chaplains was clear. Many laymen and some leading Catholic clergy in France believed that Huguenots and other nonconformists should be persuaded, or if need be forced, to accept Catholic Christianity. Obstinate Huguenots and their pastors must be isolated if their heresy was to be stamped out in France. Louis XIV, for his part, became convinced that religious "unity" was desirable (supposedly, enthusiasts persuaded him that a general conversion had already been achieved). To help finish this religiopolitical job, galleys offered punitive and proselyting services for both Chuch and State: they were prison for perpetrators of socioecomonic disorder, for rebels who declined to conform to the will of the King, and for obstinate heretics. In short, the galleys and the rigors of service at the oar were useful in the hands of French authorities because they provided varying degrees of sanctions and punishment, helping to maintain order, royal authority, and proper piety.

Hence, the galleys of France were tools for controlling and changing both the habits and minds of men. Roman Catholics, Gallican Catholics, heretics, infidels of various sorts, and even Iroquois and West African slaves who sometimes served French oars were subjected to pressures to conform in matters of faith. But as earlier indicated, the greatest pressures were reserved, in the nineties and the early eighteenth century, for adherents of the Religion Prétendue Reformée (R.P.R.), the Protestants.

And finally, French galleys had uses for all Christendom. To build and maintain galleys, to employ turcs or infidels at their oars, and to campaign with them against Mediterranean infidels was itself a contribution to the defense of the Christian Faith. Certainly the financing of such a contribution was a suitable expenditure for His Very Christian Majesty, the King of France. He, like almost every other European Christian, was committed in some degree to this defense of Christendom. The "defense" could mask many motives, of course, mostly nonreligious; but the religious element was also present in sincere, significant forms Propagating Christian belief and saving human souls were basic aims in the seventeenth-century Roman Catholic world. Pious persons, including some powerful princes, were persuaded that Moslems and infidels generally needed to be put down or restrained from attacking Christians, and that Mediterranean infidels should be confined or punished for transgressions against Christians and converted to Christianity. The Ottomans and the Barbary powers were the particular objects of such sentiments. Louis XIV participated, as almost every Christian prince was apt to do at one time or another, in some of the warfare with the Mediterranean "infidel" states, on his own terms. He took part for the benefit of his realm and "his" Gallican Church, only incidentally benefiting Christendom at large and aiding the Papacy unintentionally, if at all. But whatever his motives and sentiments, which varied over time, Louis' Galley Corps certainly did make a significant contribution to that pervasive and appealing seventeenth-century enterprise, the defense of Christendom.

Limitations of the Oar

Galleys and heavy guns were incompatible. Most of the weaknesses that afflicted seventeenth-century galleys stemmed from the use of heavy ordnance, either aboard the galleys themselves or aboard their enemies. Seagoing craft always represent a compromise among seaworthiness, speed, range of operation, and armament. A significant increase in any one of them restricts others. It is not surprising, therefore, that drastic changes ensued in the balance of these qualities when heavy cannon were brought into general use on naval vessels.

Not only were galleys extremely vulnerable to cannonfire from their enemies, they were not capable of carrying much ordnance themselves. Cannon on a galley, with the equipment and stores such weapons required, took up considerable space hitherto available for food and water — and space was always at a premium on oar-driven craft because of the large number of men aboard. Furthermore, the weight of the guns and the shock of their discharge required that more timber and heavier members be used. Designers were obliged to enlarge the overall dimensions of the vessel to carry the added weight of the cannon: the hull was lengthened to accommodate more oars, and the deck was widened with a larger overhang on either side to accommodate more men per oar.

After these interrelated changes, galleys retained much the same mobility and speed they previously possessed, but their very limited heavy ordnance was bought by sacrificing a proportion of seaworthiness and range of action.

The addition of cannon had serious repercussions on seaworthiness because the only place where sizable cannon could be emplaced was forward, within a few feet of the bow. Added to their weight was that of the heavy oaken rambarde, intended to obstruct the advance of boarders and give some cover from enemy fire to defenders and oarsmen. This weight was increased on some French galleys when the rambarde was armored with forged iron a quarter of an inch thick, weighing nearly a ton.[1] But with or without armor, this loss of buoyancy at the bow was a serious handicap which might menace the safety of the galley itself in heavy weather.

In 1690, French galley officers discussed the problem of forward logginess in connection with the efforts of Corps administrators to substitute iron cannon for the more costly bronze cannon customarily used. Galley officers emphatically preferred the bronze, naturally thinking of prestige as well as safety. But the major argument openly expressed against iron cannon was their greater weight. The officers estimated that even the few hundred pounds involved in changing the two small cannon, four- and eight-pounders on most galleys, were "of great consequence in a galley, where it is very important to diminish as much as possible the weight at the bow."[2] The galley, being "naturally overladen at the bow," could experience serious trouble even in moderately heavy weather. The officers cited the experience of the Order of Saint John, saying that the Order had already attempted all sorts of means for accommodating iron cannon on their galleys, but had finally continued to use bronze.[3] But all their arguments were unavailing. The intendant of galleys was informed in 1690 that His Majesty could not spend the considerable sum to provide the fifty-seven new bronze cannon needed for the galleys; iron cannon would have to be used instead.[4]

When stormy weather was brewing, commanders of galleys had good reason to seek refuge in the nearest port. Ordinarily, some coastal refuge was close, but even so galleys sometimes found themselves in trouble. Returning from Messina in 1678, eight or ten French galleys were obliged to jettison rambardes and even cannon to lighten bows; the captains themselves reported that it was only by doing so that they saved their galleys.[5] Rough seas made rowing extremely difficult, and in some circumstances almost impossible. All the oars of a galley had to move in unison. If heavy seas and pitching seriously interfered with the unison of movement, oars and limbs and bodies could be smashed, and the vessel itself could be endangered. Adverse weather taxed the skill of experienced oarsmen, and required the greatest exertion from them. Even hardened men were quickly exhausted by rough water. Galleys would pay a price in casualties among their oarsmen if they bucked headwinds or rough seas for even a few hours.

This does not prove that galleys could never navigate in the winter. At times they did because intervals of fair weather could occur at any season. Sorties along the coast to exercise the oarsmen, for example, were always practicable. Maltese galleys maintained regular communications with Sicily throughout the year. Spain used her galleys for the long, difficult voyage to Italy in the winter, though sometimes with serious consequences. Seven Spanish galleys sailed from "Portomaone" (Port Mahon) to Genoa in the late fall of 1697, but bad weather detained them at Corsica for forty days enroute; even so, they were more fortunate than the Spanish Sicilian squadron of that same year, which lost two galleys at sea, one of them breaking up in the Gulf of Lyons with only forty-five survivors.[6]

In France, under pressure from minister and King, winter campaigns were occasionally attempted during the seventies and eighties. One winter campaign ensued from the King's offer of transportation for several cardinals and the Duke de Chaulnes who were going to Rome for the Papal election. Unfortunately, the two galleys carrying these distinguished travellers were held up by bad weather, laying up at Genoa, beyond which the officers thought it unwise to proceed. Colbert, angered by this premature termination, said that French galleys "must not be turned back so lightly by the difficulties they meet. In the future, on such occasions, [you must] order the captains to surmount the difficulties that hinder them. They must proceed under oar in spite of the contrary winds. Nothing is of greater consequence than to put the King's galleys in a fit state to row in all seasons, to keep the sea longer than any other galleys in Europe."[7] Colbert reacted vigorously because the prestige and dignity of the King were apparently considered to be slighted. But the Duke and the cardinals were probably glad to proceed from Genoa by land.

The seriousness of bad weather as an impediment to galley operations was emphasized time and again. On at least one occasion the officers commanding an evacuation operation were informed that "since the season is still perilous for the navigation of galleys . . . [you can] destroy them if they cannot be rowed." [8] In October 1678 the Chevalier de Bethomas was given orders to patrol the Spanish coast as far south as Barcelona, but found that he was unable even to reach the Spanish coast because of the weather. "I am mortified," he said, "not to be able to execute the orders of the King . . . [but] I am obliged again to represent to you, Sir, that if the galleys continue to be ordered out so late in the season, they will be lost infallibly." [9]

In foul weather galleys were certainly less able to keep the sea than sailing vessels. A staunch defender of galleys, Barras de la Penne, stated that "their utility does not consist in doing as vessels do, nor in exposing themselves to storms. They need calm to operate with effect, just as vessels need the wind and sail." [10] Even he admitted that galleys were "under a disadvantage in fresh wind and heavy seas." [11] Storms and adverse winter winds usually kept them in port between October and the end of April, when campaigning with galleys in the Mediterranean was perilous.

Yet even in the summer, operations by French galleys were apt to be interrupted for long periods by unfavorable weather. To campaign on the Spanish coast French galleys had to traverse the Mediterranean south of France itself, and in doing so were frequently delayed for days or even weeks by adverse winds. "Many times," one officer remarked, "galleys remain for an entire month at the Château d'If [in the roadstead at Marseilles] without being able to get [started from Marseilles] to Catalonia." [12] A summer campaign on the Spanish coast was considered a long one for French galleys, not for the distance but because of the possibility of contrary winds. "Permit me to say," wrote the Bailiff de Noailles, de facto commander-in-chief of the galleys, "that it is impossible to attempt to reach Barcelona with only three weeks of victuals. To do so, as you know, Monseigneur, one must traverse the Gulf of Lyons, and M. de Mortemart was kept twenty-six days at Cette without having a single hour of fair weather to get out [of that port] in his last campaign." [13] Summer navigation on the Italian coast was usually easier; in Italy, one commentator said, "the passage from one anchorage to another is short; winds are less strong, and there is no dangerous gulf to cross." [14]

As far as French campaigning was concerned, the galley was a part-time maritime tool. The galley was seriously restricted in both the time and the place in which it could succeed. It was often unable to campaign at all, without extraordinary risk and handicap, during more than half the year. In the favorable spring and summer seasons, galley operations were hindered by storms, rough weather, or headwinds. These were serious limitations in a craft expected to carry on coastal patrols!

Seventeenth-century French galleys also suffered a serious disadvantage in their limited range of action. Sending the latest cannon-carrying galleys on a transatlantic expedition, even following the "easy," shorter northern routes of Viking voyages, was considered (in 1540) to be "rash, perhaps impossible." [15] Though galleys did operate in the Atlantic, transatlantic voyages were not practicable in the later seventeenth century. Full cargoes of victuals were seldom borne by French galleys. Their officers advised against carrying much more than the minimum because every ton decreased speed and maneuverability. At most, some said, a seventeenth-century French galley could embark a two-month supply of victuals, something over fifty tons.[16] One officer remarked that "it would not be difficult to find the means of carrying a two-month bread supply," but added that it did not seem practicable to try to do the same with wine.[17] To obviate the need to carry excessive cargo on routine missions and patrols, it was urged in 1677 that a supply base be established at the tiny port of Cette (Sète) on the southwest coast of France, to assist the operations of galleys and brigantines along Roussillon and Catalonia.[18] However, no such permanent base was set up in the seventeenth century. Instead, the usual procedure was to carry most of the supplies required by galleys aboard sailing vessels designated to accompany or to rendezvous with them. On every extended operation, cargo vessels sailed in support, meeting the squadron at predetermined points along the route. On the north coast of Italy, Leghorn and Genoa were usual meeting places. The point of meeting had to be a harbor or port offering shelter, since supplies could not readily be transhipped at sea. Secure havens for galleys were not to be found in wartime on enemy coasts, such as southern Italy and Spain, a fact that limited galley operations off enemy shores.

In the western Mediterranean, as one contemporary said, the campaigns of French galleys took them "from land to land."[19] If France had possessed a series of accessible island havens across that sea, as the Spanish did, French galleys might have operated farther afield. But the Balearic Islands and Sardinia were in the hands of Spain, as were several lesser isles, and Corsica was held by the Genoese. The French had no dependable havens between Italy and Spain in time of war. Therefore, during hostilities, they could not stay in those waters for long. For the most part, their campaigns took place along friendly or neutral coasts; their fair-weather ventures along enemy coasts were short, unless they had powerful sailing vessels in company. Even when bound for North Africa, French galleys often hugged the coast. Thus, when in 1728 a fleet sailed for an attack on Tunis, the two galleys assigned to go along, "being unable to accompany the vessels in the open sea," separated from the others, and avoided the open Mediterranean by following the Italian coast southward to join the expedition at Tunis.[20] As Barras de la Penne remarked, French galleys "rarely quit the coast without necessity."[21]

Galleys ran fewer risks than sailing vessels in coastal operations. They were less likely to be thrown onto the coast by currents and winds. Since galleys normally navigated only during the hours of daylight, they could avoid visible hazards simply by changing course. The galley could stop or reverse course in emergencies. Oars might even offer the means of getting free if a galley ran aground. But such advantages certainly did not eliminate the risks of coastal navigation. For example, a squadron of six galleys, in the act of chasing enemies, ran onto the rocks between Corsica and Sardinia on 17 June 1655, where five of the six were reported to have perished without survivors.[22] In 1662, a French galley went aground off the coast of Spain near Almería, but was luckier, the weather and time available allowing the crew, oarsmen, and even some equipment to be got off.[23] However, since French galleys confined themselves almost exclusively to coastal operations, they always faced the relatively high risks of inshore navigation, and they paid for that with many accidents over the years.

Marine accidents of course had many causes. The minister often seemed inclined to blame them on the negligence of galley officers. Officers, in turn, criticized the inadequacies of the existing charts or held them and other circumstances responsible. Criticisms were leveled from many quarters at the charts then in use, and the general state of knowl-

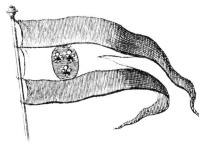

Standard of the Galleys of France

Flag of the Turkish Galleys

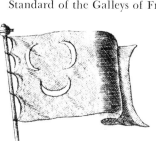

Flag of Tripoli

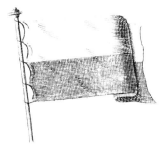

Flag of Algeria

Flag of Tunis

Flag of Castile and León
(used by Spanish galleys
of the first rank)

Flag of the Pope
(St. Peter and St. Paul
with keys, book, and sword)

Flag of Malta

Plate 1. Eight Mediterranean Flags of the Period

Plate 2. Stern view of galley, etching by Abraham Casembroodt.
Courtesy National Maritime Museum, Greenwich, England

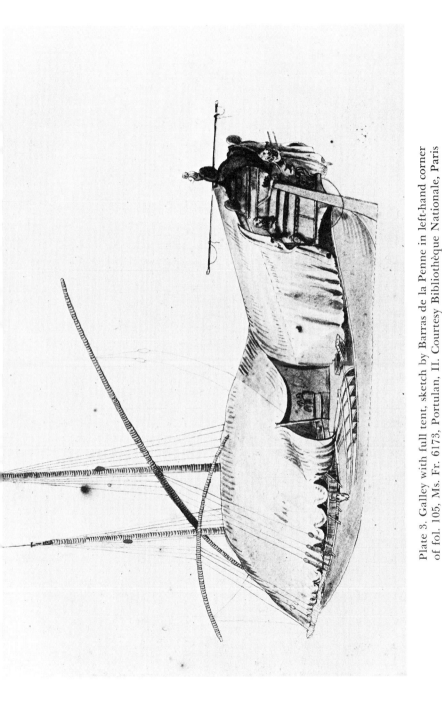

Plate 3. Galley with full tent, sketch by Barras de la Penne in left-hand corner of fol. 105, Ms. Fr. 6173, Portulan, II. Courtesy Bibliothèque Nationale, Paris

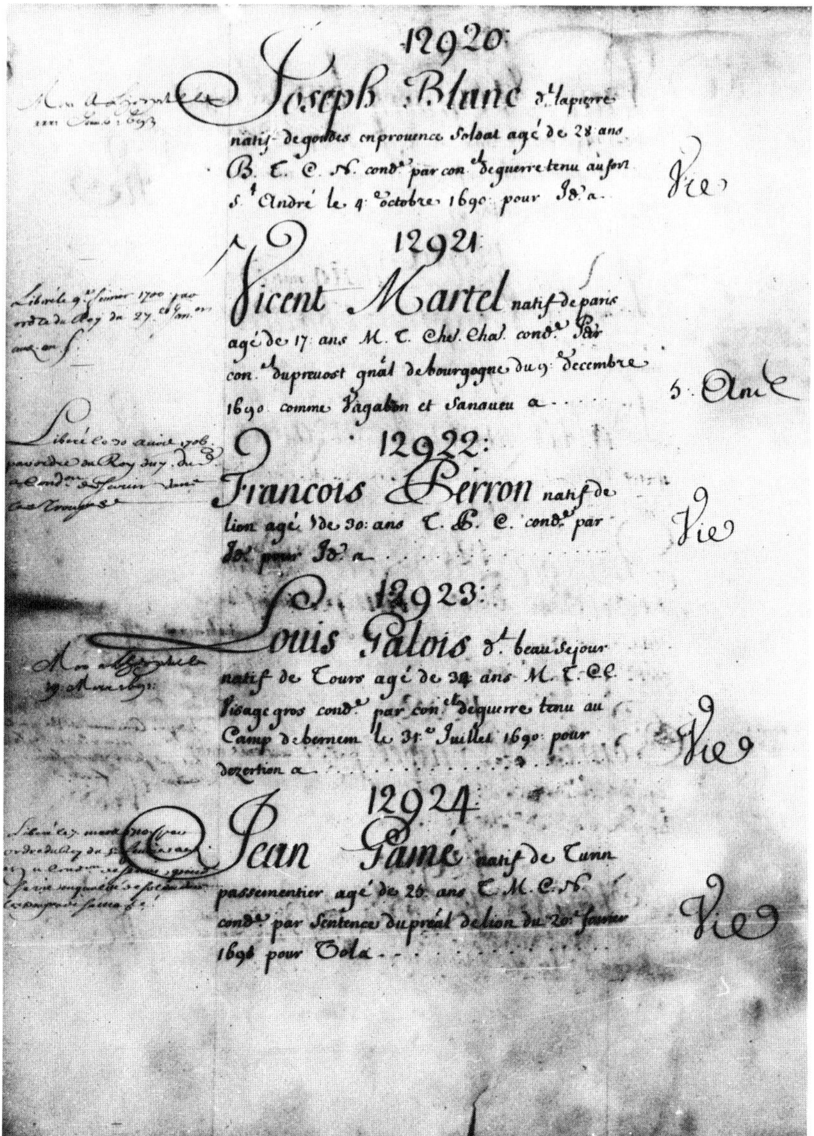

Plate 4. A page from the register (men condemned to the galleys).
Marine (Toulon), Registre des forçats, vol. 100 (1690–1694)

edge about French coastal waters in the period seems to call for more investigation than can be given to the matter here. The Corps made important efforts to prepare improved charts, though not with the care and thoroughness one might expect.

For example, when the innovation of constructing galleys on the Atlantic seaboard was attempted in 1689–90, it was accompanied by a flurry of interest and activity in making charts of the Atlantic seaboard. Galley officers were entirely out of touch with that coast, where the new galleys would campaign, and charts in their possession simply offered an often inaccurate description of the ports and principal anchorages, with some imprecise remarks on tides, winds, and distances. It was said that "nothing is more necessary for galleys than an exact knowledge of the coast and all the refuges it offers."[24] During the winter of 1689–90, teams of men surveyed the Atlantic seaboard, and prepared charts that were supposed to satisfy the galleys' needs. Of course the handful of men who undertook the Herculean task could not possibly make and record an "exact examination" of the hundreds of miles of coast from Rochefort to Dunkirk in less than a year, but the minister insisted that the charts must be finished "before the month of April" (1690). The cartographers themselves expressed serious reservations about their work.[25] Their surveys, later extended to include nearly the whole Atlantic coast of France, must necessarily have been quite superficial by modern standards. Recognition that they were faulty must have reenforced reliance on the experience of coastal pilots, a dozen of whom were recruited to serve with the Atlantic squadron. But the best available pilots and charts did not prevent the loss of galleys — indeed, shortly after their construction, one Atlantic galley was lost on the well-known banks below Bordeaux.[26]

Mediterranean coasts were of course much better known to galley commanders, not because the charts were adequate, for the records indicate that they were not, but because experience in the south was so extensive. Every galley commander was aware that the southern coast from Marseilles westward presented formidable navigation obstacles. Indeed, the coast of Languedoc was so dangerous that galleys ventured much farther out than was their wont in order to avoid its dangerous uncertainties. The perils of the Gulf of Lyons were greatest in the area of shifting banks and sands about the mouth of the Rhône. Then, too, the coast of Languedoc provided few havens for galleys: The entry to

Cette itself was narrow and difficult, and the port could barely hold fifteen galleys. At Port-Vendres, as late as 1693, galleys could not enter at all. Cape Creus was said to be dangerous because it was close to the Spanish garrison at Rosas. Essentially, this coast was inhospitable, little developed or defended. Its small towns could not provide the victuals required by visiting naval craft, certainly not for the hundreds or thousands of men who manned a major galley squadron, so supplies for the French vessels and galleys had to be brought in by cargo ships. The whole of the south coast was poorly charted, and the winds from the north and west along that coast were a problem of first magnitude. With good reason, the coast from Marseilles westward was known as "very dangerous" for galleys, even in the "good season" of the year.[27]

The Ligurian coast of Italy was much easier for oar-driven craft and better known, but farther south the portions of Italy under Spanish control were comparatively little known to French galley officers. As late as 1698 the commander of one squadron was ordered to obtain "more full and certain knowledge of ports and coasts" under Spanish control. It is significant for the operational methods and effectiveness of French galleys that even the important coast of northern Italy, immediately adjacent to their own ports, was still poorly charted and unfamiliar to French galley captains in 1698. When they sailed that coast at all, apparently they did so using neutral pilots or rule of thumb.

New marine charts were prepared for the Mediterranean in the first third of the eighteenth century. But in 1738 the charts still left much to be desired from some points of view. One commander, returning from a campaign that year, remarked that: "Very little use was made of the new charts of the Mediterranean because they are excessively detailed [à trop petit point], and because many mistakes were evident. Corsica, in particular, is not shown correctly either as to anchorages or coasts . . ."[28] One hesitates to credit or blame either the charts or the officers. We cannot know precisely, at this point, how much or how little hydrographic knowledge was possessed by pilots and the regular officers serving on French galleys. Judging from their own commentary, some of the charts were faulty in many respects. That fact intensified the normal dangers of coastal navigation, risks to which French galleys were specially exposed since they operated very largely in coastal waters. It seems certain that lack of adequate charts and technical knowledge had serious effects on the operational capabilities of galleys in particular, and perhaps on French naval craft generally.

Galleys, French and foreign alike, were vulnerable in varying degrees because of their dependence on men for mobility. On galleys the limitations of the human physique were translated into limits on operational capability. A squadron of galleys necessarily depended on the physical stamina of the men who served its oars. Storms, winds, and adverse currents and weather could quickly exhaust the rowers; prolonged periods of calm could do the same if the oars were constantly in action. Ordinarily, however, an effort was made to relieve exhausted men by allowing three-quarters or half of the rowing force to rest while the others worked the oars for limited periods of time. But even in calm less than an hour of passe-vogue, or maximum cadence in rowing, was said to deplete the strength of rowers as much as four hours of normal speed.

Perhaps no quality of the galley has been more misunderstood than its maximum speed. Speed naturally depended on many variables, including the state of wind, wave, and current, the condition of the crew and the rowers, and the state of the galley itself. Certainly, Arnoul exaggerated the maximum speed when he remarked to Colbert that there was "hardly a posthorse that goes faster." [29] Whatever the capacities of posthorses, they were certainly greater than anything the galley could do, even with the aid of favoring winds. A well-manned galley operating under oars alone could hardly exceed five knots for more than one hour at a time. The French engineer Forfait, writing in the eighteenth century, estimated galley speed at four and one-half knots for one hour only, and lower speeds for some hours following, after which, he said, the oarsmen must stop and recover their forces. Forfait's estimate does not seem low, in view of the fact that Barras de la Penne estimated that a squadron of fifteen galleys did very well to cover the distance from Rochefort to Le Havre in a month.[30] In the Mediterranean, during a voyage from Marseilles to Villefranche, Commander de Bethomas reported that he left the Isles of Marseilles (d'Hyères) "last Sunday, the 23rd at 9 o'clock in the evening with fifteen galleys. I arrived here [at Villefranche] this evening [the 26th] at six. I had contrary winds and currents all the way. All the oarsmen are so exhausted I thought it essential to give them at least one day and a night to recover."[31] In more or less continuous rowing under adverse circumstances,

Bethomas' galleys averaged something over two knots an hour for about two and one-half days. Thus, speed under oars constituted an important, but diminishing and relatively short-term advantage — a precarious advantage over a well-gunned enemy using sail alone. In a steady breeze, a well-manned sailing craft might easily outrun a pursuing galley. The galley might close the distance for a time, but the longer the chase the slower and weaker the oarsmen became. Thus, French galleys experienced great difficulties in trying, in unfriendly waters, to deal with the light, fast Spanish privateers of the Balearic Islands and Bay of Biscay. The French had similar problems operating out of Dunkirk and Le Havre against privateers in the English Channel, especially from Jersey and Guernsey. "We have tried for many days to trap or surprise some corsair . . . we chased two for an entire day without being able to take them. . . . If we had a brigantine equipped with both oars and sails, Monseigneur, none of them would escape us." [32] Calm or light and variable breezes were the conditions required, apparently, for galleys to succeed against light sailing craft in those waters; such conditions might handicap the privateers and keep their speed to a pace that galley oarsmen might, for a time, be able to exceed. But Balearic and Channel privateers, under sail, commonly outpaced galleys using both oars and sails!

Friends of French galleys were reluctant to accept all the consequences implicit in the galley's inferiority to other craft. Some of them persisted in ignoring or misrepresenting the galley's decreasing capabilities in letters and memoirs to the ministry of marine. Some even went so far as to claim that important improvements in the galley's armament could be made simply by increasing the calibre or the number of its guns. Thus, one such propagandist wrote that "there is no need to be surprised if galleys are no longer able to attack and insult vessels of war in calm, as they used to be able to do, because . . . [on vessels] the number and size of . . . cannon has doubled." He urged that the size of the galley cannon should also be increased, so that they could mount a forty-eight–pounder and two twenty-fours. He admitted that doing so would slow the speed of the galley, but said that this could be offset if a separate group of light galleys was built and equipped for use where speed, rather than firepower, was the principal need. [33]

The constructor Simon Chabert went so far as to design a new type of "galley," a stubby oar-driven vessel 100 by 30 feet, with covered decks and bulwarks 3 feet thick and sheathed with iron, and with a formidable armament of four 100-pounders, monster guns for shipboard use then. He planned to have one gun at the bow, one at the stern, and others on either side, with two mortars besides. Twenty-two banks of oars on a side, he thought, would move this floating fort.[34] Such a vessel may have had some uses, but it could hardly pass as a galley. It was, in fact, a caricature of a galley, an imaginary vessel that did little more than emphasize, by exaggerated overcompensation, the principal weaknesses of galleys: fragility, lack of firepower, and vulnerability to enemy fire.

Galleys still had special uses as collaborators with other forces in coastal defense, in some bombardment operations, in amphibious operations, and for patrols. The friends of the galley liked to call attention to the value of such craft for independent operations, such as raids on enemy coasts and towns. But for success in such undertakings, galleys needed ideal weather and a command of the sea that could be assured only by heavy ships; for example, French command of the Channel in 1690 was an accompaniment, event a prerequisite of the galley raid on Teignmouth in Devon. Such raids had nuisance value (for example, they might pin down enemy troops), but little importance.

In only one area were French galleys theoretically capable of making an important offensive contribution, and that was in running down enemy galleys. Only galleys, it was believed, could deal effectively with other galleys. This was thought to be a very significant capability, since Spain depended heavily on galleys, and Spain was the principal enemy of the French within the Mediterranean until 1700.

The Spanish galley fleet consisted of several squadrons based at widely dispersed localities. Some "Spanish" galleys were commanded by Italian noblemen who campaigned out of Naples or Sicily; galleys based in the city state of Genoa were also frequently in the service of Spain. The galley squadrons of certain Italian condottiere (the dukes of Centurione and Tursis, for example) were often in the pay of Genoa or Spain. In 1679 the French consul at Leghorn sent the minister of marine a detailed intelligence report on the dispersal of Spanish forces. According to the report, the Neapolitan squadron of Spain consisted of eight galleys, the Duke of Tursis' squadron had seven, a Sicilian squadron had six, there were two Sardinian galleys, and the contingent of Spain itself comprised seven — a combined strength of thirty.[35]

Spanish galleys regularly campaigned between Spain and Italy with the aid of the islands to which they had access. The objectives of their campaigns differed from those of French galleys because the Hapsburgs of Spain possessed holdings and connections in Italy, Central Europe, and the southern Netherlands. The western Mediterranean was a vital highway for Spain, running from Spain itself to Italy, connecting via Alpine passes with the Hapsburg domains in Central Europe, and down the Rhine to the Spanish Netherlands. Spanish galleys thus provided relatively secure transport for troops and munitions. They shuttled back and forth with orders, envoys, and funds, and generally maintained an indispensable courier service for the Hapsburg empires in Europe. French campaigns against the Spanish galleys therefore could threaten the vital strategic communications of Spain, and might also strike a blow at the archenemies of Louis XIV, the Austrian Hapsburgs.

The importance of interrupting Spain's sea communications was clearly understood in France, and had been for generations. But commanders of French naval units, both sailing ships and galleys, had serious handicaps in campaigns against Spain. First, Spanish galleys were usually scattered in small detachments at widely separated bases, from any one of which they might sail, whereas the French had no Mediterranean islands or bases other than those on the coast of France, far to the north of the usual Spanish routes in this period. Mid-Mediterranean waters were Spanish waters, because they were dotted with Spain's island possessions and connections. French galleys operating out of Marseilles or Toulon, because of their limited range, could not station themselves along Spanish communications routes in the hope of intercepting Spanish galleys in mid-Mediterranean or near insular ports of call. Without a mid-Mediterranean haven of their own, the French could remain in Spanish waters only for short periods of time, and they could never even be sure of the Spaniards' route or ports of call. In short, the French had little chance of finding Spanish galleys if they used galleys to do so.

A second handicap suffered by the French, which compounded the dilemma just described, lay in the tactical disadvantages they faced. It must be assumed, of course, that the Spanish and the French were equally capable fighters generally; two fleets, one French and one Spanish, of approximately equal numbers and strength, might be more or less equal antagonists, if both were willing to fight. But they usually were not. The Spaniards had little inclination or reason to fight. A prime object of Spanish commanders in both peace and war was the maintenance of His Most Catholic Majesty's dynastic and imperial communications.

When French and Spanish galley squadrons did meet at sea, a battle was probably the least likely of possibilities, even in time of war. The Spanish commander was almost certain to refuse battle, either by turning back or by seeking in other ways to get away. If the French happened to be athwart his line of travel, the Spanish could simply head toward one of their many refuges. With superior oarsmen (see p. 44) they could be confident of outrunning pursuers. In fleeing from French galleys the Spanish gave some observers the impression that they were afraid to fight. Clearly, there was no question of that. A Spanish squadron was likely to be numerically inferior to the French because Spanish bases were scattered and there were many problems in uniting all the forces of the King of Spain. Sometimes that was done, but circumstances rarely necessitated combined operations for Spanish galleys. Small squadrons serving in the courier service would, in ordinary circumstances, do their best to reach the safety of a port to perform the communications mission with which they were entrusted. Combat was incompatible with such a mission.

By refusing to fight, Spanish galleys doubtless helped to propagate the same mythology that was fostered by Spain's flota system and the transpacific galleons, giving the impression that the Spaniards consistently took a defensive stance, that they "lacked audacity," and that the seafaring officers of Spain preferred to run rather than fight. The fact is that Spanish sea officers served most often as transporters of bullion, troops, and supplies and as couriers of the Crown to provincial governors or tributary states; they were therefore under orders to avoid engagement whenever possible. Combat was a luxury. On one occasion Louis XIV remarked that Spain "has always regarded galleys as a bond that links her scattered possessions in the Mediterranean." It was for that reason that Louis continually urged his own commanders to seek out and defeat the Spanish galleys. Such a defeat, said Louis, would render Spain "incapable of opposing my enterprises."[36] Louis understood the Spaniards' general situation; but he may have been less understanding of his own officers' problems when he expected them to deal with the elusive Spaniards. To try to stop the Spanish galleys, to overtake them, or to give chase hoping to force a fight was a difficult assignment for the French. Encounters between French and Spanish galleys were almost certain to take place in coastal waters close to Spain or Spanish territory, near points of departure or destination for Spanish galleys. There the French had their greatest chance of finding the Spanish prey, but there, too, the Spanish could easily find refuge. To try to force a fight on an unwilling enemy is one of the most difficult and frustrating assignments in naval warfare.

To avoid a fight the Spanish needed only to equip a few of their galleys with an exceptionally numerous and strong contingent of oarsmen to facilitate escape. They had good reason for being the keen competitors they were for French buyers in bidding on prime oarsmen in the slave markets of the Mediterranean, and they had equally good reason to exert their influence to stop Malta's sales of slaves to France. French consuls reported that the Spanish maintained an unusually large number of first-class oarsmen on certain elements of their fleet — though the reports might require discounting, since consuls wanted to impress the ministry with the need to buy more slaves. The Spanish squadron of the Marquis de Bayona, comprising seven galleys in 1679, was described to the French as "better armed than any other." [37] If the Spanish did attempt to give exceptional strength of oar to some units of their fleet, as some evidence suggests they did, that fact could have given them a significant advantage, especially in view of the opposite practice that prevailed among the French. The French attempted to distribute choice oarsmen throughout the fleet to equalize the strength of all French galleys. The only exceptions to this practice were the réale and flag vessels generally, which (being larger and more prestigious) were provided with a stronger rowing force. Thus, when the Spanish equipped a few galleys with a high percentage of elite oarsmen, such a detachment could easily outrun the average French rowing force.

There were a few occasions when the French galley commanders did meet Spanish galleys at sea in the period 1660–1700, but failed to attack them, even though the Spanish demonstrated exceptional willingness to engage. The French commanders concerned excused themselves by asserting that the Spanish could not be attacked because they were slightly (one or two galleys) more numerous than the French. Louis XIV showed notable self-restraint in not relieving such officers of their commands. However, he did complain at decisions dependent on having one galley more or less than the enemy.[38] "His Majesty does not require the impossible," the minister of marine stated. One order sent to the Duke de Mortemart pointed out, "it contributes to the glory and the reputation of His [Majesty's] arms if his commanders profit from occasions when they can attack the enemy with some chance of success . . . His Majesty does not mean to suggest that 15 of his galleys must attack 22 of the enemy; but 15 galleys cannot justifiably avoid combat against 18, or 30 against 35, and so on, in proportion. This clarification of His Majesty's intentions that I am giving you will serve, if you please [as an order] in the future if such occasions again arise."[39] That was certainly not expecting the impossible, or too much from a fighting officer!

In fairness to Louis' commanders, it must be said that over the years they often received instructions that may have dampened the spark of enterprise. At times they were instructed to avoid combat with the enemy unless he was "nearly equal" to themselves.[40] Even in 1692 the commander of Louis' galleys received counsels of caution, being instructed to undertake a particular enterprise if he could do so "without too much risk"; he was also warned not to allow himself to be surprised by the enemy, or obliged to fight an unequal fight.[41] After having issued such instructions, the King might be considered to have obliged himself to tolerate some timidity. Perhaps Louis had his reasons for telling commanders, as he did in 1696, that the enemy galleys were known to be "equal in number to yours," but warning that "since the enemy knows his forces are not inferior he won't try to avoid a fight."[42]

The fact is that combats between French and Spanish galleys were extremely rare. Barras de la Penne once said, probably after 1709, that there had been only one combat between French and foreign galleys in the previous sixty years, and only two in one hundred years.[43] There was not one such combat in the entire period 1660–1700, a period when Louis constructed, maintained, and operated France's greatest galley fleet. There were many years of war with Spain in which galley commanders, apart from other undertakings, might have found and fought the Spaniard. The instructions they received from Louis XIV urged them to so. But they never fought the Spanish galleys, even though they had some chances, during over half a century. By 1700 Louis XIV or his minister of marine felt there was reason to complain of the "bad maxims" established among the commanders of His Majesty's Galley Corps.[44]

Every naval battle was a composite of circumstances, some favorable and others unfavorable in varying degrees to each antagonist at different times. Circumstances were usually exceedingly unfavorable for galleys when they were pitted against large warships under sail. Galleys might succeed if an enemy vessel could be isolated during calm, though even in that case the possibilities of success were slim because of galleys' dependence on a great number of other variables. Uniformly favorable conditions rarely occurred. And since weather was one of the variables, the ideal condition was not likely to endure for long. Notwithstanding the fact that their chances were slim, galleys occasionally did succeed in capturing large sailing vessels, including even ships of the line. Such captures offer a fair illustration of the circumstances and the rarity of the opportunities required.

One instance of combat between French galleys and a ship of the line occurred in 1702, when six French galleys operating out of Ostend, commanded by the Chevalier de la Pailleterie, attacked and captured a Dutch warship of fifty-six guns within view of eleven other Dutch men-of-war. In those same waters, the Chevalier de Langeron, a Knight of Malta, who also had only six galleys, attacked and captured a thirty-six–gun English frigate in 1707. But these two rare successes were not really representative of the power of the galley vis-à-vis the warship under sail. The Dutchman was half-manned and almost unarmed; the English frigate allowed herself to be engaged and, once the galleys had committed themselves, fought with such vigor as to occupy all the galleys and thus allowed the thirty-five merchantmen being escorted to get safely away.[45] Men-of-war under sail could not safely ignore enemy galleys, but even if greatly outnumbered, they needed only to keep up their guard by staying together. They had reason for serious concern only if isolated and becalmed in the presence of a host of enemy galleys — and even then, having their cannon double-shotted with ball or grape and goodly supplies of grenades, with some musketeers in the tops, they might actually hope to be attacked.

Questions of cost could not often be decisive where defense of the realm was involved. Yet costs cannot be ignored, and do have relative significance. Men, money, and matériel for a fleet of French galleys, given the extravagant management methods employed by the French under Louis XIV, cost as much as a considerable number of ships, frigates or ships of the line, and the heavy ships would have constituted an infinitely more powerful fighting force than the galleys. Any realistic appraisal of the value of galleys for naval operations in the seventeenth century must conclude that French oar-driven craft had little value as fighting ships; they contributed little to the power of Louis' navy and still less to his ability to command the sea. Galleys represented a deflection of French maritime energies as far as power is concerned. However, galleys served for trade and harbor defense, in a minor way,

Oars versus Sail (mixed 16th- and 17th-century inspiration)

and more important, they served Louis' policies. Louis saw himself as the rival of other Catholic princes in the Mediterranean. He demanded their respect, deference, and even fear. It was not enough that they recognize his force by staying clear of his domains. With the development of French naval forces, French "domains" and sphere of influence extended over the sea, and Louis' self-esteem was extended no less certainly. Sea power gave Louis aspirations for control of the Mediterranean; the western regions of that Sea became a French lake, or at least Louis seemed to think it was his own. Just as he sought submission from his subjects, he expected other Catholic princes and their subjects to conform to his conception of his authority and superiority. He expected the governors of French châteaux, fortresses, and maritime cities to salute his royal standard, and he wanted and sometimes attempted to exact similar deference and submission from foreign princes and their representatives.

In the seventeenth century, as now, the salute itself was the usual recognition when ships under different flags encountered one another at sea. The salute was usually rendered by firing cannon, the number of rounds on each side being equal or unequal, depending on the measure of respect, deference, submission, or honor deemed suitable. Flags were also lowered in some salutes, and distinctions were made between salutes to sovereigns, salutes to princes, and those made to the still less respectable republics. Generally, Louis sought submission. The salute became a clear-cut question of precedence. He ordered that his flag was not to be lowered to any other sovereign's, since Louis' opinion was that no other sovereign was his equal. His flag should be saluted first, with a salute appropriate to His Majesty. Then, and only then, was his commander to reply with a lesser salute appropriate to the inferior dignity and prestige of the foreigner.

Other sovereigns and governments did not take kindly to such pretensions. It was an innovation for a King of France to receive marks of submission at sea from all other sovereign princes, if only because France was a newcomer to the first rank of seventeenth-century maritime powers. In the case of England, the problem of salutes was extremely difficult. It was resolved when French commanders received orders not to render and not to expect to receive salutes from English men-of-war.[46] That was a practical solution, though not a pleasing one for Louis.

With Spain and some of the smaller, weaker Mediterranean powers, the question of salutes was less a question of power versus power than one of precedence. Of course, the King of Spain and his commanders were no more willing than the English, or Louis himself, to show submission; they did so only when they were forced. At times Louis ordered his commanders to employ force if need be, when expedient. In the winter of 1679 the Bailiff de Noailles, commanding the King's galley squadron, received the following instructions (in peacetime) to guide his conduct in the event he encountered Spanish galleys, as Louis apparently hoped he would: "My intention is that you call for the salute no matter how numerous they are, but with this difference in case they refuse: if they are approximately equal in number to [the galleys of] your command, I desire that you force them to salute. If, on the other hand, you find them so much superior that you cannot attack, you can ask for the salute, but without attempting to force them into an unequal engagement that would imperil the fleet I have confided to you." [47] The following year Louis ordered Duquesne "to prevent the sailing of the galleys of Naples and Sicily"; in event they got out, Louis' instructions required his commander to follow them "and make them salute or fight wherever you find them." Louis was implacable in his demands for submission or precedence. He complained with annoyance of "the ill-founded pretension of the King of Spain, who maintains the equality of My Crown and His." [48]

Even in the last years of the seventeenth century, Louis continued to seek salutes of submission from Spain. His galleys then served objects of high policy as well as principle, for the childless King of Spain was seriously ill, and the European princes were concerned about the disposal of his empire. Louis, among the active claimants, thought he might have to fight for the inheritance. In consequence, the commander of his galleys was instructed that his campaign of 1698 along the coasts of Italy and Spain had to serve several specific objectives connected with the question of succession. French galleys were "to make known the grandeur and power of the King" and "seek out the Spanish galleys to force them to salute." But, said Louis, since "the health of the King of Spain authorizes the assumption that his life cannot be of long duration," there are two other, "more notable" objectives to be achieved. First, to conduct a careful reconnaissance of the coasts of Italy to obtain more exact information about the ports and coasts of Spain's Mediterranean domains. Secondly, "to accustom the Spaniards and the other subjects of this prince to seeing the French, and by conduct that is full of circumspection and by honorable, albeit rather sumptuous manner of living, on the part of the commanders and other officers [of Louis XIV's galleys], to make them desire to be united with the French." These instructions were issued to the commander of a squadron of twenty galleys destined to cruise the coast of Italy, and also to a squadron of fourteen destined for the coast of Spain and to a small squadron expected to campaign on the northern Atlantic coast of Spain, with orders to go as far south as Corunna. As Louis phrased it, these demonstrations were intended "to attract the goodwill of peoples by douceur," and to create "fear and respect for a power whose superiority is well known." [49]

Similar instructions were issued for campaigns to take place the following year, 1699, when fifteen galleys sailed as far south as Sicily demonstrating in behalf of Louis. When they returned to Marseilles their commander, a Knight of Malta, reported in great detail on the circumstances surrounding the salutes rendered and received at fortresses and towns along Italian coasts. No Spanish galleys were seen. The papal galleys were encountered, and Louis' flagship rendered a salute of four cannon shots, but received only three in return! And at the Church of the Holy Trinity of Gahiette, standing on the coast in clear view of the sea, each of Louis' fifteen galleys rendered a four-gun salute, without any expectation of response, of course. The fact that Louis' Knights humbled themselves and him, in the presence of the papal galleys, perhaps annoyed the Grand Monarque. However, before the Church of the Holy Trinity, each of Louis' captains was giving recognition and indication of submission, for himself and Louis, not to the Pope but to the Holy Trinity. Farther south were domains of the King of Spain, and there the fortress commanders at every single place along the coast rendered at least as many as they received. Indeed, most places rendered to Louis' galleys double or triple and in several cases five times, the number of salutes that they received! Louis must have been pleased with much of this report.[50]

On the eve of the final disposition of the Spanish throne, Louis relented temporarily on the question of salutes, evidently convinced that it was impolitic to "sour the spirits" of other princes and governments when they were immediately concerned with the disposition of Charles' legacy. Louis' commanders were specifically ordered, therefore, not to exact salutes from Spain. Apparently, Louis hoped to influence favorably or at least to avoid exerting negative pressures on the settlement. He forbade his officers to require any salutes whatsoever at Cadiz, or at sea, from the vessels of any sovereign prince: "avoid all difficulty in that regard."[51] Conforming to those instructions, Louis' commanders were discreet. But pliability in the matter of salutes was only temporary — after the question of Spanish inheritance was resolved, in Louis' favor, he reverted to his earlier policy. Again he sought to exact salutes of submission from all princes with whom he was not at war.

For Louis, the utility of galleys was not seriously depreciated by combat weakness. All naval craft, galleys in greater measure than others, had multiple forms of noncombat usefulness. It sufficed that galleys helped to defend the coasts, kept down or at least kept away corsairs and privateers, and generally supplemented other naval craft as auxiliaries that admittedly duplicated many of the services that other vessels rendered.

As a young man, when he started building galleys, Louis believed his galleys would contribute, directly and indirectly, with victories and in other ways, to developing his prestige and to humbling his neighbors. He never lost hope, because they never ceased to contribute to some of those ends. Although victories were the least of their contribution, as late as 1696 Louis could still say hopefully, "I will be pleased if my galleys can contribute, by some dashing engagement, to the excellence of my service and the glory of my arms." [52] Louis was thinking particularly of an encounter with the galleys of Spain, or other states with which he was then at war. At that date he knew perfectly well that his galleys could not normally prevail against any well-manned warship under sail. But on many occasions, and in many ways, far more than the friends of sail realized, Louis' galleys did contribute to his *gloire* and to his self-esteem. He never would have built a fleet of over fifty galleys if they had not held promise of doing that. Nor would he have kept a corps which he did not believe added luster to his reputation and enhanced his prestige.

The Base at Marseilles

In 1690 Louis XIV had a fleet of over fifty galleys manned by more than fifteen thousand men and scores of ships of the line manned by many thousands more. That was a memorable year in French naval history, the year of Admiral Tourville's victory over the combined English and Dutch fleets at Beachy Head. The implications of that success were underscored in a startling way. A squadron of Louis XIV's galleys conducted a raid, putting a landing force momentarily ashore at Teignmouth on the southwestern coast of England, thereby announcing that Louis XIV had command in those waters, and that the French navy could bring its guns to bear on the very harbors of England; how easy it seemed for Louis to put military forces on England's shores. The English, and the Dutch as well, had more reason than ever for apprehension about the intentions of Louis XIV. With seeming primacy on the Atlantic seaboard and no serious rival in the Mediterranean, no one could predict but many imagined what he might try next.

The frightening strength of French sea power was one of the achievements of the Colberts. It was the hard-won result of thirty years of effort given to the development of naval bases on the Atlantic and Mediterranean coasts of France, to the development of the vast organization that assembled the matériel and built and manned the hundreds of ships and galleys composing the fleet. Ships of the line, the backbone of the

The Base at Marseilles

navy, were built by the score at Brest and Toulon and at the new Roche-fort base, but galleys were also a part of Louis' formidable fleet. In the years 1665–90 Louis developed the largest galley establishment of its kind anywhere in the Mediterranean and organized the royal Corps des Galères.

A newly furbished base was built at Marseilles expressly for the galleys, leaving Toulon for the sailing navy. As a base for galleys Marseilles offered advantages over Toulon and all other French Mediter-ranean ports. Size, commercial vigor, and tradition alike commended Marseilles. The ministry of marine could depend upon the merchants of France's largest commercial port to be willing and able to sell to the arsenal the stores and victuals required by the galleys. The economy of the city could easily absorb the oarsmen from the galleys as workers in commerce and industry when they were not being used at the oars. Such seasonal work opportunities were important for the Corps, and no other French port could come close to matching those offered by Marseilles. Some of the leaders of local commerce and industry wel-comed the revival of the old arsenal, for the presence of the galleys was bound to be a stimulus to the economic life of the city and, moreover, it was a major improvement in the city's sea defenses. Probably many galley officers and crewmen welcomed the move from tiny Toulon to Marseilles for frivolous reasons — the diversions offered by the larger town were certainly an attraction.

But there was also something else. The two branches of the navy, the sailing vessels and the galleys, were divided by interservice rivalries, bitter professional jealousies, and even lack of respect for each other. The quarreling of the two branches proved well-nigh intolerable when both ships and galleys were based at Toulon. Friction led to embarrass-ing incidents, with serious quarrels over pay and precedence common-place. The move to Marseilles offered a positive advantage simply because it prevented daily quibbles. The best interests of both services seemed to dictate that the galleys be established as a separate corps. Marseilles was, after all, the traditional home of French galleys in the Mediterranean. A bare forty years earlier, in 1624, they had been moved from Marseilles to Toulon with hopes that the integration of the services would eventually ensue, but those hopes had proved futile. The move back to Marseilles in 1665 therefore brought the galleys back to an es-tablished base.

Characteristically, Louis XIV decided he would make the old galley base larger than it had ever been before and more magnificent than any other. But from the outset serious problems were involved. There were bound to be many difficulties in expanding a galley base on the crowded waterfront of Marseilles. The prospect of such difficulties led the new intendant of galleys, Nicolas Arnoul, to suggest that galleys might be moved to the neighboring natural haven of Port-de-Bouc instead. But Port-de-Bouc was undeveloped and lacked "the human and material resources" that Marseilles possessed. Marseilles was preferable to "a harbor where everything remained to be done." [1] But costs and difficulties multiplied, and the consequent collision of royal and local interests significantly influenced the design, development, and even the long-term usefulness and efficiency of the galley base.

But Louis was determined to have a larger galley establishment and a larger base. Whatever the conflicts and expense, Marseilles was destined to become one of the four great naval arsenals. The harbor was dominated by Fort St. Jean and the Citadel of St. Nicolas. The site of the arsenal, enclosed by walls, stretched along the eastern and southern edge of the waterfront of the old port. Construction of the galley base had been undertaken long before by an obscure Milanese engineer; but of course the outlines of the original designs had been much changed in the process of growth and were further changed in Louis XIV's reign. No man can be named as the architect of the new galley base unless it be Louis XIV himself, who demanded its expansion and paid the bills. The orders for the extension of the arsenal, dated June 1666, issued and signed by Louis himself, were accompanied by some of His Majesty's blank lettres de cachet, the name to be filled in when (and if) necessary to remove obstacles and facilitate the work. [2]

The Colberts, father and son, had much to do with the selection of the intendants of galleys. Indeed, most of the intendants holding office for a significant length of time were associates of the elder Colbert's before their appointment or were actually related to the Colberts by blood or marriage. Nicolas Arnoul (1665–73), like J. B. Colbert himself, had long been one of Cardinal Mazarin's subordinates; Jean Baptiste Brodart (1675–84) came from a bourgeois family connected with the Colberts; Michel Bégon (1685–89) was a cousin of the elder Colbert. [3]

The intendants appointed to administer the Galley Corps after 1665 had two major areas of responsibility: first, the reactivation and expan-

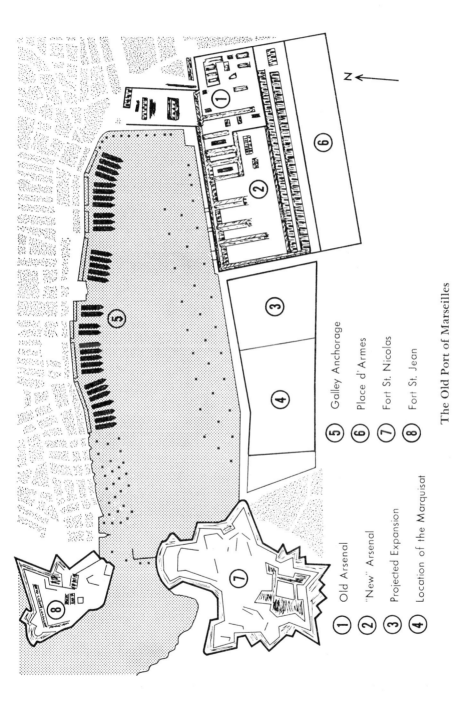

The Old Port of Marseilles

① Old Arsenal
② "New" Arsenal
③ Projected Expansion
④ Location of the Marquisat
⑤ Galley Anchorage
⑥ Place d'Armes
⑦ Fort St. Nicolas
⑧ Fort St. Jean

sion of the arsenal and, second, the construction and maintenance of a powerful fleet of galleys. In the latter, the intendants had unstinting support from the minister and King, and hence the fleet grew rapidly in the period 1665–90. Its numerical growth was a one-sided index to the growth of French sea power in the Mediterranean. As far as the King and successive secretaries of state for the navy were concerned, numerical growth of the fleet was the most important indicator of the effectiveness of an intendant's work — less attention and less steady pressure were given to the intendant's work in expanding the arsenal. In consequence, the expansion of the arsenal proceeded hesitantly and was a distinctly secondary object of expenditure; thus, it lagged behind the needs of the growing fleet. The tendency to neglect expansion was encouraged by the fact that it collided with various local interests. Significantly, the numerical growth of the fleet and the expansion of the arsenal were the two foci of a power struggle between the central, royal authority and the local authorities. In this seemingly unequal struggle, both sides won. The King got his galley fleet of unprecedented size; the échevins and their allies, for their part, in important respects were able to delay and ultimately block the growth of Louis XIV's galley arsenal.

In order to expand, the arsenal at Marseilles had to absorb valuable waterfront land immediately adjacent to the frontage already held. The development of facilities was scheduled to take place along the southern side of the old port; the galleys themselves tied up along the opposite, north shore. Hence the growth of the Galley Corps collided with urban development schemes of all kinds, including the "Plan Formiguier" dear to the hearts and pocketbooks of many échevins.[4] Although they valued the base and the fleet for the royal funds and business brought to the city, and for the protection to shipping and trade, the échevins were distraught by the King's desire to expand the base in the already crowded usable portion of the waterfront.

One can imagine the cold reception when Intendant Arnoul informed the local authorities, rather high-handedly in the name of the King, that the city of Marseilles would have to change its own development plans. Many municipal facilities along with merchant shipbuilding operations, they were told, would have to be placed elsewhere. The échevins tried negotiating, but their anguish slowly changed to exasperation and frustration. Thereafter they appear to have been predisposed to obstruct the expansion of the galley arsenal with every means at their command, fair and foul, both at Marseilles and through their agents at Court.

The navy's plans for expansion along the waterfront could not proceed at all without absorbing substantial pieces of property belonging to the Church, including the long-established buildings and gardens of the Capuchins and Bernardins standing on and near the waterfront of the old port. The cooperation of the Orders and also that of the Bishop of Marseilles needed to be obtained. These formidable conservative forces proved to be cooperative rather than obstructive. Arnoul happened to be well connected in the Church and was, of course, the most influential royal official in the region. Yet those considerations may have had less to do with the fact that the Orders were willing to sell than the purpose of the sale. What better use for land could be found than to expand a base for building galleys that would fight the infidel and piracy?

But in contrast, the échevins and other powerful merchant interests at Marseilles were distinctly uncooperative. Arnoul and his successors in the intendancy negotiated, maneuvered, and for many years reported their difficulties in contending with the powerful city councillors. Energetic administrator that he was, Arnoul encountered or aroused more vigorous opposition than other intendants. Against him the échevins or their agents even went so far as to manufacture fraudulent accusations of corruption, seemingly seeking to destroy Arnoul by undermining the minister's confidence in him.[5] The spearhead of this campaign was the échevins' Paris agent, but his obvious mistake, and that of the échevins, was to try to use false evidence when they might have found real evidence that could have served their purposes. As it was, Arnoul was able to "prove" his innocence and to earn even stronger support from the minister.

But Arnoul did receive a significant rebuke from Colbert in which both basic policies and Arnoul's self-interested economic machinations were discussed. "I find," said the minister, "that you have quite inconsiderately deprived the city of Marseilles of the only place suitable for the construction of merchant vessels." The minister was at pains to point out certain defects in Arnoul's methods: "The maxim that I take to heart [and the one] which guides my conduct in all things, is entirely opposed to yours." Colbert went on to say, significantly, that his own method and objective was to encourage "by all possible means" the construction of merchant shipping and the augmentation of the commerce and navigation of the realm. "I believe it is more advantageous for His Majesty to have merchant ships [he specified 40, 50, or 60 merchant ships built at Marseilles each year], belonging to his subjects, than for him to build for himself 12, 15 or 20 [vessels] which can only serve for war, and will not produce the double advantage that those built by merchants bring. Conforming to this maxim, if I had two localities at Marseilles for constructing vessels, and one of them was more spacious than the other, I would give it to the merchants without difficulty."[6] Such remarks coming from the minister of marine were especially significant in 1668, when architectural plans for the galley arsenal at Marseilles were not yet settled upon. His sentiments seemed to sanction restrictions on the amount of space to be set aside for galley use. Before the end of the decade, with Arnoul's knowledge, Colbert transferred responsibility for construction and design of the arsenal to the échevins of Marseilles, even though he must have known that they were the party least apt to speed construction of a spacious royal arsenal. Loving the Plan Formiguier and lacking enthusiasm for innovations that could cost them special assessments and waterfront space, how could they be expected to expedite the overturning of their own urban development hopes and plans? By placing a share of the authority in their hands, Colbert actually re-enforced their dilatoriness and the effectiveness of their opposition to the expansion of the galley arsenal.

Thus, Colbert, as minister of marine, appears to have played a strangely equivocal role in the development of the galley base at Marseilles.[7] He was clearly not disposed to expand the base to the full extent that the King wished. Colbert indicated in correspondence with his long-time associate and subordinate, that he himself preferred *not* to see the naval establishment expanded at the expense of commercial interests, as would have to be done if the galley arsenal were to be enlarged at all! Colbert failed to force his own subordinate, Arnoul, to vacate or cede to the King the waterfront properties that he had privately acquired from the Church and was to use (as will be seen) for private commercial gain. Arnoul's ownership of that property meant that the boundaries of the arsenal could not be expanded in that direction. As a final guarantee that the commercial interest would prevail, Colbert placed power over expansion plans for the arsenal in the hands of the échevins.

Yet one can be confident that Colbert saw the long-term economic development of Marseilles as in the King's best interest. He must have expected and hoped that time would prove to the King what he himself already believed, that an *expanded* galley arsenal was unnecessary. That judgment could have been based only on the conviction that the King's desire for galleys would be of short duration or would prove to be so limited as not to require any enlargement of the facilities of the existing base. Meanwhile, Colbert wanted the merchant interests of Marseilles to prosper without being hampered unduly by the burdens that an enlarged base could entrain. But contrary to Colbert's apparent expectations, the King's interest in galleys was not of short duration — indeed, his desire to have a large fleet of them intensified. Thus, Colbert must have misjudged the nature of his master's ultimate aims, and also the extent of the use he would want to make of his Galley Corps.

Though all the intendants at Marseilles had connections with the minister, some of them very close, it did not follow that all of them were necessarily loyal, single-minded servants of the Crown or absolutely reliable instruments of the policies of either King or minister. Had Arnoul and his successor, Brodart, given less attention to their own financial interests, and bent more of their effort to the business of the King and to the satisfaction of the arsenal's needs, the galley base could certainly have functioned more effectively and economically. Expansion might also have had more chance of taking place in good time. Arnoul, in his eight years, managed to boost his own personal fortune manyfold. Not the least successful of his own endeavors were his purchases of the lands bordering the harbor, thinly disguised by vesting the titles in his wife's name. On those properties he built private wharves and a waterfront warehouse complex known as the Domaine du Marquisat that was rented out by his family (partly to the navy) for many decades after Arnoul's death. Situated on the already pinched waterfront of France's greatest commercial port, such real estate was bound to be of immense long-term commercial value. Thus, with at least the tacit permission of the minister of marine, Arnoul laid solid foundations for his family's fortunes.[8]

But the self-interested machinations of Arnoul, given the administrative ethics of the day, were relatively orthodox and discreet compared with the corruption of his infamous successor, J. B^{te}. Brodart. Brodart, also a Colbert appointee and connection, indulged his propensity for graft in an imaginative variety of ways for about a decade until finally relieved of his post by Seignelay in 1684. His misdemeanors and peculations, long blatant, had finally become notorious and, in consequence, dangerous and intolerable. At the end of his administration, the building of the galley arsenal was lagging further than ever behind the needs of the fleet, for expanding the arsenal was one of the least of his preoccupations.

The arsenal these men shared in exploiting was a royal arsenal and as such required a certain elegance. Money was lavished on certain features intended to exhibit the grandeur of the King of France; the arsenal was intended as a sumptuous display, the most impressive establishment of its kind in the Mediterranean. That intent was reflected in the design of the principal buildings and in some of their appurtenances. In some respects the designers outdid themselves. The vast armory, for example, according to some visitors' accounts, had no peer; it was one of the first structures built and was magnificent. In 1669 a lettre du Roi declared that the arsenal at Marseilles was "one of the most extensive works we are undertaking anywhere in the Kingdom." [9] Fifteen years later one enraptured visitor describing the still-expanding arsenal said he especially admired the gardens and park, and the "magnificent building" with a dome surmounted by a great fleur-de-lis. Many of the arsenal walls were painted in blue with yellow fleurs-de-lis.[10] After almost four decades of construction the base apparently ranked as one of the marvels of the time. The armory was considered its most impressive building — said to be the finest armory in Europe, it comprised four great galleries where 10,000 muskets and as many sabers were ranged in "perfect symmetry." There was a vast artillery park where visitors might see an array of 2,000 cannon and hundreds of explosive shells — the shells being one of the innovations of the eighties.[11] The ropewalks where cordage was manufactured and dried were described by one of the architects with pride as the finest he had ever known or seen.[12] Hardly less impressive were the administrative buildings, the intendant's residence, and the formal gardens. Visitors at the base might also see forges for the repair and manufacture of anchors and fittings; manufactories for oars and sails; vast magazines for the storage of victuals, general stores, and such matériel as anchors, irons, and galley oars; and building yards, basins, and wharves. It was significant that above the iron entrance gate of the new arsenal the following inscription was lettered in gold: "Hanc magnus Lodoix invictis classibus arcem/ Condidit, hinc domito dat sua jura mari."[13]

Of course, in the light of cold facts, some authorities judged the armory more impressive than practical. Colbert himself reproached Intendant Arnoul in 1671 saying it was "a ridiculous thing to put 10,000 muskets in an arms room for galleys. It would suffice if you have 6,000."[14] Colbert was tightfisted, the practical economics minister; the imaginative aim of spending for magnificence sometimes quite escaped his grasp.

Other features of the arsenal gave more persistent and significant grounds for complaint. The arsenal had growing pains, really comprising two arsenals. The first, "old" arsenal, whose designs dated from well before 1665, proved to be both awkward and "incommodious." Construction of Louis' larger "new" arsenal was undertaken on and around the same site; the new arsenal was superimposed upon the old. But by 1692 the men who knew the arsenal best, who worked at the business of building and maintaining the galleys, indicated they were convinced that the new arsenal preserved many of the defects of the old in aggravated forms.[15]

When private properties surrounding the arsenal site were acquired by the King in the face of varied opposition, the buildings standing on those lands were retained and not demolished to allow expansion to take place in a rational, economic way in accordance with the plans. Instead, existing structures were at least in part simply put to immediate use, as in the case of the convent of the Capuchins, in spite of the critical need to use the land they occupied for other purposes. In short, space that was belatedly acquired was still more belatedly used, sometimes in makeshift fashion, when used at all, to satisfy actual needs. And some of the space needed for expansion was not acquired for the arsenal at all but left in private hands. Seignelay repeatedly told the intendants that the King wanted a larger arsenal to meet the growing needs of the fleet. He wrote to Intendant Bégon in 1687: "I am surprised to have you tell me that the new arsenal for the galleys cannot be finished for fifteen years. The King desires that it be completed in five or six. To do so you must execute the plans of M. Vauban; the plans are in your hands. . . . it is the intention of His Majesty that

61

everything necessary for the execution of those plans be finished in that space of time."[16] From time to time in the following years, Seignelay issued reminders or further instructions but he did not, perhaps could not, insist.[17] At Seignelay's death in 1690 the arsenal was many years behind schedule, still far from being able to accommodate the fleet being built.

Early in the nineties the officials of the arsenal declared unequivocally that the construction yards of the new arsenal were much too small. After new basins for construction had been built, the space surrounding them was described as being "so small it cannot hold half the timber needed for a galley, and still allow enough space for the workers to work."[18] Magazines intended for indoor storage of plank were too small to hold the quantities or lengths of plank that needed to be stored for use. These magazines were only 51 feet long; the plank to be stored was 55 to 60 feet in length! This defect could be remedied by knocking out walls "to make two magazines into one, in which case the magazines will be too large, but there is no other way."[19]

The cramped and crowded condition of the arsenal was a pervasive defect. Plans for the new arsenal had called for separate warehouse facilities for each galley where the equipment and supplies needed for campaigns could be stored while the fleet was in port. Twenty of these individual "disarmament" magazines were "nearly finished" in 1692, but at that time they were declared to be so small that they could "hardly hold even the cordage for a galley"; they certainly could not accommodate all the sails, oars, tents, fittings, and other equipment that ordinarily went into storage between campaigns. And there were only twenty of these undersized magazines in 1692 for the forty galleys then at Marseilles (fifteen others were on the Atlantic seaboard by that date). Wharves that had been built alongside some of the magazines were excessively narrow and, in the judgment of the assembled galley commanders, should have been three times as wide.[20] The Quay de la Ville, which served the arsenal, was also too narrow. The whole of the waterfront "development" (the Rive Neuve) suffered the further disadvantage in 1692 of being unable to receive cargo vessels because of shallow water and rocks between deep water and the wharves.[21] Much material had to be "lightered" between incoming craft and the wharves. Furthermore, the hospital for oarsmen in the arsenal was "very badly placed" and "too small for the great number of forçats [and turcs] on the galleys" (1692). The furnaces where tar and pitch were processed had been built dangerously close to the ropewalks and magazine, with storehouses for flammables beside them — "Someday [they will] reduce the arsenal to ashes." Such facilities and also the forges and the bakeries where sea biscuit and bread were prepared, it was emphasized, should be detached from the central facilities of the arsenal to diminish the danger of fire.[22]

These criticisms of the arsenal emanated from the general officers of the Corps, and were sent to the ministry in 1692. The fact that Colbert and Seignelay had passed from the scene was probably the reason why all the officers felt free to concur. Criticism of Colbert and his administration was then commonplace, even fashionable, in the navy as in France. The circumstance immediately responsible for the complaints was the order issued that year by the new minister of marine, Pontchartrain, to proceed with the demolition of certain buildings, including those of the old Capuchin convent. Demolition of those structures and the hospital buildings was necessary and long overdue to allow space for new constructions. Among other things, new and bigger basins were needed. But in 1692 the old convent buildings were still being used as general manufactories and as workshops for making galley oars. Demolition had actually been ordered during Seignelay's ministry, but had not been executed, presumably because alternative space for these facilities was not available. Again in 1692, no prior arrangements had been made to house the displaced manufactories when demolition was ordered, and in consequence the officers of the galleys collectively declared: "We do not believe that the demolition in question can be undertaken without placing the entire service des galères in jeopardy." [23]

The defects of the arsenal were partly the responsibility of the architects who designed the base, partly that of the échevins who perennially sought to keep the base small, and partly the product of the mismanagement by successive intendants, especially the elder Arnoul. Colbert and Seignelay also bore responsibility, and some might hold that the King himself should bear a share. The King failed to decide, or to let it be known before the construction of the arsenal was planned and largely achieved, how large a fleet he desired to have. Clearly, the galley arsenal as designed and built lacked flexibility and could not readily be adapted to serve a fleet whose ultimate size no one could predict. But of course it was the King's prerogative to defer his decisions, to decide whatever he wished whenever and however he pleased. Accordingly, ministers and architects would do well to provide built-in flexibility.

As Louis XIV stood at the height of his maritime power in the early 1690's, his galley arsenal was a curious composite of virtues and faults. The galley base was impressive, magnificent in some respects, the newest and certainly one of the largest and finest galley bases in the Mediterranean, as was appropriate for the numerically superior fleet of galleys that Louis XIV maintained. But his galley base was also crowded and inefficient, an enormous, ill-planned investment. It was a paradox that Colbert, a minister preoccupied with efficiency and economy of expenditures, should have had a large share in creating, with the help of his son, a base whose design left so much to be desired and whose cost of construction and operation must have been high. Perhaps the greatest irony of all was the fact that the final arsenal was much larger than the base Colbert had wanted, and at the time of completion was too large because the King's galley fleet was then shrinking in size.

The reputation of Jean Baptiste Colbert stands as high as that of any minister of the navy who ever served the kings of France. Colbert gave the King the loyalty he prized, and on most occasions he was also obedient. He is reputed to have been "the only very great minister of marine that France has ever had." The patriot-historian, Farrère, who made that statement, later modified his view a trifle, but two decades afterward he still felt that Colbert was a "very great man." [24] Many would agree. Colbert's contemporary, the Abbé Choisy may have been close to the mark when he observed that Colbert was "always magnificent in ideas, and nearly always unfortunate in their execution." [25] Colbert was unfortunate in that his own ideas, in fundamental respects, did not accord with those of the King he served, though he nonetheless served loyally. Perhaps no definite judgment can be made of the elder Colbert alone, since he collaborated in the administration of the navy for almost a decade (1673–83) with his son, Seignelay. Their proportionate roles cannot easily be determined by anything short of a modern study of the sort made by Louis André of that other father-son team, Le Tellier and Louvois. The role of the son must certainly have become large, considering the size of the portfolio distracting the father from maritime matters. The reputations of both Colberts have bene-

Galleys at Anchor

fited by the fact that they presided over the development of the navy in a period when the level of naval expenditure and the extent of the glory and magnificence associated with it might make the work of almost any administrator of the navy seem great. Strangely, however, the record of Colbert management of the galleys was in many particulars a record of mismanagement. Subordinates connected with him by marriage, blood, or long association bear a part, but only a part of the responsibility.

Placing relatives in positions of trust as frequently as possible was, of course, a commonplace procedure in that day, especially characteristic of the government of Louis XIV. This nepotism on the part of the great and powerful clans of the time — the Colberts and their Le Tellier–Louvois rivals are obvious examples — was partly a product of familial affection or loyalty, but based mainly on the necessities of administration. Colbert required subordinates that he could depend on to be obedient and relatively loyal to his interest in the jousting struggle for privilege and power that Louis XIV encouraged among them. Colbert particularly needed reliable subordinates because of the diverse and vulnerable nature of the large portfolio he carried. Naturally, there were limits to the supply of relatives and friends who were skilled or competent administrative aides, and he appeared at times to be nearing the bottom of the roster of competents in supplying the Galley Corps. Perhaps the intendants gave a reasonable degree of loyalty, each after his fashion, to the family patron, the senior Colbert, but the same can hardly be said of their loyalty, interest, and efficiency in serving the Crown.

Many indulged in blatant machinations and fraud at the King's expense. Intendants of galleys were rarely obliged to undergo inspection. Occasionally they might be called to the capital to justify or report, but their superiors were far away. An intendant at Marseilles had the latitude and autonomy to forage for whatever personal gains could be brought to hand and was actually encouraged by the generalized system of perquisites and the custom of selling offices — though his was not among the "venal" posts. Even Colbert himself, with encouragement from the King, carried on highly remunerative, albeit more subtle and discriminating, enterprises. Perhaps the King was made to feel secure by the spectacle of his immediate associates' self-seeking at the expense of his realm and his subjects. Louis was a paternal prince but was amused by the scurrying for economic tidbits that he or subordinates spread about or permitted to fall. The cost of such largesse to himself and the realm was, in the final analysis, great; but Louis must have believed such funds were well spent or that there was no alternative to such expenditure if loyalty and obedience were to be suitably encouraged.

Colbert's countless enemies sought to multiply and magnify reports of the shortcomings and mistakes of his administration and that of his son. Indeed, after both Colbert and Seignelay were dead, a concerted campaign against them seems to have been conducted. Some of the charges were unjust or false, the baseless accusations of embittered enemies; others were closer to the truth, even if based on faulty familiarity with the facts. As regards the galleys in particular, a reading of some of the criticisms of the 1690's, such as the report of Intendant Montmort and fifteen officers of galleys in 1692 suggests that the quality of Colbert administration had suffered much from the lassitude of subordinates, much from the inability of Colbert and Seignelay to obtain the obedience they sought to exact in the name of the King. Both men were well-disposed, devoted servants of the Crown. Some degree of "failure" of this sort probably must be held excusable in almost any top administrator of that age, given the slowness of all communications and attendant problems of superintendence; even Colbert's well-known energy and sixteen-hour days could not overcome those problems.

However, Colbert was misled by his own preoccupation with economic and mercantile considerations and his predisposition to judge utility primarily in practical terms. He held galleys in low esteem as compared with the relative favor they enjoyed in Louis' eyes, and Colbert judged the need for the expansion of the galley base itself unfavorably. He disapproved of the restrictions that Louis' large-scale expansion of the galley base involved for the development of the greatest commercial port of the realm, Marseilles.

Building and Victualing the Galley Corps

aterials for the construction of galleys streamed to Marseilles from widely scattered parts of the realm and from far-distant parts of Europe. Metals came in the form of copper and lead sheets, iron plates and fittings, and some fittings of brass. Sailcloth, hemp for cordage, fine fabric for luxurious appointments aboard some galleys, and silk streamers and flags came from scattered places. Masts and spars could come from Norway and the Baltic as well as from the mountains of nearby Dauphiné and Savoy. Peasants worked in the Pyrenees to supply beech or elm for oars, and oak trees were felled in the hills of Provence or in the forests of Burgundy and Franche-Comté to be rafted down the Rhône or Durance to serve as curved pieces and knees and plank for galleys.

An important early step was taken when Louis XIV assumed ownership of most of his fleet. Previously, many vessels in the service of French kings were not only privately built but were owned and managed by mercenaries, often foreign officer-entrepreneurs and sometimes Knights of Malta. While in the pay of the King of France such mercenaries commanded their own galleys or squadrons and served under contract with the King for a specified period, receiving an agreed-upon sum. But for

Building and Victualing the Corps

a variety of reasons the services of these seagoing condottieri were not entirely satisfactory and Louis XIV dispensed with them in the 1660's. By the end of that decade only one, a Marquis de Centurion with Genoese connections, remained in Louis' employ. As late as 1669 Centurion obtained a new contract for the services of seven galleys to be based at La Ciotat. That arrangement, as it turned out, was better calculated to serve the economic interests of Centurion than the naval needs and policies of Louis XIV. Centurion never fulfilled more than a fraction of that contract, and he was dispensed with early in the seventies. The new navy thus became a royal navy and the Galley Corps a royal Corps with untrammeled royal control, better structured to serve royal interests than previous fleets had been.[1]

Initially, some of the galleys added to the fleet were constructed by foreign builders because it was easier and sometimes cheaper to buy or build abroad. For example, a few galleys were built at Genoa in the early sixties. But Colbert was fundamentally opposed to the practice of building in foreign yards; he wanted His Majesty's galleys and vessels to be constructed whenever possible in France. After 1670 almost all were.[2]

Galleys constructed by the French in the last third of the century were of more or less standard design, although their dimensions differed considerably from those built earlier and elsewhere. Many of the standard galleys used by Mediterranean princes for war or for dealing with privateers increased in size by a third or more in the century before 1650. Among French galleys there had always been differences for the simple reason that they were, until Colbert's time, built by many different constructors, often in foreign yards, and according to many different designs. Size could even be affected by the assortment of timber on hand when construction took place. But Colbert, with his penchant for uniformity, changed this. He admired the efficient methods employed in the Zaandam shipyards by the Dutch. In 1678–79, Colbert and Seignelay issued regulations specifying the dimensions of ordinary galleys: about 185 feet in length overall, with a beam of about 22 feet at the waterline; each was to have 52 oars, 26 on a side, with five men assigned to each oar. In effect, constructions should maintain a ratio of length to width of about seven to one.[3]

Oars were, of course, the distinctive feature of the galley, but in actual navigation galleys used sails much more than oars. It was to maximize the space available for oars and to minimize water resistance that galleys were long and narrow. To facilitate use of oars the superstructure of the galley overhung the hull on either side by about a third of the beam at the waterline. Hence the galley had a rather rakish V appearance from some angles of viewing, suggesting the hull lines of some carriers of a later day.

The oars of galleys were necessarily cumbersome; they had to be balanced and have flexible strength. Memoirs and even treatises were written on the oar, considering such matters as the most suitable varieties of wood, the proper size and proportions, their defects and durability, and outlining procedures commonly employed in their manufacture. Galley oars of the ordinary sort were over 38 feet long; those for larger galleys were as much as 45 feet long. Each oar had two distinct parts: two-thirds of the total length, including the blade, extended outside the bulwarks to the water; the other third, jutting inside the galley, included the grips to which the oarsmen applied their strength. In a well-balanced oar the inner third weighed considerably less than the outboard two-thirds. Beech was favored for oars because it combined tough strength and flexibility.

French galleys also carried two masts. There is no English equivalent for the French names of these two substantial sticks (*arbre de mestre* and *arbre de trinquet*), but mainmast and foremast will do. The mainmast on large galleys was about 80 feet tall and roughly 23 inches in diameter at the butt; on ordinary galleys this mast was about 10 per cent smaller. Stepped close to the bow of the French galley was the foremast, of proportions somewhat smaller than those of the mainmast. Both masts carried yardarms (*antennes* or booms) over 100 feet long to which their enormous spread of canvas was attached.[4]

The firepower was concentrated at the bow. In earlier times javelins, Greek fire, and pottery vases of poisonous vipers had been launched at the enemy. On seventeenth-century French galleys firepower was more prosaic but also more destructive, ordinarily consisting of one cannon of large caliber with at least two others (sometimes four) of much smaller caliber. All three guns were emplaced at the bow to fire forward. The single heavy gun, called the *coursier* or chaser, was usually a 24- or 36-pounder in Colbert's day, flanked on each side by the smaller pieces. In the early seventeenth century a few small swivel guns might be mounted along the bulwarks and the poop; they could do considerable damage among enemy oarsmen and boarders. But they were gradu-ally eliminated as of little use in actions against sailing ships standing high out of the water; few if any were used on the galleys of Louis XIV.

A few galleys of exceptional size were built and equipped for the French fleet. The largest of these craft was known as the *Grande Réale*, or *Réale*; then there was the *Patronne*, sometimes a *Capitane*, and a squadron leader called the *Invincible*, the latter being the smallest of the oversized galleys. Each was designed and intended as a flag vessel to carry the Général des Galères, the Lieutenant-Général, or a squadron commander. The *Réale* normally carried the highest ranking officer, the *Patronne* the next in rank, and so forth. The proportions of these oversized galleys were similar to those of ordinary galleys but slightly larger overall, employing six or seven men at each oar and a very few more oars on a side. With more oars better served, sometimes by choice oarsmen, the large galleys were expected to be at least as fast as the ordinary galleys of the fleet.[5]

These flag galleys were distinguished from ordinary galleys by size, special ornamentation, and also by the number and type of oarsmen employed. Thus, the *Réale* was the largest of the large galleys, the *Patronne* slightly smaller with somewhat fewer oars and oarsmen and with fewer slaves. Theoretically, the *Réale* was equipped with about one-third more oarsmen than ordinary galleys and about 50 per cent more slaves. The gradations in the numbers of slaves, size, and orna-mentation conferred prestige and status upon the officer in command, and hence the gradations received extraordinary scrutiny as part of the delicate question of precedence. But practical considerations did pre-dominate at times, as when the King decided that each of the fifteen galleys in the *Ponant* (Atlantic seaboard) squadron in 1690 would carry a rowing force of exceptional size and strength. Thus, questions of size and prestige were set aside for the sake of added strength of oar to contend with the tide and weather conditions of the Atlantic seaboard.

The *Réale*, flagship of the Galley Corps, bore the greatest amount of ornamentation. It carried the royal standard, of course, a large flag of white damask (or silk) strewn with golden lilies, with the arms of the King in the center. The *Réale* alone was painted white; other French galleys were red. The *Réale* carried three lanterns (others only two) on the stern. Sculptors who decorated the stern and poop naturally took special care with the flagship of the fleet. The most famous of these

71

sculptors, Pierre Puget, achieved considerable renown in his day. Some of his galley work can still be seen preserved in the Musée de la Marine in Paris.

Great sums were spent on all the large flag galleys of the fleet. Intendant Arnoul declared in 1668 that the new *Capitane* under construction "will be the most dazzling that the French have ever put to water. The entire inside of the poop (captain's quarters) will be inlaid [*marqueté*], as German cabinets are; I have brought Flemings to do the work. The exterior of the poop will be painted and gilded" and decorated with "one of the rarest sculptures." [6] When a réale was being built in the fall of 1670, the suggestions of the Général des Galères were solicited by Colbert "so that I, for my part, can do everything necessary to render this *Réale* worthy of the King, our Master." [7] In 1676 the latest *Réale* was being lavishly appointed with red velvet and gold fringes, embroideries and gold brocades; the estimated cost of the cloth alone was 109,000 livres, "not counting the lesser supplies and workmanship." [8] That was an enormous sum — many skilled workers then earned between 150 and 300 livres a year, and an ordinary galley could be built for about 28,000 livres. But the *Réale* was the showpiece of the fleet; perhaps it merited being called "a marvel of splendor and grace." [9]

Galley hulls were built either by enterprise or régie — that is, they were either built on order by private enterprise and then purchased by the King, or they were built by the King's workmen in his own arsenal using materials he supplied. The finished hulls were masted and rigged, again either by contract or régie, with the necessary masts, spars, and cordage drawn from the stores of the King. Oars were always drawn from royal magazines.

The terms of the enterprise contracts under which galleys were privately built for the King were extremely varied. One constructor, for example, agreed in 1686 to supply four galley hulls over a period of six years without any payment at all, on condition that he be given all the equipment deriving from the demolition of old galleys and all the oarsmen's cast-off clothing during that period.[10] In construction by enterprise, the entrepreneur supplied the materials. He could buy the necessary masts, irons, timber, and other materials from the King's magazines, or he could acquire them elsewhere if he found that advantageous. Some constructors bought old galleys and dismantled them, saving as much as they could of the used irons and timber for new constructions. But a great many curved timbers were needed for a galley — between 350 and 400 selected trees were cut to supply the 3,600 to 4,300 cubic feet of curved timber required for an ordinary galley.[11] Hence, constructors almost always had need of new materials. Some employed subcontractors to supply timber and other matériel for them, and others had their own gangs of men in the forests cutting and bringing timber to the arsenal on their own account. But that method was not favored by the navy, since it could involve abuse. Even the constructor Chabert cut timber reserved for the navy, ostensibly for use in the construction of the galleys he was building in the arsenal, and after shipping the timber in question under toll-exempt navy certificates, Chabert sold it privately at fancy prices. The minister bitterly criticized Chabert for that, saying that "if Chabert wants to be a merchant, he need not serve the King."[12] It was preferable, in his view, to have constructors buy their timber from the King even when they built by enterprise.

Of course, abuses could also be involved in the acquisition of timber supplies for the King's own magazines. The machinations of a Sieur de Rome, commissaire des galères, offer an example. He was assigned in 1687–88 as the royal official responsible for overseeing exploitations in the forests of the Count de Sault. He was found guilty of carrying the names of nonexistent workers on his rolls, whose salaries he pocketed; he exacted kickbacks from the men who transported timber; he sold for his own profit part of the navy's timber; he presented fraudulent certificates at the arsenal as to the amount of timber he shipped; and, finally, he sold the toppings and refuse cuttings from the trees belonging to the navy for personal gain. He escaped prosecution by making restitution.[13] Such cases supplied ammunition for persons who opposed construction by régie, and there were many who did. Indeed, there were sharp differences of opinion over which of these methods of contracting, enterprise or régie, was most advantageous for the King. In constructions, of course, everything depended on the quality of the finished vessel delivered. But constructions by enterprise at fixed and predetermined prices were often shown to be less costly than those by régie. Enterprise contracts made use of the profit motive to encourage efficiency on the part of contractors, and they involved the use of fewer salaried naval officials who could be led to misdemeanors by mercenary motives. Yet the fact was that the same constructors built the galleys, whether by régie or by enterprise; nearly all of the constructors were members of the Chabert or Hubac clans, which built most of the galleys constructed for the French navy in the century after 1650.

But galleys constructed by enterprise consistently seemed to offer savings. Sometimes a hull could be had by enterprise for 50 per cent less than cost estimates for the same hull built by régie.[14] The advantage of lower costs was the apparent basis of Seignelay's decision in 1687 to build galleys henceforth by enterprise.[15] That was an unpopular decision among the constructors. The form that their opposition took is suggested by the fact that the very next year, 1688, Seignelay was informed that the galleys then being built by enterprise under his "new regime" were defective in certain respects. "Much old wood has been employed," it was said (a strange form of complaint since old timber, if not rotted, was almost certain to be better than pieces recently cut). Complainers also asserted that under Seignelay's system of enterprise the galleys actually built were "fewer in number and much less carefully assembled" than those built by régie.[16] Whatever the case, Seignelay's decision in favor of enterprise was reversed by his successor, Pontchartrain, who decided in 1691 to revert to building only by régie.[17] In that, as in many other matters of detail, the prevailing methods of administration were at least temporarily reversed when Seignelay passed from the scene.

The men who built galleys for the King found ways to express their individuality in construction in spite of the regulations prescribed by Colbert. Construction was more an art than a science. Some of them combined caprice and frivolity with their skill, as artists are wont to do. The elder Colbert was in the habit of handing out gold medals to constructors because he believed it essential to get the best out of them. They were a small group whose services could not easily be duplicated because their secrets were handed down from father to son. Of course, Colbert disliked these men's professional monopoly. With the object of increasing their number he undertook to establish a school for constructors at Marseilles.

This school was not a success. "Faculty problems" plagued it from the start. The instructors were reluctant to instruct. The most-qualified instructor, Pierre Chabert, was supposed to feel honored by Colbert's letters announcing his nomination for the post of professor at the school-to-be. Not relishing the idea of disclosing professional secrets, Chabert had the hardihood to decline the post, and he persisted in refusal for many months despite entreaties, pressure, and threats from the minister. Finally losing patience, the minister informed Chabert that he would either teach or face imprisonment. He still refused. A commitment order was issued, declaring that Chabert would not be released "until he is more submissive and prepared to execute punctually the orders received from the King." The Marseilles carpenter-constructor finally bowed to the royal will. But that was not the end of it.

Though forced to accept the appointment, Chabert could not be made to teach. First he complained of ill health, saying his lungs were feeble, and he could not "speak in a loud voice three times a week." This ruse failing, classes began. But his instruction was superficial. Technical detail was presented so confusingly that students found it incomprehensible. Nevertheless, Pierre Chabert managed to survive the wrath of authority, and his conduct did not seriously compromise the favor he and his family long enjoyed. In 1689, when a change in construction methods was being considered, the minister warned his subordinates to "change nothing in the construction of galleys without having the opinion of younger Chabert, who is, without contradiction, the most able of them all. Do not use this new method without having consulted him."[18]

It was a compliment to the Chaberts that one of their clan was almost always given the responsibility of constructing the flagship of the fleet, the réale. When another constructor was being considered in 1670, Colbert himself wrote to tell the intendant that he had better not take a chance, "better resolve to suffer the *bizarrerie* [of Pierre Chabert] than fail to make this galley the best in the Mediterranean."[19] A Chabert built the *Grand Réale* that was put to water in 1676. It was condemned as being in a terrible state of repair and unfit for service shortly afterward.[20] But the Chaberts built a successor in 1680; another that proved to have many defects of design was built by J. B. Chabert in 1688; and the same Chabert had to build still another in 1694.[21] In the eighteenth century the Chaberts were still building réales. The aging Jean Baptiste Chabert, "reputed to be the best constructor in Europe," finished construction of a new réale in 1722, at a cost of "more than 60,000 livres," but in 1727 this "new réale" was found by the assembled officials and captains of the Corps to have serious defects, and the distinguished Captain Langeron was led to say that "it seems to me that our master constructors, who do not know the sea, should go to sea to render themselves more skilled in their trade."[22] But the Chabert reputation survived intact. In the spring of 1731 Pierre Chabert laid down a successor to this defective réale, launched in turn in August 1733.[23]

As if by habit, ministers turned to the Chabert family whenever a particularly difficult problem arose in the construction of galleys. In 1689 when it was decided to undertake the construction of fifteen galleys at Rochefort, on the Atlantic seaboard, naturally counsel from the Chaberts was sought. This costly project involved immense difficulties. All fifteen galleys were built under J. B. (?) Chabert's direction. The timber he used in constructing these fifteen galleys was undried, green timber direct from the forest![24]

Two Chaberts, father and son, also figured in a notable episode when a galley was reported to have been built in a single day (1678). The excuse for attempting the feat was the prospect that the King might be persuaded to visit Marseilles. No public entertainment could be more useful or engrossing for the King, it was thought, than the spectacle of a galley being built before his eyes in a single day.[25]

The idea of getting the King to visit the arsenal in Marseilles was in Colbert's thoughts for years. As early as October 1670, he warned Intendant Arnoul that he should be ready to construct a galley with record speed upon such a visit, keeping timber on hand precut to the proper dimensions. "Since His Majesty speaks of it often, and may suddenly decide to come . . . I urge you to hold everything ready."[26] Years went by and the King never went to Marseilles; nonetheless, successive intendants presumably held themselves ready to perform. Since the prospect of the visit was again being bruited in 1678, Intendant Brodart apparently undertook to test his preparations with a dry run; Brodart reported that the galley in question was actually finished and put to water. Some have questioned the veracity of Brodart's report that the test took place, but our interest lies in the details of the plans and preparations that Brodart described.

To construct in twenty-four hours a vessel as large as a galley, displacing some 200 tons, would be a challenge to shipbuilders of any day. It was a prodigious task in the seventeeth century, even though all the materials were presumably precut to proper dimensions and probably built into a galley at least once in advance, then marked, dismantled, and stored so they could later be reassembled as a finished vessel again. No less important than assembling materials was organizing the work force. Brodart occupied himself with that task for weeks in advance before attempting to build. When he finally did make the attempt, he explained, he had no fewer than five hundred carpenters at hand, divided into companies of fifty, each led by two master shipwrights and a foreman. Five of these companies he assigned to the elder Chabert to erect the starboard side of the galley and the others he assigned to the younger Chabert on the larboard. Each company wore caps of a different color to cut down confusion. Besides the carpenters Brodart assembled fifty nailers, with hats of another color, directed by another master shipwright, and with them two companies of porters of forty men each for carrying the timber and plank. There were also master sawyers, sculptors, and a hundred caulkers whose work was to begin as soon as the plank had been set into place. Instructions were given to each company commander and foreman to ensure that every man knew what he was to do. The work was to be done with a minimum of conversation to avoid noise and confusion – a difficult assignment.

The actual test, according to Brodart, was conducted on 10 November 1678, beginning at dawn. He said in the first half hour they accomplished the work that would ordinarily have required fifteen days to perform, and by four in the afternoon all the timber and plank of the hull had been fitted into place, the shaving and finishing was under way, and the caulkers had begun. The entire hull was caulked by ten in the evening and the caulkers spent the rest of the night inspecting their work, finally pumping water into the hull, as was ordinarily done, to test for uncaulked holes. In the early morning of the second day, Mass was said aboard and the customary ceremonies of benediction were performed while the basin in which galleys were built was being filled.

At 7:00 A.M. the vessel was floated out of the basin into the port. Masts were raised and stepped, spars were rigged, and cordage and sails came aboard, with ballast, munitions, cannon, and arms. By 9:00 A.M., according to Brodart, the crewmen were at their places, the oarsmen were aboard and chained, and the galley whose construction had begun the previous day was already out beyond the harbor chain. "Everything contributed," Brodart said, "to the satisfaction of the intendant, for it was the most beautiful weather in the world, at its trials the galley showed perfection alike under sail and oar." [27]

In the usual galley constructions there was, of course, less need for speed. Weeks were usually needed to complete construction, and when réales were built several years were sometimes taken to fit out the hull

77

But the tempo of construction was seldom leisurely during the ministries of Colbert and Seignelay. The tone was set in 1662 when Colbert ordered his subordinates "to make every effort imaginable to have six new galleys" on hand by spring.[28] No fewer than twenty were on hand by 1670, but then hopes had been raised — it was the aim to have thirty at sea "in two or three years." Furthermore, said Colbert, "you must hurry the construction of a réale" for service next spring (1671); "keep me posted" on the progress of the work, and "employ as many workers as you possibly can."[29] Year after year the intendants were told that it was not enough to build replacements alone; a larger fleet was desired. Characteristic of the haste were the minister's orders to the intendant in 1676: "His Majesty desires that the Sieur Brodart do the impossible by putting a twenty-sixth galley to sea next year."[30] Two years later it was the twenty-seventh that had to be built. "Increase the Corps each year, so that it can match the reputation that sailing vessels in recent actions have acquired."[31] Again in 1680 the intendant was told to "do the impossible" by building seven galleys to provide a net increase of two for the following year.[32]

For the administrators of Louis' galley arsenal the most persistent problem was the necessity of adapting the base to the needs of a continually increasing fleet whose ultimate size could be changed at the whim of the King. In less than three decades, 1662–90, a motley collection of half a dozen galleys mushroomed into a fleet of more than forty. The arsenal became ever more crowded. The shortage of space was reflected in the cramped conditions in which galleys were built, in the small magazines and wharves and in the fact that the arsenal did not accommodate large timber reserves. The last fact is one, and perhaps the most charitable, explanation for much unseasoned timber's being used in galleys. Proper seasoning of timber required only that cuts in the forests produce substantial surpluses of properly assorted timber over a number of years. A stockpile would then naturally develop, which needed only to be properly stored. Surely, if the arsenal had no room for storage and seasoning of the quantities of timber required, arrangements could have been made for storage elsewhere. The administrators of the arsenal solved many problems, when they wanted to do so, that were thornier than the stockpiling of timber.

Vessels built with unseasoned timber, whether sailing ships or galleys, were bound to require much maintenance and generally to be short-lived. Built into a vessel green timber dried unevenly — some pieces warped, some of those above the waterline also shrank, fittings came loose, seams opened up. No amount of care could keep such a craft seaworthy for long. Shipwrights had known from time immemorial that only seasoned timber should be built into seagoing craft. Yet in the period of rapid expansion, over three decades or more, green and unseasoned timber was continually built into galleys in disregard of experience and the ensuing waste. The constructors of galleys, the intendants at Marseilles, and the ministers of the navy (both Colberts) were well aware that the use of unseasoned timber was bound to shorten the useful life of a galley. The elder Colbert, though certainly not a seagoing man, was aware of the damage resulting from the use of such wood. If he did not know it before, he learned it in the sixties from reports on the management methods employed in foreign shipyards — as early as 1666 he was informed that the Venetians habitually seasoned their timber for as much as ten years before they put it to use. Arnoul wrote Colbert in 1669 that several recently built galleys would "soon be out of service" because of green timber; "having now dried out, they are coming to pieces."[33] Both Colbert and Seignelay are famous for having tried to stamp out inefficiency and needless expense. Indeed, in 1670 Colbert urged Intendant Arnoul to purchase timber for five or six galleys to be stockpiled at Marseilles.[34] But if such a program of purchase was attempted, it was not continued. There can be no doubt that Colbert and his son Seignelay tolerated, perhaps had to permit, the use of green timber in the construction of galleys. Certainly only a part of the reason lay in the inability of the arsenal to accommodate large timber reserves.

A related reason for the use of unseasoned timber lay in the pressing nature of timber demand for the fleet. The pace of construction was fast; new galleys were continually being ordered by the King to enlarge his fleet. The King once said he did not expect his officers to "do the impossible" in fighting the enemy, but his intendants were repeatedly under pressure to do so in the hasty construction of new galleys. At the outset, as we have seen, a few were purchased from foreign yards (p. 69), but that alternative was soon abandoned. At nearly all times the galleys in the Corps were built in France, with unseasoned timber in the reign of Louis XIV. In the 1660's the practice of using such timber was called, and perhaps was in fact, an "expedient" that could not be avoided. Colbert remarked in 1666 that "we shall not, for a long time to come, be in a position to season our timber for ten years in underwater storage as the Venetians do."[35] But demand, far from decreasing, actually increased throughout the seventies and eighties. Significantly, galley constructions halted at Marseilles in the spring of 1692 when weather stopped the shipments of newly cut timber en route from the forests of Burgundy; there were no reserves at the arsenal.[36] Barras de la Penne had reason to say in 1693 that "up to the present time, the desire of the King to have an ever larger number of galleys has made it impossible to profit from the knowledge" that well-dried timber should be used.[37] Pontchartrain, as minister of marine, made determined efforts to halt the use of green timber in 1693 and to develop reserves, but though the size of the fleet was not then being increased, the wasteful practices continued. Early in the eighteenth century, a veteran French galley officer remarked that "the Genoese do not construct their galleys in haste as is done in France; they employ nothing but well-dried, good quality timber, and their galleys last longer."[38]

The fact that French galley constructions were extremely short-lived imposed the need for constructing frequent replacements. The costs and difficulties of maintaining and expanding the fleet were thereby multiplied — and the more galleys on hand, the greater the problems. In 1673 the ministry attempted to impose the requirement that galleys be built so that they would last at least twelve years.[39] That proved utterly impracticable. In 1681, therefore, Seignelay "fixed" their life at nine years, "it being certain," he said, "that if proper precautions are taken they can serve at least fifteen."[40] But the "proper precautions" would have eliminated the use of green timber. It continued to be used, so that even a nine-year rule proved impracticable. In 1684 Seignelay had to admit that circumstances were worse. "I see with anguish," he said, "that their durability diminishes year by year. . . . It is absolutely essential to remedy this defect. Use every possible means to make them last at least as long as they formerly did. Nothing is more prejudicial to His Majesty's [naval] service than the short life of his galleys."[41]

The maximum life of a galley in seventeenth-century France was apparently ten years. Many served only two to five years. One galley, captained by the Bailiff de Noailles, lasted only three; La Perle, built in 1673, but one. La France, constructed in 1675, lasted three years, La Fidelle two, La Couronne and Invincible four, and La Rayne three.[42]

80

Building and Victualing the Corps

Of the twenty-six galleys in the fleet in 1678, the oldest was only ten years of age; the rest were eight or fewer, averaging just short of four and one-half. Nine of these, averaging just over six years of age, were judged unfit for another campaign. "The King is surprised," said the minister, "at the short life of his galleys." He was indignant, incredulous: "What produced the difference between those that last ten years, and the others that last only three or four?" [43] Such questions were asked again and again; the problem was serious and perennial. Many opinions of why French galleys lacked durability were ventured, but no systematic inquiry appears to have been made. Perhaps there was no need, since the inquiry would discover and underscore what most competent technicians must already have known — that the use of unseasoned timber was probably the most important cause.

From time to time other factors were found that could have contributed in varying degrees to the seriousness of the problem. It was noticed, for example, that galleys built by different constructors lasted varying lengths of time. In the absence of statistical evidence, it can only be said that some, especially the Chaberts and their friends, were convinced that the most durable galleys were built by the several generations of Chaberts who engaged in building galleys under the Colberts and afterward. The fact that the Chaberts had a running feud with the ministry of marine, and with the Colberts in particular, certainly did not do their reputation and prowess as constructors any harm at Marseilles. There may, however, have been some significant differences in the workmanship and materials of different constructors even though they all used the same basic designs and worked in the same port. Or the accessibility of construction materials and labor force could have been different for different constructors. But those differences do not explain why galleys built by *every* constructor of the time were short-lived.

Some observers noticed that oak timber coming from different parts of France produced galleys of different quality. "Up to the present," said the minister of 1678, "all the galleys built with timber from Burgundy have lasted less long than those built with the timber of Provence." [44] The soils and climate in the two provinces affected timber characteristics. One would suppose, however, that good oak timber from either province, well seasoned, would last more than four or five years! But a deep-seated preference for Provençal timber was de-

81

veloped, perhaps grounded partly on the close family ties many men of the galleys had in Provence. The minister apparently shared, or at least went along with, the preference, for he ordered the intendant to "get as much timber as you can from Provence because it is very much tougher and better than that from elsewhere in France."[45] Growing more slowly, the oak of Provence produced curved timber and knees that must often have been superb. The Provençal nobility owning wooded estates may have taken some pride in having their trees highly esteemed by the navy, but they bitterly resented Colbert's application of the forest conservation law (the Ordonnance of Waters and Forests of 1669) reserving their sparse stands for the navy's use. An inventory of Provençal forest resources was undertaken in 1687, and continued in later years, to find out how much shipbuilding timber was available within direct reach of Toulon and Marseilles by water and overland routes so that it could be marked with the arms of the King as naval reserve.[46] Of course, such an inventory did nothing to endear the Colberts to the Provençal nobility. But Provençal oak timber was scarce and alternative supplies had to be sought.

Considerable quantities of pine, poplar, and elm — far less durable than oak — were used in French galleys. For example, one inventory, dated 1692, included 4,000 cubic feet of elm and 30,000 cubic feet of poplar and pine along with lesser quantities of other woods; the pieces were apparently intended for exterior planking.[47] Such softwoods were notably inferior to oak as shipbuilding material. The fir frigates constructed by the English during the Napoleonic Wars proved how lacking in durability softwoods could be when used in naval constructions, even in ships destined for operation only in colder seas.[48] Yet the softwood for exterior planking could readily be replaced without necessitating condemnation of structural parts, ribs, keel, or framing of the galley. Whenever possible such members were of oak. But oak was in short supply and some softwood may have been employed throughout galley constructions. That necessitated not only frequently replacing exterior planking, but also rebuilding whole galleys.

Sea worms might also be blamed for the short life of galleys. Worms could honeycomb the timbers of a ship, and galleys, being more lightly built, were perhaps even more prone to their ravages, especially when exterior planking was of pine or fir. But the work of the worms usually took time; that was why they seemed especially pernicious in older ships. In any case, worms were seldom mentioned as a problem on the galleys. However, sea worms were reported to be extraordinarily destructive in the Messina campaign (c. 1678). At that time the minister of marine said they were a serious problem: "The concentration of worms in the port of Messina is of such consequence that it will not be possible for His Majesty to keep his galleys there during the winter, unless some remedy is found for the worms."[49] One cannot rule out the possibility, that seemed to be part of the minister's thought, that the dangers of the worms of Messina were considerably magnified by the galley officers, who had a number of reasons for wanting to end the campaign. The minister simply urged them to caulk and tar the hulls of their galleys with frequency; he promised to send all the material they needed. To replace the losses expected, principally from worms, he said, the minister ordered three galleys built at Marseilles to be dismantled and shipped to Messina in pieces. This was the only occasion when the worms were discussed as a "serious" problem connected with the durability of galleys.

Another unusual problem was discovered in 1687. At that time it was said the réale was "much ruined and dilapidated": "This condition stems from the fact that salutes are fired indiscriminately [from the réale] for all persons who visit [the arsenal at Marseilles]. To stop this, and prevent the ruin of the galleys, His Majesty expressly forbids the firing of cannon [from galleys] in the port of Marseilles for any cause, under any pretext. He further decrees that the guns on board the réale, and those on other galleys be disembarked so that only one cannon, mounted on an old condemned galley, remains to fire [at nightfall] the signal for retreat."[50] For a galley to sustain damage from her guns was understandable, especially if the cannon in question were fixed at the bow with only the usual rudimentary recoil mechanism to absorb the shock of discharges. To use guns and galleys in that way was rather a commentary on the port authorities' negligence than a suggestion that the galleys themselves were weak.

The filth of the galleys was another possible cause of their shortness of life, suggested by the minister himself. The galley was extremely crowded, carrying more men per ton of displacement than any other vessel afloat. Sanitation, a constant problem aboard any ship, was aggravated by the crowding and, according to the minister of marine, by neglect. Some thought the problem could affect the vessel as well as the men aboard her, for in 1698 one memoirist commented that "the filth of the galleys has often caused the rotting of their principal members."[51] The real influence of filth in shortening the lives of galleys was probably indirect. The obnoxious conditions aboard a galley encouraged some officers to prefer galleys that were new or recently built. Of course, there were many reasons why men liked serving on a new vessel, but the filth of an old one could be one such reason. The presence of smells, lice, and fleas — a matter of serious comment by some officers — may have encouraged the desire to seek newly built commands. The minister, seldom handling officers with kid gloves, accused them of precisely that.[52] No love was lost between the Colberts and the nobility holding commands in Louis' Galley Corps (see, further, pp. 101–105 below).

Many circumstances apparently helped at different times to shorten the lives of French galleys in the days of Colbert. But the effects of the circumstances producing short-lived galleys were remarkably reduced in the eighteenth century. In 1748, for example, there was fifteen galleys in the fleet, not counting the galère de dépôt. Five of them were over twenty years of age, and nine were twelve years of age or more. Their average age was well over fourteen years, compared with the four and one-half years of 1678. Seven of the fifteen galleys afloat in 1748 — the oldest of the fleet, except for the seven-year-old Le Valeur — were "destined to remain in the port" of Marseilles. That did not mean that they were unfit for use, because at least two of those craft, eighteen and twenty-five years of age respectively, took to sea for Toulon the very next year. Many of those galleys in the fleet of 1748 survived years more. The difference in the longevity of galleys in 1678 and 1748 is striking.[53] The difference cannot be explained by any change in the design of the galleys — the constructors in both centuries came from the same families and in all probability used the same methods (the eighteenth-century constructors were, after all, the selected, favored architects precisely because they did build galleys in the traditional way without significant change). Nor was there significant change in the sources from which timber was taken — except perhaps some slimming of the reserves in Burgundy, Dauphiné, and Provence, from which timber was drawn in both periods. One can safely assume that officers' efforts to keep a clean galley were about the same, and worms and dry rot, if any, must have been equally damaging to galleys at both times.

84

Building and Victualing the Corps

All things considered, the explanation of the longer-lived galleys seems confined to changes in the outlook of the officers commanding and handling the galleys and, most important, to improvements in the quality of the timber with which galleys were built.

Officers of the galleys directly determined, by the decisions they made, how long a galley would last. With the intendant of galleys, the officers themselves were the expert examiners who periodically inspected each galley. Their experience, their judgments, and of course, their partialities and predispositions determined whether a galley was repaired refitted and retained, or condemned to be broken up and sold. Colbert, Seignelay, and Pontchartrain all seemed to believe that the judgments of some of these officers were influenced by a willingness to indulge their own vanity and comfort. But probably more significant was the fact that the Colberts were nowhere more deeply reviled than among Knights of Malta, and one-third to one-half of the officers were Knights. The Knights as a group were bound to resent the virtually irresistible pressure placed on the Grand Master of the Order by Colbert to obtain the admission and rapid advancement of his own relatives, in one case even to the position of commander-in-chief of all the galleys of the Order, without regard for precedence. The Colberts were thereby pushed ahead of others in that prestigious Order though they lacked the qualities ordinarily required even for admission. Bitter indeed the Knights must have been at this meddling, autocratic minister, this commoner-clerk in the minister's chair.

One might also maintain that conditions prevailing in France — the life at the court and Louis XIV himself, by his policies, life, and example — encouraged extravagant, wasteful behavior and tastes on the part of galley officers. The tenor of Louis' reign and the lavish program of constructions he undertook for the Galley Corps itself encouraged the subordination of economy. Louis not only consumed and threw wide the fruits of economy out of magnanimity and for *la gloire*, but by his example undermined the efficacy of both the policy and the practice of economic order and control that Colbert sought to promote. Circumstances were different in the eighteenth century. In 1748 economy was the order of the day in all branches of naval administration. Officers, out of self-interest, were encouraged to lengthen the lives of their galleys by deferring their condemnation for sale in order to keep the decaying fleet at full "officially authorized" numerical strength. In those days, when galleys had fallen into ill repute and few new ones were authorized, a vessel stricken from the lists might never be replaced! But these matters of motive and opinion in different periods, involving dozens or hundreds of officers, are necessarily speculative and at best only a partial explanation for differences in the record of galley durability.

More definite and certain is the fact that the use of unseasoned timber was a major weakness of seventeenth-century constructions in France. Indirect evidence suggests that green, unseasoned timber ceased to be used in galley construction sometime after 1715. Of course, the arsenal must then have had more than adequate space for the storage of timber for a fleet of only fifteen. Moreover, constructions after 1715 proceeded more slowly. Galleys were no longer deemed vital in war or useful propaganda; on the contrary, they were widely recognized as merely auxiliary at best. The ministry of marine after 1715 lacked enthusiasm for galleys. The chief proponents of the fleet were the officers of the Corps, including its influential commander, who had vested interest in making certain that none of the existing galleys were lost to the fleet. Knowing the pernicious effects of using unseasoned timber, they would assuredly not have allowed its use in the few galley constructions that they managed to have authorized. The inventory of 1748 proved as well as any document could, by showing the presence of many fit galleys of relatively advanced age, that well-cured timber was being used in constructions. Had it not been used, galleys would not have been lasting as well as they were.

The intendants' administrative problems naturally increased with the growth of the fleet. The intendant, as navy's principal local representative, had most of the responsibility for procuring victuals and munitions for the Corps. The minister of the navy, of course, shared the responsibility, but he was far from the arsenal and depended on the intendant for counsel on the quality and price of the merchandise, estimates of future requirements, and supervision of the execution of existing contracts for victuals and matériel. The intendant, with the details of administration close at hand, was in a better position than anyone else to deal with details and, if anyone could, it was he who could protect the interests of the navy and the King.

The relations between the central administration and the administration at Marseilles always reflected the personality and character of individuals involved. But between some intendants, Arnoul and Brodart in particular, and the Court, there seemed to exist a much different relation than one might expect to find where the relations of Colbert with a subordinate were involved. Here Colbert's notorious bossiness was not evident or effective. For example, the elder Colbert remarked to Arnoul that he preferred to have merchants made responsible for delivering supplies to the arsenal at such times as they were needed. Arnoul, probably with an eye to the uses of his warehouse complex (the same which thwarted the sought-for expansion of the galley base), favored stockpiles of victuals and some other supplies, presumably purchased in season at low prices but necessarily stored at considerable cost! Significantly, Arnoul's method prevailed over Colbert's even though Colbert sharply criticized Arnoul's administration:

. . . the great number of buildings that I saw in your arsenal does not suit me. All those warehouses that you have built for oils, vegetables, and other merchandise that you want to buy for the galleys at times when they are sold at reasonable prices, to make some small saving, are not to my taste. . . . Believe me, His Majesty's advantage can better be found [in dealing] with merchants. Merchants have a solicitude for their merchandise that you [as an administrator] cannot match because of the sheer diversity of the responsibilities with which you are concerned. The guards that you establish [at the warehouses] will deceive you by failing to keep accurate records of the supplies, and by failing in their surveillance of the magazines. The irregularities and accidents that can befall your reserves will prove that good management can never be anything but [the figment of] imagination.[54]

Colbert and Arnoul alike had keen appreciation of the mercenary motives of men. Both were veteran administrators. Both recognized the difficulty of obtaining and keeping subordinates' fidelity in that age, especially in the shadowy service of the Crown. Economic self-interest was a lever that was better grasped, and thereby employed and controlled, than ignored or simply policed in the management of men. But the two were working for different masters. "It is an advantage to the royal service," said Colbert, "that the merchants make a profit," since small profits make big enterprises. Though he was working for the King, Colbert said he saw "no need to be always censorious and rigid with merchants, severe in judging [their] actions. One need only correct them, not blame them, when things are in some measure defective. Your merchant suppliers have need of praise and applause." Arnoul, as Colbert was aware, had angered the merchants of Marseilles when his program of warehouse construction deprived them of profits. The minister said he was sure Arnoul would soon realize how useless those warehouses were.[55] But the warehouses did have their uses: in the long run they contributed largely to the Arnouls' fortunes.

This warehousing problem was related to the victualing problem of the Galley Corps. Clearly, their magnitude entrained the indispensable need for long-term planning to obtain the diverse and extensive larder of victuals required for the Corps. For example, the following stores were among those scheduled for delivery at Marseilles during the spring and summer of 1688:

> 500 beef cattle, live or salted
> 1,500 hogs, live or salted
> 1,500 septiers (d'Arles?) of grain or
>   biscuit (septier = 44 kilos)
> 1,500 milleroles of wine (64.3 liters each)
> 50,000 pounds of codfish
> 30,000 pounds of cheese, Gruyère or Hollande
> 30,000 pounds of rice
> 1,600 septiers of vegetables
> 1,800 barrels of sardines
> 200 milleroles of oil (c. 60 kilos each)
> 200 milleroles of vinegar (64.3 liters each)
> 300 tons of firewood[56]

Intendants sometimes contracted with individual merchants of Marseilles or Provence for local commodities or occasional needs. But intendants preferred (as did the ministry) to deal with a company of merchants or their agent who would serve as a munitionnaire, agreeing to deliver most of the victuals needed over a prearranged period, usually three or six years. Contracting of that sort avoided direct dealings with many individual producers or merchants and immensely simplified procurement problems. But the middleman cost the King money. Munitionnaires were experienced entrepreneurs, usually well to do, often backed by Paris banking syndicates or fermiers. Their experience and financial strength gave the navy reasonable assurance that financial limitations of the contractor would not prevent deliveries, regardless of any scarcity and fluctuation of price. Indeed, the advantages of dealing with a munitionnaire persuaded many galley officials that a general contractor (*fournisseur général*) should be employed to supply not only victuals but practically all other merchandise as well. Rival merchant interests vied to show the advantages and disadvantages of such arrangements. Pierre Charles et Cie served as general contractor under successive contracts during the eighties and nineties but ended the century bankrupt.[57] The stakes were high.

But contracts with the navy could be immensely profitable for the merchants and contractors involved. As a consumer of clothing and food the navy was second only to the army, and in terms of construction material, the navy was the greatest consumer in France. Many varieties of aid were extended to the navy's contractors, including advances and loans. Sometimes protection from creditors was extended even to the point of having the ministry of marine exert pressure on magistrates to decide in behalf of the navy's contractor. The profits and even the solvency of a munitionnaire might depend on fluctuations in the prices of food during the term of his contract. But buying from various localities and even from abroad in anticipation of future need or demand could minimize that risk. The high prices exacted by the munitionnaires also reflected the risks and acted as a cushion against such fluctuations; indeed, some of their prices virtually guaranteed profits. A contractor might somehow get the support of the General of the Galleys (Vivonne), a powerful personage who even declared himself willing to consider the extremity of calling off a campaign because the munitionnaire was having such trouble in buying the victuals and stores required.[58] Perhaps the greatest risks the contractors faced were the arbitrary fiscal practices of the navy. Even in the halcyon days of Colbert, the navy (like the monarch himself) was sometimes short of funds. In the last two decades of the reign payments became so uncertain and fell so far in arrears that some contractors, such as the powerful Charles et Cie, were pushed into bankruptcy by the navy's failure to pay.

From the standpoint of the navy's interest, there was an obvious need for constant watchfulness. The intendant was well placed to perform that service. Among his responsibilities was an obligation to see that the terms of contracts were as advantageous as possible for the navy, that the merchandise delivered was of the requisite quality, and that deliveries were made when and where needed or promised. Particular care was required to audit the accounts and to superintend the work of the gardes-magasin, the functionaries who, in spite of a relatively small salary, carried great responsibility and were vital figures at the reception of merchandise destined for the magazines or in storage for the Corps. The distinction between perquisites and bribery was always fine, hard to define, harder still to maintain. The ministers of marine could be surprisingly lenient in making allowance for oversights and errors of judgment and often confined themselves to mere reprimands in cases of minor fraud, especially when general relations with the official were good or when he was a vigorous, effective servant of the King. Colbert dismissed (or transferred) an intendant for inefficiency, as he did the younger Arnoul after he had served only months; but the same minister tolerated Arnoul's successor, Nicolas Brodart, for nearly ten years, in spite of all his mistakes, misdemeanors, corruption, and fraud. One reason, but hardly the only one for retaining him for so long, lay in the fact that most of the accusations against him came from persons and "interests" at Marseilles hardly friendlier to the Colberts than to Brodart.

The operations of Intendant Brodart suggested some of the types of administrative malpractice that not only existed but were tolerated by the ministry even after the abuses concerned had been repeatedly disclosed and repeatedly condemned. For example, Brodart made what passed for a mistake, attributable to excessive zeal or perhaps the desire to obliterate evidence of corruption, when in 1675–76 he shipped to Messina far more victuals than were needed. When the minister learned that Brodart had (or claimed he had) literally emptied the magazines and shipped the contents to Sicily, his comment was: "His Majesty was surprised to learn how little merchandise remains in the magazines, particularly since he has always kept the magazines well-stocked, and has spent the funds needed for their maintenance every year. It is impossible that such enormous quantities could be used [in so little time] without a great many irregularities. It is your responsibility to find the cause and to deal with it in detail." [59] This method of proceeding was probably a profitable collusion between Brodart and the munitionnaire, who later was shown to be Brodart's business partner and associate. Indeed, the nature of this partnership is suggested by the fact that Brodart accepted delivery from the munitionnaire of supplies that he and his partner jointly owned. Later, perhaps significantly, we find Brodart including enormous quantities of rotting merchandise and bad wines in shipments sent overseas.[60]

Brodart's victualing contracts also involved some recurrent difficulties in matters of measures and weights, difficulties that seemed consistently to benefit the contractor at the cost of the King. For example, a contract was negotiated in 1678 that employed "measures of Provence" for the daily rations provided to galley crewmen but that gave rise to serious abuse since the "Provençal" measures used were larger than those normally employed. Under this contract the King provided more provisions per day than were needed; the "surplus" was disposed of in collaboration with "agents" of the munitionnaire. The minister ordered this arrangement changed: "The King desires that only weights of *marc* and [the smaller] measures of Paris be used." [61] In 1681 the minister discovered that these orders were still being disobeyed but in a different way. The smaller "weight of Marseilles" (differing from that of Provence, and also from that of Paris) was being used in deliveries of bread, though the King was paying for the bread by the measure of Paris, with the result that the oarsmen were receiving less bread than the King bought. The difference was doubtless profit for the munitionnaire (and Brodart).[62] The nature of Brodart's connections and collaboration with the munitionnaire became known in the ministry of marine, and in February the minister wrote Brodart: "This man Creissel, under the names of other merchants, was awarded contracts for practically all the merchandise purchased by the Galley Corps. The protection he received from you enabled him to prevent other merchants from offering to deliver goods at substantially lower prices. I would like to believe that you acted only with the best intentions in this regard; but take care that your behavior does not stand in the way of obtaining merchandise for the King as cheaply as he would wish." [63]

Hardly less questionable were Brodart's dealings with commercial shippers, whose services were needed to ship victuals to the galleys when they were campaigning. In 1675 Brodart submitted bills for freight (bottoms) supposedly needed and used in shipping 44,000 quintaux (c. 2,200 long tons) of merchandise. When the minister analyzed his accounts (with a few arithmetical errors on the minister's part), the freight bill appeared unbelievably high. Either Brodart had paid more than twice the regular rates for freight or, as the minister chose to believe, he had employed "almost twice as many ships as necessary." Brodart, one can be sure, somehow profited in the deal. In any case the freight services involved excessive costs, and Brodart was told to see that it did not happen again. He was also told explicitly to limit his expenditures for freight to a maximum of 45,000 livres.[64] But Brodart failed to stay within that limit or to adopt certain expedients recommended by the minister to effect economies. His bills mounted to over 60,000 livres. Again Brodart was merely reprimanded and not very severely at that: "you have not done as I suggested. . . . and I also see errors in yours [Brodart's accounts]; but it suffices that I tell you to take care; use all possible precautions to economize the King's expenditure." [65] Far from doing as he was told, Brodart continued much as he had before. In 1677 he submitted bills of lading for two 500-ton flûtes at 2,100 livres apiece, a very high charge for ships of that size. But Colbert discovered that the vessels Brodart had actually employed were not 500-tonners at all but vessels of 200 and 400 tons. In that light, Brodart's bills for freight were again out of line, and the minister wrote that "His Majesty desires that you clarify these obscurities." [66]

Intendant Brodart's behavior was no less reprehensible in a case when the building of ships was involved. In 1675 he was authorized to build two flûtes to assist with the transport of victuals needed for the galleys. Flûtes of 500–600 tons were ordinarily built and equipped at other ports for approximately 20,000 to 25,000 livres, but at Marseilles under Brodart's administration there were inordinate delays; a whole year went by during which Brodart assured the minister that the two vessels in question were on the way. Eventually it was disclosed that the cost of these two "cargo carriers" had mounted to 150,000 livres! Instead of building the two flûtes authorized for the transport service, Brodart on his own authority had used the credits furnished for the flûtes to construct two fighting ships of 50 and 54 guns instead. The minister was astonished! "His Majesty can hardly express his surprise at your conduct in the construction of these two ships. . . . this conduct on your part has not pleased His Majesty, and such faults will not often be tolerated." [67] The fact that such conduct was tolerated as much as it was is remarkable. But vagaries and misbehavior of many sorts were tolerated in Brodart almost as a matter of routine.

Brodart held his post until June 1684. Even then he was not discharged from the service but merely transferred.[68] The few instances of malpractice mentioned may not fairly represent Brodart's performance as an administrator; certainly he was energetic and did get things done when he wanted and in his own way. But other men were dismissed or condemned to prison, or worse, for less serious and less costly corruption and fraud. The galleys themselves were full of convicted thieves whose transgressions were socially less significant than Brodart's. Even considering the nepotism characteristic of the time, Brodart being connected with the Colbert clan, it is difficult to justify retention of such a rascal for so long. The minister tried scolding, cajoling, and threats to get Brodart to stop or to make him limit his thefts. But Brodart persisted. Finally, however, he went beyond the tolerated limits too often, too blatantly, and for too long, and perhaps in such measure that the minister's son and successor would have been compromised if, after he decided to retain the man, the full extent of his transgressions was somehow made known. Thus, Seignelay transferred Brodart after Colbert died. Michel Bégon, Brodart's successor, was reminded by Seignelay soon after he took over his post that a man charged as he was with the execution of His Majesty's orders must have a firm maxim in all expenditure for the galleys: "Never suffer any disguise of the truth in any detail of the many matters in which monies have been employed." [69] Such principles of administration were obviously respected, but they were difficult to apply in the Galley Corps. Bégon managed to do so with greater effort and in better measure than Brodart. But the high-principled character of his approach to administration, coupled with his lack of experience in affairs connected with galleys, probably were jointly responsible for his short tenure as an intendant.

The men and methods employed in the administration of the Corps enormously increased the costs involved in the achievement of Louis' policy objectives. Expenditures for the Galley Corps usually absorbed 20–25 per cent of the money spent for the navy at large.[70] Once established and built, the matériel for the Corps, both galleys and oarsmen, had to be kept in trim, maintained and replaced with regularity. Oarsmen of the kind employed could not be gathered and trained in the space of a few months or a year or two. In the last three decades of the century practically every seaworthy galley was sent out to campaign every year, manned by a crew and rowing force at full or near full strength. Practically every officer of the Galley Corps was paid a full salary each year, and the number of officers and crews steadily increased along with the fleet. The galleys themselves were replaced with astonishing frequency. Hence, expenditure for the Galley Corps under the Colbert and Seignelay administration mounted steadily and precipitously over the years in both war and peace.

If those outlays can be taken as a rough guide to the importance Louis attached to that part of his navy, it is worth noting that in the twenty-eight years after 1662 Louis spent well over 70 million livres on galleys, while spending perhaps 300 million on the navy as a whole. In the nineties at least 30 million more must have been spent on the galleys. Louis XIV was resolved, to the extent of spending over 100 million livres during the four decades of his reign, to have a Galley Corps in the Mediterranean with an arsenal whose magnificence was intended to be "proportioned to his *grandeur*." [71]

Officers and the Crown

Almost every commissioned officer on French galleys after 1680 was a nobleman. Many were also Knights of Malta, from historically distinguished noble families. For such aristocrats the profession of arms aboard French galleys was congenial and attractive. Aristocrats have often felt a special obligation to wield the sword and to command, serving either King or Church, sometimes both. Service on the galleys offered chances for distinction with special appeal to noblemen, many of whom would accept hazards willingly with the conviction that success could make their reputations and add enduring luster to their family names. In some respects galleys offered even greater chances for distinction than sailing vessels. Their tactics traditionally called for boarding the enemy, for swordsmanship and hand-to-hand combat — and perhaps such action had more attraction than the exchange of cannon fire from afar. Certainly, in any case, family tradition and ancestral preferences encouraged young men in some French families to become officers in the galley service. For example, Provençal families, Catholic and Protestant alike, had been sending men to sea for generations, and in such families there was pride in the fact that forebears had served or commanded at sea or had even owned galleys, and had loyally served the king of France.

Furthermore, service in the royal Galley Corps had appeal on religious grounds. In the seventeenth century almost all Christian churches of the West gave sanction to the "defense of Christendom," and especially to the use of force against the Moslems and the refugees, expellees, and renegades from Europe living in North Africa and the eastern Mediterranean,[1] classifiable collectively as infidels. Such people were widely held to be common enemies of all Christians. The King's galleys and many others campaigned against those infidels almost every year. Hence, French noblemen, family conscious and Church connected as they often were, Catholics and Protestants alike, could do duty as good Christians by taking service on the galleys as generations of forebears had done. Catholic and Huguenot officers served together in French squadrons, even aboard the same vessels and galleys through the sixties and seventies until the King arbitrarily excluded from his naval service all men (with a few exceptions) who would not become converts to Catholicism.[2] Until then both Catholic and Huguenot officers with pious inclinations must have reasoned that in taking service on Louis' galleys they had a double opportunity, the chance to serve both the King and the cause of Christendom.

There were also less exalted motives for serving on French royal galleys. Some men judged the chances for advancement to be exceptionally good, as they no doubt were in the sixties when Louis' expansion of his navy was creating pressing needs for additional officers. Moreover, officers in galleys were paid more than officers in the sailing navy. It was attractive that galleys, unlike sailing ships, campaigned mainly in the summer. And even more attractive was the fact that galleys campaigned almost every year; their officers were not left unemployed for years on end, as officers in the sailing navy sometimes were. In short, some men must have been drawn by the regularity of service under oars, by good pay and long vacations every year, and by the fact that galleys never made "those wretched two- or three-year voyages in distant seas."[3]

With varied motives, then, generations of French aristocrats had chosen galleys in preference to other fighting services. When the reorganization and expansion of Louis XIV's fleet was undertaken in the sixties, more officers were needed. Many untrained aristocrats were willing to serve, but Louis needed experienced officers to assume command of additions to the fleet to replace retiring veterans (such as the Marquis de Ternes who commanded a squadron of eleven galleys sent against North Africa in 1668 when he was 92 years of age!),[4] and to replace certain foreign officers (such as the Marquis de Centurion, on whom see p. 69).[5] Competent younger captains were very much sought.

Up to the sixties the Crown had usually been content to allow squadron or fleet commanders, in concert with such port officials as the intendant, to issue temporary commissions to lieutenants and sous-lieutenants for each campaign. Most of the captains appear to have been designated and commissioned directly by the Court.[6] Some men transferred from the sailing navy to the galleys; others came from the army — a suitable background because galleys did have certain military qualities. Very few Knights of the Order of Malta entered the Corps during the sixties, being deterred perhaps by the involvement of the Order in the campaign at Crete, and by friction then characterizing Louis XIV's relations with the Pope and the Grand Master of their Order. However, when further expansion of the Corps was decided upon, Colbert gave it as his opinion that there were then too few officers "of special merit in the Corps."[7] The "special merit" he thought needed consisted of being French-born of good family (nobility) and having experience with galleys — qualities that very few men (other than Knights of Malta) could be expected to possess. As we have seen, Louis had sent a mission to Malta in 1663 to seek matériel and technical help for the navy and that same mission also sought French Knights to serve as galley officers. But few, if any, were obtained at that time because the Order was already heavily committed in the campaign against the Turks on Crete. In 1668, hearing reports that the galleys of the Order had notably distinguished themselves in recent action against the Turks, Colbert sought the names of the French-born Knights who had taken part. A further indication of his preference for Knights was given by his blanket instruction to the intendant at Marseilles to obtain the services of French Knights "who have commanded, or now command galleys" for the King's Galley Corps.[8]

The forces of the Order of St. John certainly included the largest body of trained, French-born galley officers to be found anywhere. Aristocratic families in France had for many generations eagerly vied for the privilege of sending younger sons to serve on the galleys of the Order of St. John. On rare occasions men without (or with insufficient) titled ancestry were admitted to the Order, but only when their services or connections could prove that they deserved the favor and honor of being raised to noble rank. In effect, however, the Order and its galleys were the exclusive preserve of Europe's Christian, above all Roman Catholic Christian, aristocrats. The Abbé de Vertot, an eighteenth-century historian of the Order, referred to its members as "a militia composed of the most noble blood of the Christian world." [9] They thought of themselves as, and in some circles were reputed to be, an "elite of Christendom." [10] Their Order served as a training school for aristocratic officers, a veritable school of naval war. The training was of course intended to prepare men for service in the forces of the Order, but many "graduates" did leave Malta to take service in the forces of Christian princes and powers of the Mediterranean. The help thereby given to the Christian princes was incidental but nonetheless a useful and valuable service, both for them and presumably also for Christendom.

To achieve the rank of captain in the Order a Knight normally had to be over twenty-five, with at least ten years of seniority and the experience of at least three campaigns behind him. Unfortunately, Frenchmen who had risen to captaincies on the galleys of the Order were apparently unwilling to take service at the same rank, or even at higher rank and more remuneration, on the galleys of the King of France. The difficulty of making the transfer can be variously explained. In the first place, there was strong likelihood that veterans seeking permission to leave Malta to enter the service of France would receive a cool, and probably a negative reception from the Grand Master. Moreover, some Knights (perhaps many) held views comparable to those of the eighteenth-century Chevalier Luc de Boyer d'Argens, whose ideas about the religious responsibilities of Knights were probably more representative of the earlier period with which we are concerned than of d'Argens' own time.[11] D'Argens felt strongly that he had an obligation to serve his Order in preference to any secular prince. He implored his fellow Knights to consider the consequences of leaving Malta to campaign for European princes:

When a man becomes a Knight of Malta, he has the apparent intention of performing the principal duties [of a Knight], or at least he should have that intention, even if he does not. And what duties are those? To defend the Faith against the Infidels, to destroy the pirates and Mohammedans. [But] when he goes to fight against the French, the Germans and the English, he does not fulfill these obligations. He vowed to war against the Infidels, not to let the blood of Christians or to strangle brothers. . . . If you note carefully how many unjust wars are fought

98

by Christian princes, how many men they send off to their deaths, some-times simply to satisfy their personal hatred or ambition, you cannot but cherish the service of a State [the Order] that makes war only to defend the Faith and, far from taking part in the criminal disputes of Christians, regrets the passion associated so inappropriately with names of glory and love of *la patrie*.[12]

We have no way of knowing how many French-born Knights of Malta held such views. In principle, they were probably held at least by all the Grand Masters of the period, though their overt policy was necessarily flexible. When veterans left Malta for secular service, the leadership of the Order's forces was weakened and the strength of purpose of younger Knights was diluted by the bad example. No Knight of conscience could have felt entirely free from qualms in leaving, still less in slaying Roman Catholic or any other Christians, as he might be called upon to do in the service of French kings. In short, for a variety of reasons, not every Knight of Malta could or would serve in Louis XIV's galleys. Hence, veteran volunteers were few.

Colbert and Louis lowered their requirements in 1669. French-born Knights, Colbert then implied, need not have commanded galleys; it sufficed that they be able to command.[13] Under those conditions additional Knights were recruited for appointment to French commands, and a considerable number accepted commissions as subordinate officers. In 1672 Colbert decreed that all the men proposed henceforth as officer candidates should be experienced men, "should have served on Maltese galleys and should be members of the Order. . . . His Majesty desires to have aboard his galleys the greatest possible number of Knights of Malta."[14] There are several probable reasons behind this decree: First, Knights were of course experienced officers. Second, they could bring to Louis' service the immense prestige of being fighters for the Faith who had vowed to die if need be for Christianity. Perhaps it was hoped their presence in the Galley Corps might help to dissipate from pious minds the thought that Louis XIV might be a friend of the Sultan, with whom he happened, just then, to be negotiating a new Capitulation Treaty (1673).

During the years of warfare after 1672 the number of galleys in the fleet was temporarily stabilized at about twenty-five. But the need for new officers revived in the late seventies when Louis indicated that he wanted still more galleys built and manned. The minister of marine then wrote again to Malta asking for a list of twenty French-born Knights "who have made their caravans and are experienced and capable of service," but he specified that he wanted "very few Provençaux." [15] Looking to the formation of a cadre of experienced young apprentice officers, the minister decreed that every galley that put to sea should have aboard at least four Musketeers. The Musketeers were to serve voluntarily; with a few years of experience, the minister said, they would "become good captains for the galleys." [16] A corps of ensigns was also created for the galleys (1680) to give experience to young men of noble rank and to enable them to rise to posts of higher responsibility in the Corps. "Let me know the names of those you think are suited for these posts, so that I can give the King their names; but take note, if you please, of His Majesty's wish, that all of them be men of noble rank," and again he specified, "avoid as much as possible proposing Provençaux." [17]

The aversion to Provençaux requires a word of explanation. Louis' private thoughts in the matter must remain uncertain, though he was aware of the lessons of the past, taught by the turbulent history and autonomous tendencies of the peoples of Provence and Languedoc, the sixteenth-century civil wars, the mid-seventeenth–century Fronde, and continual rebellions in various parts of the realm in his own and previous reigns. All served to underscore the revolts against royal authority that took place in Provence, and at Marseilles in particular, in the years 1658–60. That episode led Louis XIV to erect Fort St. Nicholas at the entrance to the harbor of Marseilles, overlooking the town and galley base, commanding entry to the port and serving as a reminder of the King's authority. Something equally suggestive of the spirit of his administration was revealed when he visited Marseilles during a tour of the Midi and entered the town by a breach in the city walls, rather than by way of the city gates. Many men of the Midi, though they had given good courageous service, had proved headstrong, independent, and difficult to discipline. There was reason for believing that discipline, esprit de corps, and willingness to serve the Crown could more readily be developed and maintained, in the case of Provençaux, if they were employed in localities apart from their native place. Since many Provençaux normally acquired experience with seafaring vocations, such officers were perhaps better reserved for the sailing navy, then expanding rapidly, where they would help to remedy the shortage of competent officers. A proportionately large, and from the King's point of view apparently, an excessive number of Provençaux were already serving in the Galley Corps, based in the Mediterranean. Men from other parts of the realm should be encouraged to serve on the royal galleys.

Ultimately, the Knights of St. John formed the backbone of the Corps. At most times after 1670 Knights commanded about half of Louis' galleys. Many other Knights served as junior officers. In 1672, for example, on one list of twenty-one captains then commanding Louis' galleys, at least eleven were members of the Order;[18] two years later, in 1674, at least sixteen of thirty commands were held by Knights in a particular squadron authorized to campaign.[19] Incidentally, at that time only one galley captain, the Sieur Spanet, appears to have been neither a member of a titled family nor a member of the Order of St. John, and Spanet was soon afterward disgraced (for cause) and ejected from the Corps.[20] The preference shown for Knights in recruitments and promotions during the early seventies produced the preponderance of Knights found in the Corps around 1680.[21] The percentage of Knights seems to have reached its high point at about that time. But significantly, members of the Order never monopolized the higher officer posts of the Corps. In fact, their numbers fell off a bit in the nineties.[22]

"The officer is the soul of the vessel," Colbert once remarked, and "officers who add good birth and nobility to other vital qualities are the most effective officers because the soldiers and sailors have more respect for them, and are more obedient to them."[23] Colbert might have added that the real problem of obedience in the navy involved, not lowly sailors and marines and noncommissioned men, but the officers themselves. Subordinate personnel were for the most part obedient. They had to be. Their officers were authorized to use drastic forms of punishment to exact obedience. Commissioned officers could and did obtain the deference and the exact obedience that they thought was owed to persons of their station. But it is notable that in the seventeenth century, at least in the Colbert ministries, many of them did not give to the King, their commander in chief, the sort of obedience they exacted from their own subordinates.

The nature of the need for obedience among officers can be illustrated by recounting an instance of the blatant independence of a certain Jean-Baptiste de Valbelle. On many occasions Valbelle demonstrated courage, initiative, and valor as an officer, earning the nickname "Tiger" from admirers. But the "Tiger" could be rash and independent to the point of utter irresponsibility. On one occasion in 1660, characteristically, instead of cooperating in the vast and secret operation for the relief of Crete (the 1660 expedition of Mazarin), Valbelle ignored the King's specific instructions and, since that particular campaign was directed against the infidel, Valbelle also neglected his obligations as a Knight of Malta. Valbelle disobeyed direct orders from his immediate commander and fellow Knight, the loyal Commander Paul, and, braving the latter's cannon fire, disappeared over the horizon under a press of sail, resolved to go privateering on his own. For this colossal piece of impudence the Chevalier de Valbelle and his subordinate officers were condemned in absentia to the penalty of death. Of course they were not obliged to suffer that severity, and were in fact restored to royal favor afterward. Yet the offense did emphasize the imperative need for a regime of discipline among naval officers.[24]

In earlier years many officers had shown themselves too independent to be relied upon to execute orders from the Court. Independent behavior, one might suppose, could be expected when captains owned and operated galleys of their own or when the galleys of the King were "farmed out" to captains who agreed to maintain them and campaign for a fee; such captains demonstrated that they possessed not only courage and a "spirit of enterprise," but also good business sense in functioning as "fighters for hire." By the 1660's long experience had shown that the reliance on such a system of maritime mercenaries did not give the King the forces or the service he desired.

One memoirist focused attention on a few of the problems by pointing out that: "When galleys were privately owned it was noticeable that they were always defective in some respect, either because of negligence or avarice on the captain's part . . . officers were reluctant to expose their galleys to the perils of war and [to the sea] . . . galleys often quit [the] fleet for lack of victuals or for other reasons, because the captains [had] over-economized. . . . Many merchants were ruined for lack of payment from the galley captains, even though the captains had received their payment from the King . . . and lastly, it was found that . . . forçats [supplied by the King to individual captains] escaped more often, either through connivance of the captains or for other reasons."[25] Such criticisms did not apply to all captains who had held commands, but they did apply to enough of them to persuade Louis XIV and his ministers of marine that many changes needed to be made.

The most important single step taken was to expand the system of royal ownership to include all matériel. Thus, when the Galley Corps was organized (1662–65), the Crown assumed responsibility for the purchase or construction and the maintenance of all matériel.[26] The King financed and thereby presumably acquired full authority in the governance of his Corps. From that time forward the regulations of the King were expected to have greater efficacy in all matters related to officers. The officers themselves in their behavior under this "new regime" were expected to show "on all occasions, blind obedience to persons who have the honor of commanding His Majesty's arms."[27]

The regime of royal ownership was an essential step, but only one step toward enforcing and increasing the King's control. It was part of the general effort made in seventeenth-century France to increase the power of the King. But the particular problem of discipline, including the difficulties entrained by the lack of it, persisted and constituted the most nearly intractable problem faced by Louis and his ministers in developing and operating the Corps.

One basic reason for the persistence of the problem in aggravated forms lay in the venality of officer posts. Commissions, captaincies, and the posts of Lieutenant General and General of the Galleys were still being given or sold by the Crown; they were objects of real economic value that were bought and sold by qualified persons. The Sieur de Manse, for example, who was later to become Squadron Commander, bought his commission as galley captain in 1645 for 40,000 livres.[28] Louis Victor de Rochechouart, Count (later Duke) de Vivonne, who was not only comfortably wealthy but extremely well connected, had no little difficulty getting together the 700,000 livres he paid in 1669 for the post of General of the Galleys. When the de facto powers of commander in chief of the Corps passed in 1679 to the Lieutenant General, the post was purchased by the Bailiff de Noailles, member of the Order of Malta, for 170,000 livres.[29] A person holding such a commission was naturally inclined to consider it a piece of property that could be used with some latitude and from which he could uninterruptedly derive the income and prestige he supposed it would produce when he bought it. The income produced by such investments consisted of salary and perquisites, the latter being produced in large part by the exercise of powers that could be, and sometimes were, subversive of royal authority and control.[30]

Royal authorities clearly understood that this confounding of public powers and private property had the effect of limiting royal authority. As a means of reform, Colbert and Seignelay undertook a twofold program. They raised salaries and undertook to pay them regularly; and secondly, they sought wherever practicable to limit or eliminate perquisites exercised by galley officers that they considered damaging to the interest of the King. In doing so Colbert and Seignelay transgressed the interests of many officers by restriction of long-established privileges and vested interests and by substantial reductions on the returns produced by some sizable investments. This program of reform, understandably, added to the enduring opprobrium in which the Colberts were widely held and helped produce the manifold opposition of Corps officers. Though focused on the Colberts, that opposition was effectively subversive of royal authority. This team of reformers persisted nonetheless, with the King's support, and during their tenure managed to impose pervasive piecemeal increases in Crown control. But the struggle to do so was long and complicated.

Among the many manifestations of indiscipline among galley officers was the tendency to overstay their leaves of absence from the service. Hardly an unusual problem in armed forces, this assumed significant proportions in Louis' Galley Corps. Louis allowed his officers to take leave during the winter months since campaigns were not usually planned for that season of the year. Officers were sometimes authorized to take as much as six months of leave (though at the end of the century galley captains were usually limited to a three-month leave beginning about mid-November), and only about half of them were allowed to go at one time. Mere reprimand was the common punishment for lateness in returning to base, though suspension from the service (usually temporary) was sometimes imposed after repeated and seriously compromising or inconveniencing absences. But there was less disposition to be lenient when lateness prevented some galleys from accompanying the fleet on campaign.[31]

The importance and seriousness of the problem seemed to be magnified by Colbert's death in 1683. The very next year the incidence of absences without leave called forth a reiteration of regulations already issued, forbidding officers to take leave without authority and providing three months of imprisonment for the first offense and expulsion from the service for the second.[32] But mere promises of rigorous penalties did not seem to solve the problem, as evidenced by the record number of absences in 1687 when about 10 per cent of the officers designated to campaign were absent without leave. The culprits may have thought that after his father's death Seignelay would find it expedient to be lenient where so many members of such distinguished families were involved. The officers concerned were quite possibly giving vent to their dislike, even hatred of the Colberts and to their rebelliousness by showing scorn for Colbert authority. But in doing so they were also challenging the Crown authority and were speedily made to feel they had gone too far. Seignelay must have taken satisfaction in the action of the King in "breaking" a considerable number of officers. Great were the efforts of the aristocrats to avoid the penalties called for by the regulations. Even the Bishop of Beauvais was moved to intervene in behalf of a certain Marquis de Velleron (upon his second offense).[33] Of course French officers continually had more or less excusable "difficulties" in their efforts to get back to base, but Seignelay's action of the eighties seems to have dissipated, once and for all, any semblance of open challenge to the minister's authority where such matters were involved.

Another, much more painful manifestation of the problem of discipline, and one that persisted in spite of all efforts made toward its solution, was that of interservice rivalry, which was the basis for many instances of extreme indiscipline that proved exasperating to the King and his ministers. The problem was particularly evident, of course, when joint operations of sailing craft and galleys were attempted. Officers in each branch, particularly in the Galley Corps, insisted on their precedence. "Duty" to the King was forgotten in the welter of individual quarrels. Even such distinguished and loyal officers as the Duke de Vivonne, General of the Galleys, insisted that "the officers of galleys have always taken command over captains of [sailing] vessels, given equal seniority and rank,"[34] and it does not require much effort to visualize the extreme difficulties that such an attitude could and did create. All forms of interservice quarreling were explicitly condemned and deplored by the King and ministers; regulations were issued repeatedly over the years to prevent and smooth out difficulties, though never with much success. Louis XIV himself reached the conclusion that such problems were inevitable. To avoid the most pernicious effects, sailing vessels and galleys had to operate independently because "[joint] operations by galleys and vessels are nearly always incompatible." [35]

Fleet maneuvers, like many military drill procedures on the parade ground, were intended to increase efficiency and to inculcate habits of discipline and obedience. Galleys were ideal tools for such training purposes. Under oars they were capable of orderly, obedient movements as no sailing vessel was and could move in close formations. Accordingly, commanders of squadrons were informed that the King desired that "all his galleys make identical maneuvers, with the same regularity and the same exactitude that His Majesty's troops employ." [36] Even in classical times, uniform procedures and movements had been used by the owners and commanders of Mediterranean galleys. But apparently no satisfactory or suitable routine had been evolved and adhered to during the first fifteen years of the operation of the Corps. In 1681 Louis XIV expressed his hope that the recently appointed commander in chief, the Bailiff de Noailles, would "establish a discipline that has not been known up to now in this Corps, and [would thereby] avoid the confusion that has characterized maneuvers and commands in the past." [37] The minister informed the new commander that "His Majesty is persuaded that nothing can be more useful for his service," than to execute movements with "extreme exactitude." [38]

By the early nineties uniform procedures were in use. Orders issued for the campaign of 1692 prescribed in great detail exactly how the squadron of thirty-five galleys would develop its formations and proceed from one port to the next. The squadron was to form three ranks, with thirteen galleys in the forward line (the flagship in the center) and eleven galleys in each of the other two ranks following close behind in the manner of troops engaged in close order drill.[39] The position of each galley was to be determined by the seniority of its commanding officer. Entering a foreign port a squadron was required to form a single file using the detailed procedures prescribed "by the book," with special care taken to observe precedence of senior officers over their juniors. Special maneuvers were prescribed for combat situations, others for bad weather, and so on. Galley commanders were ordered to practice and perfect these procedures so that they could execute all movements with exactitude.[40]

"Close order drill" formations were impressive and had some value for developing obedience and orderly conformity, but they were harder to execute at sea with galleys operating under oars than with companies or regiments of infantry on the drill field. Close proximity to neighboring vessels in formation was certain to increase the chances for collision and French galleys had many.

The officers rather than the procedures were nearly always held responsible when collisions did take place — indeed, the reaction in the ministry tended to be so highly critical and even vehement that it seemed at times to reflect some lack of understanding on the part of minister or King, or even a tendency to indulge in harassment of galley officers. The minister decried "the frequent collisions" in which His Majesty's galleys were involved. The campaign of 1692, for example, saw three collisions take place, evidently significant ones for both minister and King heard about all three. The King's annoyance led him to remark that the commanding officers were "either negligent or incapable," and the Bailiff de Noailles received a strong reprimand.[41] The next year, "desiring to put a stop to these accidents, which are always occasioned by the negligence of officers," the minister decreed that captains and their subordinates would henceforth be held personally and financially responsible for accidents or damage they caused: "Repairs will be made at their cost, and deducted from [their] salaries accordingly."[42] Twentieth-century captains of multi-million–dollar carriers and missile ships can count themselves fortunate that such pecuniary penalties do not apply to them. The seventeenth-century penalty was of course less ludicrous: galley captains received a base pay of 3,000 livres a year, and the hull of the vessel they commanded could be constructed for between 14,000 and 24,000 livres. Apparently the minister and King were determined to require that officers be responsible for damage, as they had been in condottiere days for galleys they owned or leased.

Other characteristics of the discipline problem came to the fore when galleys arrived in foreign ports. Officers were then expected to behave themselves, at least to the extent of showing self-control, dignity, and discipline in public conduct. The minister questioned the advisability of allowing all the captains to go ashore at once, as they did at Leghorn in 1679, to dine with the local governor. "Irreparable accidents can happen to His Majesty's galleys in foreign ports in the absence of commanding officers," said the minister.[43] He may have had in mind an accident that had occurred in 1677 when the galley *l'Heureuse* blew up in the port of Cività Vecchia with the loss of many lives.[44] Officers on campaign and in foreign ports were of course especially prone to indulge their independent inclinations. They did no credit to themselves or to their King, said the minister, when they misbehaved in dealings with local populace or abbreviated religious observances or slept with women aboard their galleys. A good deal of boisterousness and carousing was tolerated in French ports even though such behavior was condemned by regulations, but it was considered reprehensible in foreign ports because it gave a bad impression of the service of the King of France.[45]

Another, far more blatant instance of independence and irresponsibility came to light in 1678 after the galleys had returned from an Italian campaign. Heavy weather had been encountered. Indeed, the weather was reported to have been so severe that the captains of some galleys reported that they were obliged to lighten their craft by throwing equipment overboard and even jettisoning cannon! On being informed of these circumstances, the minister indicated surprise "to see how many cannon were jettisoned; I believe the captains had their reasons, but the emergency must have been extreme." Two months later the minister was informed, somehow, that clues had been found to the whereabouts of some of the missing guns. Certain officers, on their return to port, were reported to have transported "cannon that they took in Sicily" to the Abbey of St. Victor at Marseilles. A royal order was issued directing the prior of the Abbey to permit a search of his premises. Cannon were discovered, which had been brought there and sold, one for 572 livres, the other for 546. The penalty? "His Majesty desires that this sum be withheld from their salaries."[46] There was reason, it would seem, for the minister's remark that officers "should not have other purposes in their conduct than those that honor, integrity, and zeal for the service [of the King] could inspire."[47]

Most of the larcenies perpetrated by officers on the King's galleys were more remunerative and less risky than the outright theft of cannon. Some of their methods were adaptations from condottiere days. In 1677, for example, it was reported that captains of galleys, preparing to depart from Marseilles on campaign, armed merchant vessels to accompany the fleet for their own account and manned the vessels with sailors and oarsmen from the royal galleys under their command, "thus weakening their rowing force, and thereby allowing many forçats to escape, since they were less well guarded on board the commercial carriers than they were on the galleys."[48] Some of the merchantmen were probably carrying victuals destined to be consumed aboard the galleys themselves. The practice of arming merchantmen for private profit was declared to be pernicious, especially contrary to the King's interest when his oarsmen were thus misused; it was ordered stopped.

Another economic use being made of galley oarsmen by the officers was disclosed in 1693 when the minister learned that a certain galley captain had "worked eight convicts [and slaves] during all the [previous] spring on a house he purchased" in the vicinity of Marseilles. In this case the minister was particularly critical of Intendant Montmort, who claimed to be surprised to learn of the existence of this abuse. "I do not know which is more culpable, to have hidden from me conduct of this sort or to have overlooked for a considerable period the fact that about a hundred convicts and slaves were leaving the galleys each day and working outside Marseilles." The minister marveled that Montmort could ignore such flagrant abuses and yet know so much detail about other matters of less consequence going on aboard the galleys.[49] The persistence of such practices in the decade of the 1690's seemed clear indication that some of the King's officers had not yet adjusted either to serving the King disinterestedly or to conforming to his regulations.

Officers of the galleys, like those in the sailing navy and the army, were empowered to recruit and appoint the noncommissioned officers in their own commands. That system of recruitment was common in the military and naval forces of seventeenth-century Europe. In making such appointments captains of French galleys received "certain small and secret remunerations,"[50] another detail of the galley system that had counterparts elsewhere. Attempts were made in 1685 and in 1689 to transfer the appointive powers of the captains to a Major of the Galleys, later to the intendant, no doubt against the wishes of some captains.[51] But in spite of many attempted changes and a series of pertinent regulations, the effective power of appointment was still in the captains' hands in 1705.[52]

This power to appoint subordinates was important. It had significant economic value for captains and was directly related to the galley's fighting capability. Every galley carried its complement of "infantry," men of various sorts who were classed as fighting men and organized by the 1690's into companies and battalions known collectively as the Corps d'Infanterie des Galères — in effect, marines who were recruited and, by the latter date, commanded by galley captains specially assigned to that work.

From the paymaster of the galleys each captain received the salaries due to his subordinates. Thus, the system of administration invited many abuses. On various pretexts captains withheld salaries from subordinates. They were authorized to deduct from salaries the cost of the clothing and equipment issued, but some captains commonly withheld more than that amount. Injustices were done, and an order condemning them was issued in 1686, requiring that henceforth the salaries due to soldiers would be paid "in full" each month, "without anything being kept from them on any pretext whatsoever." [53] In 1717, another order prescribed that if a soldier gave six years of service in the same company he should be permitted to keep his uniform even though he did not re-enlist. The captains were specifically enjoined "to allow him to keep his clothing, his belt, his sword and his laundry, without withholding anything because he is retiring, or because of the payment given [by his captain] at the time of his enlistment." [54]

Clearly, the captains' power to recruit and pay subordinates, combined with their collusive control of clothing and equipment inventories (and also rations, as will later be seen), gave them a comprehensive basis for exercising discretionary control over the interplay of interests and powers familiarly known as the commerce de galère. Not surprisingly, the captains themselves were the prime beneficiaries of this system of exploitation, and the profitable interplay of their powers can readily be seen in the padding of the muster rolls.

The rolls could of course be padded in a variety of ways, but one method consisted of the custom of "recruiting" soldiers from among the guards who were already employed on the galleys. This saved the captain trouble and probably part of the expense of searching for soldiers at Marseilles and elsewhere. Guards could be "recruited" with no trouble at all; the enlistment bounty and expense were saved, and apparently it mattered little that these recruits were part-time soldiers at best. The names of members of the galley medical staff and "many others" were also carried by the captains on the rolls as soldiers. An order of 1686 decreed that all such persons must immediately be "replaced by actual soldiers." [55] The padding of the muster rolls was a lucrative perquisite for captains since profits could derive to them from "surplus" salary, rations, clothing, and equipment. In the measure that the padding of the rolls increased, the profits of the captains were increased, though of course there were limits. Rations issued but "unused" were shared, or the product of their sale was shared, by captains with certain of their subordinates, with the munitionnaire or his agent taking a cut. Many captains appear to have indulged in these practices, at least until the issuance of orders condemning them in 1686 and 1689.[56]

The mariniers (literally, mariners) aboard galleys were "exploited" by methods similar to those used by the captains with their soldiers. Some mariniers served as oarsmen and in that capacity were known as mariniers de rame, though they usually were given the least difficult places on the oars, and served as relief oarsmen, seldom as full-fledged men of the oar alongside the forçats and slaves. Mariniers served as sailors, handling the rigging and other equipment related to the operation or navigation of the galley. But mariniers also served as soldiers; indeed, in 1674 the minister of marine approved the suggestion that soldiers and mariniers de rame could be used "interchangeably aboard each galley."[57] In short, at various times mariniers could be found performing almost any lowly job aboard the galley, and probably counted themselves fortunate when they were designated to serve as soldiers or sailors and not as oarsmen (see fuller discussion of their duties on pp. 136–137 below).

Mariniers were for the most part recruited under the system of maritime conscription that Colbert introduced. Like the soldiers, the mariniers received their rations and a modest salary from the captain's hands. Their availability as conscripts and their easy interchangeability aboard the galley made it easy for the captains to manage matters as they would. The economic value of the easy interchange varied from galley to galley, depending on such circumstances as the number of mariniers authorized for a particular campaign and the disposition and inclination of the individual captain. But if the behavior of captains in taking advantage of other economic opportunities can be taken as a measure of their ability and willingness to benefit by exercising their initiative, they must often have done very well indeed.

The galley captains seem to have shown understandable conservatism in their steady opposition to attempts to introduce changes in their relations with subordinates. They were defenders of their perquisites. One notable instance of this tendency on their part occurred in the middle eighties, when Seignelay sought to substitute the use of unpaid forçats

111

for the salaried mariniers that were being used at the oars. Forçats were particularly plentiful then since the Edict of Nantes had just been revoked (1685) and new edicts issued condemning army deserters to the galleys instead of to death. But, of course, the officers of the galleys energetically resisted the substitution of cheap and plentiful forçats for salaried personnel. Such substitutions could seriously affect their income. Perhaps there were other grounds for opposing the substitution, but the minister assumed their opposition was self-interested. Writing to Intendant Bégon in 1687, when Bégon was a newcomer in dealing with the intricate, half-hidden commerce de galère, the minister remarked bluntly, "the need that you allege, for [using] at least one [salaried] marinier de rame at each oar, has been suggested to you by the officers, in whom you have too much trust in this respect; it has not influenced me in the least, I assure you." [58]

That many captains in the Galley Corps were involved in these practices in some degree seems clear from the number and content of the reforming orders issued by the King, the ministers' attitude, and the generalized nature of the conditions the ministers' criticisms spotlight and condemn. The semiautonomous nature of intra-galley organization and management left individual galley commanders a considerable range of choice. There were, doubtless, differences in the degree and frequency with which individual officers allowed either their own interests or the King's interests to dominate their behavior. There can be no doubt, however, that the pursuit of personal interests did compromise and damage the interests of the King in serious ways.

The efforts of the ministers to limit the powers and to control the behavior of galley officers was of course the effort of the Crown to extend effective royal power. To do that, existing methods and available personnel had to be adapted to the service of the King. The ministers tolerated and sometimes even recommended practices that might now seem to have been almost as abusive as the methods they condemned. Such a minister as Colbert was naturally on the lookout for traditional or innovative malpractices that allowed private interests to take undue advantage of the difficult transition from private to royal ownership. Many recognized abuses were condemned. If some were rooted out successfully, others were allowed to creep back or to continue more or less openly in both attenuated and active forms in the realization that in the short term only a degree of change was possible. Reform proceeded that way. The reasonable course seemed to be to concentrate on controlling those practices that could be the most seriously damaging or compromising to the interests of the King.

Anyone going through the correspondence exchanged by the administrators of the Galley Corps is bound to be impressed with the effort made by the central authorities to educate subordinates and to inculcate ideas of service to the King; the central authorities' stress on administrative procedures and systematic, regular methods of functioning had as their basic object the protection of the interests of the King and the implementation of his (and his ministers') policies. The ministry implanted the idea that when galley officers, especially senior officers, behaved in a manner damaging to His Majesty's service they brought discredit and dishonor on themselves. That was an old idea — not merely medieval, but as old as the efforts of men to govern their fellows. The exaction of discipline and obedience was essential to the development of the power of any dynasty. It was bound to be a long, painful process reflecting the personal qualities of the governors, the nature of the political system, limitations of the technology and economy, and the religio-social complex of the society. All these specific aspects of the process were apparent in the administration of the Corps. It was not a task to be accomplished in a decade, a reign, or even in a century. Yet this was the basic nature of the "discipline" problem that Louis XIV and his ministers and their successors faced in the Galley Corps and in the government of France in the old regime.

Chaplains, Lower Officers, and Freeman Crew

No members of the Galley Corps have been more criticized and praised than the chaplains. Protestant historians like Gaston Tournier have published indictments of the chaplains, basing their judgments partly on accusations in surviving letters and memoirs of coreligionists, many of whom served as forçats and died at the oars or in the galley hospital at Marseilles for their faith. On the other hand, official chroniclers of the Congrégation de la Mission, which supplied the chaplain-priests (not all of them missionnaires) and had charge of the chaplain service of the galleys, have published praise of their Order, the work of its priests, and especially the work of its founder, Vincent de Paul (1581–1660), who was Chaplain General of the Galleys and has since been canonized. Such antitheses of blame and praise are characteristic of many controversial phases of the history of religion and the churches and, of course, every serious sectarian writer can justify his approach or treatment, at least in the eyes of those who accept his premises. Frequently, however, some nonsectarian road of historical interpretation can be constructed.

In this case the published praise of the galley chaplains by the Congrégation has focused on the lifetime of Vincent de Paul himself (d. 1660), whereas the published criticisms of the Catholic chaplains by Huguenot historians have focused on a later period of Louis XIV's reign, notably on the years immediately before and following the revocation of the Edict of Nantes. This convenient separation of the virtue from the vice by some twenty-five years saves the historians from the paradox and from the delicate necessity of explaining how the Chaplain General could be canonized for his work while his subordinates and followers are denounced for theirs.

Our principal concern is to evaluate some of the Huguenot criticisms of the later period. Chaplains of the galleys have been accused of all manner of extreme views and of exercising astonishing authority, especially over Protestants among the men condemned to galley oars. The chaplains were, we are told by Tournier, "the most implacable enemies of the men of our faith, and at the same time the most powerful and the real masters of the galleys." "With rare exceptions," he adds, "they were the tormentors and the terror of the Protestant galériens, and they exercised unlimited power, superior to that of the officers or even of the intendant; they communicated personally with the Court, and were always listened to, obtaining even the discharge of officers who displeased them." [1] Protestants could be expected to write uncomplimentary things about the Churchmen whose teachings they rejected and whose influence was responsible for sending their coreligionaries to the galleys. But the contents of public and private archives supply enough (or very nearly enough) evidence to sustain Tournier's sweeping indictments of the chaplains, at least for the decade after 1695. Very few chaplains, however, appear to have exceeded the authority their superiors expected them to exert, and few abused the exceptional powers and immunities that the circumstances of the time happened to confer on them as religious counselors and guardians of orthodoxy in the Roman Catholic prison that the galleys became. The record suggests that individual chaplains were under considerable pressure from their own superiors, and the superiors themselves were probably under some pressure, especially after 1695, to be more rigorous than they had shown a disposition to be before that date in the demands they made on Protestant convicts doing galley service.

All galley chaplains were under the direction of the superior of the Congrégation de la Mission, but not all of them were priests and not all were missionnaires — points that the archivist of the Congrégation insisted upon in conversation with the writer. The Congrégation was charged with providing the chaplains aboard French galleys. Vincent de Paul and his successors in the post of Superior General of the Order were concurrently Chaplains General of the Galleys and Directors of Spiritual Affairs in the galley hospital at Marseilles. But a regional superior of the Mission was maintained at Marseilles, empowered to select and to appoint, with the concurrence of the bishop, the chaplains in the Galley Corps. According to Tournier, the missionnaires succeeded in ousting the Jesuits from those posts.[2]

As long as Vincent de Paul was Chaplain General, the duties of chaplains appear to have been performed satisfactorily as a simple religious function. The routine evidently consisted of the celebration of the Mass and administration of sacraments to the Roman Catholics among crew and oarsmen, with the occasional participation of the Bishop of Marseilles. The handful of galleys in French service in Vincent's later days and the small number of priests they employed certainly made them a minor phase of the multifarious activity of the busy Congrégation de la Mission in France.[3]

But in the 1660's, after Vincent's death, the King inaugurated great changes in his Galley Corps. Within five years the number of galleys doubled, in ten years tripled, and the growth continued until the number of galleys to be served had multiplied about six times. This great expansion created extraordinary demand for galley chaplains. Assignments on the galleys could hardly have been the most attractive priestly opportunities available to missionnaires, since they were shipboard parishes comprising a motley group of slaves, renegades, criminals and Protestants, conscripts, and hard-bitten galley crewmen. Some missionnaires, following the counsel and early example of Vincent himself, might have preferred rural assignments. But individual priests did not decide for themselves what responsibilities they would carry. Some priests assigned to the galleys were habitués, ministering not only on the galleys but working at some other place in or near Marseilles as well. This doubling up was perhaps justifiable from the standpoint of the bishop as long as the chaplain's salary amounted to only eighteen livres a month. The low level of salaries, together with the rapid growth of the fleet, may help to explain why some auxiliary priests and lay brothers were recruited and assigned to help with the work. Without such help, according to the official history of the missionnaires, the needs of the Galley Corps could not have been met.[4] The authorities apparently recognized that the salaries were low, and they were raised in the seventies to thirty livres a month, placing chaplains on a par with the highest paid noncommissioned officers.[5] But the King wanted his galley chaplains to be Frenchmen, not foreigners, a fact that was brought out in the 1690's when the King objected to having Savoyards serving as chaplains, apparently believing that they could not be relied upon to be good Gallicans or to be loyal to his Galley Corps or to him, considering the prevailing tenor of his relations with Savoy.[6]

Whatever the composition of the chaplain corps and the level of their pay, word reached the Court of France in 1677–78 that they were not performing their duties satisfactorily. "His Majesty is informed that most chaplains serving on galleys are not such as could be desired in morals and manners. They often take office without being approved by bishops [of Marseilles], even without being known, [and they serve] rather for the thirty livres a month paid by His Majesty than to fulfill the duties of their profession and charge."[7] Reports received by the minister of marine indicated that the Mass and principal feasts were being celebrated with some occasional difficulties, but the sacraments were being administered.[8] The minister probably urged chaplains to make every effort to serve well, yet the reputation of chaplains was apparently not as he would have liked. The chaplains themselves complained in 1681 that the écrivains "had not the deference for them they ought to have."[9] In early 1684 the minister was moved to request that the intendant send "a list of the good and the bad qualities possessed by galley chaplains."[10] Apparently the list was heavy on the negative side. In 1685, an order was issued by the King sharply criticizing them: "His Majesty is informed that chaplains established on his galleys do not perform their duties with all the necessary vigor, and have even neglected to undertake the instruction of convicts."[11] To bring the chaplains' behavior into line with the expectations of the Court, the King's order prescribed that henceforth chaplains must "hold prayers aboard galleys both morning and evening and afterward visit all convicts and instruct them in the Truths of the [Roman Catholic] Religion"; for failure to follow these procedures chaplains were threatened with the loss of three months' pay.[12] Chaplains were expected to perform in full all the duties that the regulations set forth.

Deprivation of pay may not have been the best means of activating

missionnaires. Many chaplains had no desire or intention of conforming to this new order of worship on the galleys. That seemed evident
two years afterward when a vigorous repetition of the same remonstrance
came from the Court: His Majesty had been informed that the chaplains "very much neglect the duties of their posts and are not as assiduous
as they should be." Accordingly, the King decreed "for the welfare of
his service [and] to remedy this abuse," that all the chaplains would
henceforth be obliged "to establish an actual residence [at the port of
Marseilles]." He prescribed furthermore that salary would not be paid
to any chaplain who did not reside at the port or was not included on
the monthly roll of those present at reviews.[13] Chaplains, it was hoped,
could and would give their undivided attention to His Majesty's galleys
if they lived in Marseilles.

   Thus, until the fall of 1687 at least, the faults most criticized in chaplains of the galleys would seem to have consisted in lassitude and perhaps even neglect of their duties. Their very lassitude suggests that they
erred rather on the side of moderation and indifference than toward
the vigor and zeal with which they have sometimes been charged. As a
group the chaplains probably tended to adhere to established routine
in their ministrations on the galleys, their habits being little affected
by the fact that their charges included some of the most intractable
Protestants in the realm, and were likewise little changed by the sharp
scrutiny that was increasingly given to their work by Protestants both
outside France and by their activist coreligionists. (The Protestants considered "most dangerous," especially pastors and nobles, were ordinarily
kept isolated in such prisons as the Château d'If and Fort St. Jean at
Marseilles rather than on the galleys themselves.)

   For many years the post of superior at Marseilles was held by a "Sieur
Lorance," as the ministers of marine addressed him in their correspondence — apparently an easygoing man who had good relations with his
subordinates, the chaplains of the galleys, and also with the navy in
spite of complaints coming down from the Court. But a new superior
was appointed early in the decade of the nineties, a much more rigorous
man, a certain "Sieur" Boulanger. Boulanger had problems from the
start. He was highhanded, a disciplinarian, and he had the misfortune to
succeed a popular man. His policies soon moved the chaplains to complain and even to send memoirs and a petition to the minister of marine
himself complaining about the frequency with which Boulanger was

transferring chaplains from galley to galley. The minister eventually intervened with the Superior General of the missionnaires, Monsieur Joly, saying it is "for the welfare of the Faith and the service that a chaplain know the oarsmen of his galley." Transfers of excessive frequency compromised a chaplain's usefulness.[14] The minister supported the chaplains right down the line on a series of issues and incidents; most of the quarrels were carried to Joly and to the Bishop of Marseilles. But both these higher ecclesiastical authorities supported Boulanger. The chaplains lost their campaign against Boulanger (1695–96) and were obliged to obey him. Chaplains even suffered pecuniary penalties at the hands of the Bishop of Marseilles, who soon afterward saddled the chaplains with special tax obligations even though the minister of the navy begged him to relent.[15] Ecclesiastics and kings were equally disposed to be exacting, and ranking ecclesiastics could be almost as punitive as secular authorities where the obedience of subordinates was involved.

An outsider to this intraparty quarrel who has not seen the archives of the Congrégation can only speculate concerning its significance. The chaplains of the galleys, it appears, had fallen into a routine; their faults lay on the side of neglect and indifference, probably with moderate rather than zealous inclinations in the matter of worship, before the appointment of Boulanger. One can presume that Boulanger was brought in as a strong man to replace his relatively easygoing, permissive predecessor. The new regime of order and obedience represented not only Boulanger's personality, but apparently also the policy of his superiors in the Church hierarchy, who backed him to the hilt.

Some elements of this quarrel can be interpreted as manifestations of friction and interplay of power between Church and Crown. In a way, the struggle over the issue of "chaplain obedience" delineated the respective jurisdictions. Significantly, since the affair clearly did concern Church administration, the ministry of marine, though making Crown preferences and interests clear, held back from pressuring the ecclesiastics to act as the Crown would have liked, with relative moderation. The churchmen in authority, for their part, took the essence of the affair to be a matter of ecclesiastical discipline, and exacted obedience from the chaplains accordingly.

After the quarrel and the success of Boulanger's hard policy, the chaplains fell into line. A regime that was generally more rigorous, perhaps differing in some measure from galley to galley yet generally more exacting as regards the Huguenots, became the order of the day. There seems to be high probability that the relative rigor which characterized the behavior of galley chaplains from 1696 onward toward the Protestants,[16] in such marked contrast to their relatively moderate earlier demeanor, was the policy imposed by the superiors of their own Order and the Bishop of Marseilles. Hence the superiors, backed by higher levels of the Church hierarchy, the Bishop in particular, and not the unilateral will and disposition of individual chaplains, produced the hard policy for which the chaplains have been so much criticized.

This hard policy was also one of the principal features for which the administration of Intendant Montmort was notorious. Jean-Louis Habert, Seigneur de Montmort, Count de Mesnil-Habert, was certainly more rigorous than his predecessor Bégon had been. He is said to have been a man of extreme opinions; it is also said that his long administration (1689–1710) was the most harsh and cruel in the history of French galleys, at least as far as Protestants were concerned.[17] About the nature of Montmort's own religious opinions no easy assertions can be made. But his administration was notably harsh. He was under great pressure from powerful forces in French society that were seeking to exact compliance with the law to achieve religious uniformity in France. The exaction of obedience from Protestants was seen as the aim of the King. Even under this intendant's very nose, however, a man could be kind to Protestants, could favor them by secretly dispatching their letters as Montmort's own secretary, a certain Vialet, is known to have done.[18] But under the pressure of Montmort and their own superiors, the chaplains of the galleys were doubtless expected to comply with all royal decrees, as the intendant himself was under pressure to do.

The administrative correspondence of the ministry of marine tends to confirm the assertion of Tournier that some chaplains — and it would be surprising if there were not many, since their superiors wanted it so — sought "to provoke abjurations." This is a way of saying that the missionnaires sought to make converts. They certainly did that, by concentrating efforts on a few galleys at a time, with the cooperation of the Bishop of Marseilles and certain navy authorities. There is also much evidence confirming the charge that some chaplains "tormented" Protestant forçats in a variety of ways, as by "denouncing them to officers, intercepting their letters, taking from them their books, preventing conversations between them, and interfering in their relations with their friends outside" the galleys.[19] All these things chaplains were obliged by naval regulations to do. But some chaplains did go to extremes in these or related procedures and acts.

At all levels in the hierarchy of the Corps, as in the society of the time, there were extremes of religious opinion, but concurrently there were also moderate and even tolerant views that made their influence felt. However, the ascendancy of extreme opinion at Court and the pressure from superiors in the Order and the Church at Marseilles increased the pressures on moderates, on the galleys as elsewhere, encouraging and even forcing the persecution of Protestants. Even the relatively moderate Intendant Bégon, who showed much reserve toward the Protestant galériens, was pressed to redouble severity, and on one occasion incurred a grave reprimand for not having punished with a hundred lashes the Protestant pastor Isaac Le Febvre who did not doff his cap when the Blessed Sacrament was brought into his presence in the galley hospital.[20] Neither Bégon nor Montmort nor any other lay authority could do more at the time than moderate the effects of the pressures for a rigorous treatment of Protestant convicts. The implementation of the hard policy went forward with notorious rigor in the hands of such lay officials as the Major of the Galleys, Charles de Bombelles.[21] Louis XIV himself called a halt when he heard, in the first decade of the eighteenth century, about the floggings of convicts for refusal to kneel and tip the hat to the Host at the Mass. Louis had never ordered that adherents of the R.P.R. should be obliged to do that, and he ordered it stopped. That was probably as close as average chaplains were obliged to come to the atrocities with which they have so often been charged, though some zealots did go further. Chaplains were expected to demonstrate appropriate zeal, to equal the fervor of the Court, and forcibly to impose their beliefs. Floggings for failure to kneel were among the circumstances that moved at least one chaplain priest, Jean-François Bion, to renounce Roman Catholicism and become a Protestant.[22]

Another group of noncommissioned officers much less known than the chaplains, but who were almost as prominent and certainly as well known to the oarsmen as the chaplains, were the members of the galley medical staff. This group was headed by a surgeon general (médecin-général). Under his jurisdiction there was a barber-surgeon (sometimes with assistants) aboard each galley. There was also the medical staff of the hospitals for crew and oarsmen for which the surgeon general had a certain inspectional responsibility until the later 1680's, when he seems to have been given broader (perhaps temporary) powers in the management of hospital affairs.

The position of surgeon general resembled the situation of medicine men of all ages. The tendency was to respect or revile him in proportion as the illnesses of his patients were severe and long or mild and short. Thus, in the winter of 1679–80 when there was a great deal of sickness among the galley oarsmen at Marseilles, the persistent illness of the patients plagued the doctor's reputation all through the winter and into the spring. Writing to the surgeon general, a certain Dr. Miermand, in February in the midst of the contagion, the minister reminded him that "the King judges you and the utility of your services by their success. Let me remind you that there have never before been as many deaths among convicts on the galleys as there have been in the last four months. It is up to you to apply yourself. Find out the causes of these deaths." [23] At that point Miermand might have felt his very tenure was uncertain. The fact was, however, that his job was not in jeopardy at all. When only thirty-seven of his patients died in March, the outlook seemed improved. A total of forty-seven died in April (no record for May), but only thirty-four in June.[24]

Indeed, as far as Miermand's reputation with the minister was concerned, his failure to get along with the religious who administered the galley hospital caused him much more trouble than mere patient mortality. The minister reprimanded Miermand when he received "proofs that are only too sure" of the fact that Miermand had cudgeled a sick forçat to death when the man declared, after receiving a remedy, that the doctor was mad. "Do not allow this to happen again," the minister warned, "for I am telling you now that if you do, I will send the order for your discharge." [25] But the minister's confidence was not shaken for long: three months later he asked Miermand to list all the barber-surgeons on the galleys "and put beside the names on the list your opinion of their capacity." [26]

Six years later Dr. Miermand was not only holding his post but exercising considerably wider powers as an inspector at the galley hospital. There he had a good deal of influence on the disposition of convicts, as evidenced by a letter to Intendant Bégon. "I learn from

Dr. Miermand," said the minister, "that the Huguenots occupy a good many beds and spread a good deal of contagion in the hospital for oarsmen. He thinks the Huguenots would be better off in the prisons of the city [of Marseilles] or in the Citadel until such time as the hospital is enlarged. Find out whether it would be more apropos to put them on a vessel in the middle of the port with a detachment of guards, rather than in the Citadel."[27] At a later date the surgeon general's jurisdiction was extended to include even wider inspectional powers over the hospital for oarsmen, and he held this broader authority during much if not all of Montmort's intendancy. Not until the 1720's, under the Regency, were major administrative changes and improvements made.

Among his other responsibilities the surgeon general of the galleys was charged with superintendence of the barber-surgeons (chirurgiens). Each of these men was responsible for the three or even four hundred men aboard a galley. Their role was essentially that of ship's doctor. The barber-surgeon was part of the regular crew. In accord with the medical practice of the time, the usual patient was dispensed a concoction of sirup or herbs or pills from the more-or-less standard stock of the galley's medicine chest. There were definite limits to the small allowance provided by the King but a considerable assortment of cure-alls, supplied by the surgeon general, could come from that chest.[28] In that respect the surgeon general was a kind of master pharmacist with profits probably proportionate to his methods in graft. To supplement the medicine chest the King provided certain liquors for medicinal purposes (rafraîchissements) that probably came in bottles or casks. These came through the munitionnaire of the navy and, considering the frequency with which the practice was condemned, they were often consumed by the barber-surgeons themselves.[29]

Some barber-surgeons had sidelines. One of them, besides holding posts aboard two different galleys (presumably with more, if not double salary), maintained a shop where his remedies were sold and conducted a school where he collected fees for training surgeon apprentices and pharmacists.[30] But enterprise of that sort was rare. Indeed, it was rare for one man to hold more than one barber-surgeon post. In 1740 when a vacancy occurred, no fewer than five candidates from various parts of France sought the appointment,[31] a fact that seems to suggest that something much more interesting than the barber-surgeon's salary was involved. Indeed, there was more than a bit of graft among the barber-surgeons, as there was among most other officials of the galleys, but that was the oil that made the machinery run. Back in 1679 Miermand complained to the minister about the barber-surgeons under his jurisdiction and the abuses that they perpetrated in the treatment of the ills of oarsmen. The minister approved certain of Miermand's innovations ostensibly aimed at reform. But the minister showed himself skeptical, even cynical, about the Miermand methods: "I have no doubt that you, in continuing your efforts, will not eliminate all abuses; but carry on your efforts anyway, in concert with Brodart. Advise him of the abuses you discover that affect the oarsmen who are sick."[32] The minister knew perfectly well that the commerce de galère and the men who were part of it at Marseilles were joint authors of all kinds of abuse; he also knew that he could do little to stop it.

Miermand's methods almost always left much to be desired. The minister found it necessary on many occasions to urge him to be more willing to allow sick men to be taken to the hospital for oarsmen. In early 1681 he reminded Miermand that between 1 and 21 January no fewer than forty-seven men had died at the hospital, many of them shortly after admission. For example, "the first oarsman of the galley *La Galante* was sent only after you were solicited many times to allow him to be sent. He died the day following admission. You are wrong to be so rigid in this matter of sending sick forçats to the hospital." The minister added that the means had to be found "to remedy this prodigious mortality."[33] The King himself recognized the problem in 1685 when he condemned the barber-surgeons for not giving their patients on the galleys the necessary care. Some oarsmen die, said the decree, without receiving any medical care whatsoever. It was decreed that the barber-surgeons must do as the chaplains do: visit the oarsmen twice a day. Two barber-surgeons were ordered assigned to twenty-four–hour duty aboard the old réale, largest hospital hulk in the port, and all were ordered to that duty in their turn.[34] This regulation may have helped, but less than two years later another decree had to be issued, occasioned by the fact that surgeons "very much neglect the functions of their posts."[35] But abuses and negligence did not prevent the ministry of marine from giving the surgeon general the strongest kind of support to help him to enforce his will. In 1692 the minister informed the commander of the galleys that he was discharging a barber-surgeon who refused to obey the surgeon general, and that other barber-surgeons who did not get along, "with proper subordination," would also be "severely punished."[36] The minister wanted obedience and insisted that his own subordinates exact obedience from the men working under them.

Perhaps the most important "drive wheels" in the mechanism of the galleys, were the comites, who managed the rowing force. Not far behind them were the argousins. Comites and argousins were more generally feared by oarsmen than any other noncommissioned officers, and with reason. They had direct control over the oarsmen. A considerable number were themselves ex-oarsmen, and all had years of experience with galleys and with the ways of the men aboard them — hardly an improving milieu in the usual sense of the phrase. Certainly, a long apprenticeship was undergone by any men who rose from the ranks to the relatively exalted status of comite or argousin. Many of them could even read and write. They were apt to be intelligent, self-made men with experience that was vital to the proper working of the galley. The comite possessed knowledge and skills on which the senior, commissioned officers necessarily had to depend; he could make or break a galley as an effective machine.

La Roncière declared flatly (with exaggeration) that the comites "decimated" the oarsmen by their violence, "being something worse than the coachmen of Paris who willingly kill their horses to get the lead."[37] Tournier denounced comites and argousins for "brutality and savagery past belief," at whose hands the men of the oar "could expect no pity."[38] Both these historians based their assertions on reliable but isolated pieces of contemporary information. Comites and argousins doubtless did come from the lower orders of society — "the worst environment," Tournier insisted.[39] The blanket indictments commonly made of these petty officers, whatever their validity in particular cases, need to be understood as the product of the particular viewpoints of the men making the indictments, and of course need also to be understood in terms of the time, the place, the problems faced by comites, and the roles they were called upon to play. When comites are saddled with blame for some of the notorious abuses associated with galleys, commissioned officers are by implication relieved of much responsibility. But this passing of responsibility to the lower echelons of command is in sharp contrast to judgments made of some other historical situations, where responsibility has been passed upward through the hierarchy of command to the top. The case of the comites suggests that theirs was only a partial responsibility.

Like the commissioned officers of the galley, the comite performed a double role: he was at once a prison official and part of a fighting machine. Comites and their assistant comites, with the argousins, served as turnkeys, jailors, and administrative staff in one of the best-known prisons of their day; those functions were coupled with the job of running the ship. The oarsmen of a galley, though a varied lot of men, were all forced laborers needing close supervision and careful discipline. Revolts by galley oarsmen, led either by criminal elements or the slaves, could occur, and though they were exceedingly rare, they were feared by all the galley crew. But individual rebellion was more common. From time to time forçats assaulted guards or fellow prisoners in anger, revenge, or from unexplained motives, often in an attempt to get away. The men at the oars included a mixture of the mentally ill and hardened criminals, some of them quite capable of committing murder with any weapon that came to hand or with their bare hands if opportunity arose, along with others who would now be classed as thieves, minor offenders, debtors, and of course the slaves and adherents of the R.P.R. "Wardens" and guards responsible for this conglomerate of men could be lax and permissive only at their peril; the tendency was to use severity as the major method of control. Yet much evidence suggests that they also sought, within the limits of the rules, to be fair-minded. Prison guards can do worse than that.

But the guards did not make the rules. Sanctions of many sorts tended to encourage rigorous enforcement of the rules by noncommissioned officers and guards. They were held accountable, with their persons or their purses, for the human matériel in their charge. If any convicts or slaves escaped, the guards immediately concerned could be obliged by royal decree to pay for replacement slaves — a matter of at least a year's salary for any noncommissioned officer. If negligence or complicity in the escape was proved, the noncommissioned officer himself could be condemned to take a place at the oar.

Without condoning all the methods they employed, one should say that officers and petty officers alike were under pressure from higher officials of the Corps who insisted that their subordinates be severe. Indeed, the treatment of the oarsmen by some of the ranking members of the hierarchy and by some of the King's officials in the galley arsenal set examples of severity. There can be no doubt that the King's ordinances, many captains, and the lower officers tended to rigor in matters touching the convicts and slaves. Most men experienced with the management of galleys would have agreed with Colbert that "nothing less than the rod and chain will do" in the management of oarsmen.[40] Intendant Arnoul, to whom Colbert used this phrase, hardly needed such encouragement. He himself remarked that "our unhappy convicts sell their shirts and clothing to get drunk. I have had four or five of them punished in my presence. But the blows of the ropes and batons [*de lattes*] are nothing but ticklings for them. I have promised [hereafter] to cut off the noses of the Christians and the ears of the Turks. This severity, and more, is necessary."[41] Arnoul's biographer tells us, and there seems no reason to doubt, that he possessed an "extreme zeal" for the service.[42] His principal successors in the intendancy demonstrated at least equal zeal and severity, and their tenure covered all but five years of the period 1673–1710. One can class as comparatively "humane" the decree of 18 May 1689, devised and issued by Intendant Bégon, forbidding petty officers the use of the baton for punishment and permitting only use of the rope's end.[43] Later that same year Bégon was relieved of his post and was succeeded by Montmort, whose administration tended to inquisitorial coercion. Montmort is reputed to have ordered a forçat flogged to death and personally dealt some of the blows.[44] Much other evidence mirrors the same picture of the man. But he was not an isolated example. Even popular fighting officers of the galleys, such as Valbelle, set precedents for this particular action by Montmort.[45]

Whether following the examples of their superiors, or acting in compliance with orders received from them, or acting on their own, petty officers of the galleys could be judged "brutal" in many respects. But their transgressions against the codes of their own time and Corps were insignificant. The rigors of their jobs in a penal and military Corps, together with the comparative weakness of humane sanctions in the modern Western European sense of the phrase in their milieu, encouraged a rigor that was harsh in their day but that would only later come to be considered by most persons in authority in Western society as barbaric.

Petty officers of the Galley Corps have been criticized by some commentators as being avaricious and corrupt. They did routinely engage in many practices that are now considered graft. However, many of those practices, though by no means all, were condoned by the fiscal administration of their day. The fiscal system of the monarchy was inefficient; the bureaucracy of the King went to great trouble and expense to gather funds for the royal treasury. Tax revenues that actually reached the treasury represented only a part of the amount collected, and an even smaller part of the real value taken from the taxpayer, the rest being consumed in the high costs of collection. Hence, it was desirable to remunerate public servants by means other than payments in actual cash in order to minimize the drain on the treasury. To that end government officials were often paid insignificant salaries and were expected to augment them with perquisites — fees, gratuities, privileges, or amenities — attaching to their office. This meant, in effect, that the holder (often a buyer) of an office was frequently expected or allowed to assess, collect, and pocket for himself a considerable part of his own remuneration. Many officials were authorized, tacitly or explicitly, to exercise authority in self-interested ways, to levy tribute on those of the King's subjects who had to deal with them or use their services. As a method of financing administration under the monarchy, such practice was commonplace, but the effects of the system, often abusive, were especially pernicious in the Galley Corps. They help to explain the remark of one naval official who observed that "most lower officers [on the galleys] have no care other than personal gain." [46]

Thus, only part of the comites' remuneration came from the royal treasury; the rest they collected themselves. Their basic salary was 360 livres a year, which, even without supplements, gave no real ground for complaint. But in addition, the comite on each galley enjoyed "tavern rights," allowing him to purchase wine and sell it aboard the galley at prices established by the interplay of the comite's power and the state of the demand. This wine concession was a long-standing tradition on Mediterranean oar-driven craft, and the comites customarily received its revenue.

Many evils accompanied its exercise, and Colbert himself remarked in 1670 that "it is certain that the tavern maintained aboard galleys by comites is a considerable abuse, and should be remedied. But care and time are necessary to suppress such a well-established custom as that." [47] He suggested that Arnoul might attempt a gradual or continuing program of reform to extinguish the abuse. But thirty-five years later the comites were still "taking considerable revenues" from the tavern which they then regarded as nothing less than their "rightful inheritance."[48]

Like the commissioned officers who bought for their own use, the comites could bring wine into the arsenal, even from abroad, without paying the wine duties ordinarily levied by the city's governors. Exemptions from duties and license fees meant that wine came cheaper to comites than to other tavern keepers, and cheaper wine meant more sales and more profits. Their captive customers, the oarsmen particularly, were given every encouragement to buy exclusively from them. The comites and captains united in defense of the privilege of exemption from excise duties. The vehemence of their defense and the constancy with which the privilege was criticized by the city fathers are witness to its economic value. But the collaboration of captains and comites proved unbeatable; they managed not only to retain but over the years to extend these privileges, much to the anguish of the merchants and elders of Marseilles.[49]

The salaries of petty officers were generally modest but their remuneration was not low. Complaints that they were underpaid simply ignored the value of the perquisites attaching to virtually all positions of responsibility. For example, Intendant Brodart misrepresented the case when trying to justify the perquisites, a proceeding at which he was especially skilled, claiming that the mediocre salary of 20 livres per month received by an argousin aboard the galley made it "impossible" for him to subsist with a family without indulging in "some chicanery" on the side. In fact, an argousin received as remuneration, not only salary but food, along with fees from forçats and slaves. The salary alone, when he could collect it from his captain, put him above the scale of many workers in the arsenal. The argousin exacted one sou from each forçat or slave unchained to go into the arsenal or to Marseilles to work, as most of them did six days a week when the galleys were in port.[50] The value of such fees can be appreciated if it is remembered that the galleys were ordinarily in port during more than six months of the year and most of the oarsmen (250 or more on each craft) were permitted to leave the galley each day "to earn their livelihood."[51]

The post of chief guard (argousin réal), extant throughout the ministry of Colbert, affords one of the best illustrations of the workings of the fiscal system. His official salary amounted to 600 livres a year, with a wide range of perquisites. He collected an annual payment from the tavern of each comite. He shared with the guards the droit d'échelle involving the right to dispose of cast-off clothing (and sometimes the chains) of newly arrived convicts and slaves. Even the captains of galleys were expected to hand him about ten pistoles (about 100 livres?) on assuming a command; lieutenants newly assigned were supposed to give six, ensigns four, and the comites and lower officers "in proportion." From the oarsmen, he exacted rent on the sheds along the wharves where they offered services or merchandise when the galleys were in port. The aggregate perquisites, it was said, "produced more than 10,000 or 12,000 livres a year." [52]

The very extent of such perquisites, affecting the interests of a great many officers and men, explains why the post was suppressed about 1684. To indemnify the holder of this particular post, a new position was created and called Major of the Galleys, with a galley captain's salary, 3,000 livres a year. The perquisites of the new office affected fewer persons — or better say, fewer influential persons. The change shifted the economic burden so that it was carried by the lower strata of the Corps rather than officers. The Major was designated as "inspector of troops," and since a large percentage of his remuneration came from the King and his jurisdiction included the soldiery, the officers appear to have been relieved entirely of the burden of the older post. But this can hardly be the whole story; such posts must have had value that escapes the examiner of administrative records, or else why would individuals outside the Galley Corps bid 180,000 livres for the office of argousin réal when the revival of that office was being considered as a money-raising device in 1701; the hidden perquisites must have been substantial to elicit such an offer to invest.[53]

This discussion of the principal lower officers and their connections with commissioned officers should not suggest that every single one was involved. Individual officers might stand aloof from abuses; certainly noncommissioned officers who were technical specialists — pilots, oar and barrel makers, carpenters, and caulkers — had only limited opportunities, and took less part in the commerce de galère. They may have had a particular "commerce" of their own. But many of them had occupations in the maritime industries of Marseilles and Provence apart from the Galley Corps. Their interest and life was not bound up tightly with the administrative system of the galleys. Most of them had little or nothing to do with the oarsmen; they were set apart from the system, and from the regular petty officers who were part of it, by the fact that the authority associated with the chain of command conferred most of the remunerative ties and powers.

The lowest socioeconomic stratum of the galley hierarchy was composed of three large groups of men: the soldiers, the free oarsmen (including both conscripts and bonnevoglies), and finally the condemned men and slaves. Collectively they constituted something over 80 per cent of the men aboard. The roles and importance of the forçats and slaves will become apparent in later chapters, but that of the soldiers and free oarsmen can be examined here.

Though the soldiers and free oarsmen (mariniers de rame) performed different functions, they had much in common. They all came from the same depressed stratum of society, where they were subject to similar economic and legal pressures from the monarchy and the privileged classes. Some of them were ex–galley convicts and therefore had restricted vocational and economic opportunities outside. They lived close to the subsistence level. On that level men with or without families or dependents, in the face of want and persistent hunger, or when drunk, could be brought to volunteer for arduous and unattractive forms of employment.

As early as 1674 a total of 1,200 men were wanted, and recruits were proving hard to get. To facilitate recruitment the pay for soldiers was raised to six livres a month, a bit more than that for corporals, and nine livres for sergeants. Since there were occasions when captains found themselves bidding against one another for particular recruits, they entered into a convention among themselves in 1688. Under its terms any bounty offered by one captain to a recruit was held to be the maximum that any captain could offer to that man. If a potential recruit did not accept the first offer and tried to enlist elsewhere, he was obliged to enroll for less than the first offer made and was subject to seizure by the first captain if he did otherwise. This system, identical to recruitment methods used in some army organizations of the time, protected the interests of the captains; indeed, it guaranteed, as the convention said, that recruits "would not have the captains by the throat."[54] The captains also agreed that even if soldiers did pay off their advances or debts, they were not to be released unless they agreed to leave money in the captain's hands "to assure that they can be retaken if there is need." No soldier had the right to enroll with any other captain unless he had

131

"the consent of the captain to whom he belongs."[55] The captains certainly appear to have been in a better position to impose their arbitrary will on recruits than the King was to impose his will on his captains!

The number of soldiers on each galley was extremely variable. Their number even fluctuated with the season of the year. Winter, if the galleys were in port, found only a skeleton force of 10–25 per cent of the fighting force on hand. Even in the summer campaign season the number of soliders varied with the success of recruiters, the number of galleys to be armed, the mission to be accomplished, and even the current finances of the navy. Ministerial decision produced most of the variation. In 1674 he ordered (apparently for the sake of economy) that "all but the best 16" soldiers be discharged from each galley.[56] Three years earlier there were no fewer than 92 soldiers on each galley in the fleet.

In 1680, the galley infantry numbered 1,200 men, about 40 per galley. A memoirist of 1691 remarked there were "always" about 75 soldiers on a galley. An order of 1697, at the time of the Peace of Ryswick, indicated that the Corps then possessed more than 4,000 soldiers, organized in companies of 100 men each; finally an order of 1699 reduced the complement of soldiers to 50 per galley.[57]

Much of the fighting value of the galley, its effectiveness as an instrument of war, depended on these soldiers. Historically it had always been so. Under whatever name they served – Roman legionnaires, mailed crusaders, Knights of Malta, mercenaries, "volunteers," or conscripts – soldiers were a most important element of the galley's fighting capability. But soldiers on French galleys seldom saw any enemy at all, and were still less often called to fight. In actual fact the soldier's duties on French galleys were far less formidable in fact in Louis' day, than they could have been. A soldier was much more apt to be called upon to guard the slaves and convicts aboard than to board the enemy. Frequently, on campaign, the soldier had no occupation at all. As one officer complained they "lie down of necessity at their places on the side of the galley during the entire campaign, without activity, and without any occupation but that of guard duty [when the galley is] at anchor."[58] Since numerous other men shared guard duty on the galley, the soldiers performed even guard duty only part time.

On returning to Marseilles the soldiers could be assigned to stand guard on their own galley or on a hulk such as the old réale or in the arsenal, and they attended reviews. Some sort of review could be expected once a week; others were held once a month in the Place d'Armes or some other square where close-order drill and the manual of arms were performed. Some soldiers, with the connivance of officers, arranged not to appear. Officers and soldiers alike were pleased when reviews were held three days running to get them out of the way. The minister himself suggested they be scheduled "at the most convenient time, in order not to fatigue the soldiers or deprive them of the means of earning a living." [59]

The minister had reason to be concerned about the soldiers' means of earning a living since the navy supplied only a part of their livelihood. Ordinarily, the soldier drew full pay only during the campaign season and, if fortunate, half pay the rest of the year. To receive half pay (not always collectible), soldiers had to be counted present at reviews. In the 1670's a private received only six livres a month from which a uniform allowance was withheld. Eventually the pay was raised to nine livres per month (1695), but even then soldiers on the galleys were paid less than soldiers on sailing vessels.[60] The latter had the added advantage of a quartering allowance and "divers other favorable treatments in matters of rations, housing, and heat." This differential caused "a great deal of jealousy." The soldiers of the galleys were bitter, contending that the substantial and long-standing differential was grossly unfair.[61]

Their bitterness was increased by the difficulty of living and lodging at Marseilles "on 5 sous a day." [62] Even when they had full pay they required some other employment to support a family. The King's allowance was not intended and certainly did not suffice. "Soldiers who do not have a trade," it was said in the winter of 1694, "cannot subsist because bread of the lowest quality costs 17 or 18 deniers a pound." [63]

The ministry of marine in Colbert's and Seignelay's day, persisted in claiming that the condition of soldiers on the galleys was worsened by their officers' negligence. Recruitment, training, and discipline lay primarily in the officers' hands, and negligence was a characteristic of all three, said the ministers. In 1679 the "inapplication of the captains" brought complaint.[64] In 1681 the poor condition of the soldiers led the minister to threaten to reduce the salaries of those commissioned officers who were responsible.[65] Complaints were reiterated time and again over the years about negligent recruitment, antiquated equipment, poor training and discipline, and the economic exploitation of the soldiers by their officers (see discussion above). Such exploitation extended even to one general officer's proposing, possibly mischievously, that the soldiers' captains be given rights as heirs to the material possessions of soldiers who died.[66] To which the minister responded seriously: "The King will not under any pretext whatsoever, allow residual estates [of deceased soldiers] to be left to captains." [67]

Whatever the officers' share of responsibility, the ministers also bore some blame. Salaries for soldiers were poor. Colbert and Seignelay seemed much more concerned about the appearance of soldiers than their fighting capacities. One suspects they had in mind a sort of seagoing infantry that would rival the best that Louvois (the minister of war and their rival in the Royal Council) could put in the field for Louis' armies. Colbert did express the hope that His Majesty's galley infantry would be impressive: "Eliminate from this Corps all men who are small or poorly built. Support it in every way you can. Above all, this infantry must be well armed and well dressed. You must withhold something from the daily wage of soldiers for their clothing. See that they are all dressed alike, that their arms are alike, that all of them have bandoliers and belts, and muskets of the same caliber and length.[68]

Appearances was important to Louis, and to Colbert. Uniforms were a form of discipline. It was the captains' problem to find "impressive" men, to inculcate fighting qualities, to have their soldiers make fine appearances, and to do it all with the pittance provided them as soldier pay. The officers failed. The ministers, far from easing the task, seemed bent on making it difficult. Imagine the reaction of the officers in 1681, for example, to the minister's extreme criticisms of soldiers' appearance, and his insistence that the captains discharge "all soldiers who were 'poorly built' [malfaits]." [69]

Whatever the relative responsibility of the ministers and the captains, the soldiers of the galleys left much to be desired. Little attempt was made, apparently, to make them a fighting force. "All the measures taken up to now," one memoirist said in 1691, "to prepare the soldiers of the galleys to render the same services as soldiers in the army, have been useless . . . the soldiers of the galleys can never be seasoned or well disciplined as long as they continue to be handled as they are." [70]

Remembering that one can discount many of the strictures penned in the year or two immediately following the death of Seignelay (1690), as possible exaggerations by his enemies, more than ample evidence remains of earlier and later date to underscore the defects of this force. Galley soldiers continued to be ill paid, when paid at all, continued to live as half soldiers short on training and morale. If desertion, as reported, was one of the most serious problems facing those who administered the soldiery of the Corps, the problem stemmed from multiple causes, and was not, as the ministry pretended to believe, simply a by-product of "the bad treatment the soldiers receive from their captains." [71]

The same economic and social pressures that led many men to volunteer for service as soldiers led others to serve in the still less attractive capacity of volunteer oarsmen. Ironically, such volunteers were long called bonnevoglies. They were distinguishable on the galleys by the fact that they were not chained and were immune to the lash. Volunteer oarsmen nearly disappeared from the French service by the end of the sixteenth century, but enlargement of the Galley Corps under Colbert so increased the need for oarsmen that by the end of the sixties 1,100–1,200 had been signed on.[72] The recruitment of bonnevoglies was customarily the business of crimps, including the captain of bonnevoglies on each galley; they lured, enticed, or forced men into service, the most common and effective "persuader" probably being drink. But debtors sometimes agreed to serve, thereby obtaining advances and making themselves indentured servants at the oar. Bonnevoglies received a bit more than the subsistence rations issued to convicts, and a salary of six livres per month (as much as a soldier!). Intendant Arnoul urged that this salary be paid in advance, a procedure commonly used in Italian galleys and intended "to keep them longer in the service." [73] Advances created debts that were hard to pay off since the volunteer oarsmen were subject to penalties that either suspended salary or brought the imposition of fines; a bonnevoglie could find himself serving for years without ever being able to pay off his aggregate advances and fines.

As late as 1669 Colbert said he was still persuaded that these volunteers would be "of great utility" on the King's galleys. But soon afterward his enthusiasm apparently waned. By January 1670, on the counsel of his brother, who accompanied the Candia expedition, Colbert appears to have reversed his opinion. A serious disadvantage, he found, lay in the fact that bonnevoglies were not chained and hence could desert on the eve of campaign after extensive advances had been paid.[74] Moreover, the cost of clothing and rations for the bonnevoglie were higher than the annual cost of using convicts. A step toward abandoning the use of these volunteers was taken when the intendant at Marseilles was ordered to engage by preference those who were willing to submit to the chain.[75]

Meanwhile, in the years 1669–73, a system of maritime conscription was developed and decreed in France as a means of easing the problem of mobilizing manpower. The names of able-bodied men in the maritime provinces of France were entered on the conscription rolls in the admiralty districts, parishes, or municipalities where they lived; they were obliged to serve in the navy at intervals and in other capacities prescribed by the authorities. Thenceforth this system of conscription provided a broad background of compulsion under which most able-bodied men in the maritime regions lived and worked. The liberty of the maritime population was restricted. In effect, systematic and regularized coercion replaced the more limited and irregular coercions of the press gang. But the burden of conscription was great because the navy was rapidly expanding and the need for men was increased by hundreds and even thousands each year. Men whose names appeared on the conscription rolls were obliged to do "duty" periodically. They could be called up for duty wherever they were needed, on either sailing ships or galleys. Men who failed to make themselves available at the time and place prescribed could be classed as deserters and condemned to death or, with clemency, to the galleys for life.[76]

Under this system the very name *bonnevoglie* disappeared from official terminology (after 1672), being replaced by *marinier de rame*. These mariniers were given a choice. They could either submit to being chained and receive the usual salary of six livres a month (the standard salary for the bonnevoglie), or refusing the chain they would be paid a reduced salary of only three livres a month.[77] Many of the old-fashioned bonnevoglies, especially the Italians, refused the new conditions and left as soon as they could, as Colbert hoped they would, for he (and the King) disliked having foreigners on French galleys. An increasing number of conscripts were for some years assigned to the oar, and known as mariniers de rame. These new mariniers proved "more useful and sure" than the desertion-prone bonnevoglies.[78] Oarsmen, as one writer remarked, are "like the horse that runs away when it feels the spur." To keep them in hand they must be "bridled and chained." [79]

These conscript mariniers served a stop-gap role, to fill out the ranks when other types of oarsmen were not on hand in adequate supply. Thus in 1670, in the absence of plentiful convicts and slaves, Colbert planned to use up to eighty mariniers de rame on each galley.[80] Later in the seventies, in extended campaigns such as the Messina affairs, when the rate of mortality among oarsmen was high, conscript mariniers were again used to fill the need. Conversely, when the ministry was seeking to economize, the discharge of mariniers was usually one of the first measures employed. In the years immediately following the revocation of the Edict of Nantes, few mariniers were used because ample numbers of "obstinate" Protestants were coming to hand to satisfy needs.[81] In the period 1715–19 when economy was the order of the day, and plentiful supplies of convicts were at hand, only ten mariniers were retained on each galley.[82]

The Procurement
of Slaves

Nearly all the slaves used at French galley oars in the reign of Louis XIV and afterward were infidels. That is, slaves were unbelievers not accepting "the True God" or Christ. Most were Moslem prisoners of war; some were probably pagans or renegades. But all were infidels from a Christian point of view; as such, they could be enslaved and put to the oar. The Church of Rome encouraged the practice of enslaving infidels; it set the example itself by using infidel slaves on papal galleys, and on the galleys of the Knights of Saint John, by capturing thousands of Moslem and other infidels in crusading campaigns on land and sea, and by making a lucrative market at Malta in infidel slaves, selling to the lesser Mediterranean princes and to the kings of France and Spain. In the 1670's the rowing force of French galleys included some 2,000 of these infidel slaves,[1] not all of them from Malta of course, but practically all of them products of the perennial warfare between Islam and Christendom.

This practice of enslaving infidels gave a distinctly religious stamp to the institution of slavery in Mediterranean Europe, though both the practice of enslaving infidels and the institution of Mediterranean slavery itself, seem to go unnoticed by most modern historians of the "peculiar" institution.[2] Hugo Grotius referred to this religious or infidel slavery early in the seventeenth century. It was a custom, as he saw it,

138

already "universally received among the powers of Christendom" that prisoners of war were not supposed to be enslaved or compelled to do the labor attaching to the condition of slavery; but then he went on to say, significantly, that this custom prevailed only among peoples who confessed a common religion.[3] Grotius' comment was written early in the century. But it described no less accurately the usual treatment accorded to prisoners of war by Christian powers of Mediterranean Europe in the time of Louis XIV. Any prisoner or privateer or pirate in the Mediterranean region, any ordinary subject of a prince or power who was an infidel from the Christian point of view ran serious risk of being enslaved, and was virtually certain to be put to the chain by Christian captors if he happened to be a Moselm.

At times Louis XIV also had Christian prisoners of war put to the oars of his galleys, making them do essentially the work of galley slaves. But in doing that, Louis did not deviate from the custom Grotius described, since the prisoners thus put to the oar, being Christians, were not considered to be slaves, nor were they treated as slaves were treated.[4] In the Galley Corps, oarsmen recognized as Christians were normally classed as forçats. Sometimes mistakes were made. Language difficulties, and less excusable circumstances, help to explain why Eastern European or Levantine Christians of various sorts occasionally served for many years as slaves before it was discovered that they were Christians or before their release could be obtained. Even heretics, such as the Huguenots, though religious deviates from the Catholic point of view, did not qualify as slaves, precisely because they were Christians. Though Huguenots were subjected to extreme pressures and punishments, they were classed as forçats, not as slaves. This distinction, though it was no advantage to the Huguenots, does underscore the recognition given to religion as a basis for distinguishing between non-slaves and slaves (called *turcs* or *esclaves*). Slavery aboard French and most "Christian" galleys was reserved for infidels — that is, for unbelievers.

The Church of Rome functioned as a kind of police or inspection agency in this. While the Papacy sanctioned the capture and enslavement of Moslems and certain other infidels, at the same time it supported the deliverance of Christians being held in Moslem hands as slaves. Almost any alert Christian with piety, layman or ecclesiastic, could be involved in helping to identify and deliver fellow Christians from the hands of the infidel or from Christian-owned galleys where they might be illicitly held as slaves, and could expect the help and approbation of Christian churches and ecclesiastics almost everywhere in doing so. The Christian churches naturally opposed the enslavement of Christians, whether by Christian or infidel princes or powers, but conversely, some of them promoted warfare against the infidel and sanctioned the enslavement of infidels that ensued.

But there was significant dissent in Christian ranks about the methods that should be employed in dealing with the infidel. Almost all European Christians, Roman Catholic and Protestant alike, approved of taking a hard line in dealings with "Moslem" states. Only a small minority of Christian dissenters said, and had long been saying in different circumstances and times, that understanding should be the basis of dealings with the infidel, and where possible preaching, conciliation, and even tolerance should be the means employed. Warfare and crusading, some men claimed, were often self-defeating when conversion to the Christian faith, or persuasion to peace, were the aims in view.[5]

Such appeals were virtually smothered in divided Reformation Europe by the intensity of sectarian religious zeal and the accompanying specter of the "Turkish Menace." [6] Yet even the awesome proportions of Ottoman power and the need to "defend the Faith" did not deter some early modern pontiffs from counselling moderation, and trying, for example, to put the crusaders of Saint John on leash in the Mediterranean. Some popes "entertained grave doubts as to the legitimacy" of permitting private Knights to arm galleys for preying on Moslem trade.[7] Sixtus V (1585–90) was reportedly moved to declare that all merchant vessels passing between the Levant and any Christian port must be left free from molestation by the Order of Saint John at Malta, whether their owners were Greeks or Jews or Turks.[8] Had that papal decision been made effective over time, the campaigning from Malta against the infidel could hardly have continued for long. Urban VIII (1623–44) brought into question the very custom of enslaving infidels in the Mediterranean, or elsewhere presumably; his Bull of 1639 "strictly prohibited slavery of any kind," though he apparently had in mind the Indians in the West Indies, Paraguay, and Brazil.[9] But later, in the Mediterranean proper, in the sixties and during the pontificate of Innocent XI (1676–89), complaints from both Rome and Venice (and almost certainly also from France) moved the Grand Master at Malta to recall all his privateers (in 1669 the Order is reported to have had thirty at sea) campaigning against the Mediterranean infidel. Their seizures of booty and slaves were thereby stopped for a time. The consequent loss of revenues is said to have threatened the Order with bankruptcy. But not for long; the Order's privateers "were soon rearmed." [10]

In short, it was understood in many quarters that crusading was not the only course that could be followed; some popes and pious Christians held back from sanctioning warfare and the enslavement of the infidel as the most desirable means of "defending the Faith," or for effecting conversions, or as the method the Church should morally commit itself to employ in dealing with infidels. But in spite of the qualms expressed by individual Christians and popes, the warfare between Islam and Christendom was carried on continually in southeastern Europe, and with even fewer intermissions, apart from seasonal rests, on the Mediterranean Sea itself. The Hapsburgs of both Austria and Spain saw the continuance of such warfare as a challenge and duty that was consonant with their interests, and early modern popes were generally disposed to combat Moslems, as the Spanish Hapsburgs did, rather than to reason with them. The Church of Rome promoted crusading enterprises, and the crusading spirit was still very much alive in Mediterranean Europe in the seventeenth century, epitomized by the continued vigor of the Knights of Saint John.

Campaigning against the infidel had much attraction on material grounds. Many powers conducted periodic warfare, commissioned privateers, hired condottieri, or campaigned in a variety of other ways against infidels, and more or less intentionally aided in their capture and enslavement on galleys. Secular governments sought security, and expanded influence, trade, and the good profits to be made in booty and slaves. Slaving was one object of pirates and privateers, and an incidental phase of many major Mediterranean naval operations. The commanders of Dutch and English convoys and expeditions, for example, were glad to have any prizes and booty (such as slaves) that came to hand as they traversed or campaigned in that sea.[11] Though religious purposes were usually subordinate or even alien to this traffic, the generalized conflict between Islam and Christianity gave some unity and direction to the melee. The Church of Rome provided participants with a cloak of legitimacy having all the force that the most powerful ecclesiastical authority and organization in Christendom could provide.

Thus many variable conditions helped to sustain the institution of

slavery in the Mediterranean. Dynastic politics in the form of Haps-
burg-Bourbon rivalry, the interests of commerce and trade, privateering and seaborne banditry, all played their roles in producing slaves
and in complicating the relations of sultans, beys, republics, princes,
kings, and popes. It was indeed a melee as G. N. Clark said; [12] it took
different forms in various parts of the inland sea, the eastern Mediterranean, the Adriatic, and various waters of the West. Other differences
became apparent from year to year and markedly between the early
and the late seventeeth century. No less evident is the fact that the
characteristics of the trade in slaves were modified as the participants'
technology and motives changed over time.

Many of the slaves acquired by the French were captured at sea under
infidel flags; some were Ottoman soldiers taken at some Balkan battlefield or town and afterward sold; some were seized during raids on
Ottoman and North African coastal populations; still others were men
who had renounced the Christian faith for that of Islam. But administrators of the navy in France were, or at least gave the appearance of
being, indifferent to these distinctions as they sought to procure able-
bodied slaves of the best sorts in the cheapest, easiest way.

Naturally, not every seagoing man or prisoner of war was fit for the
oar. Many were weeded out long before they reached the prime markets
for slaves. Buyers for the galleys were interested only in men between
twenty and thirty-five years of age, sound in body and build. When
slaves arrived at Marseilles, they were examined by inspectors, usually
veteran comites, and the unfit were rejected. Careful selection was the
best guarantee that a slave would be, at least at the start of his life on
the galleys, physically fit for the oar.[13] When slaves were selected with
care, there was some justification for the reputation they had on French
galleys as the elite of the oar. Turcs were reputed to be "tall, extremely
vigorous, and very resistant to fatigue"; these were the qualities sought
in men hand picked for service at the oar. Of course when slaves were
captured, this selection process was operative only in limited ways. Yet
selection does help to explain why, man for man, the slaves could be
considered much superior to the convicts coming down to Marseilles.
It is difficult to be persuaded, however, that the slaves on the French
galleys, never more than one-third of the rowing force, could have included a significantly greater number of first-class physical specimens
than the much more numerous forçat group did. But justified or not, the

reputation of slaves for superior physical strength provided an acceptable utilitarian nonreligious justification for the use of infidel slaves. Such justification must have become progressively more useful in the eighteenth century, when the acceptability of the religious distinctions underlying Mediterranean galley slavery was diminishing for enlightened eyes.

Slaves were not absolutely required at all for the rowing force of French galleys. Convicts could serve the oars with roughly equivalent efficiency and strength, and could be acquired much more easily and cheaply than slaves. But Louis XIV was not interested in renouncing the use of galley slaves, certainly not for the sake of ease of acquisition or economy. He, on the contrary, showed himself willing, and even determined to continue using slaves even though the cost could be high not only in economic terms, but also in terms of the difficulty of obtaining and maintaining peace with Moslem governments. In this, as in some other respects, neither his desire for peace with the infidel nor his feuding with the Grand Masters and Popes prevented him from giving some occasional, ostentatious, but usually nominal support to crusading activities.

At all times, the slaves on French galleys held places as first oarsmen (espaliers) who were supposed to set the pace in the harmonious movement of oars. The farthest inboard places on the oars were given, by preference, to turcs, since those were the most fatiguing and difficult rowing positions. As a form of punishment, however, recalcitrant oarsmen were sometimes assigned to those difficult places and forced to keep up. It was also considered desirable, when the number of turcs on hand permitted, to scatter them throughout the rowing force, so that they could set examples of vigor for others. "Nothing," Colbert once said, "is as important for the re-establishment of the rowing force." [14]

Though the word *turc* passed as a virtual synonym for slave, less than half of the turcs on French galleys came from the Ottoman Empire. Most of the rest were from the coastal city states of western north Africa, especially Algiers, Tunis, Tripoli, and Salé (see the map on page 145). Judging from the single surviving register of slaves, Algerians equalled or exceeded the number of men from Tripoli, Tunis, and Salé together around 1680–81. But the number of slaves listed about two decades later indicates that supplies from Tunis and Algiers had by then sharply declined, reflecting the restraining (though by no means exclusionary) effects of Louis' peace treaties with North African states. Meanwhile, men from Tripoli and Salé had sharply increased in relative number. In the earlier period Constantinople supplied more men of eastern Mediterranean origin than any other place. Significant numbers also came from Smyrna, Alexandria, Cairo, Cyprus, and Rhodes. Large numbers of men came to hand from "Balkan" sources in a series of extraordinary "windfall" shipments received at Marseilles in the late eighties and early nineties. In the period 1679–1707 French acquisitions of slaves (judging from the register) aggregated over 7,000 men.[15]

Capture had special allure as a means of acquiring slaves because it was thought to be cheaper to capture than to buy, an impression that windfall captures seemed to confirm. One such windfall occurred in 1669 when two Algerian barks were wrecked on the coast of Languedoc, and the 104 men who survived were easily captured for service at the oar. A considerable delay ensued, and much correspondence was exchanged. At one point Intendant Arnoul said he was delighted to learn that the men would be put to the chain.[16] Later he learned it was not to be so; Louis XIV himself appears to have made the final decision which was to have the greater part of the shipwrecked men released in accordance with the recent peace treaty with Algiers. But there were some renegades among them that Louis reportedly refused to return: "the intention of His Majesty is that they be retained because no punishment is too harsh for those wretches."[17]

There were also instances, equally unusual, when the navy commissioned privateers for the explicit purpose of catching infidels for the oar. One instance of the kind took place in 1685 when the royal frigate *La Fée* was sold (or hired?) to a Sieur Poussel of Toulon, for 150 turcs. Poussel promised to deliver to the King's agent at Malta at least 50 slaves a year until the full price of the frigate was paid, and to pay 350 livres for each turc he failed to deliver.[18] Another isolated example of slave hunting by the navy took place in 1720, when a flotilla comprising a royal frigate, a flûte, several barks, and ten other small craft was dispatched with a contingent of some 500 soldiers aboard; the enterprise sailed from Toulon to raid Moroccan coasts for slaves.[19]

French, Dutch, and English naval vessels on convoy duty or on station in the Mediterranean scared up prizes when they could, and sold their crews as slaves if they happened to be infidels. Thus in 1677, some Eng-

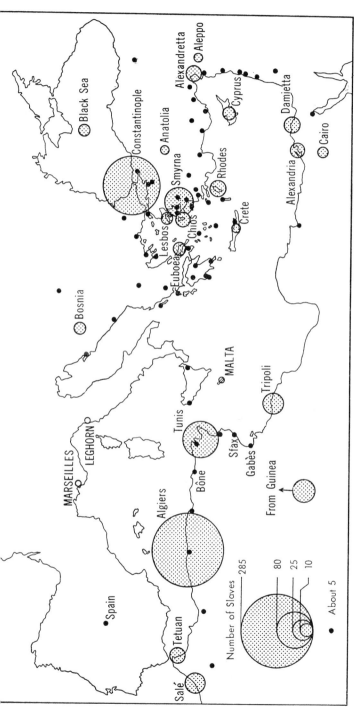

Origins of Slaves (about 1,050) Serving on French Galleys around 1680

Note that over 100 east Mediterranean and North African places supplying only one or two slaves each are not shown. Other points of origin are not shown because they were not identified (or are unidentifiable) in surviving fragments of the register. Note also that many hundreds of slaves who came to the galleys from Algiers and the Bosnia region in the decade or so *after* 1680 are not shown. Leghorn and Malta, principal slave markets, and Marseilles itself are shown in capital letters.

lish naval vessels, having taken some turcs, brought them into Leghorn for sale.[20] The following March saw the arrival of the *Portland*, commanded by Admiral John Narbrough, with slaves that the French consul at Leghorn attempted to buy.[21] Several years later, in 1681–82, the French consul at Genoa reported the prospective arrival of an English naval vessel with 150 or 200 turcs for sale; he made ready to buy by getting in hand 30,000 livres in cash and bills of exchange. On 11 March 1682 Admiral Herbert arrived off Sardinia with 30 turcs for sale.[22]

Merchants who dealt in slaves could be found in many Mediterranean ports, large and small. Captors therefore had many possible outlets. It was to tap widely scattered sources that French slave-buying expeditions were occasionally dispatched. But most French buying took place in the western Mediterranean, at a handful of markets where only a few intermediary hands were involved. Not all slave markets in that region were open to the French, and there was no single market of any consequence where the French navy could claim a monopoly, except of course at Marseilles. Buying abroad, French needs had to be met in the face of competition. Markets at Neapolitan, Sicilian, Sardinian, and Majorcan ports were usually dominated by the Spanish. Competition came, too, from such princes as the Pope and the Duke of Tuscany, both of whom had galleys to maintain. Lisbon and Genoa only intermittently supplied French buyers or their agents with slaves. Adriatic ports were also a restricted preserve, where the French bought few, if any, until the later eighties. At some ports the French had to pay tariffs on exports of slaves. In fact, there were only two major markets where French buying was long sustained: Malta and the free port of Leghorn, the former becoming progressively less important for the French as a source of supply.

The Knights of Malta, pledged to war with the infidel, nearly always had a supply of infidels on hand that could be sold as the Order chose. But since many of the slaves were owned by the Order itself and, according to Vertot,[23] were held in a manpower pool until campaigns were prepared, the market was best tapped on an occasional basis by a resident buyer (usually a Knight) who could purchase newly arrived slaves as opportunities presented themselves. At most times, demands were not readily satisfied at the Malta market. Thus in 1663–64, when Louis sent the "Chevalier de Gout" (de la Guette?) to buy 200 turcs, Grand Master Cotoner, trying to be cooperative, had some slaves assembled and, in spite of grumbling among his Knights, allowed the French agents to choose those deemed proper for the oar.[24] But this procedure was extraordinary, and did not make friends for the French among non-French Knights.

The far-reaching struggle for Crete must also have had adverse effects on the Malta market. Before 1645 Crete had served as an important base for privateering, where victualing and refitting could be done and slaves could be marketed when taken in central and eastern Mediterranean campaigns. Crete had long been a thorn in the side of the Ottomans, as Rhodes had earlier been, and as Malta itself still was. Imagine the damage that could be inflicted, and the slaves and other merchandise taken by Christian predators using Crete as a base of operations, situated in the midst of Ottoman possessions, close to the sealanes between Alexandria and Constantinople. The loss of Crete as a base of operations in 1669 seriously restricted all Christian privateering in the eastern Mediterranean, especially that conducted by the vessels and galleys from Malta. It must have cut the supplies of slaves from the east, giving the Order fewer to sell. From then on, and considering his strained relations with the Grand Master and Pope, the Order could hardly have desired to sell any slaves at all to Louis XIV. But of course the Order could not openly refuse to sell to France, considering the vast extent of its privileges and property within Louis' domains. Perhaps the furthest they could go was to claim they had few to sell and place export duties on shipments of slaves.[25]

In any case, intense antagonism and other difficulties affected sales of slaves to France in the early 1670's, producing the opposite of the plentiful supplies and preferential treatment that Louis (through his ministers and agents) claimed he deserved. Colbert was incensed by the tax of 55 livres a head imposed on slaves exported from Malta to France in 1671; the French consul was told to seek total exemption from that levy.[26] In the early seventies, French consuls at Malta reported that they had contracted with Maltese and Savoyard captains, who promised deliveries of slaves of various sorts. Curiously, just after Louis' negotiations for a renewal of the French Capitulations agreement with the Porte had borne fruit, it was reported, to Intendant Arnoul, that Knights of Malta had just taken some 1,200 prisoners in action with the Turks; Arnoul said he thought those slaves might offer "a splendid chance to strengthen the rowing force of the King."[27] Of course, in buying those slaves, Louis would have violated and possibly destroyed his new agreement with the Porte.

But Louis did want to buy slaves, of acceptable kinds. To encourage his consuls at Malta to find them, Louis promised to reward the Knights serving him in that capacity with the captaincy of a galley upon the delivery of 200 slaves. Some such device was needed to get Knights to show the necessary zeal and loyalty for his service, because they faced so much opposition within their own Order in trying to buy for France. Two Knights working as consuls did supply enough slaves to obtain their captaincy, the Chevaliers de Piancourt and de Tincourt. However, each of them took many years to supply his quota, and Louis' minister of marine implied that he doubted their zeal. Under their auspices, and that of their successor, the Chevalier d'Escrainville, the Malta market almost completely dried up for the French. D'Escrainville was a notably ineffectual buyer, by far the least successful of the three. During a period of fifteen years he supplied barely 200, and many of them were rejects that had to be returned.[28]

Louis was somewhat better served by his consuls at Leghorn. A relatively new and bustling free port on the north Italian coast, Leghorn was a convenient entrepôt, with liberal laws and a large degree of religious tolerance for the day, that attracted merchants who were troubled elsewhere. Some Dutch and English vessels made Leghorn a regular port of call. Christian corsairs also frequented Leghorn, bringing in slaves for sale. The port became a very significant regular source of slaves for the Galley Corps.

The work of Leghorn consuls as buyers of slaves throws light not only on the local market, but also on the general character of the trade and on some of the special problems faced by the French in acquiring manpower for the oar. Particular insight is afforded by some of the correspondence of François Cotolendy, French consul at Leghorn for 1670–91. Cotolendy can hardly be considered "representative," since the length of his service as a buyer distinguished him from most others.[29]

One of Cotolendy's problems at Leghorn was the competition, whose bidding naturally raised prices and interfered with his buying. He claimed that Spanish buyers and buyers for the papal galleys, and Neapolitans, Genoese, Tuscans, and even Englishmen, were at times his competitors. But most of all he complained that Frenchmen were topping his bids and occasioning trouble, and it was on his insistence that an order was issued in 1678 forbidding French merchants to buy slaves at Leghorn, Genoa, and neighboring places.[30] About Spanish and Neapolitan competition he could do little or nothing. But when the English entered the market as slave buyers for a brief period in 1673–75, Cotolendy eliminated their competition by "the convention we have made to share among ourselves all [the slaves] that either one buys, so that neither will raise the price for the other." [31] The minister of marine thought Cotolendy exaggerated the intensity of the competition, and complained that Leghorn prices were too high.[32] In turn, Cotolendy complained, first to Intendant Brodart and in 1677 to the minister himself, that his navy drafts were neither promptly nor fully paid at Marseilles, and that persons presenting his orders to pay received "bad treatment" of various sorts, "which is the reason why many [businessmen] of this city will no longer accept my letters of exchange, even when I give a bonus of 2 per cent." [33] Letters drawn by other consuls were also discounted heavily, in such measure that it was deemed essential to draw on Lyons instead.

Once purchased, slaves were both a problem and a source of profit for a consul. Transportation was one problem. The captains of many merchant ships were reluctant to take slaves, and some refused to have them aboard at all.[34] Slaves were dangerous cargo; if a merchantman with slaves aboard happened to fall prey to a North African corsair, there might be especially unpleasant consequences for her captain and crew. This risk was less serious out of Leghorn than from more distant ports. At Leghorn, moreover, the squadrons of French galleys that cruised the coast of northern Italy could pick up slaves.[35] But the galleys usually appeared only in the summer, and if slaves were purchased in the fall, many months might pass before they could be put on the galleys. There was an added problem of transport out of Leghorn stemming from a royal edict of 1669 that forbade French merchantmen coming from the Levant to embark or discharge any cargo in Italy; hence, a good many French merchantmen never even touched at Italian ports.[36]

But far from being a burden to the consul, delay could be profitable. With good management, a consul might make substantial profits by working slaves as laborers while they were awaiting shipment to France. Slaves were usually quartered under guard in a municipal slave compound or workhouse-prison. Of course, illness, accident, or death could befall a slave while on the consul's hands, but such risks were not great. Illness might involve the loss of wages and some expense for medicines.[37] If a slave did die or escape, the loss involved would be assumed by the King, so long as such accidents did not happen often. Such ill luck could bring a tongue-lashing, as it did for Cotolendy in 1682 when he was informed by the ministry of marine that "the King is very ill-satisfied with the lack of care you took in the choice of slaves. It is extraordinary that five should have died while on your hands, and that you should have bought a cripple. This indicates extreme negligence on your part in the inspection made before purchase." The ministry thought it still more extraordinary that five others should have died on the hands of Consul Aubert at Genoa the previous month! Roguery was expected, and commonly suspected.[38]

Consuls often bought slaves through intermediaries. This procedure dissociated them from open participation in transactions involving slaves from "sensitive" sources. Obviously, it was undesirable for a French consul to buy Algerians after Louis had signed treaties of peace with Algeria. Thus, when consuls were offered slaves in unbreakable lots, they found it useful to employ neighboring merchants to buy for them. Other means were also employed to disguise purchases, since anonymity was also desirable for the sake of safety in shipment and for that of the ship employed; ownership was sometimes registered in the names of persons other than the consul, with an official destination other than Marseilles. But probably few people who were seriously interested in knowing what went on were fooled by facades of indirect purchase, disguised ownership, and fictitious destination. The Ottoman and North African governments were not.

On a few occasions, Cotolendy reversed his role and sold slaves. In the 1680's, when a great many new hands were becoming available for the oars, the ministry decided to dispose of "worn-out" slaves no longer fit for the oar. In the "housecleaning" of 1686 four old turcs were sent to Cotolendy. He reported selling them at what he thought a good price: 30 piastres a head. But four more arrived soon afterward, and then another four. For the lot of them he managed to get 120 piastres, but insisted that he wanted no more to be sent. The minister congratulated him on the sales, and also promised to send no more. Other means then had been found to dispose of invalid forçats and turcs.[39]

Meanwhile, recognizing that the enslavement of the subjects of Moslem states would not conciliate or improve French relations with them, Louis sought to minimize the use he made on his galleys of slaves from Moslem powers with which he had, or was seeking to make, treaties. This eliminated some sources of supply, and also resulted in the loss of some slaves, since many were returned or exchanged under the terms of the treaties he and his officers made. But the treaties were thereby much strengthened.

This whole problem could have been avoided, of course, had Louis simply renounced the use of slaves on his galleys. But he was determined to have slaves, and this determination, combined with the restriction of supplies, resulted in a "shortage." Clearly it was an artificial, contrived sort of dearth. Perhaps Louis felt he should use slaves since most other Mediterranean princes having galleys used infidel slaves. Perhaps he wanted to use them for the sake of relations with the Gallican clergy. The general character of his relations with Rome makes it likely that Louis welcomed the opportunities thereby afforded to continue his ongoing feud with the Pope. His efforts to obtain these unnecessary slaves involved him (as could be predicted) in novel difficulties with the Pope. He could pose, through much of the struggle, as a peacemaker obliged by his desire for peace (with Moslem powers) to find substitute sources of infidel slaves for his galleys; Louis could appear to be forced, to be led inadvertently into conflict with the popes simply because they supported and sanctified an everlasting struggle from which he was trying to extricate his realm. Public relations, his image as an enthusiastic buyer of infidel slaves, and some pleasing incidental successes in his quarrel with Rome were probably much more important to Louis than the few hundred unnecessary slaves he acquired.

Rome for its part was firm in opposing the use of Christians as slaves; at the same time, Catholic religious, working among the oarsmen aboard Louis' galleys, managed to convert many non-Christian slaves brought to Marseilles. In both these respects the Church moved to thwart, or was put in a position of seeming to thwart, Louis' efforts, throwing him back to using Moslems from traditional Mediterranean sources of supply, thereby undermining, or seeming to be trying to undermine, the peace treaties he had made or was seeking to make with the infidel states. Here was a contest that Louis seemed to enjoy, one in which he chose to engage. On one side, then, was a succession of Popes and Grand Masters of the Order of Saint John with the interests of the Church of

Rome in view, seeking to promote defense of the faith and continuation of crusading war; on the other hand Louis XIV, dominated by worldly, secular, and personal aims, wanting to strengthen his control of both the Church and the State in his realm, to promote the interest of his dynasty and France, and to pose in the service of these objects, as a crusading prince, yet at the same time sincerely determined to maintain peace with the Mediterranean infidel states.

Russians, presumably Christians, were regularly available on the Constantinople market, and were used by the Turks on their galleys. Some of Colbert's subordinates expressed qualms about putting Russian Christians to the chain, even in a "semi-slave" capacity as bonnevoglies. For example, the elder Arnoul said, "It would be a great advantage for me if they would agree to serve as volunteers, and thus heal the scruples I have about holding Christians on the galleys in chains." No such scruples bothered the minister of marine; orders were issued to acquire the Russians. "It is certain," he said, "that we must profit from all possible opportunities that present themselves for strengthening the rowing force of the galleys; that is why, if you find you can get Russians from Constantinople, the greatest possible number must be bought. I shall instruct M. de la Haye [French Ambassador at Constantinople] to give all the help he can to those doing the buying." [40] Considerable numbers of such Russians appear to have been purchased in the sixties, to be worked as indentured (and chained) bonnevoglies until they worked off their debts, including the price of their purchase.[41] But in the early seventies, the use of bonnevoglies was at least temporarily renounced (see pp. 135–136). It was hoped that other means, either purchase or conscription, could supply the oarsmen desired.

The idea of using Russians, and also Greeks obtained on comparable terms, was revived about 1673. In that year, much uncertainty was expressed as to whether or not a group of Greeks, captured by the vessels of the King, *should* be put to the oar, and whether or not the French had a "right" to keep them.[42] But by the summer of 1674 the doubts seem to have been resolved. The Chevalier de Piancourt, then consul at Malta, contracted with a corsair who sailed under the flag of Savoy to deliver schismatic Greeks to Marseilles for 60 piastres a head, a low price indeed compared with prices then being asked for turcs. The consul, it appeared, had no personal qualms about purchasing Christian Greeks as slaves. He stood to gain if the contract was approved, and he argued for it strongly. He said the Duke of Savoy was then at war with "these Greeks"; the Greeks would be captured under the Duke's flag, and Louis' flag need not be involved at all. By a curious coincidence he was able to report that "some days ago there arrived here [at Malta] the Superior of the Recollets who guard the Holy Sepulchre [at Jerusalem]. He complains of the attacks made on the Recollets by these Greeks on Easter Sunday. He says the Greeks do them [the Recollets] more harm than the Turks. Men of this sort would be suitable material for the galleys." [43] The consul also pointed out that Greeks were (often) seafaring men, and that the Venetians manned their galleys with Greeks. The minister wrote his response on de Piancourt's letter: "Good, he can purchase the Greeks." [44]

After this surprising approval, de Piancourt told a number of corsairs that the King of France was willing to buy "all Greeks found on Turkish ships that fall into their hands." Since a large percentage of the shipping under the Ottoman flag was manned by Greek Christians and other non-Moslem subjects of the Ottoman Turks, the corsairs could offer many men of these types. But the consul reported that they also found it difficult to believe that they were free to sell such Christians as slaves — they insisted "that His Majesty obtain assurances that they would not be oppressed or troubled in their traffic either by the Pope or by his Inquisitor at Malta." [45] Perhaps the consul was simply expressing the corsairs' sentiments, but he was also stressing the pertinence of the views, and authority, of Grand Master Cotoner, the Inquisitor, and the Pope. Such a contract for slaves, if approved by the minister of marine, would place Louis in the distasteful position of being obliged, if he wanted to buy slaves, to obtain permission from the Inquisitor and the Pope. No one could imagine Louis XIV asking permission.

Louis' minister of marine was told — exactly when is unclear — that the use of Greek Christians on French galleys was no longer desired, and Intendant Brodart was warned in turn (in late 1676) that when buying Russians from Constantinople he must take care not to allow his buyers "to mix any schismatic Greeks with the Russians." As a matter of policy, the Russians were evidently acceptable bonnevoglies, but Greek Christians were not. Later a curious "secret" contract was made with a corsair named Cruvelier, whose agreement provided that the navy would buy Greeks, but only in a ratio of one Greek to five Turks. Within a few weeks after his arrangement was approved, the clauses relating to Greeks were abruptly cancelled.[46] And soon afterward Brod-art was told unequivocally that the King did not want any more Russians either: "in case you have given any orders in this regard, revoke them." [47] These instructions constituted a definite and long-standing decision that forbade the purchase of Russians from Constantinople or any other market. That decision was perhaps precipitated by the rumor circulated in 1678 that some of the "Russians" then serving in the French rowing force were not Russians at all. When investigation disclosed that there were about twenty Poles on the galleys, orders were issued (April 1679) for their release.[48] Louis evidently wanted to avoid the discredit that could derive from knowingly using Christians as slaves or even as bon-nevoglies on his galleys.

The very next year, 1680, Louis' feud with the Order of Saint John took an interesting turn. The Inquisitor at Malta, according to Consul de Tincourt, was strongly opposed to the sale of Christians, including Christianized Turks, to the French; the Inquisitor even went to the extremity of excommunicating Tincourt for selling Christianized Turks as slaves.[49] Tincourt reported that when he tried to send two baptized Turks to Marseilles for the galleys, the Inquisitor had them seized, and imprisoned one for safekeeping. Tincourt said the slave in question be-longed to the King of France, but "once inside these prisons I can not get them out except by means whose consequences are not to be desired." He added that there was no hope the Grand Master would openly in-tercede on Louis' behalf: "He is an Italian, and you know in what re-spect Italians hold the Inquisition." [50] That affair too may have been concocted as a lesson for Louis, teaching where the limits of his authority lay, and where that of the Inquisitor and Rome were supreme.

The drying up of the Maltese market and the scarcity of slaves at Leghorn gave added impetus to Louis' quest for substitute slaves. West Africa could provide slaves, brought from Cape Verde. The French min-ister of marine was enthusiastic about this source. Neither high prices nor any other hindrances seemed, at the outset, likely to impede the use of such slaves. They could be supplied by the Senegal Company in almost any quantity desired, and of course the Company was eager to provide them; Colbert probably saw to that. Northern neutrals or the Dutch would probably consent to transport them, as they did much else in wartime. As for the capacity of West Africans for the oar, Colbert remarked optimistically that "these *naturels* do unbelievable labor in all American colonies; there is reason to believe they would be very suitable for the galleys, if treated well." [51] Recognition of these advantages, plus the fact that West African slaves could be acquired with minimum difficulty and expense, must have helped to commend them. Equally evident, no doubt, was the great advantage of drawing on a source that could not involve complications with North African Moslem states. From the practical standpoint of service and accessibility, these were probably the best conceivable substitutes Louis could obtain for Mediterranean infidel slaves.[52]

But not all naval officials shared the minister's enthusiasm for the West African slaves or his confidence in their capacities as oarsmen. Some outright opposition to them was expressed. Part of it was predictable conservative response to change. Opposition could certainly be expected from persons whose economic interests were tied up with the procurement of slaves from conventional sources — the merchants and shippers of Marseilles and others dealing licitly and illicitly in Moslems could not expect to share in the West African traffic, for the Senegal Company had exclusive rights. Opposition could be expected also from Knights of Malta. Having vowed to defend the faith and destroy pirates and Mohammedans, Knights probably preferred to enslave infidels from Mediterranean sources, rather than to have West Africans (who might also have been Moslems) working the oars of the galleys they commanded. The continued use of slaves from Mediterranean sources was bound to be more beneficial to the slaving traffic of their Order, and any slaves from an outside source would cut into that traffic. Considering that the captains of about half the French galleys were Knights, and that many junior officers were also Knights, the influence of their preferences could have been strong. In any case, the minister of marine was moved in 1679 to tell Intendant Brodart that one of his principal duties must be "to persuade the captains of the value of the blacks." [53]

Actually, the primary spokesman for the varied opposition to blacks had been Brodart himself. Adamantly against their use, he even opposed the idea of using West Africans experimentally, suspecting perhaps that "experimental" use could easily lead to permanent use. His uncompromising opposition had led the minister to say to him in November 1677 that "His Majesty has been surprised at his intendant. Without ever having tried to see whether or not blacks can work the oar, he decided absolutely that they are not fit to serve." [54]

As early as 1676 the minister proposed to merchants of La Rochelle, who were engaged in the African trade, that they arm a vessel, under the English flag since it was wartime, to bring 200 or 300 blacks from Africa.[55] Nothing seems to have come of the idea until nearly the end of the war. But the minister and King were evidently determined to give blacks a try. Brodart was uncooperative to the extent of refusing comment on the plans that were being made, though the minister repeatedly pressed him to explain his views. Finally the minister chided Brodart in January 1678, and again the following month, saying, "You have written me nothing on this subject; you could not have forgotten an affair of such importance as this"; but there was no response from Brodart, at least for a considerable time.[56]

The Senegal Company agreed to deliver to Marseilles 200–300 slaves of premium quality at 130 livres a head, an attractive price since a prime turc cost 350 livres or more.[57] An early shipment of 77 blacks, arriving in April 1679, included 38 who were judged too young to serve, but the quality of those accepted left little to be desired. According to Colbert, "The King has never had stronger or better-built men for his galleys."[58] At least three more shipments were delivered in 1679–80. Of the more than 300 men delivered, the inspectors at Marseilles accepted 273.[59]

The minister ordered that special care was to be given to any of the new arrivals who appeared to be sick or debilitated after their voyage on the slavers. Indeed, the minister, always attentive to detail, seemed to do everything possible to enable the blacks to "succeed on the galleys." He appointed a Monsieur Mariage to teach them French and to serve in the meantime as translator and overseer. He ordered that the blacks should be separated from forçats and turcs when the galleys were in port because a bad example would be set for the newcomers by the veterans of the oar. He wrote the Superior of the Congrégation de la Mission at Marseilles asking that a member of the Order be appointed "to instruct them on the lights of our Religion, and make them fit to be Christians."[60]

The minister urged Brodart to send reports on the condition of the blacks and their performance at the oar because "that is, at present, one of the most important matters of concern to the galleys."[61] The minister went so far as to say that "the ease with which we can get these slaves will enable us to put thirty galleys to sea." Perhaps in the future, he enthused, we can use them to equip some galleasses as well.[62] Part of the minister's solicitude for the West African blacks stemmed from the apparent importance of the newcomers as possible substitutes for slaves from the usual sources of supply. But there were also grounds for anxiety about the apparent deterioration in the physical condition of the West Africans being held at Marseilles: from the start it seemed possible that they might be receiving improper care. As early as 1679 the minister learned that eighteen of them had died in the hospital for oarsmen.[63] That was hardly encouraging, but perhaps there was reason to believe that they died of the aftereffects of their voyage on the slaver. The condition of the survivors should soon improve.

In December 1680, the minister was pleased to learn from the superior of the Congrégation that during the winter (1680–81) the blacks would be given religious instruction. "There is nothing," the minister wrote Brodart, "more important for the Glory of God and the service of the King than to make them all Christians. Do not fail to contribute as much as you can to the success of that good work." [64] The following August the minister expressed his satisfaction when he learned that a "very considerable number of the blacks are now capable of being baptized," and he urged "continued application in this important work to complete the instruction of those that remain at Marseilles." At that date fifty were considered to have been converted to Roman Catholic Christianity, and the Duke de Vivonne had them baptized.[65]

Though the minister appeared to approve the enterprising work of the superior and his missionnaires among the West Africans, he could hardly have done otherwise considering the prevailing opinion at Court in the early eighties. The bubbling approval he gave in this matter seems out of character, excessive and unconvincing considering the nature of the religious opposition to the employment of Christians as galley slaves. One might expect him to view with mixed feelings the successful conversions among the West African slaves, since only their heathen or, in some instances, probably Moslem condition — in either case, their dissociation from Christian belief — justified their condition of slavery in the eyes of the Church. The success of the missionnaires in effecting conversions removed the reason for enslaving them, and would almost certainly be followed by Church-inspired objections to their continued employment at the oar.

In contrast to their improved spiritual condition in 1681, their physical health was reported to be notably worsening. The treatment they received at Marseilles was obviously unsuited to the needs of debilitated men. Diet on the galleys was poor, without supplements. Until the fall of 1681 these Africans were given the ration ordinarily given to French convicts, which was kept purposely scant, ostensibly to encourage the men to work. The ration consisted (officially) of two pounds of bread or sea biscuit a day, three ounces of beans in soup, oil (or lard), salt, and sometimes a little wine.[66] All oarsmen were given a modest "sea-ration" supplement while on campaign, but in port all oasmen were expected to work and thereby earn extra food. From the standpoint of modern penology the system of work had positive merit, when applied with healthy men. And the system had the notable virtue of saving the King a tidy sum on food for the ten or twelve thousand men on the galleys during most of the eighties and nineties.[67] But the West Africans necessarily required some time to learn the peculiar ways of their work-house-prison. Pulled out of their own society and lacking the experience, skills, and even the language needed for many types of work in their new environment, and kept apart from the experienced oarsmen as much as possible, they were certain to have difficulty getting supplements for their ration. As early as February 1681, they were reported "suffering and dying from the winter and cold," in spite of the fact that the minister earlier urged that they be housed in heated buildings.

But the winter weather and short rations were not alone responsible for the fact that they were reported, in August 1681, to be "dying every day."[68] Their overseer and translator, Monsieur Mariage, seems to have had a hand in the matter. At his own request, he had been made responsible for feeding and maintaining them, and his request had been approved in the hope of improving their condition. But three months after Mariage assumed these duties, the minister had reason to reprimand him. It was then disclosed that the West Africans were still being grossly neglected and abused: "His Majesty has often ordered special care for the blacks at Marseilles; yet now he learns that they are barefoot. It is very important to protect them from the cold, to clothe them fully, and to give them shoes, even though that man Mariage pretends that for what it would cost the King [to do that] he could give them eight ounces of rice with beans [a day?]."[69] Shortly afterward, it was disclosed that Mariage "abuses the trust confided to him by converting part of the subsistence to profit for himself."[70] The minister asked

Brodart "to see if he can be discharged without prejudice to the slaves. If so, let me know, and the King will discharge him forthwith. But in case he must still be retained, he must be watched."[71] Mariage was dealt with, but by the following February (1683), only 98 of the original 273 blacks remained alive.[72] Several years later, since the 86 surviving blacks were considered "useless and at His Majesty's charge," the minister approved their shipment to the West Indies for sale.[73]

The attempt to use West Africans did not prove that black slaves were physically unfit or less suited to the oar than other slaves. Yet one commentator expressed precisely that view, or excuse, when he remarked in 1682 that "the purchase of blacks is an expenditure from which one gets almost no return because, being unable to endure the fatigues, they are unsuited to the galleys."[74] Such an opinion was strangely inconsistent with the fact that the labor of West African slaves was the basis for plantation and mining economies in all the Americas. It was still stranger considering that Moslem blacks were normally present among the turcs who gave such satisfaction at French galley oars. Identifiable blacks from Moslem lands having Mohammedan names were present both before and after the period 1679–82, when the shipments from Cape Verde began to arrive.[75] Apparently the blacks from Mediterranean sources of supply were deemed useful; only the blacks imported in unlimited numbers from Cape Verde were deemed unsuited to the oar.

Some stigma may have attached to Louis' use of the same kinds of slaves owned and employed in large numbers by West Indian merchants and planters, or to his using a kind of slave that no other Mediterranean prince systematically used on his galleys. West African slaves were not the usual prisoners of war, but simple laborers. No particular prestige attached to their use comparable to that attaching to the use of men who were the subjects of governments identified by the Church as enemies of the Christian faith. Moreover the slaves from West Africa seemed peculiarly prone to become a burden and embarrassment to Louis in that they attracted such extraordinarily intensive "instruction" efforts by the missionnaires, and responded so readily to their proselyting efforts. After accepting the elements of Christian faith, such slaves qualified themselves for release, and earned the intercession of missionnaires as pleaders for their liberation from the oar. Louis, the ministry of marine, and the King's officers at Marseilles had many persuasive reasons for making their negative judgment on the utility of West Afri-

159

can blacks on French galleys. No significant effort was afterward made to secure further shipments.

Even as blacks were being "proved" unfit for the oars in the decade of the eighties, Louis' "need" for new sources of slaves was intensified by the series of treaties he extracted from the North African state of Algiers. The agreements with the deys of Algiers in 1681 and 1684 were of special importance since Algiers was the largest and strongest of the North African states, and their treaties set a pattern for the others. Those in 1681 and 1684 were simply truces, as most earlier agreements had been, even though the later treaty included a clause declaring the signatories intended to keep the peace for "one hundred years." A new, more durable agreement with Algiers was reached in 1689. As far as the interests of the Galley Corps were concerned, the treaties from 1684 onward were said to have resulted in the release by 1690 of no fewer than 700 turcs.[76] The peace treaties signed ultimately with Tunis, Tripoli, and Algiers legally eliminated most of the traditional sources of Moslem slaves for French galleys.[77]

The implications of these treaties were clearly understood. In the ministry of marine, peace and the promotion of trade were clear-cut objectives; Colbert declared in 1682 that if it were not for the trade involved, he would rather have war with the Barbary states than allow the men from those cities to be returned.[78] His opinion may have been influenced by the knowledge that the number of Algerians held in France was larger than the number of Frenchmen being held at Algiers. But reservations on the part of mere naval officials, even at the ministerial level, were not enough to prevent signature of the treaties of peace. The treaties themselves suggested that Louis had important political and religious objectives in view, as well as the Colbertist aim of promoting trade. Perhaps he also had some notions about a possible far-reaching Mediterranean empire for himself and for France. But about his immediate objective there can be no doubt: his aim was peace with the North African infidel states.

The implementation of the treaties was a difficult matter, partly because compliance with treaty terms depended on the cooperation of the officials of the navy at Marseilles and ministry of marine at the capital. Problems speedily arose. The officials at the arsenal, as the Algerians must have expected, were not dependable when release of able-bodied slaves were called for by treaty provisions. Such reluctance to

The Procurement of Slaves

release able-bodied turcs was notably apparent in March 1682 during a Moroccan emissary's stay in Marseilles. Slaves from Salé and other Moroccan dependencies, then in French hands in contravention of treaties, were hidden by naval officials on an island in the roadstead, and others were concealed on the upper floors of the hospital for oarsmen to delude the visitor.[79] That same month efforts were made to force slaves on the galleys to write letters home to Algiers misrepresenting the state of affairs at Marseilles; approving words came from the ministry of marine, "It is fine to force the Algerian slaves on the galleys to write as the Sieur de Beaujeu requests; mistreat them for that purpose if you must, but His Majesty thinks that the threat alone will suffice."[80]

Almost a year after the treaty of 1684 had been signed, the dey of Algiers complained in a letter to Louis that few Algerians known to be held by the French on their galleys had been released and returned. The dey said, "The officers at Marseilles have kept most of the slaves to be returned under the treaty of peace, and instead they have brought us sick and crippled slaves from the Levant who are not from Algiers."[81] Though close to 400 turcs were released at a relatively early date, the Algerians claimed that less than half were Algerians, while authentic Algerians remained at Marseilles. "It is not as a favor that we claim the release of the Janissaries remaining in France; they were included in the treaty" and should be returned, complained the dey.[82]

There seem to have been acts of bad faith on both sides, and much mutual suspicion. Plantet asserted that "it is certain" that the officers of the navy "showed regrettable unwillingness" in finding and delivering the slaves whose return was called for by treaties.[83] Relations were specially bitter in 1684 because both sides resorted to the atrocity of blowing prisoners from the mouths of their cannon.[84]

Even when the King and minister had the best possible intentions, and wanted full compliance with treaty terms, the translation of their intentions into action was uncertain in many matters of detail. The mechanism of acquiring and managing slaves in the Mediterranean presented opportunities galore for negligence, subversion, and worse. Its characteristic complexity played into the hands of men who preferred not to comply or who might be ill disposed to maintain peace. Some slaves from treaty powers were virtually certain to be acquired when privateers were captured because the subjects of several North African principalities frequently served together on a single vessel; thus, the

161

crew of a prize, whatever its flag or its origin, would be likely to include a number of men who should be returned to one or another North African city. Understandably, shipments of slaves from such ports as Melos or Malta or Leghorn were commonly composed of men of divers origins. The officials at Marseilles could argue that they felt an obligation, since they were interested in keeping a steady flow of slaves coming in, to purchase any able-bodied man who arrived. For that reason, and others, they accepted many men from treaty states, knowing that they should be returned or exchanged. Such men tended to accumulate at Marseilles, and they were commonly worked on the galleys while awaiting shipment to their "treaty-protected" place of origin. But sometimes months or years went by without their presence being reported to the ministry, or without orders being issued for release or exchange under treaty terms. Once a man's name was entered on the registers of slaves, he could easily be forgotten or overlooked until he was no longer of any use at the oars; then he was likely to be noticed, for he was at His Majesty's charge.

"Infidelities" on the part of Louis' subordinates in complying with the provisions of treaties were at least encouraged by the King's example of giving high-handed, arbitrary treatment of the deys and beys of the North African states and their emissaries to France. Many subordinates hardly needed encouragement to give vent to their repugnance and hatred for infidels. The desire of many in the Corps to keep all the infidel slaves they had led naval officials to be "insensitive," even to wink at the violation of treaties to avoid worsening what they saw as the shortage of slaves. But of course there were multiple violations of treaties on both sides, following the treaty of 1684 and that of 1689. At least some of the authorities in North Africa and France alike, we can be certain, had a flexible attitude, tolerating transgressions and overlooking infidelities in remarkable degree, perhaps partly on the assumption that it could not be helped.

Yet this disposition to flexibility, present in unusual degree after 1689, when French relations with Tunis and Algiers were notably tranquil, needs more explanation. Perhaps it was a fair measure of the "progress" made that the number of Algerians arriving for the galleys during the period 1689–1707 was reduced by three-quarters or more, as compared with the previous period. However, a great number of Algerians (and other North Africans) were put to the oar in spite of the treaties, so there *was* ample justification for renouncing the treaties and renewing warfare with France, as had often been done before. But several considerations, taken together, go far toward explaining the unusual degree of reluctance to seize the ready-made excuses for resuming hostilities. There was the trading and privateering advantage for them to keep the peace with France and make prey, as Louis desired them to do, of the shipping of France's enemies. And there must also have been respect for the destructive bombardment fleet that Louis repeatedly used against them during the "punitive decade" of the eighties. Louis' new mortar ships rendered the North African states weaker than they had been before vis-à-vis the French; they could no longer renew war with France with anything approaching their traditional degree of immunity to retaliation.

At the same time, however, the North African governments must have come to realize that Louis XIV was different; the pretentious, powerful Louis was determined to maintain peace with them, albeit on his own terms and with the imposition of conditions only partly acceptable and in some ways highly disadvantageous for them. They had to deal with a "peacemaker" carrying a club, one who claimed (to paraphrase him) that he willingly granted peace on terms he could not expect from his enemies if they had enjoyed over him the superiority he enjoyed over them! No less persuasive for the North Africans, perhaps, was the fact that Louis, in his quest for peace, flouted the crusading purposes of the Pope and the Knights of Malta — the two most implacable enemies of infidels. After their experience during the eighties, the North Africans must have had difficulty conceiving Louis in a peacemaking role. But they were patient, and played along with his colossal vanity and power. After he had extracted a new treaty from Tripoli in 1693, Louis proved he could rightly claim a role as a peacemaker, at least as far as French relations with North Africa were concerned. After that date the infidels would not have done Louis justice if they had failed to recognize that he was adhering as well as he could to the terms of peace. French relations with Tunis, Algiers, and Tripoli then entered an era of relative calm and peace.[85]

Meanwhile, Louis and his ministry of marine looked to Canada for possible slave supplies. This possibility was ready at hand; as administrators of colonial affairs, ministers of marine well knew that there was an Indian problem in New France. Some of the Indians made serious problems indeed for the settlers. The struggling settlers and the navy alike might reap some benefit if some of the troublesome redskins were shipped to Marseilles for use on the galleys. The notion of gathering slaves from the sparse Indian population now seems utterly impracticable. Yet it may then have seemed reasonable, or at least plausible at first sight, that if thousands of blacks could be gathered out of the vastness of Africa and shipped from east to west, some of the troublesome Indians might be gathered and sent the other way; the principal difficulty would consist in getting the Indians together to send.

Whatever the dubious rationale of this project, it was hardly a scheme calculated to be helpful to the missionary efforts of the Recollets, Jesuits, and other religious who were active among the North American Indian tribes. In fact, the whole plan was kept secret from them. Louis must have thought there was no reason why the religious should be told in advance that his interests were to take priority over the salvation of Indian souls in New France. Some such thoughts may have been in Louis' mind when he gave orders in 1684 to the Marquis de Denonville, Governor General of New France, "to do everything possible to capture [in the forthcoming war] the greatest possible number of prisoners from the Iroquois Indian tribes; ship them to France for the galleys at every opportunity." [86] Capturing Iroquois was no easy task in the forest. The French Canadians were reduced to preying on some friendly Iroquois who sometimes brought fish and game to Fort Frontenac for sale. The Indians evidently thought themselves secure because the Church had its missionaries living and working among them.

Thus in 1685 we find the Governor General not only planning war with the Iroquois in accord with instructions, but asserting to the minister of marine that the Iroquois had to be "exterminated." [87] The Governor General and Intendant Champigny used trickery to declare war on the Iroquois. They apparently hoped, by that method, to take a sizable number of prisoners at the start, including some Indian chiefs. To this end, Indians of several Iroquois tribes were invited to take part in a powwow and feast. "They knew nothing of the impending war with their Iroquois kinsmen and came trustingly, with their wives and children, in a party of about two hundred." [88] After the feast, French troops suddenly arrested the Iroquois guests. About forty of the braves thus captured, including several chiefs, were soon afterward shipped to France and put to the oars of Louis' galleys. They were treated com-

164

paratively well. For example, the minister of marine decreed that the Iroquois need not be shaved as slaves usually were, and that they need not be chained "provided you are certain they are thus secure, and will not escape."[89] At first the Iroquois were fed standard rations, as the blacks had been, but later, since it was claimed that they too needed more than the usual fare, the minister ordered that their rations be increased.[90] It was reported in 1688 that the Indians were docile, getting along well with their religious instruction, and receiving the sacraments.[91]

Meanwhile, the Governor General was instructed to continue fighting the Indians and sending prisoners to France. "It is [now] certain," wrote the minister, "that these men, vigorous and accustomed to hardship as they are, can be of service on His Majesty's galleys."[92] But able-bodied Iroquois braves were seldom taken prisoner. The Denonville expedition against the Seneca (Iroquois) tribes in 1687 encountered deserted villages and ambush, and took only a few stragglers as prisoners; some of the prisoners taken simply served, it was said, as food for the Governor General's cannibal Indian allies.[93]

The Iroquois, for their part, were bent on obtaining revenge and the return of their chiefs. They ravaged the countryside far and wide and massacred the French at Lachine, in the very environs of Montreal. Denonville admitted that sending Iroquois braves to France for service in the galleys had "very much contributed to irritate the Iroquois against the French."[94] But he could justifiably pass responsibility for that action to others, as he did in writing to the minister of marine in 1687 that he was obliged to obey blindly the orders of the King. At Denonville's request, re-enforced by that of the returning Governor General Frontenac, the King consented to have the captive Iroquois sent back to Canada. "His Majesty is pleased to use these savages to make peace with their nation, it being inconvenient in present circumstances to continue this war."[95] Accordingly, the twenty-one remaining Iroquois embarked at La Rochelle for New France. Thirteen (some sources say three) survived to reach Canada in the fall of 1689.[96] The Iroquois nation proved an illusory source of slave supply. Substitutes for North African Moslems had to be sought elsewhere.

But perhaps the Iroquois experiment, though not productive of significant numbers of slaves, did underscore the lesson Louis seemed disposed to point up for the Papacy: in his realm, France and the colonies alike, where secular affairs were involved, his policies, his acts, and his will must prevail. The Church and all the ecclesiastics in the realm — and Louis certainly included among them Mgr. de Mont-morency-Laval, Bishop of Quebec, who persisted in claiming his juris-diction came direct from Rome — whatever their claims and pretensions, must recognize royal authority and be obedient to the King. The in-terests of the Church and the pursuit of objectives not conforming to royal purposes, must be subordinated to the objectives of the King, even to his whims.

Meanwhile, in Europe, the later stages of a great and decisive war were unfolding; a turning point was reached in the struggle between the Hapsburgs and their Eastern European allies on the one hand and the Ottoman Empire on the other. That struggle promised a variety of substitutes for the Moslems coming from maritime North Africa. Ottoman armies drove into southeastern Europe (with secret encourage-ment from Louis XIV) and laid siege to Vienna in 1683. King John Sobieski of Poland and the Duke of Lorraine successfully raised the siege, and the next year papal diplomacy produced the Holy League comprising Poland, the Hapsburg Empire, and Venice. In the decade and a half that followed, Christian European powers mounted a suc-cessful crusade against the Turks, winning some sensational victories and forcing intermittent but general retreat of Turkish armies. Louis held aloof from this Christian-infidel conflict for a time, obstructing the efforts of the members of the League, apparently hoping to see his Hapsburg enemies weakened in warring with the Turk while he strengthened himself. But he was thwarted by the successes of the League. Eventually, he brought France openly into the war in the West.

The French minister of marine was early aware that the succession of Turkish defeats and retreats meant that substantial numbers of Moslem prisoners of war were coming into their hands. Notable successes were won by the Austrian forces in Hungary (Mohacs, 1687) and by the Venetians and their maritime collaborators, the Order of Malta, the Papal States, and Tuscany. Hence in the middle eighties Louis' min-ister of marine could look to the members of the Holy League, especially to Venice and territories occupied by Austria, as possible sources of slaves for French galleys.

The Venetian Republic, ordinarily, was a poor market for slaves, at least as far as the French were concerned, but the minister of marine had hopes. Maltese sources reported in 1685 that the Venetian army had "sacked the free port named Arta" (a minor commercial rival of Venice) where "they took 450 Jews or turcs as slaves."[97] That very year, the French Ambassador to Venice, de la Haye, received orders to ask the Venetian Senate to allow French merchants to buy turcs. The Senate responded that it had "no knowledge that any are sold from our maritime dominions, considering [our own?] needs," but later thought it wise to add, soothingly, to the representative of Louis XIV that "there has never been the least hindrance to purchases of that sort."[98] Official permission to purchase, as this was interpreted to be, had no immediate value according to the French consul, Le Blond. When writing to Seignelay in the summer of 1686, he reported finding "no Turkish slaves" that he could buy, "either in Venice or its environs, because the Venetians use them all in their galleys. Not a single one has been seen [offered for sale] since the war."[99]

In Dalmatia, Consul Le Blond did manage to secure a small lot of Turks; that shipment pleased the minister in France, and produced the promise of a "gratification from the King" provided he could "send to Marseilles as many as 150 or 200 as good as the first ones you send."[100] But Le Blond's correspondence and the results of his efforts through 1687 suggest that some of his friends and business associates in the upper Adriatic were interested in doing what the Venetian Senate appears to have been disposed at first to do: to persuade the French that Adriatic markets held nothing for them. The French persisted, however. Finally, the Venetians apparently offered to trade Turkish prisoners of war taken before Chios for vessels belonging to the King of France. That was an interesting proposition, one the minister of marine wanted to hear more about.[101]

The prospect that slaves might be bought from the Austrians seemed an even more intriguing, but also more remote possibility, at least for France. The Emperor was not likely to be willing to sell slaves to Louis XIV. Yet slaves might perhaps be obtained indirectly. Tincourt reported from Malta in May 1680 that he had written to the Governor of Croatia, "a Grand Croix in our Order," to try to buy slaves.[102] Later, in the winter of 1683–84, news was received from Leghorn that the Emperor was sending 600 slaves to Naples for the galleys of Spain, and 400 to Rome for the galleys of the Pope.[103] In 1687 the Emperor was reported to have sent another 150 to the Grand Duke of Florence "to re-enforce his galleys."[104] Such rumors, or news, enlivened French interest, as it may have been intended to do.

The initial French effort to buy slaves from the Emperor was openly made at the highest level. The Prince of Dietrichstein, lord high steward at the Austrian Court, was approached in the fall of 1684; it was said that the "greatest possible number" of slaves were sought for French galleys; could he help?[105] The French perhaps thought that the Emperor might see an opportunity to embroil Louis with his Turkish friends through the sale of Turkish prisoners of war taken in the Balkan campaigns. However, the only apparent result of the initial approach was to persuade the minister of marine that French efforts to buy should thereafter be more discreetly made. The minister resolved to send a secret agent to Hungary to buy.[106] The "Italian merchant" selected for this secret mission was the Sieur Chevalier de Salis, known as "Baptiste Fedeli," who "does not speak French"; his instructions were issued in April 1687 (in French).

This secret agent visited Vienna, Raab; Budapest, and Gratzen; his instructions called for the purchase of up to 500 able-bodied men twenty to forty years of age "for the galleys of Italian princes," delivery to be made at Trieste. In less than two months he reported that the "Germans" (Austrians?) had already "disposed of most of their slaves"; perhaps they used some on Danube galleys, but in any case the Emperor either would not sell or made exceedingly difficult conditions for the sale of those he said he would sell.[107] Meanwhile, in a move suggesting limited confidence in his agent, the minister of marine dispatched a Sieur de Louvigny to Venice with similar instructions to buy slaves and to send them to Leghorn or Genoa, using French or English vessels (or French vessels under the English flag) to minimize risks in transit.[108]

Le Blond remained active in seeking out and bidding for slaves as far afield as the Aegean (Negropont) and in the Adriatic at such markets as Ragusa, Zara, Buccari (Imperial Istria), and Venice itself. Concurrently another agent was commissioned in 1686 to buy Turks in the train of the Venetian army.[109] As if to add to the confusion, French consuls at Malta, Genoa, and Leghorn were showing active interest in the prospects of purchasing slaves, and some of them took significant shares in the limited purchases made in this "Adriatic market." The consul at Malta, for example, was very active. In late 1687 he reported a firm contract for the purchase of 200 slaves and an invitation to bid for 500 more with a Neapolitan merchant whose Vienna agent reported that he had obtained permission from the Emperor to export "whatever quantity of slaves he wished" from the Empire; this must have made it seem to the French that the Austrians freely exported slaves when the buyer could consign his shipments to Naples or Malta.[110] This same Neapolitan merchant, while dealing with the consul at Malta, was concurrently committed, apparently, to deliver slaves to Consul Le Blond at Venice.[111] Aubert, consul at Genoa, was also involved in negotiations to purchase slaves of Austrian origin "taken at Buda[pest] and in Dalmatia" at prices more than double those Le Blond agreed to pay.[112] Aubert had his own agent operating right under Le Blond's nose at Venice.[113] Cotolendy of Leghorn was also meddling in what Le Blond considered his territory; apparently they were both using the same agent. Imagine Le Blond's sentiments on being blamed by the French minister of marine because he "lacked assiduity" and had "contracted with persons not able to keep their promises." [114]

This welter of overlapping and contradictory efforts to buy and sell were damaging to the interests of all buyers, especially the French, who were bidding against themselves at every turn. In effect, they posted advertisements all over the region that the Grand Monarque was attempting to purchase the subjects or ex-subjects or soldiers of his ally. But perhaps secret agent de Salis had some advantage in being where the slaves were actually scheduled to be sold. He did not tarry with the discouraging prospects he found at the prisons of Raab and Budapest, but moved south to where the armies were actively campaigning. Early summer found him near "Essek" (Esseg), and his letters of 27 and 30 July 1687 described the encounter of the Imperial army and the Turks, and also the fact that slaves could be bought. The minister said he hoped for 300, and in mid-September sent a letter of exchange for 12,000 gold ducats; [115] merchant Fedeli was also authorized to draw on an Italian bank at Cologne.[116]

In late September came the splendid news that the Imperial Chamber had consented to sell 600 slaves for 54,000 livres (add 10 per cent for transit to Trieste). A bargain it seemed, at one-third the prices common in the usual Mediterranean sales of the day.[117] Meanwhile, the French minister of marine ordered three ships dispatched to the Adriatic from Marseilles, each with its special agent aboard. The greatest importance was said to attach to hiding the fact that the slaves were destined for the galleys of France — not easily hidden when one of the vessels was a royal flûte with an "Italian" captain and the other two, nominally English, had French officers and soldiers aboard.[118] Delays ensued. Then it appeared that the consent of the Imperial Chamber to export slaves was not enough. Permission was also needed to purchase the slaves! Still worse, reports of the number of slaves that could actually be bought were progressively cut from 600 to 300, to 200 and less, with reports that competitive bidding was going on, and that Le Blond's agent was bidding against merchant Fedeli. Eventually, 164 slaves reached Trieste. Of the three ships from Marseilles, the royal flûte finally sailed (15 December) after waiting in vain for four months for a cargo of slaves; the two "English" vessels were still at "Piram" (probably Pirano) after waiting almost five months for their overdue cargo of slaves; but they finally did receive that partial lading of 164.[119]

These complicated affairs suggest how difficult and subject to misrepresentation, corruption, and missteps the process of purchasing slaves for French galleys could be. In spite of all, however, French agents were kept in the field, and by persistence managed to buy substantial numbers of slaves, including many hundreds from the new Adriatic (Dalmatian, Hungarian, Bosnian, Moreote) sources in the years 1689–93. The basic negotiations and purchases were carried on amid the myriad of offers and counteroffers described. The exact numbers obtained cannot be known because the relevant pages of the registers of incoming slaves for those years have been lost. Some published works suggest that Austrian archives might supply significant details; Hungarian national sources in Budapest are not of help.[120] But French records do make it certain that many hundreds of men were acquired, and that many, probably most of those from the Balkan sources, were shipped to France via Italy, many passing through the port of Leghorn (Cotolendy's preserve) and others through Genoa en route to Marseilles.

Evidently it was assumed in the ministry of marine that the men being acquired from the new Adriatic-Balkan sources of supply were classifiable as infidels, and hence were suitable slave material for the oars. Eventually, however, even though they were apparently considered physically and otherwise fit on arrival, it appeared that many were not so fit. A considerable number, for vague reasons, came to be considered undesirable at least as early as 1692. Then the Bailiff de Noailles, Lieutenant General of the Galleys, began insisting that a considerable number of the slaves, and the Bosnians in particular, were "malingres" (sick and puny?) — usually a vague term of disapprobation, implying in this context a lack of energy or capacity to work, but perhaps meaning something more. At Noailles' urging, it was decided that these slaves should be given larger than ordinary rations — an extra half ration of bread and half measure of wine. But the minister was moved to express his surprise "that these turcs who serve well on the galleys of the Pope, the Grand Duke and Genoa cannot do the same on those of the King." [121] Finally, at the end of 1693, it was decided that no more Bosnian slaves would be accepted, "or at least none unless they come with an equal number of Levantine turcs," [122] evidently because their usefulness was somehow seriously impaired. In some cases the "impairment" could have been physical, but their religious condition may also have given pause to a man such as Noailles. The slaves could well have been a mélange of Moslems and Christians, possibly including some sectaries, Bogomils, or other neo-Christian heretic-outcasts. Perhaps they were also proving responsive, as the blacks and redskins had been, to the missionnaires on the galleys. Either of these possibilities would help to explain the contrast between the attitude of Noailles, the Knight, and that of Surgeon General Pellissery and Intendant Montmort. Noailles was disposed to be firm but kind to them; these others leaned to rigor and severity. But whatever the case, the decision was made to require equal parts of Bosnians and "Levantine" turcs in future purchases of slaves. For practical reasons that requirement probably shut off imports from that source of supply.

This Balkan buying appears to have been Louis' last serious endeavour to acquire slaves from "non-sensitive" sources of supply. From the eighties onward, and particularly after 1693, the percentage of slaves in the rowing force gradually fell because of his treaty exchanges with North African states. The probability seems to be that the vastly increased numbers of forçats coming to hand after 1685 were only partly balanced by slaves from Adriatic and Balkan sources. Both the proportion and numbers of slaves at the oars declined. There were still 1,002 slaves in a rowing force of 5,600 in 1712. However, in that year the ratio of slaves to convicts (roughly 1:5) was abnormally large because some thousands of forçats had just been released or impressed for service with the army in Spain. Nor do those figures sufficiently stress the fact that few slaves were then being bought. Their total number was falling steadily, so that by 1746 there were fewer than 200 slaves in a total of over 3,000 oarsmen.[123]

In conclusion, it should be emphasized that the decline in the number of slaves was not the result of any generalized shortage of slaves or any change in Louis' desire to have slaves. Instead, this significant decline was produced by the frequent releases and exchanges of prisoners with the infidel states, and can be taken as a measure of Louis' success in obtaining and preserving bilateral peace and trade treaties with them. Louis believed the interests of the realm were best served by making treaties with Moslems, by detaching France from the perennial Mediterranean milieu of religio-political-trade war, and by collaborating where practicable with the "infidel" powers against common (Hapsburg and other) enemies in both East and West. French efforts to procure trade treaties and peace with the infidel illustrate the fundamental character of the clash of his policy objectives and those of the Popes. But Louis' employment of infidels, his persistent, far-reaching, and notorious quest for slaves, even though they were not needed at all to sustain the operations of his galleys, must be seen as part of his "pose as a zealot of Catholicism." [124] He wanted it said that he and contemporary Popes were in essential agreement in sanctioning the use of infidel slaves at galley oars.

Condemnations to the Oar

Until comparatively recent times men who broke the law were apt to be subjected to public punishment, sometimes to mutilating corporal punishments as well. Those condemned to the galleys for life in Louis XIV's reign were branded with the letters *G A L*. That brand denoted condemnation to the oar for a capital crime. In the first quarter of the eighteenth century, when authorities in France thought that the punishments for some sorts of crime were not sufficiently severe, it was decreed that all instances of theft from churches, by men or women, would henceforth be punished by branding with the letter *V* (*vol*, theft; *voleur*, thief), and at the same time it was also decreed that all persons condemned to the galleys, even for terms of years, for any crime whatsoever, would likewise be branded with the letters *G A L*, hitherto reserved for capital offenders alone. At mid-eighteenth century these brands were still used. But some thoughts of moderation and penal reform were stirring — the "enlightenment" was dawning, in limited ways, in some quarters of France. Hence in 1750 Louis XV issued new letters patent on the subject, suggesting that the ineradicable letters of the brand *G A L*, obviously a mark of infamy, should not be made on a man more than fifteen days in advance of his actual departure for the galleys. This change in the timing of the branding was made so that those who enjoyed royal clemency, and thus had their penalty commuted, were not irreparably marked before the decision to commute the sentence was made.[1]

As these examples suggest, many different means were devised for the punishment of crime, and sentencing to the galleys for a term of years or for life was but one. Galleys were prison ships, where men were held for long periods. To be sent to their oars was certainly constraint and punishment. In this respect galleys may have been an exception to the general rule, described by Marcel Marion, that in the old regime prisons were not usually thought of as institutions for punishments, but simply as places of "detention to keep an accused [in custody] until he was judged, or as a mode of restraint to force a debtor to pay."[2] Galleys served all these functions, and could perhaps be described more accurately as workhouses than prisons.

Jails were costly both to construct and maintain. In France of the old regime they were too few and too small in proportion to the incidence of crime. In a jail in France (as elsewhere), a man usually had either to pay for his keep or to have someone else pay for him. If a poor man other than a debtor had the misfortune to be put into jail, he might languish for a time, but there was a good chance that some agency of the Church or some municipal workhouse (often staffed by religious orders) would take him in hand and, in return for his labor, would provide work and at least enough food and shelter to sustain life.

Knowing these circumstances, magistrates could not responsibly sentence many men to long imprisonment. Instead, they traditionally meted out a variety of low-cost public and corporal punishments. Corporal punishment was not only cheap, but was thought to have salutary effects on the offender and the general public as well.

Jean-Baptiste Colbert saw obvious advantages in maximizing the number of able-bodied lawbreakers who were condemned to the galleys instead of to the wheel, dungeons, jails, or the usual prisons. On the galleys such men could expiate their crimes by serving their King. To implement these notions, Colbert wrote to many judicial officials, including the chief magistrates of the parlements, emphasizing the King's desire to re-establish his Galley Corps and his hope that they would be zealous in obtaining oarsmen (i.e., in imposing sentences to the oar). Colbert exerted pressure in many quarters to have more men made available for the oars. He was not the first to exert such pressure. Other men, even good King Henry IV, had in earlier times tried to multiply sentences to the oar and to lengthen the terms to be served. Perhaps Colbert worked harder in exerting the pressure, as he did at most other projects he undertook; he wrote more letters to more magistrates, and his letters survive in greater number. He earned praise from the King he served for his energetic application to the work, by which it is said that he managed to "put more than 1,000 good [able-bodied] men in the galleys in less than one year's time." [3]

Great and regrettable though Colbert's pressures may have been, they did not produce all the oarsmen Louis wanted. Indeed, in some quarters, by some magistrates of the parlements for example, pressure from a minister of the Crown was almost certain to be coldly received. Opposition from the parlements was traditional. Added to it, in the case of Colbert's administration, was a significant scattering of opposition based on the very nature of his methods and responsibilities. Among other things, Colbert raised taxes, created new sources of revenue, reorganized administration on many levels, and generated an intense and widespread opposition to himself, his policies, and much that he was thought to represent. Many powerful vested interest groups and individuals, in addition to his long-time foes, Louvois and Le Tellier, were among his enemies. Thus, many factors helped to explain the difficulties he experienced in obtaining increases in the number of condemnations to the galleys.

Some magistrates of the parlements reacted by doing exactly the reverse of what Colbert wanted. The "record of over 1,000" condemnations in a single year was probably achieved several times between 1661 and 1683, but special circumstances helped, as when the risings or rebellions of the sixties and seventies were put down and the number of condemnations increased in consequence. Few large increases seem to have been obtained simply by the method of pressuring regular civil officials or magistrates of the parlements. It remains to be determined exactly how far short of hopes and expectations the results of dealings with the magistrates were, but there seems little doubt that greater numbers of condemnations were obtained from other authorities and by other means. [4]

To Colbert, it seemed a needless waste that criminals were so frequently punished with the penalty of death. He willingly agreed with magistrates on many of the points at issue — that death was often well deserved, that exemplary punishment was required to deter others from falling into like error, that nothing short of the death penalty sufficed for the punishment of certain types of crime, and that in some instances declarations or decrees of the King were needed to change the statutes under which condemnations could be made. Yet he urged French magistrates to consider condemning able-bodied offenders to the galleys whenever possible, particularly as a suitable substitute for the penalty of death. In all this, it must be admitted, Colbert was involved in certain unfortunate inconsistencies. He was recommending galleys as the punishment for lesser crimes and suggesting identical punishment for the correction of capital crimes of all but the most heinous sorts. This could hardly have seemed reasonable or persuasive to magistrates who were sooner or later bound to become aware that condemnation to the oar for a term of years was, in actual practice, tantamount to condemnation for life. Most magistrates saw things with some measure of concern for justice and equity; it was expediency that underlay the methods and policies of the minister and King, at least where the procurement of convicts was concerned.

Thus, we find Colbert writing to the public prosecutor at Grenoble, saying that the King was "daily increasing the number of his galleys" and describing the pressing need for oarsmen. "Therefore," he said, "you cannot be too exact in the execution of his orders to convert the death penalty to that of galleys." One intendant, for whom such suggestions from the minister's pen were evidently equivalent to command, promised "to amass as many as possible since His Majesty has need." [5] But as could be predicted, some stubborn resistance was encountered. The First President at Dijon had the boldness to respond to the minister that a royal declaration or at least a lettre de cachet was needed if judges were to moderate the death penalty. He might have added that the King would have no assurance, even then, that the magistrates would do as he wished. Crown appointees, executive authorities, and the police proved most willing to conform to Colbert's wishes. But they too seemed touchy at times, as when one intendant remarked that it was not his fault if the number of convicts being sent to the galleys had declined.[6]

The authority of the Crown was most strikingly evident and effective in obtaining condemnations to the galleys in cases of rebellion, or where crimes were committed directly against the authority of the sovereign. In such cases the designated leaders were made to suffer some horrible form of public execution, thus serving as examples. Others who did not

176

happen to be labeled leaders got off with lighter penalties, such as condemnation to the galleys for life or for a term of years. That was the
case with the rebellious Boulonnais of 1662, who were so desperate as
to take up arms against the King's tax collectors in the so-called War of
Lustucru. Their insurrection included some thefts, assaults, brigandage,
destruction of crops, and worst of all, defiance of the King's authority.
No monarch would tolerate that sort of opposition from ordinary subjects. An overwhelming force of troops was sent, accompanied by the
King's judiciary. The "most guilty" of the leaders were executed. The
septuagenarians and boys were released. But the able-bodied men, to
the number of 476 from the region, were sent to the galleys.[7]

Some of the "convicted" Boulonnais managed, by force of money, to
get off or get away; some escaped en route to the galley base at Marseilles.
Two years after their condemnation, some of those who had been sentenced to life terms in the galleys but who had money or influential
friends were negotiating with the authorities for release. As early as
1666, perhaps as many as 55 Boulonnais had been able to obtain release
by supplying a slave (or the price of a slave) to take their places at the
oars. Others, not so rich, were less fortunate. In 1669 they were still serving the oar, and at that time one Corps official remarked that they would
not be released until they had supplied a slave as a replacement. An inventory of forçats prepared in the early eighties listed at least two dozen
of the unhappy Boulonnais still serving the oar. Nine were destined
to be deported to America in the various shipments dispatched from
France between 1682 and 1689, presumably to the West Indies, where
they probably became indentured servants. Two others, for no specified
reason, were released and allowed to return home in those years. They
must have communicated to friends and family the fact that some of
their fellows were transported to America; they also could have reported
that four fellow "rebels" had died in the galley hospital between 1682
and 1685. Yet there were still at least twelve Boulonnais in the galleys
at Marseilles. Six of them were finally released in different batches in
1694 and 1695; four others died at the oar, the last of them in 1698. The
last two continued in the galleys until the end of the century, being
released in 1701 and 1702 after almost exactly forty years in the galleys.
By that date, the lesson on rebellion must have been well learned. The
example that was made of the Boulonnais illustrates not only the exercise of arbitrary executive authority, but also throws a little light on

"justice," the socioeconomic character of recruitment for the oars, and the methods used to maintain royal power.[8]

Desertions from the army and the navy were capital crimes in the day of Louis XIV, punishable by death, and Colbert and Seignelay sought to have those penalties commuted to life sentences on the galleys. The system of maritime conscription itself produced deserters, but the system was difficult to establish and troublesome to enforce.[9] After trying without success to induce French seamen to return to France from foreign maritime service, a royal edict forbade Frenchmen to reside abroad without special authorization or to serve on the crews of foreign ships, on pain of galères perpétuelles.[10] Failure to register or to appear when called to serve could eventuate in trial or summary arrest and in condemnation (in person or absentia) before a court martial empowered to impose the death penalty. In practice, this penalty was commonly commuted to a life term at the oar. The registers of men convicted before 1676 suggest that such commutations were common even then, even though the letter of the law did not allow galères perpétuelles as a possible alternative until September 1676.

Some military offenders, including a few army deserters, were used in the 1660's, the latter under an evidently temporary statutory authorization; it was then said that "if deserters from the army continue to be sent to the galleys, our needs will soon be filled." [11] But in the 1680's Seignelay found himself faced with such need that the penalty for army desertion was changed, once again, from death to galleys. One naval officer later remarked that Louis XIV was "touched by the representations of M. de Seignelay" that excessive numbers (he said thousands) had been executed for desertion from the army; in any case, a royal decree of 4 December 1684 moderated the penalty so that "in the future all deserters from the troops will be condemned to have their nose and ears cut off, [to be] marked with a fleur-de-lis on each cheek, and sent to the galleys [for life]." [12] The next year a galley officer complained that he had received six deserters "who are all young and will do good service." But he added that "if the severity practiced of not leaving any part of the nose on the face is relaxed, they will [in the future] be better, because it is noticed, Monseigneur, that after a little work the difficulty of breathing notably diminishes their strength, so that they have to be relieved." [13]

Though not fully enforced, this measure helped for many years to increase the size of the rowing force. Without it, one commentator asserted, "it would not have been possible to man forty galleys." Whether or not that was the case, the fact remains that deserters constituted one of the largest groups of convicts at the oars.[14] In 1717 the galleys lost this source of manpower when the death penalty for desertion was re-established. But the galley officers did not soon forget the usefulness of deserters. In 1723, after the plague at Marseilles and Provence had wiped out hundreds of oarsmen, and again in the 1740's in different circumstances, galleys officers sought restoration of the penalty of galleys as a substitute for execution.[15] Finally, in 1749 after the Galley Corps had been formally abolished, the desertion penalty was changed, and in some acts of condemnation, referred to as the galères des terres.[16]

A wide range of other offenses could also be punished by consignment to the galleys, and such broad "eligibility" was distinctly encouraged by Colbert, who informed various officials that the King desired to have "the greatest possible number" of guilty persons consigned to the oar.[17] As late as the first two decades of the eighteenth century, magistrates were still employing the penalty of galères perpétuelles for theft, forgery, and a considerable range of lesser offenses. In the various registers that include the names of convicts, theft is second only to desertion as a ground for condemnation to the galleys, usually for terms of years rather than life, yet effectively for life. Persons convicted of such crimes as blasphemy, perjury, and falsehood (involving oaths) could also receive life terms in the first third of the eighteenth century. The roll of convicts was further lengthened, as late as 1739, by the inclusion of men serving for unspecified reasons, "after trial," "without condemnation," and many for whom the registers read "sans dire pourquoi."

Such vague phrases did not necessarily mean a man was sent without being condemned by some official or judicial authority. Clerks of the Galley Corps were at times responsible for vague entries in the registers. When a forçat had any share in the loss of documents relating to his own trial or condemnation, the officials of the galleys recorded that circumstance beside the man's name, and also recorded "life" as the penalty to be served. Vagueness about the grounds for condemnation could, in some circumstances, work to the advantage of the forçat concerned. A man convicted of an especially reprehensible crime such as blasphemy or sacrilege might be better off without having the specific nature of his conviction on the record at Marseilles. Many men condemned to maximum penalties stood to gain from doubt, and the magistrate (or clerk) may actually have done them a good turn by failing, intentionally or not, to record the specific charges or conviction. Less fortunate, certainly, were the circumstances of some unfortunates sent off to the oar when merely "suspected" or "accused" of some crime. Examples in the registers demonstrate that vague suspicions and unproved charges could send men to the oar.[18]

Clearly, one need not have committed a crime to be sent to the galleys; to be a gypsy or to be apprehended for begging or vagabondage was sometimes sufficient reason, in practice if not in actual law. Gypsies had long been subject to harassment and arrest on trifling evidence. They were taken in hand for theft on almost any arbitrary pretext or suspicion, and during the reigns of Louis XIII and Louis XIV the long-standing harassments to which gypsies were subject in France (and elsewhere) were intensified, evidently as a concomitant of heavier sanctions to conform and obey in all sorts of matters. A long series of edicts (1634, 1656, 1665, 1666, 1673, 1678, 1682) declared that these "Egyptians" were not wanted in the realm and that they must leave, sometimes "within one month," on pain of condemnation to the galleys.[19] But this repressive series of decrees was unevenly applied in the provinces. Generally, they were not well enforced, as their repeated issuance and a great deal of other evidence, including lists of convicts, tends to suggest.[20] Perhaps very few officials entertained opinions resembling those which led Intendant Arnoul to say that when vagabonds and other do-nothings (apparently including gypsies) were put into the galleys instead of being put out of the realm, the world was "unburdened of the rubbish with which it is so heavily charged."[21]

From 1540 onward, many royal regulations prescribed the penalty of galleys for vagrants, vagabonds, and other gens sans aveu.[22] This last category could include many who might be considered parasites or socioeconomic misfits in a secular state, regardless of the justification for their nonconformity, individualism, or hapless condition. In Richelieu's day officials of the state aimed "to purge Paris and other cities of vagabonds and gens sans aveu," and thought it possible to send them to the galleys "without doing them any injustice,"[23] the thought being, apparently, that in the galleys these unfortunates would at least be assured of having the food and clothing to survive. One law issued as late as 1656 ordered police and judicial officials to arrest an astonishing variety of men for the galleys: gypsies, vagabonds, sturdy beggars, "vaguans des Landeds" (of Gascony), discharged soldiers, counterfeiters, salt smugglers, malefactors, and other gens sans aveu — a range of "offenders" that could include a very large number of individuals and that allowed wide discretionary powers to authorities.[24] Thus, even at the outset of Colbert's ministry, there were precedents for many of the efforts he made to recruit for the oar under exceptional procedures, by executive or police action "without any ceremony or form of proceedings at law." In his own time many new royal orders were issued (in 1666, 1673, 1678, and 1682, for example) explicitly providing for such arbitrary arrest without formalities of trial.[25]

With Colbert, such legislation evidently proceeded at least in part from the opinion that idleness was dangerous or reprehensible, and could be "cured" or avoided if work was provided and "lazy" men were pressured to work. But he was not consistent in this or in his attitude toward the punishment of social, economic, and other forms of nonconformity of the types commonly involved in vagabond life. At different times and in different situations, he suggested handling it with varying degrees of severity. He sometimes sanctioned extraordinary haste and arbitrary conduct in condemnations; at other times he expressed preference for conformity with standard judicial processes because, as he once observed, "a variety of difficulties can otherwise ensue; animosity or other vicious purposes can put poor people" to the oar.[26]

Yet in twentieth-century eyes, a confused and exaggerated severity is the tendency usually associated with the letter of the law in seventeenth-century France. The maze of bureaucracy and the rigor of the law were an ominous backdrop of society. Legal penalties could be avoided by some people. The rich, by spending money adroitly, almost invariably managed to avoid them. Litigation could be lengthened or shortened, depending on the wealth, influence, and desires of the persons and interest groups involved. Men lacking knowledge and influence were usually unable to modify or multiply or give direction to procedures, or to obtain costly appeals, or to sway the verdict. The poor therefore felt the rigor of the savage penalties prescribed by the law in infinitely greater measure than the economically or socially privileged orders of society. A great many more such condemnations to the oars would have resulted had the letter of the law been applied; often it was not. It would appear that the principles of justice and equity were ill-served when some men could be kept from the oar while others who were no more culpable, but far less lucky, were sent to the galleys.

Some provincial and municipal authorities in France showed reluctance to implement the legislation issued by the Crown. The parlements were less cooperative than royal authorities would have liked. Their resistance appears to have been a continuing characteristic, even though pressures exerted on them by royal authorities increased in some respects after Colbert came to power. But as courts having the power to condemn to the galleys, the parlements were a very important source, perhaps the most productive single source of long-term condemnations to the oar until well into the eighties. It was at about that time — the mid-eighties — that the penalty for desertion from the army was changed from death to galleys. Thus, the military courts and parlements alike gave strength to royal authority.

It was in the eighties that the great influx of Protestants began to reach the galley base at Marseilles. A minority of Protestants must at all times have been included among those condemned to the galleys. But from 1680 onward, many hundreds (and after 1685, greater numbers) were sent to serve the oar because the public practice of their religion had been officially proscribed. They were victims of Louis XIV's policy of seeking to impose religious uniformity in France. Many authorities having the power to condemn to the galleys showed themselves extraordinarily willing to cooperate with the King's indicated policy. In doing so they contributed substantially to the number of available oarsmen, and also to strengthening royal authority.

Condemnation to the oar for life or "à perpétuité" was the usual penality for offenses against legislation relating to the suppression of R.P.R. The revocation of the Edict of Nantes itself (1685) reiterated these penalties. It specified, among other things, that Protestant pastors must leave the realm within fifteen days after publication of the revocation. All other subjects of the King adhering to the R.P.R., as well as those recently converted to the Catholic faith (called the Religion Catholique, Apostolique et Romaine), were expressly forbidden to leave the realm or to assist at any services or meetings connected with the R.P.R. Laws relating to these and other matters carried the galley penalty, and with their later amendments, provided the statutory basis for a large number of condemnations to the oar. Most of the condemnations that actually involved Protestants could be classed in one of three inclusive categories:

attendance at Protestant religious services, assisting or harboring a pastor, or attempting to leave the kingdom or assisting others doing so.[27]

The proportion of Protestants included among the shipments of convicts sent to the galleys varied. One devout, perhaps well-informed, but certainly cautious seventeenth-century writer who was himself one of the galériens estimated that well over 600 Protestants, sent for reasons connected with religion, were on the galleys as early as June 1686.[28] This figure may err on the conservative side, considering that 2,378 new convicts "good and bad for the oar" are supposed to have arrived at Marseilles in the two full years 1685–86,[29] whereas the number of convicts of all sorts arriving annually in the *early* eighties (pre-revocation) was said to average perhaps 500 a year.[30] The implied increase of over 100 per cent seems small, considering the general impact and effectiveness with which the revocation legislation of 1685 was applied. It probably takes little or no account of the hundreds of R.P.R.'s (and others), many of them unfit for the oar but also including some able-bodied men, all of whom were shipped to the West Indies after 1685. In any case, the influx of Protestant convicts continued to be large in the years immediately following the revocation. At least 250 Protestants were said to have been sent to the galleys in 1689.[31] Many hundreds of additional adherents of the R.P.R. were condemned in the half century that followed, making a grand total estimated at between 2,000 and 4,000; Gaston Tournier, working with literature, archives, and private papers in France and elsewhere, collected well over 2,000 case histories.[32]

There is no doubt that in many places in France, as well as on the galleys themselves, Protestant convicts received exceptionally harsh treatment. It could hardly have been otherwise, considering the intensity of the religious sentiment and antagonism of the time. Magistrates, police officers, and guards all along the line were under special surveillance and under pressures that discouraged leniency and sanctioned severity where adherents of the R.P.R. were concerned. Even the usual consideration given to rank or family connections or social distinctions tended to be lessened where the case concerned a Protestant. The Protestant Baron de Salgas, who could have claimed the right to serve on the galleys "in the manner of nobles" — that is, as a soldier with a sword at his side not employed at the oar and not put in chains[33] — was kept instead in double chains and treated with exceptional harshness, and when his release was finally arranged through the intervention of the King of England with Louis XIV in his behalf, Salgas was kept on the galleys for at least four months after his release was authorized by Louis XIV because "it pleased M. le Cardinal de Noailles [then Archbishop of Paris] to have him retained" while attempts were made to obtain cancellation of the order for his release.[34]

Neither physical weakness nor old age seems to have constituted a disqualification for shipment to the galleys in cases where adherents of the R.P.R. were concerned. Of course, physically feeble and defective persons were never wanted at Marseilles for the galleys; old men and youths were almost entirely useless at the oars. But many such persons who happened to be Protestant (along with some who were not) were sent to the galleys. In short, many overaged, underaged, or physically incapacitated convicts were sent, and in the aggregate must have constituted a large percentage of the invalids on galley administrators' hands in the later eighties. Many of them must have been included, too, among those invalids sent to the West Indies in those years. Another consequence of these unusually indiscriminate condemnations consisted in the fact that a high percentage of the older, weaker, and very young men sent in the chains became casualties or died en route or soon after they arrived at Marseilles.[35] But it was said by the minister of marine to be the will of Louis XIV that Protestants "suffer longer than others" at the oar, and that "no man condemned for reasons of religion could ever leave the galleys."[36] There were many exceptions to this rule, of course, some made under the influence of foreign princes or powers, who sought the release of Protestants at various times. But assuredly, among the most effective types of legislation, as far as the recruitment of Frenchmen for galley service was concerned, were the measures directed against the Protestants in the eighties.

Regulations connected with the enforcement of the salt and, later, the tobacco monopolies also produced large numbers of oarsmen. As a means of raising revenues, the monarchy in France sold salt and tobacco monopolies. Groups of financiers and businessmen acquiring such rights were allowed, for specified localities and times, exclusive rights for the manufacture or importation and sale of such commodities. Since large amounts were needed for both industrial and consumer purposes, monopolists who bought the right to produce and sell the salt had opportunities for enormous profits, provided they managed to maintain their monopoly. Tobacco, being a luxury, did not have the importance of salt, and since tobacco was for the most part imported from afar, the tobacco monopolists had an easier task in maintaining their monopoly. Yet the two monopolies involved many similar problems. The organization and controls established for the two were similar, and at times the same groups of tax farmers controlled both salt and tobacco sales. Both types of monopolists were armed with extensive search and seizure rights, and the penal "codes" with which they were equipped (especially the proclamation of September 1674 on tobacco, and that of May 1680 concerning the salt tax (gabelle)) were similar in many respects and equally ferocious.[37]

The greatest vice of this vexatious system of taxes and finance was the greed and rigor of the monopolists themselves. In administering their privileges, they had little or no compassion for consumers, and no mercy for persons who transgressed their monopolies. They sent delinquents and petty thieves and smugglers to the prisons by the hundreds. Over the years many thousands of salt smugglers were sent to the galleys, most of them recidivists. In the eighteenth century Necker, the finance minister, estimated that the contrabanding of salt led annually to 2,300 arrests, to the confiscation of 1,100 horses and 50 vehicles, and to 300 condemnations to the galleys. Marion assures us (paraphrasing Mollien) that there was "an enormous distance" between the letter of the law and its execution near the close of the old regime.[38] But in Louis XIV's time, and even in the earlier eighteenth century, there seems little ground for thinking the salt monopolists were hindered or were lax in making condemnations to the galleys.

Among the men they condemned to the galleys some were, and many more became, invalid or otherwise unable to work the oars. Being useless as active oarsmen, such men were simply chained up by the navy on the hulks where other old, sick, and invalid men were kept along with hospital overflow. It was the navy's practice to give rations and a sou a day to each of these invalids, except the smugglers. The salt and tobacco monopolists themselves, said naval officials, should feed their own. The navy would feed able-bodied men arriving at Marseilles as long as they could work the oars, but held that the responsibility reverted to the monopolists when their prisoners were no longer of value on the galleys of the King.

In assuming this responsibility, the salt and tobacco farmers showed much laxity which affected men designated for the galleys as well as those who had already done service aboard them. Their failure to pay for the invalids' rations was profitable, and sometimes intentional, though it must usually have been simple negligence or oversight on the part of local agents of the tax farmers. But whatever the causes, some failures of the sort did take place at both ends of the line, in the prisons in which the convicts were held to await the coming of the chain bound for Marseilles and on the hulks where invalids were held. In 1678, for example, three salt smugglers were lying in the prisons of Moulins and Bourges waiting to be taken to the galleys, one a paralytic and the other two, 60 and 73 years old, lacking limbs. Understandably, when the conductor taking the chain of men to the galleys stopped to collect the accumulated prisoners, he left these three behind. They would have been a burden to him all the way to Marseilles, and useless for the galleys when and if they arrived. The minister of marine was informed that they had been left, and he, in turn, told the salt monopolists: "if it is necessary, for the well-being of your monopoly, to keep such men on the galleys, then you must meet the expense involved in sending them, and [you must] feed and keep them when they get there." [39] Whatever the unknown fate of these three men, their case was "typical"; they doubtless found themselves with ample company, either in their own prison or, if they did reach Marseilles alive, on the hulks. No fewer than 487 invalid salt smugglers were reported to be on hand at the galley base in October of that very year (1678).[40]

In 1684 the intendant of Soissons described a group of smugglers awaiting the chain for the galleys (seven for salt violations and four for tobacco), of which there were five "who were only children from ten to thirteen years. All eleven men, women, and girls were in a sort of dungeon not thirteen feet square . . ." The intendant ordered the jailors to remedy that situation and to see that it did not recur. At the same time, conditions at Vervins were hardly better, apparently, with convicted salt smugglers being kept "at the bottom of a dry pit, into which they descend by a ladder, and where sunlight is never seen." [41] Writing to the salt farmers in 1695 the minister of marine reminded them of the condition of the men they had sent to prison: "I have told you before that they are almost nude, and equally in need of nourishment. I write again to tell you this, so that you can order your subordinates to give them better bread and, at least once a day, some soup. Even if the will of the King did not oblige it, your charity will excite you to make this small expenditure."[42] The tax farmers found charity and the profit motive difficult to reconcile. But the spirit of charity was commendably alive among some of their contemporaries. In 1716, for example, it was disclosed that the Dames de la Charité of Dijon had provided for convicts in the local prison during the preceding nine years, and were then seeking funds to continue their work.[43] Apart from the limited charity available and any funds they might have had on entering prison, the only resources available to men condemned to the galleys was a sou per day provided by the King to enable them to survive "while they are in the prisons waiting to be conducted to Marseilles."[44]

Some forçats condemned to serve at French oars were obtained outside of France from foreign princes who had few or no galleys of their own. Monaco, Lorraine, and certain west German principalities sometimes chose to use French galleys as a prison. The ducal dynasty of Savoy periodically supplied convicts from its territories for service at French oars before 1680, though the dukes sometimes complained about the failure of the Galley Corps to release convicts at the expiration of their prescribed term and about other irregularities.[45] Such difficulties, and the generally widening gulf between France and the House of Savoy, made the latter increasingly reluctant to use French galleys. The desire to supply oarsmen could hardly have been enlivened by such overbearing letters as one from Seignelay in 1685 to the sovereign Prince of Savoy, in which Louis' minister assumed his Master's mien in remarking that "His Majesty has asked me to write," since he is informed that you have "a considerable number [of forçats] at 'Villefranche' who are not usefully employed."[46] That very year, of course, the dwindling sympathies of Protestant Swiss were "utterly extinguished" by the revocation of the Edict of Nantes.[47] In the eighteenth century, the King of Poland and Her Electoral Highness the Countess Palatine sought "permission" to send their convicts to French galleys.[48] Bourbon family ties also underlay the temporary transfer of some hundreds of "homeless" Spanish galériens to France in 1742, after a raid by an English squadron had burned five Spanish galleys at St. Tropez that year.[49]

Of less importance, in terms of the number of men involved, was the occasional use made of Spanish prisoners of war as oarsmen (see p. 139 above). Fragments of Richelieu's correspondence with Sourdis suggest that prisoners of war of Spanish and Portuguese origin served on French galleys during the later years of the Thirty Years War;[50] in 1659 a lettre du roi authorized the release of numerous prisoners of war who had served on French galleys for "many years." [51] As that suggests, prisoners serving in the galleys were not always released immediately after peace treaties were signed. Indeed, negotiations were under way in 1684, six years after the Treaty of Nimwegen, to arrange the mutual release of prisoners of war held by France and Spain aboard their respective galleys. Even those belated conversations may not have brought about the release of all the prisoners held, since the Ambassador of Spain to France asked in 1688 that the subjects of the Spanish King then serving be liberated, and when that request was finally brought under consideration at Versailles, in December 1689, the minister of marine had to request information concerning "those that have survived." [52] In 1691 a treaty was signed between France and Spain providing for the mutual exchange of "navy prisoners," but the French envoy sent to implement that agreement was privately instructed to delay and obstruct the execution of its provisions: ". . . without appearing to delay needlessly, put off this inspection, the result of which cannot but be disadvantageous for the King, since it is estimated that there are fewer Frenchmen on the galleys of Spain than there are Spaniards on those of France." [53]

In spite of efforts to prevent their being sent, many men besides salt smugglers arriving at Marseilles were found to be physically incapable of useful service, a fact that angered Colbert because such men occasioned needless expense for the King. "Care must be taken that the convicts sent have the health and strength to serve well." [54] A circular of 1672 to that effect recommended that "no criminal over fifty-five years of age be condemned to the galleys, unless he has the strength and health necessary to serve usefully." [55] But neither should the convicts be too young. One complaint brought before a session of the naval officers concerned the fact that five boys had been attached to the last Brittany chain, "the eldest of whom wasn't fifteen years of age. They cannot render any service on the galleys; on the contrary they are led by the convicts and turcs to crimes which are only too common on the galleys. Hitherto it has been customary to liberate them and use them around the arsenal. But since there is reason to fear that in returning to their homes they will fall again into the same bad habits, it is decided . . . to send them as indentured servants to the [West Indian] Islands." [56] Generally, naval officials believed that men between twenty and thirty-five years were best for service at the oars.

Equally burdensome and useless for the oar were the crippled and incurably sick. Men maimed or disabled in arm or leg or those with hernias were not wanted at the galley base. Only the salt and tobacco monopolists were authorized to send invalids to the galley base routinely, and they were expected to pay for their rations there.[57] Colbert warned, however, that although physical disability was a reason for omitting to send men to the galleys, it should not serve as a pretext for escaping the "more rigorous" penalty of death, if merited.[58]

Men judged suitable for the oar at the time of their condemnation were not apt to remain able-bodied for long in the seventeeth-century prisons of France (or elsewhere). As the Count de Roannes explained, when describing a group of forçats newly arrived for the galleys, some were thin and tired "only because they have stayed too long in the prisons after their condemnations, laden with irons in dungeons, and without having enough bread and water to nourish them." [59] Prisons of that day were neither suitable nor intended for long-term incarcerations. Thus the intendant of Poitou, reporting twenty "good and vigorous" convicts on hand, asked that they be taken soon, "the sooner the better, so that they won't die, and because the judges are more disposed to give this penalty when they see that their prisons do not remain long encumbered with convicts." [60] But men condemned to the galleys might wait half a year or even more.

Men might also manage to escape before their dispatch to Marseilles could be arranged. Provincial prisons were notorious not only for the bad conditions in which their inmates lived but also for the ease and frequency with which prisoners were reputed to be able to escape. At Moulins, sixteen convicts escaped "by the main doors," with the complicity of the turnkey and concierge.[61] At Rennes it was the turnkey alone who was "accused of having provided a piece of iron to pierce the prison wall." In that case, haste was made "to judge" the turnkey so that he could be included with the convicts in the chain about to depart for Marseilles.[62] Such escapes had greater notoriety than frequency, one suspects; yet perhaps they did justify the apprehensions of Pontchartrain, who advised that "the stay of these unfortunates in your prisons can only be distressing, and can have very dangerous consequences." [63]

Certainly the prisons from which galley oarsmen came were no more humane in the seventeenth century than they were when their shocking characteristics were described a century afterward in the famous prison surveys of John Howard.[64] Writing to M. de Miromesnil, Pontchartrain described the "bad nourishment" given in the prisons of Saumur, Angers, and Tours as a cause of high mortality among the convicts: "They have nothing to eat but very bad bread, and are so weak when taken [from the prisons for the trip to Marseilles] that they can support neither the fatigues of the roads, nor good nourishment, dying as soon as they are given enough to eat. The irons with which they are laden . . . also render them unable to serve [the oar]. Convicts [in the prisons] are obliged to be seated at all times, which gives them gout and other ailments in the legs that make them permanently invalid." [65]

Many convicts, waiting in prison to be sent to the galleys, having been obliged to sell their clothing to their jailors in order to live, needed shoes and clothing as preparation for the long march to Marseilles.[66] In Colbert's time minimum needs of this sort, "to protect them from the bad weather," were sometimes met with royal funds. But in the mid-1680's, when additional funds were needed to meet the extraordinary needs created by the high tide of deserters and Protestants, the funds were not increased and may even have been reduced.[67] But whatever the case, the consequences described to the minister by the public prosecutor at Dijon were lamentable: "I must say . . . regarding the clothing, it is only with difficulty that even shoes are provided, particularly since, in recent years the chains have become more numerous than before. It is this that has caused the loss of many of these unfortunates. Without clothing or underclothes, and exposed to the injuries of the air, they easily contract mortal illnesses on the march, and die along the roads or on arrival at Marseilles." [68] Of course, the administration did not intend to create any such situation; it developed as a by-product of ill-advised economies and a confusion of financial responsibilities that was only partly remedied. Unhappily, problems of a financial sort were especially difficult to unravel in the administrative "system" of the old monarchy, and this particular problem persisted in less aggravated form even in the eighteenth century. In 1716 the accumulated debts for clothing furnished to convicts by the parlements of Burgundy, Metz, and Besançon in 1707–15 were still unpaid. After 1689 the expenses were customarily paid (at least in part) by provincial officials, with the expectation of reimbursement by the treasurer of the Galley Corps; the Corps did make reimbursements up to 1706. One official writing to the minister commented: "I will not attempt, Monseigneur, to tell you to what degree I am fatigued by the complaints of merchants who have furnished shoes and clothing in years past." The sums due amounted to 7,421 livres.[69]

In other respects as well, the financial methods of the monarchy fell short of providing the services intended and needed. Defects were strikingly evident in the recruitment and remuneration of men who conducted the chains of convicts. Understandably, conductors were a hard lot. "The best of them," as the Marquis de Ternes observed, was "much more concerned with his own interests than with good and loyal service [to the King]." [70] The system under which they worked was intended to assure continuance of the service of chains at minimum cost to the King, in effect to guard the King's financial interests from damage at the hands of unscrupulous conductors. But the interests of the forçats were not similarly protected. Indeed, the system actually encouraged greed and self-interested brutality on the part of conductors.

Men destined for the galleys were chained together in groups of fifty to several hundred at a time and marched to Marseilles in the charge of a conductor, assisted by guards. These "chains," as the troops of convicts were called, had long been used but were ill organized and poorly controlled, Colbert thought, when he came to power. They departed at irregular intervals and travelled irregular routes. He undertook to reorganize the service, as he did many others, establishing approximate itineraries for the principal chains, and branch routes to assure the gathering of scattered convicts from prisons situated off the principal arteries. See the map on page 192, showing the Paris chain moving from Rouen or Paris up the Seine Valley and eastward, gathering convicts from much of nothern and northeastern France, thence moving southward via Dijon, to Châlons-sur-Saône where boats were usually taken down the Rhône as far as Avignon, from which the chain marched overland to Marseilles. The Brittany chain originated at Rennes, gathered convicts as it moved up through the Loire Valley, finally reaching Lyons, whence it also followed the Rhône southward. Another, the "Guyenne" or Bordeaux chain originated at Bordeaux. Its route led up the Garonne Valley southeast as far as Toulouse, thence reaching the Mediterranean or going overland to Marseilles. Convicts from the prisons of much of Languedoc and from Avignon, Provence, and Dauphiné were conducted to Marseilles in small groups, often by guards

Approximate Routes of Chains Marching to Marseilles

from local prisons, and of course the distances they traversed were relatively short.

A more definite impression of this "system of chains" can be conveyed by a breakdown of the "arrivals" at Marseilles over a specific period of time. Thus, for example, during the period from June 1685 to December 1686 (inclusive) a total of over 1,771 men arrived, individually or in groups. Almost four-fifths of them came to Marseilles as components of the Paris, Brittany, and Gascony chains. Those chains averaged 180, 110, and about 70 men respectively. Since five Paris chains arrived in this period (about eighteen months), men arriving via the Paris chain alone aggregated over 900 of the total. Smaller, more frequent arrivals came from such points as Grenoble, Nîmes, and Perpignan (aggregating

Condemnations to the Oar

over 230 men). The authorities of Aix and Marseilles itself condemned to the galleys a total of 79 men in the period. Others dribbled into Marseilles from widely scattered parts of the Midi, and two dozen came from abroad (Avignon-Carpentras, Monaco, Turin).[71]

Men who joined one of the major chains close to its point of origin marched the greatest distance. A man in a Paris chain might trudge hundreds of kilometers during a trek that commonly required 26 to 28 days.[72] On the march each convict was collared with a thick band of iron about the neck, and linked either in single or double file with others along the length (or with lengths) of a central chain. The iron collar and chains for each man were exceedingly heavy.[73]

Conductors were paid a fixed sum for every living convict they delivered at Marseilles, regardless of physical condition. Thus, the conductor of the Paris chain received 40 livres a head for the convicts delivered at Marseilles from distant prisons, such as those of Rouen and Picardy, 30 livres for those from Paris and Dijon, and so forth. The per capita fee was intended to cover all the conductor's costs: subsistence and housing for the chain, carts and drivers for the sick and exhausted, horses for the conductor and his assistants, wages of assistant conductors and guards, the cost of the boats used in descending the Rhône. Anything beyond the cost of providing such services was the conductor's remuneration; it was, in short, a system of enterprise rather than régie. Economic sanctions thus encouraged speed and tended to keep costs low.

The following is an itemized list of the expenditures ordinarily involved in conducting a chain of 100 convicts from Paris to the galley base at Marseilles, with total estimates based on a 26-day trip in 1676:

	livres
Collar and chains for each convict @ 6 livres each	600
Two argousins @ 50 sous each per day, or 5 livres per day, for 26 days	130
12 guards @ 30 sous each, or 18 livres per day, for 26 days	468
One driver @ 26 sous per day, 26 days	32
Three horses @ 3 livres per day, 26 days	78
Food for 100 convicts @ 2 sous each per day, 10 livres per day, 26 days	260
Food for conductor @ 50 sous per day, for 26 days	65
Candles (burned all night) and straw to bed the convicts @ 40 sous per day for 26 days	52
Boats, Châlons to Avignon	300
Total	1,985
Incidentals and cost of return (est.)	500
Total	2,485

These estimates appear high in many particulars, as might be expected in an account prepared by a man seeking to show that conductors were not overpaid at 30 livres a head. The local populace was obliged to furnish shelter for the chain, usually in barns or stables.[74]

Occasionally, conductors apparently sought to cut expenses by reducing the number of guards, but such a practice was dangerous since it could encourage revolt or facilitate escapes from the chain, and it was apt to bring severe official reprimand when the chain arrived.[75] To prevent such dangerous relaxations of security, regulations promulgated in 1686 required two argousins (usually mounted) and ten ordinary guards for every 100 convicts.[76] In general, significant economies could be effected only at the expense of the convicts. Trifling ones might be made by cutting out straw for bedding, reducing the number of carts, and so on, but most important were economies made in food and drink. The ration prescribed by royal order for each convict — to cost two sous a day — consisted (prices permitting, and at best) of two pounds of fresh bread, a half pound of beans, and a half pint of wine.[77] The comparatively humane Intendant Bégon urged the minister in 1685 to forbid conductors "to retrench anything on this ration," and not to allow them to give it in money, because various abuses then ensued: "The assistant conductors and guards . . . prevent the convicts from buying the necessary rations along the road . . . and sell the necessary food at double its cost."[78] Among the causes for mortality in the chains, Bégon said, was "the lack of food . . . and failure to provide the quantities prescribed" by royal decree.[79] At his urging a regulation was issued in February 1686 prescribing certain improvements in the diet to be provided for convicts in the chains. A further regulation of 1693 provided that the following would be supplied daily to each member of a chain: soup of herbs and vegetables, half a pound of fresh meat, two pounds of bread, one measure of wine, and eggs or a piece of cheese.[80] Further improvements were made later.[81]

Some convicts, like the Protestant Jean Marteilhe and twenty-two coreligionaries accompanying him, obtained comparatively favorable treatment because they were apparently well supplied with money, having a common purse of 700–800 livres. A payment of 100 écus exempted them from the cudgels and bullwhips of the guards, and gave them access to the carts when they were too exhausted to go on.[82] Other convicts, less supplied with friends and funds, fared much less well. The alms or charity monies given by relatives or sympathetic people at the start of the march or along the road usually did not go far toward satisfying needs or the greed of conductors. Up to 1688 some nutritional benefits no doubt derived to some convicts from the fact that wives were allowed to follow the chains. But usually, after the chains reached Marseilles, the wives became "a public charge, the greater part of them having nothing on which to live," yet were unable to decide to return home; "there are also some who lead a scandalous life, and others who manage to contribute to forçat escapes." [83] For these several reasons, the wives of men condemned to the galleys after 1688 were not to be allowed to follow the chains, but there is evidence that some did so surreptitiously.

The rules drawn up by Bégon and accepted officially for the governance and improvement of the behavior of conductors specified, among other things, that the alms given to the convicts of the chain as a group will be divided "equally among them." According to the rules, conductors and guards were "forbidden to apply any part [of such funds] to their own profit, on pain of the galleys; nor can they exact anything from convicts for good treatment, or on the pretext of 'soap' (savon, ou colier?) which are the terms they use to relieve them of all the money they can get." Conductors, Bégon added, must also "provide carts for the sick without requiring any payment from those who ride," as they were accustomed to do.[84]

Shortening the time required for the trip could be a source of profit for the conductor, though no other party to the enterprise would seem likely to benefit by it. Taking about one month of travel as "ordinary" for the Paris chain,[85] it is apparent that a single additional day spent on the march could mean much higher costs in such expenses as wages for guards, food for convicts, and forage for horses. The longer the chain, the greater the conductor's monetary loss from delay. For example, the added cost of food for convicts alone, at the official rate of two sous a day per head, would amount to 20 or 30 livres a day for chains of 200–300 men. The longer the chain, the greater the incentive to speed. These circumstances help to explain the frequently high incidence of mortality among convicts on very large chains. The sick and exhausted were forced by whips to trudge on at the pace of the others. When a convict fell on the road and failed to respond to the usual whipping, he was "detached and led or dragged" to a cart and thrown aboard.[86]

195

Bégon, an enemy of speed in the conduct of chains, urged that the march be limited to four lieues de France (approximately 5½ miles) per day on leaving Paris and only three in the provinces, when the chain was presumed to be more fatigued. "After four days of march there will always be one day of rest." These prescriptions were written into a royal regulation for the conduct of chains, issued in February 1686.[87]

But it was easier by far to legislate than to regulate the conduct of conductors. The abuses proscribed did not disappear in practice, as continuing official complaints and mortality in the chains attest. Reports of bad treatment on the road were especially frequent in the later 1680's, perhaps because exceptionally large numbers of convicts were involved, and because the King's regulation made known the fact that certain abuses were officially proscribed. Perhaps also the numerous Protestant convicts and their friends, having no sense of "guilt" for the commission of crime, and in some cases having powerful connections both in France and abroad, were less hesitant than the usual criminal convicts to criticize conductors' malpractices. Their situation was also more apt to elicit sympathy, in some circles, than that of criminals.

These bad conditions occasioned some revolts. Individual attempts to escape were of course ever-present possibilities. But concerted revolt was also a very real possibility, especially with the larger, more dangerous chains. The Paris chains were most subject to revolt, being generally the largest and passing nearest to French frontiers across which the escapees might hope to make their way. Few concerted efforts to escape were as successful as the rising that took place in the fall of 1697. At a point between Lyons and Vienne, 68 convicts managed to escape from the Paris chain, and 5 others were killed in the attempt. Perhaps significantly, the conductor involved had a bad record, in the sense that his chains in earlier years had on several occasions sustained high mortality en route. But the successful revolt of 1697 was followed by a series of later risings; revolts took place in the Paris chains of both the spring and fall of 1698, both times unsuccessfully, with casualties among the convicts.[88] These several revolts, along with high mortality in the chains, exceeding 10 per cent of the convicts in some larger chains, and continual complaints about the bad conduct of conductors not only from convicts and their friends but also from officials of the towns through which the chains passed — all these circumstances finally moved the navy to appoint a royal official, a commissaire des galères, in 1701 to accompany the Paris chain and to superintend in person the execution of royal decrees regulating the chains.[89] Later in the eighteenth century, a commissaire accompanied each of the long-distance chains.

Complaints from the convicts and others were not usually much credited by those in authority, as is suggested by the belated official response to complaints. Referring to such complaints in general, and to a particular case before him at the time, Commissaire Rozel remarked that: "Since these men often complain without reason, or for very little reason . . . it does not seem to me this complaint merits much attention. I see it as my duty, however, to take the liberty of informing you, in order that this conductor knows that nothing happens on his route of which Your Grandeur is not exactly informed."[90] Reaction to criticisms leveled at the conductor of the Brittany chain of 1689 was typically disparaging: "they appear to me, by the depositions of witnesses, to be without foundation."[91] But this port official went on to say: "I have not failed to reprimand this conductor strongly for having mistreated the peasant who drove the cart of convicts, and I have no doubt that he will in the future give him the things he needs with less violence."[92] In general, if the men composing a chain were in comparatively good physical condition on arrival at Marseilles, that was taken to signify that the conductor had treated them well. Thus, after inspecting a chain of 229 of which only 3 died on the road, Intendant d'Héricout commented that "all these convicts appeared to me to be in good condition, and only 3 were put in the hospital on arrival, which is rare for so large a number, and which proves that they were well treated en route."[93] When losses were heavy and the condition of a chain was poor on arrival, the conductor might be blamed. But there was a tendency to find excuses for conductors. The poor condition of the men could be attributed to the effects of overlong detention in the prisons, or the blame could be shifted to ailments unidentified by the medical practitioners of the day; there were also some attempts, apparently, to find blameworthy the treatment received immediately after they arrived at Marseilles, as in 1662: "The salt smugglers [recently arrived] continue to die from a sickness said to proceed from ennui and distress. But I protest, by Almighty God [Dieu vivant] that they are eating good bread and good beans, in which I have from time to time put meat, to make the bouillon better . . . I would think myself unworthy of the mercy of God if I connived with someone for the diminution of their life and daily bread." [94]

At other times, when a feeble chain arrived, it was the weather that was blamed. Winter weather could be deadly for ill-fed and ill-clad convicts on the march. As early as 1663 doubt was expressed as to the advisability of dispatching chains in the winter months. Writing to the minister in January 1663, the intendant remarked: "We have interrogated all the forçats in the last chain, which arrived four days ago, conducted by the Sieur Farin. We have found that their complaints were not significant enough for proceedings to be taken against him. In fact, I have sent him his release for 64 with 1 dead, noting [however] that 18 died on the roads and 2 after being liberated by M. le Chancelier, which makes me think that the rigor of the winter is not very suitable for the conduct of convicts." [95] Though it was manifest that the weather was responsible for fatalities, that fact did not prevent the frequent dispatch of winter chains in later years. The year 1666 saw a mid-January chain en route from Paris. Mid-December the next year saw another on the road, "all young men of 25 to 35 years, to each of whom I have issued a pair of shoes, and breeches and drawers, for the ice and rigor of the season [otherwise] would have felled them before the reached Châlons." [96] Two decades later the effects of the winter season were still being felt by men in the chains, because they were still being dispatched in that season. Noting in 1683 that a Bordeaux chain had been forced to halt for some days en route because of bad weather, Seignelay observed that "it is very important to dispatch the convicts only in the months of April and September. His Majesty desires that you determine whether or not the departure of chains can be fixed for those times." [97] A short time later April and September were, in fact, fixed as regular months of departure, and conductors were expected to make themselves available at the starting points at the appropriate times." [98] But the rule, however well intentioned and necessary, was not thereby established in practice. Three years later, when a chain was about to depart from Paris in November, Seignelay himself wrote to the conductor concerned, not objecting to the season of departure, but rather to the lack of clothing provided because, as he said: "we are now in a season when it is necessary that they have the clothing the King ordered." [99]

April or September departure had advantages for the convicts if the debilitations of the prisons were not much lengthened. But at those

198

seasons, wagons and teams were often fully employed in the countryside, and hence were difficult and often costly for the conductor to obtain. Peasants and proprietors were said to hide their wagons; others refused to allow their vehicles to be used. The conductors themselves complained about the weather, called attention to the bad effects, and explained, as one said, how "troublesome for these wretches" bad weather was. Conductors were quite aware that convicts needed more clothing than they were supplied, and more food too perhaps, but conductors were hard put to supply additional food, and could not give clothing, they said, on the budget they were allowed.[100]

In 1744, after April and September had been accepted and established as departure times for chains, the intendant of Strasbourg remarked that "every year there are disputes between the conductors of the chain and local officials along the road about the vehicles needed for the transport of convicts."[101] Perhaps there were other plausible reasons for not departing in April or September, or for sending additional chains at other times, but as late as 1712 the desirable schedule was not uniformly observed; a January chain of 313 arrived that year, after losing 56 dead along the road. "It is not yet possible to judge precisely the state of this chain . . . because these men are utterly fatigued."[102] A December chain of 353 arrived the next year, but only ten died en route.[103] Of those reaching Marseilles, however, 88 were in the hospital the day after arrival.

It is not possible to indicate with any precision the proportions of able-bodied and invalid convicts in the chains that arrived. Mortality en route and invalid condition on arrival were variables, certainly more severe and more frequent in the period 1660–1715 than in the half century thereafter. It was to the earlier period that Bégon referred when he remarked that it was "unquestionable that more than half [of the convicts] perish or become invalid before their first campaign" at sea.[104] Bégon may have been referring not only to the conduct of the chains, but also to those who did not live through the "training period," or apprenticeship at the oars, and to those men who never left the prison in which they were held awaiting the arrival of the chain. In the eighteenth century, the condition of chains was gradually improved. Mortality among convicts en route in the 1740's ranged from 3 down to less than 1 per cent; and a comparable decline took place in the incidence of sickness and disability among arrivees.[105]

Life Aboard

Convicts coming to Marseilles were met at the city gates by detachments of guards. This special security force accompanied the chain and its wagons and conductors through the city streets. Progress must have been hard and slow on that last leg of the trek. The shouts of the guards and the clanking of irons rose in a chorus louder than the usual bustle of the narrow streets. Onlookers gaped from windows and doors as the chain approached and passed. Guards brushed pedestrians and spectators back to make way, and to hasten the dragging procession of men in chains, winding painfully down to the old port, finally coming to a halt near the city hall or before the residence of the intendant of galleys.

Ordinarily, the new arrivals were "received" immediately and assigned to the réale or other old galleys serving as receiving ships. That was a temporary assignment, usually for a few days or a fortnight, the length of the stay being determined by the immediate need for oarsmen and the convenience of the Corps. As soon as practicable, however, they were divided into five or six classes, according to their physical condition and promise. Veteran comites and the doctor handled the business of judging quality and condition. Theirs was a crucial decision determining which of the several classes of work a man could perform at the oar. The first class was "choice," the others were lower grades according to estimated strength and capacity for work at the oar. The lowest class comprised the sick and unfit.[1]

The newcomers were then parcelled out so that each galley received a share in proportion to need. That was a delicate, important problem since the oarsmen of each galley, it was thought, should be a good match in collective strength for the rowers of sister vessels; unless they were equal, or nearly so, the better-manned galleys forced the oarsmen of the weaker ones to make extraordinary exertions to keep pace. Such exertions, when long continued, produced casualties that compounded the troubles of the weaker galleys and increased disparities among the various craft. There was sharp rivalry among galley officers; each wanted to maximize the number of choice oarsmen assigned to his rowing force. The captain's reputation was at stake in this, since the quality of his galley's speed and maneuvers naturally reflected the quality of the men serving its oars.

Various devices were employed to assure a reasonably equitable distribution of new oarsmen when the need was especially keen. The method employed on one occasion (at Dunkirk rather than at Marseilles) was described in detail by Jean Marteilhe, a convict who lived to publish memoirs describing some of his experiences: "We were led to the Parc de l'Arsenal, and made to strip nude, so that all parts of our bodies could be inspected. We were felt all over as though we were fat cattle at market. The inspection over, we [sixty men] were put into classes, [rated] from strongest to weakest, and then we were divided into six lots, as equally as possible, and each comite drew a chance to select a lot." [2] Marteilhe mentions having heard, before the lots were drawn, that the comite aboard *La Palme* was especially harsh and that those who happened to be included in his lot were not to be envied. After the drawing took place, and not knowing his own fate, Marteilhe turned to a man standing nearby, asking to what galley his lot had fallen. " 'To *La Palme*,' the man replied. Marteilhe cursed his terrible luck. 'Why are you any less fortunate than the others?' the man asked. 'Because,' said Marteilhe, 'I've fallen into an inferno of a galley, whose comite is a demon or worse.' " Marteilhe did not know that he was speaking to that very comite.[3] But as events turned out, fate was kind; his new comite, according to Marteilhe, went out of his way to prove that his reputation as a devil was not justified. Without entirely rejecting Marteilhe's claim, it does seem evident that the behavior of the comite in

FIGHTING SHIPS AND PRISONS

question may have been influenced by the fact that Marteilhe had some powerful friends and access to funds. In any case, Marteilhe enjoyed comparatively favorable treatment at the hands of the man.

Shortly after their arrival, a clothing ration was issued to new forçats and turcs. The usual ration consisted, in 1676, of two long shirts of nightgown length, two pairs of trousers, a pair of stockings, and a red wool stocking cap. In addition, each forçat was issued a jacket and cloak every other year. Garments came in two sizes: small and large. Each man was responsible for maintaining his wardrobe, doing his washing as opportunity arose. Worn-out clothing was replaced at the King's expense on the first of January every other year, with half the rowing force receiving their replacements in odd years, the other half in even. The old garments normally were turned back to the clothing contractor when new ones were issued. No shoes were issued for use aboard the galley, since it was not expected that the galérien would go very far afoot! But when men were allowed or ordered to leave the galley for work details of various sorts under guard, shoes were issued temporarily.[4]

A forçat was expected to take care of his clothing, and not be so careless as to lose any part. He was certainly ill advised to sell any of it. Lost articles were replaced at the King's expense only if lost on campaign. To be certain other losses did not take place, a royal order of 1688 required comites to conduct a clothing inspection every Sunday; any clothing missing on those occasions was replaced at the expense of the forçat or slave concerned.[5] Most forçats and slaves eventually accumulated some funds that could be used to meet this charge. Argousins and comites were held responsible for clothing issued. Thus an oarsman who lost or disposed of garments was certain, at the very least, to irritate the men who policed his daily life!

Persons knowing the attractions of the south coast of France for vacations might suppose that wintering on that coast would be pleasant. But the winter season in the south could be rigorous, at least for galériens. The chill and violence of the mistral coming down from the north made winter garb indispensable. To live for a winter in chains aboard a galley, even with a jacket and cloak and under the tarpaulin-tents that were hung (see Pl. 3), could be a bitter experience. Forçats who sold clothing usually did so for drink or from some extraordinary motives. No forçat in full possession of his faculties would sell jacket or cloak, knowing he would have to face winter and his comite afterward. In January 1670, for example, Intendant Arnoul, with unusual solicitude, remarked that a "thaw" had set in at Marseilles "for which I'm glad because of the poor forçats." [6] At Toulon, the wind and cold were equally severe. One memoirist, adding to inter-city rivalry, remarked that Toulon was "more exposed to winds [than Marseilles]; such winds force the galleys to strike their tents, thus leaving the oarsmen entirely exposed to the cold and rain; on one occasion the galleys were three days and nights in that condition, not daring to raise their tents; that never happens at Marseilles." [7]

Whatever the differences on other matters, there was unanimity of opinion that winter cold took a heavy toll. For galleys based on the Atlantic, as many were during the two decades after 1689, it was worse. Fifteen galleys wintered at Rouen in 1690–91 and many precautions were taken, including the use of a double clothing ration and double tents sent on emergency requisition from Marseilles to protect the oarsmen from the freezing Biscay and North Sea weather.[8] In general, as far as protection from the elements was concerned, it would seem the King did well by his forçats and turcs. His clothing ration was certainly more generous, and more nearly adequate, than his ration of food.

There was no seasonal variation in the adequacy of the food; rations were scant but barely adequate the year around. As mentioned earlier, the official allowance consisted of two pounds of bread or sea biscuit a day with bean soup, oil (or lard), salt, and sometimes a little wine.[9] Though there were occasional supplements on holidays, and even if he received all that he was supposed to receive, the fare could not satisfy an able-bodied man. As far as the King's interest was concerned, the ration had two great advantages: it was cheap, and it encouraged oarsmen to employ their extra time and energy earning money for supplementary food.

Slaves often received a slightly larger ration than forçats — in 1669 Colbert thought they might be overfed. He warned Intendant Arnoul that "many persons experienced in galley affairs say that our rowing force cannot be good because you allow the slaves too much liberty and you feed them too well. There is nothing more damaging to the quality of a slave than [to be] fat and overweight. You should reflect on this." [10] Galley officers, under whom the oarsmen worked and some of whom took a cut from rations, evidently did not share Colbert's fears about the possibility that the oarsmen, whether forçats or slaves, were becoming fat and pampered on the King's ration. On the contrary, one informed the minister in 1676 in no uncertain terms that "all the officers are persuaded that . . . the bread and beans that forçats receive aboard the galley are not sufficient for their maintenance, or to make them good oarsmen."[11]

Several years later a change in the ration was seriously considered by top naval administrators. Their approach was cautious — judging from the minister's dispatches, some might say parsimonious. "For a long time it has been proposed that the King improve the diet of his galley oarsmen; beans with oil, it has been claimed, is not enough. Because of the increase in expenditure that a change would involve, and because the forçats have always been maintained on the present ration, His Majesty has refrained from changing anything in this regard up to now. However, complaints concerning the weakness of oarsmen have led me to order an on-the-spot investigation to determine how the forçats could be given a more substantial ration without unduly increasing expense. His Majesty feels that the expense would not run to a very considerable sum if they were given rice four times a week, with some fresh meat in the cauldron; they could be given a little wine to sustain them on the [other] three days when they have only beans and oil [with their bread]."[12] Intendant Brodart, to whom these instructions were addressed, responded with a counter proposal. He suggested that the ration be increased with four ounces of lard a day instead of the rice and meat (perhaps the lard would have been more profitable to his friend the munitionnaire). But the minister rejected that scheme. He insisted that the meat and rice would make a satisfactory soup. He spelled it out further when he said that part of the meat could be given to the sick, and the rest to the vogue-avant: "In this way it will cost much less, and the effect for the galleys will be salutary, because the vogue-avant will be more energetic, and the [other] forçats will seek to become vogue-avant in order to be better nourished."[13]

The addition of rice to the ration did improve the diet of galley oarsmen. In later years, many further changes of various sorts were proposed and some were made. At least one allowed the munitionnaire to substitute some other food for the meat that was ordinarily supposed to be distributed to the oarsmen.[14] As late as 1748, a galley official reminded the minister that the King's ration left much to be desired: "You know,

Life Aboard

Monseigneur, that the King's ration does not suffice for their subsistence, and that not only humanity but the interests of the service require that they be able to procure more substantial nourishment." [15] Such statements do not authorize indictment of royal policy, nor can such a statement as this be taken as a fair representation of the adequacy of the oarsmen's actual diet. It is difficult at a distance of several centuries, and it was also difficult for Colbert and Seignelay, to estimate the adequacy of this diet for different individuals even when the exact quantity the men were supposed to receive is known.

The King's ration was variable, and so was its adequacy. It became less satisfactory for oarsmen when the ability of the individual to obtain supplements decreased with excessively long or frequent campaigns, illness, advanced age, or when officers made excessive demands on his funds. When supplements could not be obtained over a considerable period of time, the health of the individual forçat was apt to deteriorate; dietary deficiency could easily become a critical problem on an excessively long campaign when oarsmen were cut off from supplements at the very time they were making maximum exertions at the oar. Of course, the campaign ration was ordinarily larger than the port ration, but even so, it did not equal the ration that most forçats were able to buy or scrounge for themselves from private sources while in port.

A great many factors affected the diet and health of galériens. Much depended on individual constitution, but there were also a number of significant environmental circumstances that were apt to affect anyone — no matter how strong or how good his general health. After all, forçats did not always receive their full ration. Both quantity and quality were fixed by royal decree, but that did not mean that each ration was measured, weighed, or analyzed. There was short weighing, false measuring, cheating, corruption, and graft of unbelievable sorts all along the line — part of the effects of the system of gratuities and perquisites, of which the twentieth-century tip is a reminder. Bean soup might be ladled out in a very rough manner and measure, and the term used to designate the ration of bread that was actually issued aboard, *main de pain*, suggests its possible quantitative variation.

Hardly less serious were variations in the quality of food issued. The minister himself expressed concern about the high mortality among oarsmen during the campaign of 1675 (in which 475 oarsmen died!). His investigation led to the conclusion that "the bad quality of victuals, about which the Duke de Vivonne complained . . . had much to do with the extraordinary number of deaths." To forestall a recurrence of the problem, he ordered Brodart to apply himself assiduously "to examine the quality of the victuals furnished during the course of the forthcoming years . . . [and] not allow any biscuit or other foodstuffs to be embarked until they are inspected and found to be good quality." He also told Brodart that "His Majesty has spoken strongly to the victualers on this subject; they have promised to do a better job next year than they did in the year just past."[16]

There were times when the damaging effects of graft and ignorance worked together on the galleys. After all, the dietary and medical knowledge of the age was rudimentary, and did not always enable the minister to act in the best interest of the oarsmen even when he was striving to give them strength. That was part of the problem with diet in general; it was also the problem with wine. The ministers, like most men of that age and others, believed that wine had significant value as both nutrient and stimulant. Hence special care was taken to add wine to the ration when French galleys were out on campaign. That addition raised morale. And wine was a safer beverage than water; a barrel of wine certainly contained fewer bacteria than a barrel of water from streams along the coasts of Italy or Spain. Hence Intendant Montmort was close to the truth when he expressed the prevailing sentiment in 1691 that "it would be very prejudicial to the forçats" if they drank less wine, though his reason was that "they need to be fortified and solaced because of their long campaigns at sea."[17] In the 1740's, as a supplement to the diet of forçats engaged in heavy labor around the arsenal, one naval official strongly recommended wine to make them fit for work: "All things considered, I feel that an increase in the wine ration they receive ashore is the course of action most agreeable to them, the easiest for the service, and the least expensive for the King."[18] Perhaps he was right. Certainly there was widespread conviction that a good pot of wine a day was needed to supplement the King's ration, but there were a few well-intentioned dissents on the value of alcoholic beverages. The Count de Roannes expressed the opinion in 1694 that cider was contributing significantly to diarrhea; he therefore substituted meat.[19] Of course there was awareness of the pernicious effects of overindulgence; a royal ordinance of 1686 forbade comites and tavern keepers' giving more than one pot of wine a day to any forçat on the galleys.[20]

Life Aboard

Wine did not become part of the daily ration until well into the eighteenth century; the King's drink for convicts was water. Water was cheaper. Besides, a regular ration of wine would interfere with sales at the tavern aboard the galley, whose profits went to the comite and indirectly enabled the King to pay the comite a small salary. The comite's wine was readily available aboard the galley; it could be had at the tavern (*cantine*) just below the level of the main deck in the center of the galley. On Sunday, after mass, the tavern was open. Wine could be purchased by the pint or the pot. The tavern closed after the Ave Maria (vespers). Though a forçat was officially restricted to a pot a day, that regulation must have been impossible to enforce if the will to obey was lacking in both buyer and seller. There can be no doubt that the tavern was a focal point of interest on the galley, for forçats if not for abstemious turcs; the operation of the tavern was an important preoccupation for a majority of the men aboard.

The effect, and one object, of the operation was, of course, profit for the comite, the assistant comites, and their aides. There were various business arrangements, including the extension of credit to oarsmen, aimed at maximizing the demand for wine among forçats and slaves. One might suppose, at first, that every forçat would be a willing customer, and that little difficulty would arise within the limits of the pot a day. But an unusual buyer-seller relationship existed between forçat and comite. The comite was a combination of warden and chief petty officer, straw boss and wine merchant, with almost unlimited powers over his captive customers. Forçat buyers were hardly in a position to haggle over price. Nor could they go elsewhere to buy. Indeed, the forçat could not with impunity even refuse to buy at least a minimum.

Comites often employed a trusted forçat as tavern keeper (*tavernier*). The tavern keepers' methods were well established even in Colbert's day, for wine had been sold on galleys in medieval times. The practice, had been highly developed to maximize the comites' profits. Abuses associated with sales of wine were apparently as old as the tavern itself, and they persisted in spite of proscribing ordinances, as the reiteration of those ordinances suggests. One of these, issued in 1678, condemned the tavern keepers who "sell wine at prices higher than the legal maximum . . . distribute wine in measures that are not accurate, and often mix water with the wine to increase the quantity." This ordinance was read aloud and nailed to the mast of every galley. It provided penalties to be imposed on forçats and comites alike if the abuses recurred.[21] Nonetheless, they continued. There were later complaints that wine was not only diluted, but diluted with seawater instead of fresh, this being declared "the most common cause" of sickness on campaign.[22]

An investigation undertaken in 1693 disclosed that it was then the custom each morning for the tavern keeper "to receive a main de pain" from each banc. "In return, the tavern keeper gives a little wine to be divided among the forçats of the banc as the members of the banc see fit; as a result, one ration of bread is lacking [each day] from each banc." [23] Two years later a report to the minister by a galley captain, the Chevalier de Breteuil, disclosed that this custom still prevailed. Comites required forçats to sell part of their ration of bread to the tavern keeper for wine by threats of rough treatment in forthcoming campaigns.[24] "Many argousins" entered into collusion with comites "to force these unfortunates to carry their bread to the tavern." Comites and arousins alike "are devils" said Breteuil; they "daily invent new means to tyrannize and steal from oarsmen." [25] These were strong words from a captain, but Breteuil did not leave it at that. He emphasized the difficulty of proving the existence of such abuses. An inspector called to hear a complaint, he said, heard only from a single oarsman. It is his word against the comite's. "Afterward, the complainers will be punished in secret by the comite; the captain will be none the wiser." [26] Breteuil also pointed out that "the favorites of comites are the ones who work all week, [and] Saturday evening begin to carry their money to the tavern for drink . . . [and continue] all Sunday until evening . . . eat nothing and take only wine for two days." [27] One can be certain, he said, that such men are not worth much at the oar. On such fare a man "burns his liver and stomach, becomes dehydrated, debilitated and gaunt." [28] In 1700 one memoirist asserted that "most noncommissioned officers have no other occupation than that of profiting from the taverns and the oarsmen." [29]

To say that a fully-manned galley was crowded is to understate the case. A galley on campaign was swarming — between 350 and 500 men were confined to an area about 170 feet long and 40–45 feet wide. Barras de la Penne admitted that the galley was so crowded that crewmen could not sleep in a prone position; when everyone was at his post, there were "only heads from prow to poop." [30] At the bow, in an area perhaps less than one-twelfth the length of the ship, were quartered 30 sailors. In the central three-quarters of the galley were 250 to 350 oarsmen chained at their benches on either side of the coursier, a central runway of planks a few feet wide and slightly raised running from rambarde to poop. Even the poop, reserved for the captain and officers was small. This shoulder-to-shoulder density was perhaps an accurate picture of the galley under some circumstances. However, campaigns were the only times when every officer, soldier, crewman, and oarsman was aboard for a significant length of time; officers, crewmen, and oarsmen did not sleep at sea, though the notoriously lazy soldiers usually did.

At the Oar

When on campaign, galleys normally headed into some haven in late afternoon. If the coastal region was thinly populated or the nearby towns were small and poor, the oarsmen assembled beds for the officers. With relative ease the beds were set up on stilts just above the bancs, resembling tables about three feet wide and six feet long; beneath each one a banc of oarsmen slept. A woolen or horsehair mattress was brought up from the hold and placed on the bedboards, then sheets and blankets. If there was a chance of rain, as there often was, a canopy was raised over each bed by a rope and pulley attached to the great tent that was raised in inclement weath to enclose the galley as a whole. The result was three or four (at most half a dozen) small tents standing within a large tent. Each officer had "a bed fit for an angel," said Marteilhe, who helped make up such beds but slept on the deck beneath. "Fit for an angel, perhaps, but not for a sailor!"[31]

This bed-making routine was accomplished quickly so that officers could retire whenever they pleased. The oarsmen ate their bread and beans, and at nightfall, when the boom of a gun sounded retreat, the whistles of the comites ordered the forçats and slaves to lie down for the night. Throughout the night no oarsman "could stand erect, nor speak, nor make the slightest stir. If one of them was obliged to go to the side [the head] by nature's necessities, he had to utter the cry 'à la bande,' but could go only if the guard on duty gave his permission with a cry of 'va' [go]; [otherwise] a profound silence reigned aboard all through the night, as though the galley was deserted."[32] On the prow of the galley, not covered by the great tent, the sailors sometimes slept under tarpaulins. Soldiers dozed along the bulwarks — that is, along the top of the narrow overhang on either side of the deck. The oarsmen slept on the deck or in their bancs as best they could, pleased if they did not have to contend with the intrusion of the thigh-sized butt of the oar in their limited space. In normal circumstances, the officers and crewmen, except for comites and guards, slept ashore. They ordinarily did so at Marseilles during the seven or eight months, or more, that the galleys were tied up in that port each year. Hence the forçats and slaves, the guards on duty, and a few others were the only ones who had to put up with crowded conditions aboard — they alone contended year round with the smells and lice and fleas; they alone knew intimately the smoky, lamp-lighted interior of the great tents that warded off winter winds and chill; they alone partook of the bean soup prepared in the fougon, the kitchen some eight by nine feet where meals for more than 400 men were sometimes prepared.

There were thieves aboard the galleys, and there was theft. After all, theft was at times the most frequent cause for judicial condemnation to the oar, and there might be some justification for the reputation of a galley as a "raft of thieves." It was recorded of a thief named Ambreville, renowned even among forçats for his deft pickpocketing, that a bishop told him in jest that he knew his reputation and was watching his purse. When the bishop debarked he still had his purse, but he lacked his pectoral cross! Several versions of that story are told. Barras de la Penne in the eighteenth century mentioned that visitors were officially asked not to bring stilettos or purses aboard, for fear they might be relieved of them by the forçats. Both forçats and turcs were found guilty of stealing and selling irons and other objects — even chains — from the arsenal. When thefts of jewels and other small objects took place in Marseilles or neighboring towns as far as Avignon, the intendant of galleys was apt to be alerted, since the forçats were known to serve as fences.[33]

To punish thefts and other transgressions and to keep oarsmen obedient and disciplined, various punishments were used. There were several variations on the age-old punishment of running the gauntlet, as described in a memoir of 1681 on punishments for forçats. The malefactor was required to run the length of the coursier and as he passed each banc the oarsmen struck at him with the wooden-handled mop they used to clean their banc.[34] By mid-eighteenth century there were at least six other punishments officially authorized for oarsmen: (1) putting them in handirons; (2) chaining them with short chains or double chains to bulwalk; (3) sending them out to work at heavy labor for many days running and retaining the money they earned in order to repay their debts; (4) the bastonnade or flogging with a rope's end or "white" cord; (5) bastonnade with a tarred rope; (6) repeated bastonnade on successive days, with many or few strokes each time depending on the age of the recipient and the nature of the offense. On the galleys, as in sailing navies, flogging was a common punishment. Its severity could readily be adapted to suit the seriousness of the offense. Thus, four or five forçats guilty of selling part of their clothing ration to buy drink were ordered flogged by Arnoul in 1666; he oversaw the punishment himself and promised worse penalties for any additional offenses.[35]

In another case, a turc "of mediocre robustness," who stole irons from the arsenal and went into the city to sell them, reportedly "received a total of more than 250 lashes with a rope's end in three separate floggings, but without disclosing [the name of] the receiver of the goods. He was incommoded for nearly a month without danger to his life. One can thus judge the amount of punishment that can be imposed."[36]

Apart from any humane consideration, it was obviously in the King's interest not to have able-bodied oarsmen sustain any crippling injury as a result of punishments. Numerous ordinances were issued from the mid-sixteenth century onward whose purpose was to prevent crippling injury to oarsmen by unauthorized, careless, or needlessly severe punishments. Of course, mere legislation did not prevent that sort of thing from occurring. Certainly it was exceptional for a comite to be brought to court-martial, as one was in 1689 after a forçat died from the ill treatment he had inflicted. This comite was intended to be an example.[37] In the early eighteenth century, as a precautionary measure, even captains were deprived of the right to inflict the bastonnade "on the spot"; it could be inflicted only by permission from higher authority. In 1723 the captains petitioned Commandant Barras de la Penne to regain the right to employ this penalty on their own authority, but he refused.[38]

In the same year Barras was counseling moderation, one of his fellow officers was of the opinion that the death penalty (ordinarily by hanging) was not severe enough for certain offenses. The Count de Roannes called attention to the case of a recent premeditated attack by a forçat on a noncommissioned officer, from which the officer died. At his execution shortly afterward, the forçat did not repent his crime, and Roannes felt that the offender had gotten off too lightly; in his opinion the forçat should have been broken on the wheel. "With your permission" said Roannes, "I will do that in the future when the crime is premeditated, because none of these miserable forçats has any fear of the gallows." [39] In the spring of 1723 a further indication of officers' opinion of punishment was given in a report to the minister by the Bailiff de Langeron:

Since I have the honor to be attached to the service of the *Réale*, it is my duty to inform you of occurrences aboard that galley on the eleventh day of this month. . . . M. de Gardane, the Aide-Major of the Galleys, had come aboard the *Rèale* to carry out the usual inspection that the Aide-Major of the Week makes each day at nightfall. A forçat of this galley handed him a petition on behalf of the oarsmen as a group. The petition requested that their argousin be relieved of his duties. This unanimous request appearing [to be] a conspiracy and mutiny, the Aide-Major ordered that handcuffs be put on the forçat who presented the petition. This order was no sooner given than all the oarsmen stood up and began to chant aloud: "point de menottes" and "point d'argousin" ["no handcuffs," "no argousin"]. This obliged M. de Gardane to leave, and to report this to the Captain of the Guard as an insurrection.[40]

The cries of the oarsmen continued throughout the night and apparently could not be stopped. However, the next morning, in the presence of the Bailiff de Langeron, "the oarsmen did not even murmur when handcuffs were put on the whole lot of them," and the Bailiff remarked that they seemed "as compliant and as submissive as one could desire." A court-martial was meantime hurriedly assembled, with the object of trying the man who had presented the petition. The decision, handed down later the same day, declared that the petitioner, "the said Claude Leger Poclet, forçat of the galley *Réale* . . . being convicted of writing and presenting the petition in the name of the oarsmen . . . and of being the chief of the insurrection on the said galley . . . is condemned to be hanged and strangled until dead in the full view of all the galleys . . . the twelfth day of the month of April 1723." [41] The explanation for the haste and severity of Poclet's punishment lies in the fact that the affair was interpreted as an insurrection. Petitions by more than one person were then expressly forbidden in France, even for law-abiding subjects. The right of collective petition was not won until 1789. [42] There were, of course, other circumstances that called down the death penalty. Certain moral crimes were punishable by the extremity of burning alive (though that practice was very rare), but nothing rivaled the fear and abhorrence in which mutiny was held. [43]

It is evident that the circumstances of life aboard the galleys created a real need for the *missionnaires*. Their concern was for the spiritual welfare of men aboard the galleys, and also for their physical welfare when they were in the hospital, where the management was at least partly, if not entirely, in their hands. It is not possible to know the extent to which Vincent de Paul was able to influence the behavior of the French chaplains who were his subordinates during his later years. He left a personal legacy that could have served as inspiration; though his passing perhaps presaged a temporary deterioration among the chaplains on the galleys, the tradition of humane good works left by Vincent was not forgotten or ignored in the galley hospital.

The regular medical staff of the galley, the barber-surgeon and his assistant, sometimes had little to do. At other times a high incidence of illness among oarsmen created a pressing need for hospital services for both the galley oarsmen and the crew. In 1625–26, for example, aboard one galley with a rowing force of about 270, "there were always more than ten men sick, often more than twenty, even thirty, and some weeks they were up to thirty-five or thirty-six. Special care was taken that they were well fed; the captain furnished one half pound of mutton a day [per man?] and rice and wine, but in vain. The mortality was very high. On that same galley . . . the dead numbered twenty-five between January first and the ninth of May 1626." [44] Such conditions were certainly exceptional, particularly since the galley in question had not recently returned from campaign but was merely anchored in port. Yet the problem of health and the need for a hospital was ever present with the galleys. The preamble of the King's decree establishing a galley hospital emphasized that the oarsmen were "often infected, often sick," and "a great number die because they are not in a hospital where they could receive the necessary care . . . the rowing force of the galleys is thereby weakened to the point of being useless for the service of the state."[45]

The need for a hospital was clearly recognized early in the century by Henry IV but the permanent, widely celebrated galley hospital at Marseilles was not established until the 1640's. The founding of the hospital was the joint undertaking of powerful private persons, some churchmen, and the King. This joint sponsorship was one of the hospital's most significant strengths, making for durability. Without the King's consistent financial support, both at the outset and on a continuing basis, the hospital could not have been the effective institution it was. Earlier efforts to establish a permanent hospital did not succeed precisely because of the inadequacy of private means over the long term. When chartered in July 1646 the hospital was set up as a private corporation, not as a royal hospital. The institution was thereby made independent of control by self-interested lesser functionaries of royal bureaucracy. Its administration was in the hands of charitable persons, lay and religious, helping the sick in the service of God and the King.

At its founding the hospital received 9,000 livres a year from the King, increasing within five years to 12,000 livres a year.[46] In addition, the King paid a subsidy of 3 sous a day per patient, which aggregated about 55 livres a year for each patient.[47] These funds supplemented the income from an endowment established by Madame d'Aiguillon, which returned 6,000 livres a year for the hospital.[48] Thus, the hospital administrators had at their disposal some 18,000 livres a year, plus 3 sous a day for each patient under care.

The galley hospital was always of rather modest size, but in its first half century it did expand. The new rooms and beds were more than justified by growing need. For example, the total number of oarsmen was about 6,500 in 1670, and over 12,000 in the 1690's. This increase in numbers, accompanied by vigorous campaigning, literally inundated the hospital with patients. In 1682 the overflow was such that two old galleys had to be used as an annex to the hospital, each accommodating about 200 patients.[49] The problem was even greater a decade later — in October 1691 there were 1,170 patients, a fact that disturbed the minister when brought to his attention. Later that year, however, the number fell to under 800.[50] The decade after 1685 was one of the most active in the history of the hospital. Expenditures by the institution stood between 30,000 and 37,000 livres a year before 1685, but rose to at least 90,000 livres in 1693.[51]

The large number of patients in the hospital did not signify that forçats and turcs were lightly permitted to leave the oar for the hospital. Hospitalization was not easily obtained precisely because galley administrators were fully alert to the possibility of feigned illness; serious effort was made to make certain that only those oarsmen in real need of care were taken to the hospital. As a general rule, galley officers and administrators believed that weak or sickly men could best be kept on the galley. "Many forçats, who seem to be worthless, become very good" oarsmen under the care of their comites. On the other hand, "it is evident that all the forçats in the hospital are weak."[52] The Duke de Vivonne remarked that the "good forçats" realize that "a stay in the hospital only weakens them and makes them prone to even worse sickness when they return to the galley. For this reason many of them will not go to the hospital, will not be treated elsewhere than on the galley."[53] Colbert agreed: "It is certain that the stay of forçats in the hospital weakens them extraordinarily."[54] It was far better, he thought, to keep the forçats out of the hands of the hospital staff. "I am persuaded," he wrote Surgeon General Miermand, "that you take good care of all the forçats who fall sick [on the galleys]." To help distinguish those who really needed to be hospitalized, Colbert suggested that Miermand "keep a special register of the forçats who enter the hospital, put a mark beside [the names of] those who die, and try to learn to distinguish the principal symptoms of their maladies."[55] The minister was often officious; yet Miermand needed much more surveillance than he received.

The position of the hospital staff was not enviable, for it must have been difficult for them to contend with ministers of marine like the two Colberts. Directives were drawn up to govern the functioning of the hospital, indicating the titles of the staff and even the nature of the hospital routine. The staff included physician(s?), supervisors, clerks, laundrymen, nurses and aides, kitchen helpers, and cooks.[56] Invalid oarsmen were frequently used in some of these positions, and as a further measure of economy some old or invalid turcs were kept at the hospital as servants; they usually served without salary, but the hospital fed them.[57]

According to the prescribed hospital routine, the day began at 3:30 A.M. when the kitchen helpers and orderlies, most of them convicts, were awakened by the guard. They rose and bustled about the building preparing soups and remedies to be administered at 4:00 A.M. when everyone else arose. The rooms were "perfumed" and, wind and weather permitting, aired. At 4:45 A.M. the staff had prayers. At 5:00 A.M. concentrated perfume was released, and sometimes incense was burned to dissipate pernicious vapors in one of the large sick rooms, where patients and staff then gathered before an altar for mass. At regular hours through the day, remedies, soups, and varied foods were distributed to patients; rooms were cleaned and pots were emptied; beds were made twice daily. Bedsheets were supposed to be changed at least every fifteen days as were the patient's clothing and towels. The physician visited patients morning and afternoon. Those afflicted with venereal disease, malignant fevers, and scurvy were lodged apart, sometimes in a special building, their afflictions being considered communicable. As an added precaution, the laundry of such patients was bleached.[58] A separate quarter of the main hospital was reserved for turcs. Hospital accommodation was provided separately for members of the crew, but toward the end of the separate existence of the Corps, the declining number of forçats apparently allowed a section of the forçat establishment to be set aside for crewmen. Visitors and sightseers were permitted. There was a time when sightseeing tours were guided by a trusted turc who carried before him an incense burner to dissipate the odors and who collected 30 sous from (well-to-do visitors) at the exit.[59]

The hospital staff was in many respects independent of the officials of the galley arsenal. Such independence was an advantage for the hospital, but it was also a source of difficulty. Some Corps officials thought the administration of the hospital much too self-sufficient and made it clear that they wanted control. In consequence, a quarrel was carried on for many years between intendants and hospital administrators. Embittered correspondence from both sides went to the minister of marine. Intendants Arnoul and Brodart, in particular, sought to have the King transfer the administration of the hospital to them. For a long period they tried to uncover grounds for criticism and complaint strong enough to justify that extraordinary step. One letter specifying complaints came from Brodart's pen in 1676. The nature of his grievances throws a good deal more light on the parties to the quarrel than on the quarrel itself. Brodart began his letter with "sadness," he said, "that monks and [other] pious people so often do mischievous things on the pretext of devotion to charity." He was referring particularly to the preferential treatment given in the hospital to a certain turc:

I have complained before, and with good reason, about this turc named Louis. He is a man that the hospital administrators have taken under their protection on the pretext that they baptized him (turc though he is), and that he has thus been made Christian. They have given him the name of the merchant by whom he pretends to be sponsored [Louis Bonneau]. In consequence [of his conversion], they prevented his going on campaigns with the galleys for many years. I am more severe than my predecessors. I didn't want him to stay any longer in the protection of that hospital, where he is making trouble. So last year I had him brought back to the galleys. He made the campaign aboard the galley of M. le Chevalier de Forest. [The hospital administrators] were scandalized by this, and by my refusal to return him. A short time later they bought a turc [a replacement being often required before a slave was released], and [they] all came down last April, just before the departure of the galleys . . . This turc [Louis] is a very bad man, a great sodomist; he only became a Christian to escape. . . . I beg you not to give [him] his liberty, and to be agreeable to having him taken into custody, and sent back to me . . .[60]

This case of Louis Bonneau, the Christianized turc, was not in itself a great issue with Brodart; the case was merely an incident, though a significant one, in his continuing campaign to discredit the hospital administrators and bring the independence of that institution to an end. Brodart's efforts were not so inept or as futile as this incident might make them seem. There were men in the ministry who were jealous of the semiautonomous status of the hospital, and perhaps a little apprehensive, as Brodart may have been, that it could serve as a vantagepoint for outsiders to become acquainted with the workings of the galley administration. The galleys were, after all, both a defense and a prison institution, and appropriate security measures could be justified for both naval bases and prisons. It is worth noting, however, that Brodart's accusations and the misdemeanors he disclosed could have had precisely the reverse effect of that sought by Brodart if they had been brought to the attention of the King, on whom powerful religious influences could be brought to bear. In any case, some significance must attach to the fact that Brodart was relieved of his own post as a direct result of his complicity in maladministration and graft; his accusations were perhaps grounded in a desire to distract attention from his own abuses.

Brodart continued his campaign against the hospital for years, and though there must have been rejoicing within the hospital at his departure the struggle had only just begun. Other men at Marseilles, and in the ministry of marine, claimed that the hospital was a logical part of the galley administration, whose control was too important (or potentially lucrative) to be lightly renounced. On several later occasions, special investigators were appointed by ministers to probe the hospital management. One investigator, D'Ortières, called attention to a number of practices he found abusive. The victuals purchased and used by the hospital were of poor quality, he said, and hospital officials only managed to hide this fact "by secretly threatening to return complaining patients to the galleys; therefore, the oarsmen don't complain [about the hospital food]." D'Ortières claimed that "nearly all members of the hospital staff [some being forçats and slaves] are nothing more than manservants to the administrators, who give them such jobs by way of compensation. Most of them are knaves [fripons], really incompetent. They have often been found carrying away meat and bread and other things. Yet nothing has been done about that." [61] He also complained that there was too much furniture because the administrators could simply requisition it, and that the administrators guarded their prerogatives and authority with "unconquerable jealousy and prickliness . . . even to the point of refusing to give . . . the names of the forçats who die in the hospital." He declared himself convinced that "as long as the administrators are allowed to make independent expenditures, and are empowered to appoint members of the hospital service staff," it will be "impossible to avoid abuse." [62] This bitter quarrel may help to explain why many galley officers disliked sending oarsmen to the hospital. Both Intendant Arnoul and the Duke de Vivonne agreed, at one point, "not to send any more." The needs of the oarsmen did not allow that decision to stand for long, yet Colbert himself affirmed that their decision was well taken.[63] The history of the hospital for oarsmen remains to be written, but the glimpses afforded here put its lay and religious administrators in a very favorable light.

Written communication from forçats or slaves to persons outside the galleys was at all times illicit, unless supervised or inspected. As one memoirist remarked in 1751: "It must be agreed that criminals such as the galériens are not supposed to have any dealings with other men. They can appropriately be regarded as cut off from the body of society. Deprived of the amenities of civil life, malefactors cannot rightly exercise the liberties of writing and receiving letters, unless with the participation of the persons to whom their discipline is confided." [64] On this matter there was probably near unanimity of opinion among galley administrators. Communications arriving for men serving in the galleys were generally handled with considerably more indulgence than were those going the other way. But correspondence in either direction was considered a privilege. The privilege of receiving ordinary mail had to be paid for by the galérien, or by someone else for him, quite apart from any postal charges in the transmission. In general, communication was likely to be favored by the noncommissioned officers inasmuch as it offered immediate gains for them in the form of the fee exacted for permission to write, with the possibility of considerable future benefits if it brought money to the hands of the slave or forçat concerned. The dangers of forçat correspondence were of course well understood; care had to be exercised to be certain that the exchange did not result in the concoction of plans to escape, and care had also to be exercised lest the communications of slaves to Moslem potentates occasion criticism of France for not complying with terms of her treaties or other obligations.

The most rigorous supervision was reserved for the Huguenots' correspondence. But even they were allowed to write their family and friends, and it was deemed necessary to issue a special ordinance in 1696 requiring that galley officials take particular care to censor such mail.[65] A considerable amount of uncensored correspondence took place as well, in spite of rigorous surveillance. Many letters from Protestants addressed to their coreligionaries in various parts of France, the Swiss cantons, Holland, and England reached their destinations. Some survive in public archives and others in private hands, notably in the Antoine Court Collection in Geneva, the Musée du Désert in the Cévennes, and Bibliothèque Protestante in Paris.

Officials at Marseilles were especially concerned lest oarsmen's correspondence disclose matters that could bring criticism upon them from the minister or other persons at Court. One communication of the sort they particularly wanted to intercept reached the minister in 1729 and survives in the archives: a forçat petition, without signatures, complaining about a number of abuses. As a matter of fact, the abuses described were already known at the ministry. But the document's arrival did create annoyance and consternation at Marseilles, where it was not known precisely what the petition contained. In letters from Marseilles, the Count de Roannes disparaged the petition as the work of a cabal: "If the least injustice had been done, it is certain that I would have received twenty petitions from them because all the oarsmen, and likewise the crews, regard me as their father. You must therefore consider the content of the petition false from end to end." [66] Perhaps the minister recalled that Roannes had earlier sought permission to substitute breaking on the wheel for execution by hanging,[67] and had also had a share in the trial and execution of petitioner Poclet.

Of course these matters of discipline and punishment, and many other details of life aboard the galley, were only incidental to the prime function of the galérien, the service of the oar. Whether a convict doing penal servitude or a slave doing his master's will, every oarsman was part of a team. The sovereign and master required of him all the physical energy he could give toward making his oar and the galley a formidable instrument. Many of the King's functionaries had a hand in assuring that the oarsmen gave the services sought; but none was more intimately associated with that task, or more directly responsible for his performance and his welfare than his comite. An effective rowing force on any galley owed more to the comite and his assistants than to anyone else. The comite's powers very soon became apparent to the new arival. The comite decided what position on the oars each man would take. An oarsman could literally be worked to death if assigned to a place beyond his physical capacity; the effort required at different positions was very unequal. Turcs, as we have seen, were preferred for the most difficult positions. The newcomer could hope that his assignment would be commensurate with his energy, strength, and endurance; but physical strength was only one of several factors determining where he served. If a galérien were interested in easing his circumstances, he was given to understand he should make service to his comite his first occupation; if cooperative, he might carry lighter irons, or could even be assigned to the comite's own banc (or an assistant comite's), where oarsmen customarily were exempted from the lash and shared the leftovers from the table. In effect, men assigned to the bancs of the comite and his assist-

Life Aboard

ants were servants. Those were known as the "bancs respectés." "All the forçats aspired with ardor to be assigned to the banc of the comite and assistant comite." [68]

The inboard section of a galley oar approached the circumference of a man's thigh, and was thus too large to be handled effectively; hence the oar had to be equipped with an oaken manille that could be grasped in the hands of the five or more men who worked each one. Pulling a galley oar demanded coordination and dexterity, qualities at least as important as physical force. Most important of all, perhaps, was a sense of rhythm and the ability to work with precision as part of a team. The series of rowing movements was signaled by words of command and the regular sounding of a percussion or tympanic instrument, and was accompanied by a liberal distribution of "tickles" from the lash to eliminate off-beat performances.

These movements, and the ability to perform them rapidly, constituted a skill that oarsmen had to learn. Unless both the oarsmen and their comites knew what they were about, serious accidents occurred. Arnoul reported one accident in 1671, when new oarsmen were being trained and good comites were in short supply: "the ignorance and resulting mistake of an assistant comite crippled nine men . . . four of whom died"; but the accident, he said, "was partly the fault of those who were injured." [69] Just as horses are broken to the saddle, so men had to be broken to service at the oar. And after they had learned the rudiments, skill had to be developed by practice. There was, according to one galley officer, "no occupation that required more practice than that [of the oar], not only to exercise the oarsmen and make them resistant to fatigue, but also to make them familiar with the various maneuvers required." [70]

The training required by new oarsmen was best given before they made their first campaign. They were sometimes exercised, as practice at the oar was called, aboard galliots in the harbor at Marseilles, and on galleys maneuvering around the Château d'If in the roadstead of Marseilles or along the coast. Under Arnoul in the 1670's, it was customary in peacetime to send practice galleys four or five miles out to sea to exercise in both spring and fall, when campaigns were not being carried on. Even in the impoverished days after the death of Louis XIV, when there were hardly funds to pay officers' salaries, the oarsmen were continually exercised, weather permitting, in the waters near Marseilles.

The comparatively calm and protected waters around the Château d'If, a small island fortress and prison off Marseilles, were considered a particularly good training ground. Better still, in the opinion of the Marshal de Tessé, were the waters farther east, near Toulon. "There's no roadstead in the Mediterranean more suitable to break, train and exercise oarsmen than the Îles d'Hyères. Even the most poorly manned galleys run no risk there . . . with sea room for rowing, and for all sorts of maneuvers [with galleys] under sail." [71]

The business of exercising oarsmen was an important preoccupation of all galley powers, just as essential as well-kept rigging, or as snug pistons would become in a later day. One objective of any galley campaign, even wartime campaigns, was the exercising and conditioning of oarsmen. Often the galleys of Spain and her Italian allies could not be found or drawn into action by the French. Even so, when a French squadron returned after a campaign with no direct action against the enemy, one object could always be held to have been achieved: the oarsmen had been well exercised.

Frequently, individual galleys or squadrons of galleys made forays explicitly to exercise the oarsmen. Such was the purpose of the Marquis de Fornille's campaign in 1699. He was informed that the King had "resolved to dispatch the best of his galleys in three separate squadrons to exercise the oarsmen, and by their armament and the number of his vessels, to make known along all the coasts of the Mediterranean, the care that he takes to maintain his naval forces." Fifteen royal galleys campaigned the Italian coasts on those instructions, and others evidently appeared elsewhere that year with the same objectives.[72]

No minister of marine appears to have been more keenly aware than Colbert of the need to exercise the galleys. He saw no reason why the King's oarsmen should confine their exercising to the summer campaign. Writing in 1662 he indicated his desire that the galley "go out along the coasts during the forthcoming winter, at least in good weather, so that the rowing force is exercised all year round, [with care taken to] mingle new forçats with the old to teach them to row." There were a number of occasions in the last three decades of the century when fall and winter campaigns followed on the heels of summer. The officials of the ministry and the King persisted in overlooking, or ignoring, the pernicious effects of winter campaigns on a rowing force (see pp. 32–36). Winter weather — particularly rough seas and winds — was inherently dangerous if only because of the extraordinary exertions at the oar that it could entrain. But more important than that, the King's ration did not go far toward satisfying physical needs even in the summer, and recuperation after a summer campaign was slow. When a winter campaign followed closely afterward, the damaging effects were compounded.

The particular difficulties attending the conduct of both winter and summer campaigns were made evident in some of the correspondence dealing with the difficult campaigns of 1669–70. In late November 1669, the Duke de Vivonne wrote to Colbert indicating that the 150 oarsmen sent to him earlier as replacements had been especially needed on the three galleys whose forces had been most depleted. Those replacements had made it possible for the three weak galleys to accompany the others from the Hyères to Marseilles, even in the face of a stiff breeze. The squadron as a whole, he said, had "lost a very considerable number of oarsmen, but by great good fortune, very few good men were among the dead. The best of the oarsmen resisted not only the fatigues of the voyage but also all the other inconveniences against which we had no defense: the tainted water, the bad bread . . . and the cold that took us by surprise." [73] Two months later, in February, Arnoul sent a more detailed account of the same expedition to the minister, enclosing the latest roster of the oarsmen and an explanatory letter: "You know how many we lost in Crete [the recent expedition], from which they are still dying every day. The weather here now is making me apprehensive about the galleys that have been sent to Cività Vecchia. The cold is so intense and so extraordinary that I am giving two quintals [c. 200 lbs.] of coal daily to each galley, and the oarsmen are all shod with stockings and shoes or sandals (which cost me nothing beyond the labor of making them up since I already had sufficient old leather on hand). Nonetheless, not a day passes but that they fall sick, principally of frostbitten feet. You can see by the roster for each galley how many are lacking." [74] In these accounts, involving recovery from the ill-fated expedition to Crete and a campaign to Cività Vecchia in bad weather, it is evident that many factors were involved in the physical condition of the rowing force. There can be little doubt that winter weather aggravated the ill effects consequent on other circumstances; certainly weather could worsen any debilitation, such as that carrying over from the long march to Marseilles, or any persistent ill effects of campaigns in which an oarsman had taken part.

Even summer campaigns in good weather could produce casualties and mortality among the oarsmen. Indeed, one galley commander wrote to Colbert with a note of pride, saying: "I cannot omit making known to you that only thirty-six forçats died during the campaign, which is incredible good fortune [*bonheur*], for we lost more than eighty last year, and in other years the galleys of Malta have lost three hundred in making the same navigation that our galleys made this year, the air of the coasts of Spain and Sardinia being very unhealthy." [75]

One must consider, however, that very few oarsmen were obliged to sustain, in any one campaign, the effects of all the adverse circumstances that could be encountered. Most galley oarsmen managed to serve and survive a number of years. The compounded effects of fatigues in the march to Marseilles, the inadequacy of the rations received, the labor in working the oars, the tainted food and water that was sometimes consumed, the incidence of communicable disease among the crowded oarsmen, and countless other circumstances help to explain why there were few really long-lived oarsmen on French galleys. Yet some hardy souls did survive twenty, thirty, or more years at the oar.

Life Ashore

If oarsmen had lived the year around on the galleys without being able to work aboard or ashore, they could not have served the oar or the King of France with much effect. Work was an opportunity to improve both their diet and their general condition of life, and to give them some hope. Oarsmen were allowed to spend most of their days in port working at trades and professions or as laborers in the galley arsenal or Marseilles. The money they earned was the basis of the commerce de galère, by which the King and his navy, galley officers and crewmen, guild masters and entrepreneurs made gains. They all "exploited" the oarsmen. Wages paid to oarsmen were abysmally low; but there was no lack of work. If a man arrived at the galley base with a sound physique and was willing to work, he was likely to find the means to survive and buy food and wine to supplement his rations, whether he had previously been seaman, artisan, merchant, peasant, or laborer. With luck he might even be able to earn and save enough money to buy his way out of the galleys.

Some convicts and turcs had tiny shops in the baraques along the wharves adjacent to the galley anchorage; others labored daily, except Sundays and saints' days, on the galley itself at some trade or handiwork. Some worked at widely scattered places around Marseilles. Others left the galley daily at dawn with pertuisaniers accompanying them for regular or occasional work in the metropolis. Another group left the galleys to work in the naval arsenal itself.

The men working in the baraques were for the most part self-employed. Their occupations varied with previous experience — there were tailors, hatters, shoemakers, lacemakers, wigmakers, engravers, and even portrait painters; other men, more or less self-taught worked at wood carving, knitting, button making, or polishing coral and mother-of-pearl. This work was, of course, kept under close surveillance by inspectors, headed by a major of the port. The major and his aides patrolled to see that the stalls were never closed while occupied and to guard against any roguery within. Of course they willingly accepted small gratuities from the workers in the baraques, over and above the shop or stall rental. But generally, the artisans marketed their wares and services, either hawking their work at shops of craftsmen in the city or selling to passers-by. Though they experienced some trouble because of the opposition of some guildsmen in Marseilles, the men in this group, nonetheless, worked in their shops and stalls in comparative independence and tranquillity.[1]

Most galleys had at least one convict entrepreneur aboard, perhaps a businessman or master craftsman before his arrival in the galleys. Such artisans, aboard the galley, could function as overseers or even as merchant-manufacturers, employing other convicts. After all, the convicts aboard were a cross-section of the unprivileged rural, small town, and urban French working class of the time; many of them had no vocational skills that were of direct use to them on the galleys. One galley officer remarked that "most convicts on the galleys are men without a trade." Whether or not that was the case, most convicts took employment, if only as manual laborers, or learned some trade before they had been in the galleys for long. The comites had ways of dealing with those who showed reluctance to work; one memoirist asserted that slackers were obliged to carry a cannonball around with them all day until they went to work or learned a trade.[2] The entrepreneur served a useful function by teaching the rudiments of a craft or skill to other convicts and by employing them as apprentices. Such apprentices were no doubt ill paid for their work. But their apprenticeship did give them some income, and as the quality and volume of their production rose, they were paid more. Ordinarily, the products of their labor were turned over to the entrepreneur, who was apt to be the man who supplied their tools and raw material. The entrepreneur, in turn, marketed the finished products to wholesale or retail buyers.[3] This system, as is apparent, worked in much the manner of the putting-out system that was a normal feature of industrial production in Europe at the time. But abuses commonly associated with the putting-out system were apt to be much aggravated by the sanctions available to the employers, and the conditions of servitude, on the galleys.

Galley officials fostered this type of manufacturing enterprise in a variety of ways. The most experienced galley officers were persuaded that it was necessary to have convicts on each galley who had considerable funds, so that they could make advances of money, materials, or tools to other oarsmen. As one official remarked, the entrepreneurs "enabled others to subsist" by giving them work, by distributing silk or cotton thread for the manufacture of stockings, gloves, and other goods. The important role and the privileged status of these convict entrepreneurs is illustrated by a letter of 1740 to the minister from the Count de Maulevrier, a high-ranking galley officer. He explained that a certain entrepreneur had been "condemned to a double chain and confined to his galley, *L'Hardie*, for having attempted to escape." But these restrictions seriously interfered with the convict's business enterprises, and he was offering, said Maulevrier, to post bond of 1,000 livres as a guarantee that he would not again attempt escape; he also desired "the privilege of going into the city from time to time in the usual manner [chained to a turc or another convict and in the company of a pertuisanier] to attend to his affairs." Maulevrier sanctioned these requests saying that "since this convict has the greater part of the oarsmen [aboard *L'Hardie*] working for him . . . [he] deserves some relaxation of the customary restrictions."[4]

Equally useful services were performed by a few other convicts who worked aboard, or near the galley, in the unlikely role of educators. In the navy there was a recognized need for petty officers educated not only in the ways of the sea but also in the elements of reading and writing. To serve this need, Colbert saw to the enlistment in 1670 of a number of boys, twelve or thirteen years of age, orphans or the sons of petty officers, called prouvers. They were to be "reared and instructed to serve as comites or petty officers,"[5] and their education was confided to convicts. Though it is uncertain how many performed these teaching services, at least one was apparently thus employed on board each galley. In the 1680's six prouyers served on each galley in the nominal charge of the comite or an assistant comite, and they were required to take daily instruction in reading and writing from a convict aboard the galley where they served. In time, these classes came to include children other than the prouyers, for the most part children of junior grade commissioned officers. Probably the low cost of the instruction was a principal attraction. But the education received at the hands of convict teachers, in some instances at least, left something to be desired. The convicts, it was said, gave children "bad examples, to say the least," and in the 1690's many children were withdrawn from classes that had become objects of "public notoriety." [6] Finally, in 1706, since "it was not desired that the children be left in ignorance," a different sort of school was set up in the galley arsenal at the instigation of the Court. The École de Vertu was the name given to the new school, conducted by chaplains instead of by convicts. It was reported that here the children, including the prouyers, were taught "to know and to pray to God, and to read and write, with much success"; other reports were less complimentary, indicating that in the chaplains' school the children learned only the catechism and pilotage. After the death of Louis XIV in 1715, the Navy Board decided to abolish the École de Vertu, claiming that the instruction was unprofessional. In 1716 a certain Chaplain Michel was seeking a pension as additional compensation for his instructional services. The Conseil obliged the children to return to convicts' instruction aboard the galleys.[7] A decade later, in 1726, prouyers were ordered sent to Malta for instruction in the duties of petty officers, perhaps as a sort of postgraduate program for prouyers, under the auspices of the Order of Malta.[8] After all, it had been in imitation of the Order's methods that Colbert had formed the first group of prouyers in 1670. In any case, by giving useful training to petty officers, their children, and the prouyers over a long period of years, convicts added the profession of teaching to the range of their other occupations aboard the galleys.

Among the convicts to be found aboard the galley all day almost any day were many older and some weak or debilitated men whose physical condition forced them to conserve their strength by remaining on board. The sickest and weakest were ordinarily transferred to special galleys, usually hulks, destined to remain in port. Some other convicts were ordinarily kept aboard as punishment, or because they had attempted or were suspected of planning to escape. These men often carried chains of

heavier gauge or even double chains. Any man who showed himself in-
dolent, contrary, or generally uncooperative was likely to be abandoned
by the argousins, "and employed daily at the chores and fatigues of the
galley and arsenal" without pay and thus without any supplement to
the King's insufficient ration, with the result that "they soon became
sick from lack of nourishment and overwork."[9] In contrast to these,
there were a few other convicts selected for favored treatment by officers
or noncommissioned officers. A case in point was Jean Marteilhe, who
was employed by his comite as a personal lackey.

Convicts going into the city were often regular employees in the shops
or manufactories of the guild masters of the town. Many, in the early
eighteenth century, were employed on a monthly basis by the masters,
some of whom had numerous convicts in their employ. In 1702 no fewer
than 77 merchants, manufacturers, and artisans in Marseilles employed
convicts. These employers included masters in the linen trade, carpenters and cabinetmakers, shoemakers, buttonmakers, wheelwrights, locksmiths, blacksmiths and armorers, cutlers, pinmakers, founders, silk
workers, saddlers, workers in mother-of-pearl, wool combers, makers of
pulleys and chains, dyers, sculptors in plaster, pewterers, furriers, papermakers, and makers of measures and scales. The guilds governing these
trades entered a collective agreement with the Galley Corps in 1702.
Duly solemnized before a notary, this agreement set forth the terms under which convict labor would be supplied from the galleys, and suggested the general conditions of employment that the guildsmen would
provide. Each guild agreed to appoint a syndic to oversee the conduct
of three of its own members who employed forçats or turcs. Each syndic
was to submit an annual report to the navy's commissaire in charge of
oarsmen, and this report was required to be "an honest and exact description" of the oarsmen's behavior and treatment. It was further
agreed that none would be supplied to any master not "known to be of
careful and irreproachable conduct." When a master chose some convict to work for him, the argousin from his galley could not substitute
another, unless a change was justified by the master's abuse of the predecessor. The employers agreed to pay, for each convict used, twelve sous
a month to the argousin of the galley from which the convict came,
this sum to be paid in addition to the wages paid to the convict himself.
To ensure that the King's interest would not suffer by the escape of convicts in the custody of guildsmen, the guilds mutually and collectively

guaranteed payment of 1,000 livres to the King in event of successful escape, and rewards and expenses if an escapee was recaptured.[10]

This agreement formalized arrangements that had been in force, or in the process of development, for many years past. In France and elsewhere in Mediterranean Europe, slave and convict labor was commonly employed for industrial purposes when available. It had long been so at Marseilles. Indeed, forced labor had come to play an important role in the economic life of that metropolis by offering real advantages: whether skilled or unskilled, it was cheap. One memoirist writing at Toulon in 1662 underscored the cost advantages when he pointed out that twenty convicts could be employed for the wages of "four médiocre [average?] freemen."[11] Another writer spelled out the same differential in other terms, saying that convicts cost only five or six sous per day, whereas free laborers received at least twenty.[12] Since the labor of oarsmen was certainly less costly than that of freemen, it is understandable that there were bitter complaints from the guildsmen when, from time to time, galley officials ordered oarsmen kept aboard their galleys, as, for example, after a series of escapes. That happened at the end of January 1748. After the convicts had been kept aboard for a month, the master artisans of the city claimed, and proved to the satisfaction of Intendant d'Héricourt of the Galley Corps, that they were being ruined.[13]

Another body of men, apparently not covered by guild agreement, performed a variety of unskilled chores, serving for example as porters and watercarriers. They usually worked at such tasks in pairs, carrying a load suspended on a pole or bar between them. Many others labored in groups of half a dozen or more as stevedores or in the building trades; others worked as gardeners and even as household servants. Turcs were more often employed as domestic servants, though perhaps less frequently after 1695 when a law was promulgated requiring employers of turcs to pay 1,000 livres for any that escaped.[14]

Altogether, the men who went into the city, skilled and unskilled, forçat and turc, aggregated 1,400–1,500 men daily in the early eighteenth century (1707).[15] Of this number, over half were ordinarily skilled workers employed by the guild masters. These totals represented a decline from the levels of the last two decades of the seventeenth century, when the total force of oarsmen in the galleys was at its peak. Still later, in 1747–48, when the total rowing force had fallen to 4,200–4,800 men, those who worked in the city numbered 700–800.[16]

Convicts were not free to work or to go where they pleased in the city. There were restrictions. Employers were forbidden to use convict labor where bodily injury might result — thus damaging part of the King's rowing force. But experience proved to galley administrators that the two most serious dangers threatening the King's oarsmen in the city were escape and venereal disease. Time and again the pertuisaniers were informed that they must not, under any circumstances, allow their charges to enter "any house, or cabaret or other public place." Nor could they be permitted to rent rooms or basements in the city, as it was discovered they were doing in 1693.[17] In 1698 it was decreed that henceforth guards would be required to pay a penalty of six livres for each convict found to be afflicted with venereal disease; any guard found guilty of taking convicts into a house of prostitution would himself be put to the oar in chains for a month or more. The penalties imposed on the convicts themselves were of course even more severe,[18] and punishment was also meted out to the women who consorted with convicts in the city or who disguised themselves as convicts in order to be smuggled into the baraques on the wharves. These latter were deemed deserving of severe punishment. An order of 1688 decreed that women found in the baraques or in the rooms of soldiers and crewmen of the galleys would henceforth be condemned by court-martial to have their noses and ears cut off and in that condition would be led about the port as public examples. But repression, as later cases proved, did not have the full effect desired.[19] Down to 1748, repetition of these legislative prohibitions and penalties suggests the persistence of the problem.

Oarsmen who worked in the naval arsenal engaged in a wide range of occupations. Many performed heavy physical labor, but there were also skilled workers. A list of employees drawn up in 1706 shows that eight convict clerks were then employed in the office of the intendant, and ten others held posts in other administrative offices at Marseilles. They were paid 7 livres 10 sous a month. Ordinary civil employees performing the same services were paid wages of 20 to 50 livres a month.[20] Convict metalworkers were employed in the forges of the arsenal, and in Colbert's day the manufacture of anchors for the navy was largely carried on by convicts.[21] Apparently sailmaking also occupied some of them in the 1680's when the minister urged the advantage of having convicts in that trade; the King's outlay for the manufacture of such matériel, it was said, could thereby be reduced.[22] Unskilled convict labor was continually employed to move timber, masts and other heavy stores, equipment, and supplies around the docks and arsenal. Work gangs, comprising scores or hundreds, worked at cleaning the basins where ships were built and launched, dredging the port of Marseilles, and excavating for various construction projects. Detachments were occasionally sent to dredge the Canal of Arles (1669) and Port de Bouc (1695), or to undertake other work where much manual labor was needed at minimum cost.[23] In the early eighteenth century, detachments of two or three hundred convicts and slaves served at Toulon on a semipermanent basis, performing a variety of skilled and semiskilled tasks in the construction of sailing vessels.[24]

An observant visitor at the waterfront of Marseilles, noticing that there were not many turcs in the group working aboard the galleys, could have been informed that the turcs ordinarily left the galley each morning to work in the arsenal or in the city as manual laborers. Most turcs unlucky enough to get into the galleys were fishermen or seamen, and though some possessed a knowledge of shipbuilding arts, they apparently did not ordinarily have other industrial skills that they could use at Marseilles. But turcs enjoyed high repute as workers in the port and naval arsenal nonetheless. It was said that turcs were "adroit at anything you want them to do" in the arsenal.[25] Thus when the ministry was informed in 1689–90 that the local labor available around Rochefort was not sufficient to assure completion of the galley constructions planned, it was decided to send slaves from Marseilles to help out. Orders were issued for 100 to travel by sea to Cette, thence by canal to the Ponant, a distance of some 600 miles to Rochefort to assist in the construction of the galleys then being built at that port.[26]

The potential usefulness of turcs led the ministry of marine in 1692 to establish a special school in shipbuilding arts to give some of them special skills. About 100, mostly those too young to work the oar, were to be enrolled to learn the art of caulking galley hulls. They were to be paid three sous per day beyond their ordinary ration until they were "skilled enough to have their pay increased." Fewer than 100 of these young turcs were found to be available, and a number of "enfants de bourgeois de Marseille" were enrolled instead on a "temporary" basis, "until the young turcs are sufficiently numerous to make up the 100 student-apprentice quota for the school."[27] Young turcs and young bourgeois had in common a useful degree of detachment from the interests of the proletarian free workers, whose jobs they were to be trained to perform. Of course it was useful for young bourgeois to learn the value of hard work and a little spending money, and useful also for the young slave apprentices to increase their earning power by developing this skill, but the increase in their earning power was not the only objective in view.

The ministry was keenly aware that the cost of slave and convict labor was low compared with the cost of hiring free workers. Significant economies could be effected by using forced labor on works undertaken by the arsenal, and savings of an indirect sort could result if entrepreneurs who contracted to do construction jobs around the arsenal on a job or project basis were assured that they would be free to use oarsmen as laborers. Obviously, there were limits to the amount of forced labor that could regularly be employed without drying up the necessary pool of free laborers. But economy was the primary consideration from the ministers point of view, and the employment of oarsmen contributed to that because their labor was "controlled." The ministry was prepared to send oarsmen to any port facility where they seemed to be needed.

Free laborers did not welcome forçat and slave competition. They seldom do in any society. But in seventeenth- and eighteenth-century Marseilles they had to become accustomed to having a large pool of forced labor ordinarily available to their employers during nine months of the year, with the result that wages were kept at a relatively low level. A free worker might wish to improve his circumstances, as by changing his place of residence to some other city. He might move to other coastal areas, but such moves involved difficult problems, including problems with the administrators of maritime conscription. Most men living in coastal regions of the Midi had little choice but to tolerate the competition or wage-lowering potential competition of slave labor. Men from the galleys often worked beside free laborers in the city, at the port, or in the navy arsenal and shipbuilding yards. But the freemen did complain — sometimes bitterly — and occasionally some of them did more than just complain. At Marseilles in 1693, a group of freeman caulkers tried to halt the work of the young slaves then being employed in the building of merchant ships, but to no avail. Indeed, a decree was issued by the minister of marine in defense of the slaves, who were declared free to work without being troubled in any way by freeman caulkers.[28] Five years later, in 1698, a comprehensive ordinance forbade any worker of Marseilles, whatever his trade, "to maltreat any forçat or turc" employed in the arsenal on pain of a fine equal to three months' salary.[29]

The competition was most keenly felt by freemen when work gangs of convicts were moved out of Marseilles to other ports, particularly to small ports along the coast where jobs were scarce and freemen were unaccustomed to having convicts contending for their jobs. Gangs of convicts were moved to Toulon from time to time in the early eighteenth century, and even at that relatively large and populous port their presence in the labor market was nothing less than disastrous to the indigenous working class. The intendant at Toulon asserted, on one occasion, that "an infinity of workers, barbers, shoemakers, porters and others" had almost no work after the arrival of the convicts. He added that the sailors customarily employed as day laborers in the arsenal had lost their jobs.[30] All this mischief was attributed to the presence of a single galley at Toulon; the problems evaporated when that vessel was withdrawn. But in 1720, we might add, at the solicitation of influential businessmen at Toulon, who were navy contractors, and certain other persons, a request was submitted to the ministry of marine for 200 skilled convicts to be sent anew from Marseilles. The galley Éclatante brought them and was immediately disarmed, the intention being to stay for a considerable time. The oarsmen aboard were placed at the disposition of the navy contractors and businessmen at whose instigation they had been sent.[31] Another group was sent to Toulon in the 1730's. Economy was then the order of the day in the navy. Accordingly, the minister ordered substantial reductions in the wages of freeman port workers, including those at Toulon. In the expectation that the workers whose wages were to be cut might leave their jobs, a considerable number of convicts were readied and sent to Toulon from Marseilles. The convicts' wage was then only six or seven sous a day, whereas wages for free workers in ordinary times were twelve (or more) at Toulon. It was apparently a concession to the free workers that the convicts sent to Toulon were employed in port work only three days a week, "so as not to lay off too many free workers."[32] In effect, convicts and slaves were used as a convenient means of controlling free workers and of keeping their wages at levels deemed suitable to the interests of the State.

Convicts and slaves were also employed at Marseilles in bagnes. Similar establishments, often resembling prison compounds or stockades, existed at many other Mediterranean ports where slaves and others were confined for security purposes. Bagnes had long been established, for example, at Malta, Leghorn, and Tangier. The establishment of a bagne at Marseilles was proposed to Colbert as early as 1669. He accepted the idea that a bagne was perhaps necessary, not only to hold convicts and slaves in security ashore, but also as a place where they could work.[33] He ordered study of comparable establishments on Malta and in Italy with a view to developing a bagne at Marseilles, but he warned the intendant that any such new establishment should occasion "as little expense as possible."[34] The studies and plans made at his instigation had no immediate issue, perhaps partly because the vigor of French galley campaigning in the two decades that followed made a bagne seem superfluous. Louis XIV thought that his galleys should campaign in spring and fall as well as in the summer of the year. In those years when the oarsmen were campaigning six months or more, a bagne had at best limited utility. A bagne for Marseilles never seems to have been attractive to Louis as an economy measure.

The idea of a bagne was brought up again in the 1680's, then proposed as a means of dealing with the pressing problem of invalids. Invalids had become exceptionally numerous as a result of wholesale sentencing of Protestants, deserters, and others to the galleys, and vigorous campaigning by large fleets of galleys. Any man who was unable to serve the oar was classed as invalid, whether by reason of age, loss of limb, debilitated or diseased condition, or other physical incapacity. Such men were ordinarily kept aboard prison hulks at Marseilles. Such invalids had in many cases little or no work. By special concession, the King allowed each invalid a sou a day to supplement their regular ration, but even so, they languished aboard their hulks. The number of these invalids increased from the early 1680's onward. In 1683 the two hospital galleys together held 400.[35] A decade later, in the fall of 1693, no fewer than 2,000 invalids were being held, even though a great many had been disposed of in the intervening years. It seemed essential to get rid of them. M. de Bombelles calculated that each of these men cost the King 62 livres a year in food and clothing alone, making a total of 124,000 livres a year for men who were utterly useless on the galleys.[36] Various expedients were tried in the eighties and nineties to reduce their number, to ease the extremly crowded conditions aboard the hulks, and to reduce the useless expense. The establishment of a bagne was judged to be the most promising solution to the problem, but in 1695, as one memoirist remarked, "the war does not allow His Majesty to build bagnes for such a large number of invalids."[37]

In the spring of 1700 however, after peace had been temporarily restored, Pierre Charles, long an important navy contractor, and a group of Marseilles investors were awarded a contract by the navy to organize and manage a bagne at the base. Charles et Cie agreed to erect a large building on land owned by the King adjacent to the arsenal to provide living and work space for 2,000 or more invalid oarsmen. It was to include warehousing space, equipment for manufacturing, space for food storage, kitchens, latrines, and other facilities that would be needed by workers. The entrepreneurs agreed to make an initial outlay of 100,000 livres, to be repaid by the King within five years; their contract was to run for eighteen years. But since erecting the bagne would take time, the King placed a warehouse (the magasin général) at the disposal of the entrepreneurs to house the enterprise "temporarily" — an expedient doubtless convenient and profitable for the entrepreneurs. Necessary structural changes in the warehouse were completed in the fall of 1700, and the bagne actually went into operation and production as a manufactory in early 1701. Unfortunately, the entrepreneurs soon ran into difficulty, and by mid-1701 Charles et Cie, burdened by heavy debts from earlier enterprises, was bankrupt. Charles himself fled the country with some of his associates. But the bagne continued to operate over the years (1700–48) quite effectively despite changes in top management; the managerial and production methods adopted under the terms of the original contract of 1700 remained the basic pattern.

The contract of 1700 described the bagne as a place where convicts and turcs from the galleys could be lodged and maintained; could learn trades; could contribute to increasing the manufactures of the realm; and could contribute some self-support. It was in accord with these initial purposes that many hundreds of invalids were taken from the galleys and prison hulks and lodged in the bagne to work. But the new entrepreneurs refused to accept invalids whose physical or mental condition limited their usefulness as workers in any way! They were allowed by the terms of the contract to be selective, and only "able-bodied invalids" were accepted. Those judged to be too old or too weak, or who had lost arms, hands, or fingers, or whose eyesight had been seriously impaired, were left aboard the prison hulks, as were the R.P.R.'s by specific order from the Court. In consequence, fewer men than had been anticipated were accepted. To make up the full complement of workers promised by the contract with the entrepreneurs, able-bodied oarsmen were taken from the active galleys and assigned to the bagne. Presumably only the weakest of the able-bodied were sent, and their assignment was temporary; but the original contract specified that oarsmen "on the galleys" could be obliged to accept the opportunity to work for the entrepreneurs of the bagne. Its supposed function as a haven for invalids was thus subordinated to a new intended role as a workhouse-prison.

The significance of the change, and that of the bagne itself, was perhaps most clearly understood by the petty officers of the galleys. They saw that when men moved from the galley to the bagne to live and work, they were lost (some thought they "escaped") from their control. An oarsman making such a move no longer bought wine at the tavern on the galley, no longer paid a daily sou to his argousin to be unchained for work in the city, port, or baraque. He was lost to the galley as a consumer of the goods and services petty officers sold. Petty officers were touched in a most sensitive spot, their purses. The bagne was therefore bitterly opposed by most petty officers as an undesirable, impracticable innovation. Their spokesmen denounced the original contract with Charles et Cie: "It is not possible to teach trades to invalid convicts, the youngest of whom are fifty years of age, and nearly all [of whom] are sixty to seventy-five." "Nothing," they said, could be "more pernicious for the kingdom and the galleys than this contract" for establishing a bagne.[38] In response to such critics, one of the entrepreneurs of the bagne remarked ironically that the new establishment had only one defect: "It is a place that reduces the profits of comites, and that is a capital crime." [39] Failing to prevent the establishment of a bagne, the petty officers became alert critics of its administration, and at times the entrepreneurs were damaged by their criticisms; but the bagne itself was firmly rooted. Seeing its success, a considerable number of galley officers appear to have made common cause in prosposing an alternative bagne, with themselves as entrepreneurs; they proposed establishing a bagne général for 6,000–7,000 men in 1704![40] Though this visionary proposition got a negative reception in the ministry, there is no doubt that within a few years, the petty officers did manage to increase their representation on the administrative staff of the existing bagne, and in fact appear to have gained de facto control over its administration.

Though it was part of the initial purpose of the bagne to economize royal expenditure, that object appears to have been lost from view in actual administration. The building where the bagne was established was owned by the King. The structural modifications required to make it suitable as a bagne were paid for by him. Argousins from the galleys served as guards in the bagne, and their salaries and some other charges incident to the guarding of convicts and slaves in the bagne were paid by the King. The King assumed the cost of clothing for the non-invalid convicts and slaves in the bagne, and that of all the necessary chains, the mattresses, tarpaulins, and cooking equipment. Sick men were taken to the hospital and cared for at the cost of the King, and he assumed all charges incident to the conduct of spiritual life. These conditions characterized the establishment down to 1716. Conditions varied in different contracts, but the variations did not alter the fact that a substantial proportion of the administrative costs of the bagne were borne by the King; entrepreneurs of the bagne were the principal beneficiaries of the royal largess, and the supervisory employees in the bagne took another smaller cut. Incidentally, the invalid oarsmen well enough to work in the bagne enjoyed some benefits. They had a generally better standard of life as a result of their work in the bagne than they had in the hulks.

The entrepreneurs of the bagne were not run-of-the-mill businessmen. At the outset, through the association of the Marseilles banker Jean-Baptiste Milhan and the receiver general of Provence, Nicolas Simian, the company must have enjoyed the respect of the Marseilles business community at large. But the influence of these men was soon overborne. They were pulled down and out with the bankruptcy, disgrace, and flight of Pierre Charles, whose demise may have been related to the fact that the navy was very heavily in his debt, and he in consequence could not pay his own bills. When that first group of businessmen went out, André Dautan and his associates took over. Dautan was one of Pierre Charles' original associates, identified in the original contract simply as a "bourgeois"; he was, in fact, an active salaried official in the Galley Corps. But it was not as a royal official that he took over the bagne; it was, instead, as leader of a company of private persons seeking private profit! Apparently no conflict of interest was thought to be involved — the orthodoxies of business morality differ in place and time, even though the profit objectives and possibilities remain comparable.

The connections enjoyed by this second set of entrepreneurs were helpful in obtaining the initial contacts, and important in obtaining highly favorable contract terms. In fact, there is reason to believe that a search of notarial archives would disclose that these men were partners or agents of others, perhaps powerful, high-ranking men, in whose interest (as well as their own) they were authorized to act. The extent of the advantages enjoyed by the entrepreneurs strongly suggest that some powerful, partisan official influence was at work in their behalf.

The basic, continuing advantages have already been noted. But that was only the beginning. Contract terms included exemption from all excise taxes — royal, provincial, and municipal — on raw materials brought into Marseilles for use in the manufactory and on wine and foodstuffs for those employed in the establishment. The market advantages accorded to the entrepreneurs included an agreement by the ministry to buy from the bagne, by preference, all sailcloth, shoes, clothing, textiles, and other products produced that could be used by the Galley Corps. Since it was confidently hoped that the bagne could do more than supply the Corps, the entrepreneurs also enjoyed exemption from French export duties on those of their products destined for foreign markets.

These advantages were quite overshadowed by still more remarkable privileges accorded to the contractors in the matter of labor force. The oarsmen who composed the greater part of that force were actually subsidized workers not requiring remuneration large enough, in itself, to enable them to live. The amount and form of the subsidy varied in the various contracts signed by the entrepreneurs of the bagne. For example, in the contracts of 1700, 1701, and 1704, the King agreed to pay a subsidy of two sous a day for each convict or turc used. This payment more than covered the entrepreneurs' outlay for that part of the food and clothing they supplied to men working in the bagne. It was later reduced to 15 deniers, but with the condition that "His Majesty will remain charged with their maintenance and subsistence"![41] The contracting entrepreneurs could pay nominal wages because the wages paid did not have to cover the workers' necessities of life. Their contracts did oblige them to scale the wages to their workers "according to their capacity and the work they perform," but the scale was extremely low compared to the scale prevailing for free workers doing similar work.[42]

The organization of production in the bagne offered an easy solution to problems of absenteeism and lack of discipline with which many early manufacturers were troubled. Bagne workers lived and were fed in the manufactory, and slept on large mattress tarpaulins stretched out on the upper floors. Workers rose at dawn each day, went downstairs to the workrooms, and were already at work within a quarter of an hour after the gun in the arsenal had sounded reveille.[43] Of course, the entrepreneurs were forbidden by clauses in their contracts to employ oarsmen at any work that could "alter their health or diminish their strength." Such clauses were designed to protect the King's interest, but it was deemed no less fair and just that the interests of the entrepreneurs should be protected. Contract clauses provided [44] that convicts and slaves who "maliciously waste the raw materials or merchandise confided to them, or who throw them away [into the latrines], or who break or damage their tools, will be obliged to pay for such merchandise or tools with their labor, according to values determined by the commissaire." Workers "who leave their work and assemble to drink at hours other than those designated for meals, or who take more than the time prescribed for meals, will remain manacled in their places for a day on [a diet of] bread and water." [45]

To facilitate payment of their workers, the masters in the bagne were authorized by the King to issue "card money," that is paper or lead tokens, "in quantity sufficient to cover the daily wages." At the end of each month, at the latest, the entrepreneurs were obliged to convert these tokens into coin. They commonly took a commission for effecting this exchange. Though "all persons of whatever condition" were expressly forbidden "to take an exorbitant commission in converting tokens to coin, it is not clear what percentage of value would be considered "exorbitant." In fact, the rate at which card money was exchanged for coin, in 1708 for example, was extortionate. A convict was obliged to give six sous in card money or tokens for one sou in coin.[46] But he was probably well advised to accept the prevailing rate and make no complaint. His best course was to spend his tokens in the bagne. He was expressly forbidden to take card money or tokens out of the bagne on pain of confiscation; outsiders were forbidden to receive them on pain of 500 livres fine.[47]

The greater part of a convict's wages were apt to be spent in token form. As on the galleys themselves, the oarsmen could easily spend money. The most convenient and most popular place was the tavern, where all forms of tender, including credit, were honored. The tavern of the bagne was operated by comites, who brought their know-how from the galleys. When first established, the tavern in the bagne prospered too well. It was said that "the greater part" of the convicts' earnings then went to the tavern; indeed, the minister found it necessary to reprimand the entrepreneurs of the bagne, writing in strong terms, "I repeat that these convicts are not given to you to make the tavern pay, but to make useful products for the commerce of the realm." [48] But according to a memoirist writing in 1732, conditions had improved. He noted that "wages paid . . . in 1731 amounted to 41,048 livres, while the receipts of the tavern amounted to only 25,729 livres." [49] Though most of the convicts' money was thus spent for drink, at least part of the remainder went for food. Some, one memoirist wryly remarked, "are not content with their ration," which was "not sufficient for people who work" and therefore "they buy meat and other edibles." Bread, cheeses, fish, cooked meats, and other commodities were commonly peddled in the bagne by the convicts themselves or even by petty functionaries, and could be purchased either with card money or coin. Peddlers in the bagne, no matter who they were, had to have prior authorization in writing from the entrepreneurs, obtainable on payment of a fee.

As has already been implied, a wide variety of "fees" were collected, some in card money or tokens and some in coin, and such payments accounted for a substantial portion of earnings. The amount absorbed by fees depended, primarily, on the convict's work. Thus, a man going into the city on business, as men in the bagne were allowed to do under guard, was obliged to pay one sou in coin to his argousin each time he went. If a convict was ambitious or vigorous, and wanted to maximize his time at work, he could arrange to be unchained early each morning, and, in the evening, he could be one of the last taken to the sleeping hall to be chained for the night. Such an arrangement could usually be had for five sous a week (card money). Skilled workers and those working in a supervisory capacity had to buy this privilege; convicts who laundered clothing (usually four launderers in each hall) and those who worked as assistants at the tavern (three in a hall) were expected to pay this fee as a matter of obligation. Ordinarily, about sixty men in each hall were allowed the privilege of being unchained on Sunday or a saint's day; the fee for that privilege was one sou in coin. All the fees and perquisites mentioned here were paid to the argousins and their assistants because it was in their hands that the chaining responsibilities lay. In 1708 it was conservatively estimated that each of the work halls produced fees for its two argousins aggregating 1,400 livres a year. Each argousin received half of the 1,400 as his "gross." Of the 700 he received, half was has own, certainly a substantial addition to the regular salary of a non-commissioned officer. The other 350 livres was used to pay his aides — two assistant argousins and two cabin boys; there were also four convict aides in each hall who assisted with unchaining each morning and re-chaining at night, and who received "some small share of the take." [50]

The organization of manufacturing operations in the bagne was comparable in many respects with that on the galleys themselves. A few men worked independently at self-appointed tasks. Others, and notably those with the least skill in a trade or profession, worked for some convict artisans, some of whom had six or eight men, including apprentices, in their employ. In the bagne these convict entrepreneurs did not play the important role they did on the galleys. But their services were appreciated in the bagne, as on the galleys, because they trained apprentices and thus contributed to higher productivity and revenues. There were also a few freeman employers in the bagne, master artisans who took apprentices. These freeman masters sometimes relied on selected convicts to oversee and inspect the work of their fellows. When necessary, convict employers or overseers could leave the bagne, as they left the galleys, to go into the city in connection with their work under appropriate guard, but of course they paid an appropriate fee to an argousin.

Whatever the organization of the production, all workers in the bagne were subject to the control of the entrepreneurs, and all possible effort was made to see that every transaction or activity taking place there contributed to profits. Much, but not all, of the work performed helped the entrepreneurs produce supplies for the navy. They contracted to supply sails, tents, tarpaulins, stockings, shoes, and other articles of clothing destined to be used on the galleys themselves. Thus in July 1702, shortly after the bagne was organized, about four hundred men were employed at stocking manufacture, with seven or eight convicts supervising and inspecting the work of the others.[51] Production of this type was particularly favored by the managers because it could easily be taught and controlled by them; they disliked small-scale, individualized production. Their views and interests were quite consistently supported by the commissaires, naval officials presumably representing the interests of the King. In practice, however, most of the commissaires appear to have been little more than puppets of the entrepreneurs, lobbyists who explained the entrepreneurs' desires to the ministry of marine. Commissaire Rozel, for example, argued for the entrepreneurs against the interests of the King, misrepresenting to the minister, intentionally or not, the nature and amount of the cost involved for the King and those for the entrepreneurs — minimizing those of the King, exaggerating in his accounts the outlay of the entrepreneurs.[52]

Such commissaires were particularly useful to the entrepreneurs during the early years of the bagne. The War of the Spanish Succession created extremely heavy demands on the royal treasury. Financial crisis during that war led to heavy depreciation of bills drawn on subtreasuries to pay government contractors. The entrepreneurs of the bagne, as navy contractors, received such payments. They suffered losses on many occasions when they used them to pay for merchandise delivered to the navy's arsenals. They naturally complained about their losses, and tended to exaggerate. Losses of that sort constituted one of the usual risks for government contractors, particularly in periods of war. But government contracts, though fraught with great risk, could be enormously profitable for entrepreneurs who survived the crises because contracts gained entrée to privileges. The commissaires played an important role in the production of "profit," repeatedly representing to the ministry the dire need of the entrepreneurs. They were at least partly responsible for obtaining successive moratoria issued by the King in 1711 and 1712 on debts owed by the entrepreneurs. After the war, they were not only paid, but enjoyed the exceptional favor of being reimbursed for losses suffered on their depreciated bills of exchange![53]

The organization and operation of the bagne at Marseilles made it apparent that the King, not the entrepreneurs, carried most of the financial load. No less evident is the fact that within the bagne the convicts and turcs labored under oppressive conditions, though hardly more oppressive than those they experienced at the oar. Clearly, the principal beneficiaries of the bagne were the entrepreneurs. The petty officers and supervisory personnel took a smaller cut. But the oarsmen themselves also had a share — a much smaller share to be sure, and less clearly defined.

Though candid preferences and opinions were rarely recorded, and were in any case subject to many pressures, most oarsmen, both able-bodied and invalid, considered themselves better off in the bagne than on the galleys. There can be no doubt that it offered greater attractions for invalids than life aboard the rotten hulks anchored in the port, where the perennially crowded conditions and lack of remunerative work could lead only to physical degeneration and death. Though some of the entrepreneurs described their bagne (1703) as a "place of tranquility for the convict, a winter harbor where he can recover and increase his strength," [54] for both invalid and able-bodied men, the bagne was a workhouse. Even the entrepreneurs did not try to pretend that it was a pleasant place for a lazy man; the term *tranquille* does not describe a dawn-to-dark routine of work. Yet the bagne offered better shelter for the winter than any galley could. An oarsman might recover from the debilitation of campaigns by being assigned to the bagne. The work there was apt to be sedentary, and one could, if he chose, buy food to supplement his ration of bread and beans. In any case, both invalid and able-bodied oarsmen were led to volunteer for service there soon after it was organized. "Able-bodied volunteers go to the bagne," claimed one of the entrepreneurs, "because they are better off there, and because they earn more than they do by working in the city." [55] One of them asserted that a convict in the manufactory earned "9, 10, 12 and even 14 sous a day [card money was probably meant]." The entrepreneurs went so far as to claim that convicts in the bagne were "infinitely happier than the freeman worker." [56] But one entrepreneur added his opinion that they should not be allowed to "amass money, for which they have no use except to bribe people in the city to facilitate escape." The wage scale should be "reformed," he said (lowered), "so that the best workers cannot earn more than five or six sous a day, and the weaker three or four." One entrepreneur also claimed that unless this "reform" was made, he could not continue his work. He said he would be obliged to abandon his manufactory because he was "operating at a loss." [57] However exaggerated these claims appear, the fact remains that they were apparently persuasive in the ministry. In 1730 and 1732 the wages were "considerably reduced" by Intendant d'Héricourt because the entrepreneur was "in difficulty." Up to 1732, at least, the bagne offered some advantages for the oarsmen, including economic advantages, over the galleys themselves as a place of life and work.

But the bagne possessed one other advantage, one that was probably more significant than any other from the able-bodied oarsman's point of view. Once an oarsman was assigned to it, he was unlikely ever again to be brought back to the galley. In the eighteenth century, only a small percentage of the galleys in port and fit for the sea were actually sent on practice cruises or campaigns. Hence if the galleys assigned to campaign were in need of additional men, their deficiencies could be made up by selecting oarsmen of galleys remaining in port. Captains were unlikely to draft men from the bagne, where invalids and sedentary workers afforded wretchedly poor material for the oar. Most men would give anything to be freed from the oar, and no doubt many paid for the privilege of being transferred to the bagne — to escape the oar, perhaps also with an eye to better shelter and a bit more to eat.

The bagne was one of Marseilles' major manufactories in the eighteenth century.[58] It did long service for the Galley Corps as a producer of naval stores and general merchandise. It was no doubt a "high costproducer" as far as the King's interests were concerned, but it gave employment (even to invalids who otherwise would have had little work or no constructive employment at all), better shelter, and more to eat to many men. Royal funds were often expended with less salutary effects. Furthermore, the bagne had long-term value as vocational education for men who came to the galleys with no previous trade or manufacturing skills. For others, disciplined productive work was itself an opportunity for rehabilitation.

Apart from these well-established, regular employments on board the galleys in Marseilles and in the bagne, oarsmen were engaged from time to time in extraordinary occupations. For example, they served as pumpers aboard sinking ships on more than one occasion and as a fire brigade for the port of Marseilles. But perhaps most dramatic was their work during the plague that spread through the coastal provinces of southern France in 1720–23, halving the populations of Marseilles, Aix, Toulon, and the countryside.

Several features of this plague created demand for the oarsmen's services. Its coming was long heralded, intensifying fear and dislocation inspired by its specter and spread. From 1718 onward, reports were received at Marseilles describing violent and recurrent outbreaks in Egypt, Smyrna, Aleppo, the Ionian Islands, and Salonica.[59] Health officers redoubled preventive measures. But in spite of all precautions, including quarantine, the plague reached Marseilles in the spring and early summer of 1720. Slowly it spread, a few new cases at a time. Thousands fled in alarm. Health officers in surrounding areas soon erected a quarantine around Marseilles and its inhabitants, in the hope of isolating the pestilence.[60] Then, in July and August it began to spread through the city like fire, with murderous effect. Panic ensued. Thousands of people locked their doors against the plague, against friends, neighbors, fellow citizens, venturing on the deserted streets only for food. Few persons even attempted to carry on their usual jobs, however necessary. Merchants either fled their shops or were victims themselves. Notwithstanding the cargoes of grainstuffs sent, for example by the Pope and other authorities, famine was a terrible accompaniment of the plague.

Even more difficult to find than food were corbeaux to carry and bury the dead. The unburied, neglected dead soon could be counted in the hundreds, and by early August, matters were out of hand. The échevins petitioned the commandant of the galley base for help. As the Chevalier de Rance later reported to the ministry of marine, "we gave to Monsieur de Pilles and the échevins twenty-six of the convicts who were recently freed [but who had been unable to get out of the city because of the quarantine]." [61] These few were only a beginning. On 21 August 1720, thirty invalid convicts were transferred to the control of authorities in Marseilles. The ministry was assured that "the only convicts being used for this service are those sentenced for minor offenses." A few days later twenty more men were sent — "the inhabitants, paralyzed with fear, cannot bear the sight of the numerous dead in the houses and streets." Before the end of the month fully half the convicts committed to this work were sick with plague or dead. The commandant reported and asked approval of the petition for the transfer of 80 more, explaining to his superiors that this aid was being given "without inconvenience [to the navy] since these men [invalids and "rejects"] are useless on the galleys and the cost of feeding them is thereby saved." [62] The Chevalier de Rance wrote in similar terms: "We are dischargeing the galleys of useless men." [63] His action was approved.

Meanwhile the plague had begun to attack men aboard the galleys themselves. By 26 August, 225 lower officers, soldiers, and oarsmen were in the hospital, and 130 had died. From July 1720 to July 1721, apart from the mortality among the corbeaux, the total rowing force of 6,100 was reduced by only 882 as a result of turc and forçat mortality.[64] The hospitals of the region were in a pitiable state: nearly all the nurses and orderlies were sick or dead. Convicts had to be sent to help. It was said toward the end of September that "the convicts sent to the hospital to serve the sick remain there only a few days before they die themselves." [65]

Most of the convicts who fell sick speedily died; there were, however, some forty convalescents at the hospital who were put aboard one of the galleys to separate them from the others.[66] By mid-September four successive Capuchin chaplains had died while serving at the hospital, leaving the patients without spiritual aid; it was reported that the galley chaplains unanimously agreed that they would quit rather than accept assignment to the hospital.[67] If the spirit of St. Vincent had deserted them, it remained very much alive in the Bishop of Marseilles, who went himself among the sick and dying in the arsenal and town.[68]

By 6 September the city had received 260 convicts corbeaux. They were "extremely helpful," said the échevins; they buried 10,000 dead. But the situation was worsening. "Nearly all" the convicts previously given to the town were by then sick or dead, and those remaining were totally insufficient. There were untold numbers of dead in the houses, and "2,000-odd corpses have actually lain in the streets for many days, causing general infection." [69] The city sought another hundred convicts and with them (if they were guilty of crimes) forty soldiers and some officers; the officers were promised 10 livres a day, each soldier 50 sous, and "when it pleases God to deliver the city from this evil, 100 livres paid as a gift to each one remaining alive." [70] Even in the crisis, purses were held tight. But the men were sent. Before the end of September, twelve convict butchers had taken the places of those who had died or fled. In the months following, fifty-two other convicts distributed grain. A temporary hospital was thrown up by convict carpenters. Other convicts cleared the streets of debris, including furniture, bedding, and clothing thrown from houses by inhabitants fearing that contagion from those objects might communicate infection to them. By October 1720, it was estimated that 30,000 had died in the city proper, and another 5,000 or 6,000 in its environs.

Meanwhile the plague had spread east to Toulon and likewise to nearby Aix-en-Provence. Both these cities obtained convicts to remove and bury their encumbering dead and to care for victims. Aix was heavily hit and in November 1720 requested 40 or 50 convicts for hospital work; the arsenal sent a dozen.[71] The galley *Éclatante* happened to be at Toulon in the fall of 1720 when the plague broke out; seventy-five of its oarsmen were drafted to bury the dead. The following spring the contagion reached a high pitch — Toulon lost almost 14,000 people to the plague, about half its population — and there was desperate need for more men.

But it was decided not to take any more from the *Éclatante* in order to "save the good workers [skilled craftsmen]" who remained aboard; fifty other oarsmen, apparently "inferior" sorts, were selected at Marseilles and sent to Toulon, and by early May another fifty were sent. By mid-May only twelve remained in service, so still another hundred had to be sent.[72]

The plaque persisted in various parts of Provence until 1723. In all the urban areas affected, convicts helped the local population deal with the crisis. Between 800 and 1,000 took part in the work. A few of them, it is known, attempted to escape; but the vast majority did their dangerous jobs with remarkable resignation, devotion, and effect. They were partly motivated, no doubt, by the repeated promises that they would be liberated if they worked well and survived. Nearly all of them contracted the disease; almost two-thirds of them died.[73]

The labor of oarsmen had many uses, humanitarian, naval, and economic, but from many points of view the economic connections were especially significant. Oarsmen were allowed to save. Even "lifers," condemned to galères perpétuelles, were allowed to have savings and dispose of property by testament. Slaves were also allowed to accumulate funds. In this respect their status resembled that of prisoners of war rather than that of the usual slave of modern times, though in most other respects their treatment closely approximated that of slaves. Ordinarily, an officer, an écrivain, or the captain held oarsmen's savings — indeed, oarsmen were usually required to hand over for safekeeping any sum of dangerous size.

It was useful, indispensable, for oarsmen to work, to earn and to have funds. Galley administration was based on the assumption that oarsmen must be made to contribute to their own maintenance insofar as they could; the product of their labor was dispersed, as we have seen, piecemeal fashion to pay for their keep and to compensate their "keepers" — the officers of the Corps and the King.

Since oarsmen ultimately gave nearly everything they had in the form of labor and earnings, one might well ask if conditions might not have been improved had they simply been forbidden to possess private funds? Then, if the product of their labor had been placed directly into official hands, much abuse might have been avoided. But as must be apparent, such an arrangement would have withdrawn a keystone of the whole system of administration and finance. If such a proposal for "reform" had been made to a galley officer of the time, he would probably have responded by asserting that oarsmen would work well only when they believed they had a chance for gain. If their earnings were confiscated outright, oarsmen would have felt little incentive to work; it would have been necessary to motivate their work ashore by the same means employed to make them activate the oar — using lash or baton. That method was neither so cheap nor so effective in the long run as a system based on the interest of hungry men in obtaining the means of survival in the commerce de galère.

The work of oarsmen ashore and their earnings were the basis for an intricate system of exploitation. Yet the striking abuses of this venal system should not obscure the "benefits," or better say, the relative advantages that were incidentally conferred on slave and convict oarsmen. In spite of predatory inroads on their earnings, the average oarsman usually did have enough left to supplement whatever portion of the King's ration he actually received from his officers. There were some choices he could make in the disposition of part of his earnings. Most galley oarsmen had enough to eat. If they had little liberty, yet they had more than the inmates of most prisons of their time. And they did enjoy a greater measure of "security" than most of the King's "free" subjects were likely to have — perhaps a more significant comment on the general conditions of life in society than on the magnitude of the advantages oarsmen enjoyed. But galériens were also far more certain of having remunerative work than the peasant or proletarian free subjects of the King, and for inmates of the galley prison, work had a special value. Whether it consisted of heavy manual labor or the practice of a trade, work could mitigate misery. Work could afford a modicum of satisfaction to men who would otherwise have borne the added burden, and deadly effects, of combined idleness and chains. The men who worked in the galleys or learned a trade, as one forçat letter-writer said, could "more easily take the right road and marry," if ever he was able to get out of the galleys.[74]

Releases and Escapes

Any man who began to serve at the oars of Louis XIV's galleys was apt to do so for the rest of his active life, unless he had money to buy his way out. It made little difference whether he was condemned to serve a life term or a very few years. As long as a man could work the oar, any legal limit on his sentence was likely to be ignored. This was not a result of official negligence, or ignorance, or purposeful inhumanity, or any intention to increase the penalty for his offense. At least in theory, men were retained in the galleys beyond their term in the seventeenth century because the King needed their services.

Several years were required for a man to become accustomed to handling the oar and hardened to its fatigues. Not all men lived long enough to complete that training, and therefore those who did so were valued for their experience and hardiness. The rowing force was weakened, and the interest of the King ill served, it was thought, when seasoned oarsmen were released after serving a mere apprenticeship. Hence, as long as galleys were wanted for campaigns, releases from the oar were rarely granted until infirmity or age produced disability, unless outside influence was involved. This rule applied both to forçats and turcs, but not to Protestants. Religionnaires were not, if they had been sent to the galleys for religion-connected offenses, normally released at all, unless they became converts to the Roman Catholic faith, and even then they seldom obtained anything but indentured servitude in the West Indies. A great many regulations pertained to release, some theoretical and others practical. Some were the dictate or preference of the King himself. Others were decreed by ministerial authorities. Most appear to have been the product of administrative custom at Marseilles, of galley officers, or of medical and spiritual authorities associated with the Corps. In the aggregate, it might be said that the rules and customs constituted a system. They did not produce uniform procedure or equity in releases. That could hardly be expected from procedure that was primarily designed to make galleys effective operational tools for campaigns, and that also reflected both the policy and whimsy of the King and his bureaucrats and jailors, and that only incidentally rendered any consideration to equity or justice.

Until the last two decades of the seventeenth century, the rules on releases were dominated, in practice, by the idea that able-bodied men were needed at the oars. Many negative maxims were corollaries to this. For example, no releases were granted to second offenders or to any man whose condemnation represented commutation of another penalty; men guilty of an "atrocious" crime were in the same class and, as late as 1746, the class of "atrocious" crimes was large: high treason, poisoning, arson, theft from a church, blasphemy, counterfeiting, and forgery. To be guilty of any of these made a man undeserving of royal grace, presumably unfit for release and reintegration into society.[1] All the property of a man condemned for life was supposed to be sold and he was legally dead, which constituted a serious obstacle to his return to society. Lesser offenders could usually obtain release only after they had served longer than the term to which they had been condemned. Thus, thousands of men serving limited terms, usually of three, five, seven, or nine years, were released only after twenty or more. Hundreds of others served thirty or more years of life terms and then were shipped to America, or died in the service without being released. "Mort à l'hôpital" was the marginal annotation and epitaph for tens of thousands of men condemned to the galleys.

In general, three questions were likely to be asked about a man being considered for release: Is he invalid, disabled, or too old to be of use and hence "at the King's charge"? Can he supply a replacement — a slave or the price of a slave? Has he served the term to which he was condemned? In the seventeenth century, an affirmative answer to all three of these questions was a general prerequisite for release.

If physical examination revealed that a man was physically or mentally defective, he could be classed by medical authorities as invalid and transferred to a prison galley or hulk. He might live there for years in the company of amputees, men with damaged hands or feet or limbs, or extreme hernias, or with loss of sight or hearing; the aged; the insane; and some with debilitating diseases not thought to be contagious. All these lived together, usually on galleys considered as useless as the men aboard them. They were expected to work if they could; if a man was believed to be uncooperative or likely to try to escape, the standard treatment was not to allow him to leave the galley, where he was kept constantly chained, subsisting on the King's ration. Subsisting in any of these conditions, and if he was *not* a Protestant and had *not* been condemned for an "atrocious" crime, he had a fair chance of eventual release. If he had saved enough to supply a turc (or money payment instead), his chances of release were greatly improved. But in either case, if he behaved himself and enjoyed the favor of his argousin and comite, his name might eventually be included on one of the lists of burdensome invalids recommended for release. But as this description suggests, the sending of the name and favorable action by the minister was predicated on a great many "ifs."

Forçats serving abroad the galleys were of course well aware that invalid status was considered a prerequisite for release. Oarsmen simulated various incapacities; some bribed their way to invalid status. Upon assuming his duties, Brodart was instructed by Colbert to take special care to unmask the efforts "always used" to pass off able-bodied men as invalids. Forçats even attempted self-mutilation to incapacitate themselves; of course such actions were condemned by galley officials, and the punishment for purposeful mutilation was death.[2] This rigorous rule appears seldom to have been applied. When the ministry received a list of seven oarsmen who were said "to have maliciously allowed their feet or hands to freeze to make themselves invalid," the minister responded saying that it was the King's decision that the men concerned were never to be liberated unless additional reasons for their invalid status were proved.[3] To discourage self-mutilation, it was decided (as early as 1671) that efforts should be made to disparage invalid status as a prerequiste for release.[4] Invalid status retained its essential importance, but an effort was made to add other conditions to make invalid status less obvious a condition for release and hence less attractive to oarsmen. Beginning in the early 1670's, for an indeterminate period, ten or twenty of the eldest forçats who had given long service were to be released each year. The apparent theory was that this would encourage men to serve long and well at the oar; as a policy it could "only have a very good effect," said Colbert.[5] But of course invalid status continued to be a general prerequisite for release.

A man's financial condition was almost as important for obtaining release as his physical or mental condition. Oarsmen with money enjoyed an incomparable advantage. Even able-bodied oarsmen, in some cases, were able to obtain release by supplying replacements. For example, a certain Frionnet was promised his liberty on condition that he give thirty turcs in his place; subsequently he seems to have brought the price down to ten turcs or the monetary equivalent.[6] For the average invalid, it usually sufficed to supply a single turc or the money for one. The ideal candidate for release was the term offender who had "done his time," was invalid, and was able to pay for a turc. But such men were rather rare. Colbert had to lower the standards and contented himself with getting as much money as possible from each candidate. In 1678 the minister wrote Brodart in regard to a group of a hundred invalids over sixty years of age, whose names the King had already approved for release: "It is difficult to believe that these men have not earned something since they have been in the galleys; you can easily find out how much they have. See if you can get something from each one of them or from most of them — a turc or some money toward the purchase of a turc — 100 to 300 livres. His Majesty leaves the matter of the amount to you." [7]

Money paved the road to release in other ways too. To persuade men to act in behalf of his release, a man needed money. The King himself took payment for releases, and administrators of the Corps were thereby encouraged to do the same. More or less numerous releases took place on what might be called fraudulent grounds. Such releases were subjects of memoirs of complaint in the eighties and nineties. One such report of 1691 by the captain of one galley, de Viviers, claimed that the King's regulations had long been flouted. "The self-interestedness of commandants, and that of the intendant, and above all that of the clerks and men who work under them have contributed to render royal regulations null and void. . . . [The intendant] seeks to assure himself control over the choice of invalids proposed for release, without allowing the captains to have any say in the matter." No less guilty, in Viviers' view, were the clerks and lesser officials. They profited from "negligence in the choice of invalids," by managing to include on the rolls sent to the minister "not only actual invalids, but many of the best men in the galleys, who have the means of putting a turc in their place and at the same time of giving [the officials] considerable sums." [8]

Viviers had complaints of his own to air. On returning to Marseilles in 1688, he said he found that five of his best oarsmen, two turcs and three forçats, had been released during his absence. "These five, all first oarsmen, were liberated under false pretenses, as I proved to the intendant." All the other galleys were similarly treated, said Viviers, but without their captains having complained "either because they did not know any better, or out of consideration for the intendant, whose responsibility it was, or because someone has imposed silence on them, or because they have scruples in meddling with the liberation of a great number of poor unfortunates." But the worst aspect of the result, as far as Viviers was concerned, was the fact that after a large number of good men were liberated from the galleys, the captains, himself included, were obliged to take aboard new arrivals or even semi-invalids for the next campaign.[9]

More might be said than Viviers chose to say regarding the abuses of the captains themselves. Most captains wanted "choice men," and naturally, they opposed liberating first-rate oarsmen. But captains were inclined to overlook, even to favor, the release of third-rate oarsmen, since the replacements might be stronger. It was with reason that the minister warned that some captains "imagine a forçat is useless when he isn't a first- or second-class oarsman." [10]

Colbert sought in the mid-seventies to guard against abuse in releases by fixing forçats and turcs permanently on galleys where they served. When they were moved about, their length of service, term of condemnation, and even their identity tended to become lost — even names were changed. Multiple "mistakes" and "oversights" prepared the way for illicit releases.[11] When attached to the same galley with the same officers and men for years, the able-bodied oarsman could not so easily be reclassified as invalid; there was less chance to cover or excuse illicit release. But in the 1680's and early 1690's, larger numbers of galleys and great numbers of newcomers, including Protestants and deserters in increased numbers, helped produce confusion of identity; still greater confusion was introduced in 1689–90 by the new galleys built at Rochefort. Hundreds of oarsmen from Marseilles and a number of chains regularly directed to Marseilles went to the several temporary galley bases on the Atlantic seaboard. Further confusion must have resulted from the recruitment of many hundreds of peasants in the coastal provinces and the conscription of others to serve on the Rochefort-built galleys as salaried oarsmen. Eventually, this mélange of men was divided: part of them stayed on the Atlantic galleys, most of the peasants were discharged, and the remainder of the forçats and slaves were sent back to Marseilles. Such transfers of large bodies of men and the irregular ways in which they were acquired and held created convenient confusion over the identity of the oarsmen, and must have created problems to which the security system and bookkeeping used in Colbert's day could be adapted only with difficulty, if at all.

The illicit release of able-bodied men and the retention of invalids helps to explain why invalids were ever more numerous during the eighties, but other factors were of greater importance. Campaigns, especially those of many months' duration and those taken in the winter, wrecked many able-bodied men. "Reflect," Brodart wrote the minister in 1676, "that last year 500 forçats died [on campaign] and in addition, the galleys left behind more than 200 invalids; with those on hand here, that makes nearly 500 [invalids]." [12] That was the toll for a single campaign, and there were campaigns every year though not usually so costly. Finally, new chains arriving at the base often included invalids.

In sum, more invalids came into the navy's hands than were released in the period 1670–90. In the 1670's one old galley was set aside as quarters and hospital for invalids; by the early 1680's, several galleys were being used for that purpose.[13] When Bégon became intendant in 1686, about 1,400 invalids were on hand — a continuing unnecessary expense and a serious problem.[14] Of course the problem was not new, but it was Bégon who first attacked it with notable vigor at a time when its magnitude was great.

In recurrent fashion, before Bégon's administration, the American colonies of the French had been used as a dump for invalids from the galleys because it was believed undesirable for many reasons to try to reintegrate such men into French society. Transportation was encouraged by the fact that the minister of marine for the navy was also responsible for administering the colonies. But the transportation of invalids to the West Indian colonies involved disadvantages, known at least as early as the 1660's. La Guette then reported that when such men had been sent to the colonies in the past "a good number of them died." [15] Bégon, two decades later, must have thought that the earlier misfortunes attending transport to the colonies had been "exceptional" and perhaps avoidable. In any case, Bégon proposed and the King approved in 1685 sending 86 "useless" Negroes on hand to the West Indies, and they were sent.[16]

At the same time Bégon began to wrestle with the more serious and difficult problem of forçat invalids. Forçat invalids had little hope of release in France; as we have seen, the King consistently showed himself opposed to the idea of permitting lifers to re-enter French society.[17] This was not mere perversity on his part. The return of a man to his native place after he had been condemned to the galleys for life involved tremendous problems of human adjustment: being legally dead, the returnee had no property or rights, and experience showed that there were apt to be delicate situations in the relations of the returnee and persons connected with his original arrest, imprisonment, and condemnation. Yet the rule that lifers would not be released seemed to mean that invalid forçats were indefinitely on the hands of the Corps, unless they could be sent out of France. Hence Seignelay sanctioned Bégon's idea of getting rid of them by shipments to the West Indies. After obtaining royal approval, he ordered that invalids of various types — term offenders, lifers, and men condemned to the galleys by the salt farmers — be sent to America at the King's expense, the last group at the tax farmers' expense. He also observed that "in order to take the greatest possible advantage from the shipment of these forçats, they should be sold as indentured servants to the inhabitants of Canada and the Isles, according to their strength and the service they can render."[18] The minister ordered Bégon to prepare a memoir on the "monetary value of the sugar that the inhabitants of the Isles St.-Christophe [St. Kitts], St.-Martin, and St.-Croix must pay for the invalids distributed to them." He wanted to know whether the cost of shipping them would be covered by their sale.[19] Whatever the details, the King (and the tax farmers as well) were unburdened of a considerable long-term expense. In 1686 alone, at least 821 invalids were sent to the Americas.

Bégon and Seignelay showed satisfaction as successive shipments were dispatched, but the forçats were remarkably ungrateful for the efforts made to transport them to the "promised land." Some, in fact, were violently opposed. In 1686, when the time arrived to take down the names of men to be sent to America, the forçats aboard one galley actually rebelled. As reported by the Bailiff de Noailles to the minister, "There was a revolt on the galley *La Vigilante* eight days ago. Some [forçats] threw themselves on the register [in which names were being written], and tearing up the pages, put themselves in a state of defense. The sieurs Dumont and d'Espinay, and the guard corps stopped the tumult with a few sword thrusts . . . The criminals were tried and the two most guilty were hanged on Saturday as an example . . ." [20] The officers were partly to blame for this affair, the Bailiff said, because they had told the forçats that only those who wanted to go would be sent to America. Noailles remarked that the forçats "had drunk a little more wine than usual"; but we can be certain that their opposition to being shipped to the West Indies had rational grounds. To be sent to America meant exile. A man thereby lost virtually all hope of seeing again friends or family in France. But perhaps most decisive were the rumors about the earlier invalid forçat "emigrants," who had found it difficult or impossible to adapt to the slave economy of the Indies.

Seignelay and Bégon could also have known these facts from their files. Either they did not credit the reports, or they assumed that conditions had changed or would be different on different islands. They were aware, however, they faced an immediate problem, disposing of the many hundreds of invalids on hand. Soon after the new shipments were sent to America, the minister was informed by the governors in the West that the islands were "surcharged" with forçats. In 1690, when Bégon proposed sending invalids to Cayenne, he was turned down flatly by the minister, because, "the King is informed of the disorder caused by the forçats previously sent to the Isles, the greater part of them having died of misery or fled to [our] enemies." [21] Indeed, by 1695 the governors of West Indian colonies had tried to get some of the remaining invalids sent back to France, "not knowing how they could be used" and having them at their charge.[22]

When invalids could not be shipped off to the West Indies or Canada, they accumulated. One memoirist suggested in the early 1690's that since they were so burdensome to the King, perhaps some of the 2,000-odd men then at hand could be liberated on condition that they serve as soldiers aboard the galleys; after all, some ex-forçats served on galleys as petty officers. Many arguments were marshalled against the scheme.[23] Yet the expense was undeniable: each invalid cost the King 62 livres a year or more. There were over 2,000 invalids. The grand total, some 125,000 livres a year, was not an unbearable burden for a monarch who gave away such sums to courtiers and friends and who spent scores of millions on Versailles but such expenditures were not to be compared. In the Galley Corps and especially when forçats were concerned, 125,000 livres bulked large. Therefore, serious thought was given to disposing of these useless men who occasioned needless expense. Some invalids, it was admitted, had to remain on the galleys because they were considered good for nothing or because they were guilty of "enormities" or of lesser crimes that "cannot be corrected." It was supposedly for the latter sort of men that the bagne was established in 1700.

But there were other invalids and near-invalids who, in the early eighteenth century, were considered fit for soldiering. Their strength would probably increase, it was said, if they received their liberty. They could usefully serve either in the regiments or in the garrison troops of His Majesty.[24] Numerous proposals of this nature were made in the 1690's, and during the hard years of the War of the Spanish Succession (1701–13) hundreds of recruits were obtained in this way. Especially after 1708, being desperately pressed for soldiers, the King consented to release hundreds of men from the galleys, many of them invalids and lifers, on condition that they serve with his troops in Spain. A list of over 1,500 such "recruits" was sent to the minister in 1712, and that was an unprecedented number of men to be recommended for release at one time. Ultimately over 2,000 men were released and sent to Spain. All the maxims and rules were forgotten in arranging this exodus. The principal criterion of selection appears to have been financial: Does the forçat want to serve with the troops in Spain and, if so, how much will he pay? Thus the contingents of "invalids" for Spain included many "valid" men, still quite capable of serving the oar. It was reported later that "some of the best men in the galleys" went to Spain. Many paid bribes to be sent. Bribery became so notorious that Marshal d'Estrées and the Regent himself took note of it in 1716, saying that "the public was not so charitable as to believe that these men had not paid [bribes to] the clerks and scribes, or that the galleys of the King were ruined for nothing."[25] Officials of much higher rank than clerks must have shared the proceeds. The Sieur de Rozel, commandant at Marseilles, defended this release of able-bodied men by pointing out that they "have to make a long and difficult march [to Spain]" and there face "the necessity of making war in that burning climate"; in his opinion, that was "a more proper way for them to expiate their crimes than to leave them tranquillizing at Marseilles." [26]

A more delicate problem was that of getting rid of invalids who were or had been religionnaires. The King was steadfast in his contention that no Protestant would be released to return to French society; the Church naturally opposed their release and reintegration. Though Protestants were, in most cases, technically condemned to the galleys for their failure to obey the orders of the King, the grounds for condemnation and retention were fundamentally religious in nature. That was apparent in the fact that the King did grant releases (albeit rarely) after a religionnaire had renounced his Protestant views and embraced Catholicism. Many cases illustrate this policy of favoring conversion by grants of release — for example, fifteen religionnaires released "in recognition of their good conduct," with the expectation that they "would not fall into error again." D'Estrées asked in 1717 for a list of "forçats religionnaires convertis who are doing their duty" so that releases could be granted "to those who are fulfilling it best." [27] Released converts were often sent to America, but occasionally some went back to their native place or were sent back as examples for others. But in general, the King would not consent to a man's release if he remained a Protestant. Explicit exceptions to this rule arose in 1698, when, following the Treaty of Ryswick, Louis consented to the release of a number of French Protestants who had been taken prisoner while serving aboard English ships captured by the French, [28] and when the Dutch Ambassador, Heemskerk, reported that after his multiple petitions the King had consented to release a certain number of religionnaires. [29] But these were special cases, strongly supported by a foreign power.

Louis XIV remained unmoved by entreaties from abroad throughout the negotiations for peace in 1713, even when plenipotentiaries of the United Provinces, the United Kingdom, Prussia, and other states tried to negotiate the release of religionnaires held on French galleys, and the treaty of peace finally signed at Utrecht did not call for their release. On that issue, Louis would not allow himself to be forced. Within a month, however, Louis did consent to release 136 "incorrigible" Protestants (religionnaires obstinés), on condition that they leave his realm, along with 47 others who had become converts in order to remain in France; in 1714 he liberated 44 others.[30] This seems to accord with the views of some historians who contend that Louis took a somewhat softer attitude toward the Protestants at the very close of his life. When the old King died in 1715, the Regent, of whom the Protestants had high expectations, consented to a few more exceptions to Louis' policy; liberty was accorded to 96 Protestants in 1716–17.[31] But these releases did not herald the advent of a more enlightened policy, as French and foreign Protestants apparently hoped it would. As d'Estrées pointed out in 1717, a serious disadvantage of releases granted to religionnaires obstinés was that they had the effect of destroying the work of the missions seeking conversions. "If they have hope, no new conversions will be seen."[32] The years that followed saw religious persecution continued. Protestants served on French galleys through the first two-thirds of the eighteenth century, and relaxation of policy in the matter of releases came only in the 1740's, and then very gradually.

The action of the Navy Board in the decade after Louis XIV's death underscored the fact that the "enlightenment" had not dawned. The Conseil resorted again to shipping invalids to the American colonies. As early as November 1715 twenty-one men were ordered sent to the West Indies. The captains of merchant ships at first refused to take them aboard unless they were paid 60 livres per head, but finally were obliged to take them as indentured servants.[33] In the spring of 1717 thirty-eight "vagabonds" were arrested in the environs of Paris, and being deemed of no use on the already overcrowded galleys, they too were sent to the colonies.[34] The Conseil de Marine was unaware of or ignored the fact that earlier shipments had not been wanted by colonial administrators, who reported that "the greater part" of the men already sent had "died of misery."[35] Lessons on colonial policy, however, were not easily learned in the ministry of marine. The West Indies, at least, was considered a dumping ground for unwanted men and remained so even in the 1720's. Imagine the chagrin of the 239 corbeaux who survived their dangerous labors during the plague of Provence, to be informed by decree that they would receive the promised releases only if they consented to be sent to the West Indies.[36]

The turcs presented special problems in the matter of releases. Their status was indefinite. Some turcs captured by the French in wars with the North African states were technically prisoners of war. Others had been purchased in slave markets, such as Leghorn and Malta. But the status of the turc, the manner in which he had been taken, his port of origin, and other details mattered little on French galleys; nor did it make much difference as long as he served French galley oars. If his status was equivocal, it was convenient for the service that it remain so until the question of release arose. Even then, a turc could be considered a slave or a prisoner of war, as suited the interest of the King and his administrators. If the monarch decided to resell a worn-out turc on the slave market, the turc was clearly considered a slave. If the King signed a treaty for the exchange of some of his turcs for French prisoners held by North African states, the turc was a prisoner of war. More ambiguous still was the status of eastern Mediterranean turcs from the Ottoman Empire, with which Louis had friendly ties and some of whose subjects were more or less surreptitiously enslaved on French galleys.

Generally, however, utilitarian rules applied to turcs just as they did to forçats, and turcs were retained as long as they were useful at the oar. Having served to the end of their strength and being classed as invalid, they constituted a form of "surplus" or waste destined to be dumped or sold for whatever they would bring. Seignelay shed light on the official attitude toward the problem in a letter to one of his Italian consuls: he said the King was aware "of the great number of invalid turcs on his galleys who are causing expense, and from whom His Majesty derives nothing. He has resolved to be rid of them. To this end, he has ordered that they be sent to you for sale [on the slave market at Leghorn]." [37] Worn-out turcs did not bring much on the Italian market, but they did defray the expense of their shipment and sale. There were disadvantages to that method of disposal, as the consul pointed out, and other methods were tried. One method proposed by Arnoul was the exchange of invalid turcs being held at Marseilles against invalid Christians being held by North African states. Colbert approved the idea and in 1673 ordered Arnoul to take whatever measures he thought necessary to bring about such exchange.[38] But Colbert had some second thoughts: "An awkward disadvantage could result if some [of the turcs] were returned to Algiers and Tunis. They could inform the Divan how many turcs from those cities are present on the galleys. That would produce a demand that they be returned; His Majesty's refusal could lead Algerian corsairs to capture merchant vessels belonging to the subjects of His Majesty." [39] This hesitation may have been motivated by the desire to protect commerce; it may also have been grounded on the desire to block the exchanges about to take place.

Certainly it did not facilitate exchanges to insist, as Colbert commonly did, that each turc should be obliged to pay the King for his release. The amount depended, apparently, on how much he could pay. The intendant received a suggestion from Colbert, in the King's name, that some turcs could probably provide able-bodied slaves to take their place, "in which case His Majesty will grant them release. As for the others, since they are entirely useless to the service, His Majesty desires that the means be found to send them to their own country in exchange for an equal number of old Christians." [40] Those orders, issued in 1676, appear to have become standard operating procedure for releases of turcs in the years immediately following. They were repeated in 1677 and 1678, with the added proviso that 100 écus (300 livres) from a turc was acceptable in lieu of a replacement turc.[41] Thus the turcs, like their fellow oarsmen, after being exhausted of physical usefulness, were drained of financial resources, and then, having become a liability, were considered ripe for release or exchange against those of the King's subjects held in slavery abroad.

Treaties were the usual means of bringing about exchanges of invalid turcs for invalid Christian slaves. However, sometimes exchanges took place even when existing treaties were in other respects void. Nor were all the turcs released under treaties invalid men, though doubtless some galley officers preferred that they be so. Unfortunately, from their standpoint, a great many able-bodied oarsmen were among the several hundred turcs released in the early 1680's under the treaty arrangements made, again and again, with Algiers. For example, among fifty-six turcs approved for release to Algiers in May 1685, only ten were invalids.[42] It must have seemed futile and foolish (from the naval viewpoint) to release able-bodied men, the cream of the rowing force, in the interests of amicable relations with a North African potentate who might soon make some excuse for resuming hostilities. As a punitive gesture, or perhaps to hide the fact that turcs were held, one memoirist thought it might be a good idea to get rid of the Algerian invalids by sending them to the American colonies. But Seignelay ruled that out because "invalid turcs can be turned over to the Algerians in event peace is made with them, and [they] might even facilitate the negotiation [of peace]." [43]

Releases and Escapes

Louis XIV would have agreed with Seignelay on that. The King made it clear that his intention was to use the slaves on his galleys for the implementation of his policy of obtaining and maintaining peace with the Mediterranean Moslem states. Hence his views on releases of turcs, from the early eighties onward at least, contrasted sharply with the views of some galley officers. Louis sanctioned regular and effective program of exchanges with the North African treaty states, involving the release of all prisoners of war held as slaves on his galleys, able-bodied or not. Clearly he gave the preservation of his treaties of peace with the infidels high priority. The preservation of the slave contingent on his galleys was, by comparison, a matter of no consequence at all.

To effect the actual exchanges of prisoners, Louis was apparently disposed to rely on the help of religious. Until 1683, when the principal concern was to arrange the release of Christians held in North Africa, or to get rid of old and invalid turcs, the Redemptorist orders and the navy functioned with a minimum of surveillance and hindrance. Both made use of the Papacy's "Apostolic Vicar of Barbary," Père Le Vacher, who doubled as French consul in Algiers until his death (by execution) in the bombardment campaign of 1683. The whole consular operation as far as releases of Moslems was concerned was thereafter conducted under relatively careful ministerial surveillance, and, in accordance with the King's "peace policy," the number of slaves on the galleys shrank in spite of the efforts (described on pp. 160–172 above) to obtain substitute slaves from non-treaty sources.

Both able-bodied and invalid turcs were included in releases after 1690, quite indiscriminately, and the earlier stress on "man for man" exchanges appears to have been dropped. It was assumed that the North African governments would release all Frenchmen held as soon as practicable, and there was no apprehension about the possibility that France might release more slaves than the North African treaty states did. The interest of both peace and trade treaties was to be served regardless of numbers. Among the many rosters of turcs drawn up, one listed thirty "turcs de Tunis on the Galleys of the King that His Majesty orders be transferred to the directors of the Compagnie du Cap Nègre," and about the same time (1692) 210 turcs were ceded to the Divan of Algiers.[44] Turcs were released from the galleys because their liberation could serve the higher policy purposes of the King. Sometimes they were explicitly given as gifts, as with the release of eight turcs in 1691 for presentation to the Algerian envoy visiting France.[45]

A very few releases of turcs continued to be arranged under religious auspices. The Redemptorists (in this context perhaps especially the Trinitarians) devoted themselves to the liberation of Christians being held in infidel hands, and in carrying on that work they occasionally sought the liberation of a turc from French galleys for exchange against a particular Christian being held abroad. Such was the purpose in 1721 when they sought release of a turc whom they planned to exchange for the Frenchman, Ramond Dicasse(?), native of Valence in Guyenne, who was then held in Morocco as a slave. The proposition was initially declined by authorities, "in view of the small number of turcs on the galleys." But the religious apparently persisted, and eventually the turc's release was arranged.[46] The religious of the galley hospital, mostly missionnaires, only with great difficulty managed to obtain the release of one turc whose part they took because of his work in the hospital and because he had become a Christian.

Conversion to Christianity was one means, outside the context of treaties, by which aged or invalid turcs might obtain release from their chains. Even suspected renegades, or "men found among the turcs," as on privateers, were sometimes held "until they profess the Roman Catholic faith."[47] But for a turc, the act of becoming a Christian had sweeping implications; conversion might break the chains that held him at the oar, but it did not confer freedom. A Christianized turc could not readily return to his Moslem homeland. Indeed, in seventeenth- and eighteenth-century Marseilles, he was surely a man almost alone, ostracized by his own people and alien to the French. A few individuals managed to do reasonably well in these circumstances. In 1694, the King ordered the release of a Tunisian turc named Noé Chaban, "on condition that he embrace the Catholic Religion and pay the 400 livres he offers, and [that he] continue the commerce he conducts on the galleys, by which a number of forçats subsist."[48] Small numbers of Christianized turcs at Marseilles are occasionally alluded to in the documents, and possibly they had some group life of their own. A letter dated 1717 indicates that there were then sixteen Christianized turcs at Marseilles, and it was said to be a long-established custom for each of them to be issued a daily bread ration by the arsenal officials. When a question arose as to the authority for the issuance of those rations, no written authorization could be found, but the rations had been issued for many years past. Without the rations, it was said, they would "perish of famine," being "without vocation, unable to work and unable to return to their native country because of the change of religion." The Navy Board, in response, authorized "continuation of the established charities." [49]

Many of the turcs were liberated over vigorous opposition of men of the Galley Corps who considered turcs the backbone of the rowing force. Because of the King's treaties, exchanges, and occasional gifts of slaves to foreign potentates, and the accompanying shortage in the markets supplying suitable types, the proportion of turcs in the rowing force gradually declined between 1680 and 1720. The fewer turcs there were, the more tenacious the officers appear to have been of those that they had. In 1723, when a few old but still able-bodied Moslems offered 800 livres apiece for their liberty, twice the amount usually sought in forçat releases, the officers strongly opposed their release. The Count de Roannes declared that the captains and all the comites were of the opinion that "even the worst of the slaves is absolutely necessary at his oar, even if he is nothing more than a quarterol. M. de Vaucresson and I are of the same opinion." Two of the turcs were fifty years old, and each had spent thirty years at the oar. But their age and experience, said Roannes, only increases their value, especially for the instruction of young, incoming turcs. "They can still serve for some years . . . My advice is to liberate none." Clearly, there were few left and the officers wanted to keep every one! The ministry of marine made an issue of these cases, and even the officers eventually had to concede that releasing the handful of men involved would not break the Corps; indeed, they were moved to admit that their release might even infuse new strength in the rowing force if the money offered for release was used to buy young and vigorous replacement slaves.[50]

Given the rigor of life in the galleys and the uncertainty of release, attempts at escape were frequently made. As in any prison establishment, security was a thorny and perennial problem, one that was never solved — no matter what measures were taken, attempts to escape were bound to be made. And with luck, patience, determination, and a lifetime to give to the effort, a considerable number of men were certain to get away using novel, unpredictable, or even age-old techniques known to prison wardens in any age. Chains could be sawn or filed; guards could be found asleep, evaded, or bribed; and in Marseilles, one of the largest cities in France, many hands offered aid out of kindness, compassion, or for a price. One intendant, who knew well the problems of keeping men in chains at Marseilles, urged a subordinate to remember that "all the world is against you."

Without hope of total prevention, the best course for galley officials was to reduce the number of escapes by all possible means. Distinctive clothing and haircuts for oarsmen of different types hampered efforts to escape. Special care was exercised to prevent disguises and tools being smuggled into baraques or aboard with the aim of escape. Mutilating punishments, such as facial brands and the cutting off of noses and ears, were inflicted on recaptured escapees. Escape was made more difficult by the method employed in anchoring galleys in port, with their sterns to the wharf and fifteen or more feet of water on every side. Guards stood post on the stern and patrolled the wharf night and day. In buildings ashore where forçats worked and in the hospital, windows were barred. In the hospital a two-hour patrol was maintained day and night, and in 1676 after three forçat patients had sawn through the bars of several windows to escape, a double grillwork of bars was installed. Thereafter, all escapes from the hospital appear to have been made by the doors.[51]

One of the major preoccupations in the management of galleys in the 1660's was the "conservation of the oarsmen." A long series of regulations were issued, many of them modeled on the practice of the galleys of the Order of St. John, though of course modifications of detail were continually made. No rigid set of rules would do. As early as the 1660's, La Guette stopped the practice of allowing oarsmen to go into Marseilles alone or unchained. He decreed that those going to the arsenal or the city to work would go in pairs, with a forçat and a turc chained together, and in the case of two forçats, a term offender chained with a man condemned for life. Thus coupled, the expectation was that the differences in language, religion, and outlook would impede efforts to escape. He sought, with no permanent success, to stamp out the abuses of argousins and other petty officers who were led "by certain avaricious interests" to favor rather than prevent escapes. He thought that any oarsman who informed on another man should be rewarded (he recommended only two écus), but if one escaped without the others of his banc having given any warning, he thought they should all be punished with sixty lashes for three days running and should be separated. Deeming it essential to keep the oarsmen out of pious hands, he decreed that none would be lent to religious houses as workers "because on pretexts of piety they help them escape, even giving them religious habits of disguise." [52]

But whatever the thoroughness of reforms and regulations, neither La Guette nor any other jailor could forestall all the opportunities of escape that accident could offer or that intelligent men could devise if desperate and determined to be free. One could hardly anticipate, for example, the impromptu seizure of a boat by 7 turcs and 3 forçats in 1672; they threw their officers overboard and got clear of the chains of the harbor before any alarm was given. An officer rushed to inform General of the Galleys Vivonne. He was dining at the time, but Vivonne (on that occasion) was a vigorous man. He ordered out the felucca and the caïque of the réale, and he himself gave chase. The culprits were caught about six miles at sea. Another surprise, equally difficult to foresee, was delivered by six oarsmen sent to the cemetery in company with several guards and a priest to bury the body of a fellow forçat. They overpowered the guards, threatening them with death at the least outcry, and locking them and the priest in the chapel. They unchained themselves and made good their escape through a breach in the city walls. [53] Colbert appears never to have been fully reconciled to the fact that there was no hope of eliminating all escapes. Regulations were his answer to this as to problems of almost every sort. He was also influenced by his suspicions, sometimes well founded, about the complicity of guards in escapes, but even the most alert and reliable of guards could not prevent unforeseeable escapes.

Under constant criticism from the ministers, Corps officials were forced to recommend suitable reforms; to that extent, Colbert's pressures were effective. Improvements of detail could almost always be devised. Officials also recommended that the whole guard system needed to be improved, making the easy suggestion: the number of guards must be increased. Finances were an obstacle to that, but when suggesting specific changes in 1674, Intendant Arnoul suggested the quartering of soldiers on each galley as a security measure. His recommendation was at least half applied when soldiers were ordered to sleep aboard, it being assumed that their very presence would be a useful security measure in itself. But as a minimum, Arnoul thought, a guard corps should be put aboard the réale and the two galleys at the extremities of the line of anchored galleys; he also thought it wise to provide at least four sentinels per galley, two at the stern and two others at the bow.[54] These suggestions apparently were not put into effect. In 1676, Intendant Brodart could still complain, in explaining how escapes took place, that there was usually only one guard per galley at night, who, he said, "remains on the poop and sleeps most of the time." In turn, he urged the need for guards "to make the rounds" every night, and suggested the addition of roving sergeants to patrol the wharves.[55]

But aside from number and distribution, the quality of the guards left much to be desired. Guards not only slept at their posts, but they were found guilty of complicity in many attempts to escape. That should not be surprising, said Brodart, for the guards are "often worse than the forçats themselves." He called attention to the fact that two argousins had disappeared from a galley one night in the company of the forçats they were supposed to guard; two others were condemned to the oar by a court martial for complicity in another escape. There were others too, he said, who had not been condemned by court martial "either because it could not be proved they had contributed to the escapes, or because they were supported by their captains."[56] Immediately after receiving this report from Brodart, the minister informed him that he was coming to Marseilles in person to investigate the real reason for escapes, which were occurring with inexcusable frequency. Indeed, there had been a number of serious security incidents that year, the most serious in April 1676, when twenty-three forçats escaped. This disaster angered Colbert: "Such disorder has been unheard of during the tenure of all the intendants who served before you at Marseilles, and what is even more extraordinary, is that you did not inform me at the time!"[57] Less than four months later, forty-six men destined for the galleys made good their escape under the minister's very nose from the Tour de Saint-Bernard in Paris.[58]

If the minister actually went to Marseilles, his subordinates doubtless told him of the many reasons for successful escapes, the most important of which was good luck. But Colbert would have made every effort to determine whether or not any degree of responsibility could be attributed to the guards involved. The logic of doing so was obvious, given the possibilities of self-interested behavior inherent in the jailor-prisoner relationship aboard the galleys (see pp. 126–128 above). A significant step toward controlling temptation was taken in 1676. The ministry then decided to withhold salary from guards in the amount of

300 livres for each oarsman who escaped their custody, even though the guard was not proved to have connived at the escape.[59] The salary withheld would serve to purchase a replacement for the oarsman lost and, secondarily, to punish the guard. If complicity was proved, the guard himself was put to the oar to replace the man who had escaped. This system of "binding" did have the effect of making guards attentive to business and cut down on the profitability of prearranged illicit getaways. But it could still be worthwhile to allow an oarsman to get away if the bribe was large enough to cover the salary and risk.

It was precisely this fact, apparently, that moved the navy to increase the fine for escapes to 1,000 livres by 1682. That was about four times an argousin's official annual salary and many times a guard's gross pay. Few guards could pay such a fine out of private resources. But since occasional escapes were bound to occur, no matter how careful the guards were, there was need for some defense against accidental getaways. Therefore the argousins constituted themselves as an Argousin Corps and entered into a formal agreement with the navy, their employer, in 1682. By its terms they made themselves collectively responsible for the payment of fines that were imposed when escapes took place. Any argousin from whose custody an oarsman escaped was to pay, from his own pocket, 250 of the required 1,000 livres; the Argousin Corps in the 1690's assumed responsibility for paying the other 750. The navy agreed, for its part, that an argousin responsible for retaking an escaped oarsman would receive a reward, or credit, of 200 livres, and other persons participating in captures could receive as much as 100 livres apiece.[60]

This novel distribution of responsibility offered certain advantages. It afforded the argousins some protection from an exorbitant fine; it protected the King's interest, for it placed the individual argousin under the surveillance of his fellows and restricted his ability to connive with oarsmen bent on escape. But it did not entirely obviate the possibility of corruption because, as one memoirist pointed out, "an argousin who took 400 livres from a forçat to let him escape could easily pay his own share of the [resulting] fine." [61]

As a matter of fact, the argousins' fines were seldom paid but were allowed to accumulate as a long-standing debt. The fact that nothing was done for many years about enforcing payment constituted a significant loophole in the security net; indeed, the whole system of collective responsibility thereby became a farce. Although the argousins' self-interest would theoretically compel them to police the behavior of their colleagues, escapes could be arranged and paid for by bribes as though the system did not exist. Recognition of these circumstances underlay some overdue modifications that were made shortly after 1700. The fine was reduced from 1,000 livres to 600, and was thenceforth to be paid by the argousin involved in the escape. But in actual practice the argousins were still allowed to accumulate their obligations. Finally, in 1707, the King sought to impose payment. Short of funds, he used their debts as an excuse for reducing expenditure; thenceforth, half their salaries were withheld toward liquidation of the accumulated obligations. For many years afterward the argousins tried, as a Corps, to get their whole obligation written off; they finally managed to do just that, in 1717, when their remaining debt in the amount of 212,327 livres was cancelled.

But the navy was quite aware that it had been ill used, and in the new arrangements made to guarantee responsibility for escapes, it was agreed that the fines would be only 400 livres and would, without exception, be paid immediately. The King also decreed that the responsibility of recapturing escapees would henceforth be entirely in the hands of the argousins; royal mounted police were told that they need not concern themselves.[62] Guards were thus obliged to pay the fine first and then, presumably, self-interest would lead them to retake the escapee, at their own expense, to recover the fine.

The merchants and manufacturers of Marseilles who used oarsmen for their part agreed that when an escape took place, their syndics would immediately seize such of the employer's property as was necessary to pay a 1,000-livre fine. Any merchant found guilty of aiding an escape could be condemned to serve at the oar himself; if the escapee was retaken, the merchant who had lost him was required to pay the 60 livres and all rewards.[63] Somewhat modified in 1712, this arrangement remained in force until its cancellation at the end of 1749, when the galleys and their worker-oarsmen were moved away from Marseilles to Brest, Rochefort, and Toulon, where similar arrangements were subsequently made.[64]

There are some fragmentary statistics on the total number of escapes. That record shows that between 1682 and 1707, no fewer than 664 oarsmen escaped from the King's galleys, and 366 were never recaptured.[65] Other escapes that took place in those years went unrecorded. Yet, within

270

the limits of the official figures, considering that there were around 10,000 oarsmen on the galleys at most times in those years, and almost 15,000 at certain times, it was a tribute to the effectiveness of the security measures that a mere 366 got away in twenty-five years. That would mean that only one or two men per 1,000 escaped in any given year.

The Transition to Prisons

An event long and impatiently awaited by many European princes occurred in 1700: King Charles II of Spain died, childless. By his will and testament, the last of several versions, he left his empire to Philip of Anjou, grandson of Louis XIV. The crowns and territories of the empires of France and Spain were to be controlled by the Bourbon dynasty; two long-time enemies thus suddenly became allies. Other claimants to the Spanish empire were embittered, and in many quarters there was also apprehension about the threat that this new "union" of two empires posed to the tranquillity and balance of the powers. Few European princes had reason to believe, on the basis of experince, that the French Bourbon dynasty could be depended on to use such an augmentation of power in peaceful, accommodating ways. Louis XIV, for his part, anticipating the negative reception Charles' testament in his favor was certain to receive, decided to move against the opposition before they moved against him. The War of the Spanish Succession was the result. In taking on almost all the other powers of Europe, the two collaborators needed to make changes in the composition of their armed forces, including their galley establishments.

Until then the maintenance of fleets of oar-driven craft by both France and Spain was partly justified by their long-standing rivalry (see pp. 20–22). Thus Louis XIV himself said in 1701 that his new ties with

Spain justified some cuts in expenditures for oar-driven craft: "The accession of my Grandson . . . to the Crown of Spain moves me to think that I can, with no inconvenience . . . eliminate ten [of the galleys of my fleet]." He also ordered the retirement of a number of older galley captains — not to reduce further the size of the Corps, but apparently to reassure younger officers about the stability and permanence of the Corps, and their future in it, "my intention being [that] the effects of retrenchment fall solely on the oarsmen and the crew."[1]

Part of the significance of Louis' reduction in the size of the Corps lay in its timing. On the eve of a war that promised to be long and hard fought, Louis' expectations for galleys were not high. The French Corps had reached its largest size (55) in 1690 and had shrunk to an official strength of 40 by 1700. Other galley users were showing much more acute dissatisfaction with the oar. North African states had virtually abandoned their use. Shortly after 1700 the Grand Master Perellos of the Order of Saint John, a practical as well as zealous man, invested a large personal fortune in constructing and equipping major sailing units because galleys had proved ineffective and perilous tools against infidels in well-armed sailing ships. The Order continued using galleys for many decades more, as did the Papacy. Yet, as Louis XIV's own Marshal de Tessé pointed out in 1712, "everyone [?] says and believes that the Galley Corps is only a mediocre part of the navy."[2]

We can only conjecture why Louis decided in 1701 to maintain as many as 30 galleys, manned by an oversized Corps of aristocratic officers, and continued to do so until the end of his reign. Less open to conjecture are the reasons why the Regency reduced the fleet first to 26 galleys in 1716, then to 15 in 1718, and why Louis XV continued to keep a fleet of 15 for thirty years more, until the Corps was officially abolished in 1748.[3] One thing is certain: all these governments must be counted as supporters of the oar, though not on the scale that Louis XIV had been.

Among influential preservers of the Corps, the most notable was Jean Philippe, Chevalier d'Orléans, a natural son (b. 1702) of the Regent himself.[4] He was General of the Galleys from 1708, and from young adulthood onward showed himself actively interested in the exercise of that charge. As General (for a record length of time) and Grand Prior of France in the Order of Saint John, he maintained a splendid residence at Marseilles and showed himself extremely, even ridiculously tenacious of every prerogative and privilege that a general and grand prior could exercise. His blood connection with the royal family and the social customs of the old regime required that he be treated with the uncritical deference due a prince; his personal disposition led him to sharpen the requirements in order to cut a better figure.

Another prestigious and influential friend of the galleys held the post of Lieutenant General, the old Marquis de Roye. He valued his post to the extent of acquiring its survivorship for his son, Jean-Baptiste-Louis de Roye de La Rochefoucauld, Duke d'Enville (b. 1709). While waiting for this child to become old enough to command, the marquis passed the post to a succession of veteran galley officers. Thus the charge of lieutenant general was passed in 1717 to the Chevalier Le Bouillier de Rance, squadron commander and at that time actual commander of the Corps, aged 93 years. When he died three years later the post was passed to the Count de Roannes, who retained it until his death in 1734 (at 86). He in turn was succeeded by d'Anville, who served only until 1744. Each of these men was tenacious of the status quo and his vested interests. With the Chevalier d'Orléans they constituted the spearhead of the defense of the Galley Corps against its detractors and gave the Corps some of the extremely conservative, aristocratic characteristics that marked its later days.[5]

After 1701 there were far too many officers and men in the Corps. Their average ages increased as the recruitment of young men slowed down, a process that was accentuated when a considerable number of able young and middle-aged commissioned officers transferred to the sailing navy. This aging process was particularly apparent in the twenties and thirties, when command of the Corps itself and that of many individual galleys as well was in the hands of septuagenarian and even older men who had risen to positions of command well back in the previous century.

In line with Louis' policy of making the more drastic reductions in the crew, many noncommissioned officers and crewmen saw their posts evaporate. A handful of the crewmen were accorded small pensions in the early 1700's, but such bounties became progressively more difficult to obtain and to collect as the financial condition of the monarchy worsened in the War of the Spanish Succession. A few displaced crewmen were taken on as guards along the Rhône and Durance waterways or in the ports of Languedoc, Provence, and Dauphiné, posts recommended "to help them to subsist for the rest of their days."[6] But lower officers faced unemployment, and to avoid it many of them consented to transfer to the sailing navy based at Toulon; others, in the later years of the war, went to the army.

It was a different story for the oarsmen. With them, the fact that fewer men were needed to serve galley oars was grounds for smiles, not groans. At least 2,000 oarsmen became "surplus" in 1701. But of course men continued to be condemned to the oar; an average of more than 1,000 convicts were received each year between 1699 and 1715.

The arsenal and the city of Marseilles itself could not provide work for that many men. The bagne became the first of several expedients devised to deal with the problem of unneeded convicts and the financial outlay they occasioned. We have noted the expedient used in the War of the Spanish Succession, when well over 2,000 surplus convicts were released to serve in the army between 1707 and 1712. An unknown number (certainly many hundreds) were shipped off to the West Indies as soon as the sea-lanes were again open to French ships at the end of that war. A group of religionnaires was released at the behest of the foreign powers shortly after the signature of peace in 1713, and a few more were let out in 1716. But with the fleet itself inactive in the postwar years and the navy's funds drastically reduced, the cost of maintaining several thousand surplus oarsmen seemed especially burdensome. The search for solutions was intensified.

To cut off part of the flow of convicts at the source, change was sought in the punishment for desertion from military service. From 1717 onward, desertion was punished as it had been a third of a century earlier, with the penalty of death instead of galères perpétuelles. This probably reduced by at least one third the average number of convicts arriving at Marseilles each year.

The burdensome surplus of convicts at Marseilles encouraged adoption of the practice of releasing men after they had served their terms. The salt smugglers, being among the least serious offenders, were logical first choices for regular release. It was a happy coincidence that the practice of regularity in releases — that is, release at the end of the specified term of condemnation — coincided with the principles of justice and equity. Respect for those principles does not seem to have had much to do with bringing about their observance in the navy's treatment of convicts. But perhaps the example of regularity in practice during and immediately following the war generated pressure for similar handling of other men later. Judging from the documents, naval officials were not particularly sensitive to the inequities involved; but the convicts must have been very much aware of them, and they did have some spokesmen or advocates in positions of authority after 1715.

One variety of inequity that attracted the attention of the authorities stemmed from differences in the laws against contrabanding salt and tobacco. The law on contraband tobacco called for the penalty of galleys without specifying the term, whereas the laws on salt specified a variety of penalties.[7] In consequence, men guilty of similar or identical contrabanding offenses received terms of two years, three years, or life for the same offense. Complaints about such inequities began to be recorded after 1713. Such complaints were actually taken under consideration by the Navy Board of the Regency government. After extended discussion, at the behest of the Regent himself in 1718–20, the decision was made that smugglers of salt and tobacco would henceforth be treated identically; all would serve three-year terms.[8]

But clearly, most of these reforms in condemnations and releases resulted from changes in the needs of the State. Those needs were effective prerequisites to reforms in the old regime. Humanitarian considerations, or equity, or other theoretical conceptions seem to have been implemented in practice only, or almost only when they happened to coincide with the interests of the State. But whatever the mechanisms, by the decade of the twenties the convicts in the galleys other than Protestants were frequently being released promptly at the expiration of their terms of condemnation rather than being retained as long as they were able to serve. This constituted significant evidence of the transformation taking place in the Corps. Having lost virtually all usefulness for foreign policy purposes, both warfare and prestige, and being used by the navy for little more than occasional river and coastal patrols, the eighteenth-century galley was useful almost exclusively as a prison. These facts explain the increasing tendency to treat men condemned to the galleys as prisoners, rather than as navy matériel.

The penitentiary features of the galleys were also underscored when the ministry of marine decided, beginning about 1725, to withhold the King's rations from oarsmen on days when they worked en baraque or in Marseilles. This action seemed justified because most "oarsmen" were in port the year around, year after year — they were not really oarsmen at all. Reduction of their rations was simply recognition of the fact that the product of their labor was being used to enrich private persons and galley personnel rather than to support the oarsmen. Later the ministry of marine became convinced that oarsmen should provide their own food as long as they were able-bodied. This change gave explicit recognition to the prisoner status of the erstwhile oarsmen; making no contribution to the oar, they could not get subsistence from the navy.[9] The Corps was becoming a self-sustaining prison.

The decline of the fighting galley was also evident in campaigns. French galleys played no significant role at either extremity of the Mediterranean, either against Spain or the Ottoman Turk. Only in forays against North Africa did they have even a pretense of utility, but North African waters (as earlier seen) were not favorable for them; only three times (1717, 1728, 1742) were galleys even included in eighteenth-century expeditions to North African waters. Seven of the ten expeditions sent, 1717–42, to the North African theater were composed exclusively of sailing vessels. The first time galleys were included, neither sailing nor oar-driven craft reached the North African coast at all. In 1728 the two galleys sent, with their half dozen cannon, must have made a distinctly minor contribution compared with the eight other naval vessels with their hundreds of guns in the bombardment of Tunis and Tripoli. The third time, on the infamous expedition of 1742 against Tabarka, off the Tunisian coast, three of the four galleys dispatched were put out of action en route when an epidemic spread among their oarsmen. The captain of the single galley that did arrive, also the senior and therefore commanding officer of the whole expedition, saw 800 Frenchmen taken prisoner by the Tunisians and the expedition repulsed.[10]

The more usual employments of galleys after 1713 consisted of parades and campaigns in quest of salutes. Between 1716 and 1738, at least a dozen squadrons, usually composed of four galleys, were ordered out to patrol for prestige and salutes. One such squadron, in 1727, involved a parade by six galleys along the coast of Italy as far south as Palermo, where French galleys had not been seen since 1678. In 1734 eight galleys worked south along the coast of Spain as far as Gibraltar in a fruitless search for privateers from Salé. Galleys also carried dignitaries between France and northern Italy. Thus, in 1724, two galleys carried two cardinals to Italy to take part in a conclave electing a Pope; in 1731, the King ordered four galleys to transport the French ambassador to the Holy See, the Duke de Saint-Aignan. Missions of that sort were perhaps memorable or even enjoyable for some of the galley officers involved. But galley officers spent little of their time on such expeditions. They generally stayed at Marseilles, where they enjoyed an attractive and interesting life in spite of the fact that the Corps was steadily losing prestige. At Marseilles there were seldom any officers of the sailing navy to be dealt with. The life itself was good: plentiful housing and entertainment was available for those who could pay, and galley officers could. The average captain received a base salary of 250 livres a month (as much as a workman received in a year). Senior officers also had valets or an allowance for valets — most of them seem to have kept more than one, some had seven or eight, and one had ten.[11] Captains, and others in proportion, had table allowances from the King of as much as 3,000 livres a year, and d'Orléans had 3,000 a month. Marseilles offered opera, concerts, and art. In addition to many official and semiofficial ceremonial occasions, galley officers organized entertainments of their own, such as open air balls.

A few details about one such affair, held in the summer of 1728, have survived because that particular ball called forth an order from Barras de la Penne, then one of the eldest officers and Commandant of the Corps. In his order he offered some advice and disclosed some significant details about the social role of the galleys and their officers in Marseilles. The site of the ball in question was the square in front of the city hall facing the waterfront where the galleys tied up. Apparently the officers scheduled the ball in that public square without consulting city officials, and officials had complained about a serious incident. Barras began his reprimand by observing that "When officers are giving a ball in front of the city hall, it is only courtesy to inform the échevins to get their approval. But I think it would be better not to give the ball in that square at all, so as to avoid the accidents that the flames of the torches could produce in the port, where it is forbidden even to pass with a lighted torch." By holding the ball elsewhere, it would be possible to avoid exposing the affair "to the insults of the people assembled around the square. Having no respect for the flag, [they] can cause trouble, and necessitate calling out the guards armed with bayoneted muskets to put it down." On any future occasion when a ball is given on that square, said Barras, the soldiers lining the edges of the circle of dancers should be armed "only with their swords," not with muskets and bayonets.

Their swords would suffice, he said, "to prevent the crowd and the common people from entering the circle [of dancers]." [12]

Galley officers had vested interests in the preservation of the galley and its traditions. They must have managed to cloak or ignore its practical infirmities; they sought to carry on as though the oared vessel was still an effective fighting machine conferring prestige on the Crown and themselves. Many officers still defended their galleys out of conviction against its modern, empiricist critics. The Bailiff de Mirabeau and the Chevalier de Pilles, for example, both Knights of Malta, wrote memoirs seeking to demonstrate the utility of oar-driven craft.[13] The most assiduous and "scholarly" spokesman for galleys was Barras de la Penne, who spent years preparing a long treatise in defense of the galley, several versions of which still lie unpublished in the Archives de la Marine. Even more influential than he, of course, was d'Orléans; not until after his death in 1748 did the ministry of marine abolish the Galley Corps.

For all their prestige and connections, galley officers must have been keenly aware of the institutional decay going on before their eyes. They had only to look about them to see the diminishing number of galleys tied up, and the deplorable condition of many that survived; everywhere about the base was evidence of decay. Many officers serving in the 1730's could remember a time in their own careers when the King demanded an ever larger fleet of oar-driven craft, when expansion was slowed only by lack of oarsmen or exhaustion of the supplies of timber at hand. The former bustle of the arsenal, once filled with the sound of carpenters, sawyers, and smiths echoing across the waters of the old port, was much subdued; the early eighteenth century saw few galleys built, unused timber was reported rotting in storage. Even some of the bakers' ovens, no longer needed at Marseilles, were ordered sent to Toulon for the sailing navy.

Galley officers must have had special regrets about the diminishing number of turcs among the oarsmen. With their distinctive clothing, moustache, and reputation for physical strength, turcs were a feature of the old fighting galley, significant symbols especially for the Church, but also for the Crown. In earlier times turcs had been bought in battle with blood, and more recently with money when they were acquired at all. But the Navy Board and later the ministry of marine resisted and postponed such acquisitions, claiming the purchase of slaves was inconsistent with naval economies and with the unmistakable superiority of sailing warships. In the minds of galley officers, however, reductions in the number of slaves suggested the debilitation of their Corps. Declining numbers of turcs implied loss of strength and importance, and brought the numerical ascendancy of the convict labor; it emphasized the fact that as galleys lost their utility as fighting ships, their value as prisons remained. Galley officers could hardly have relished the loss of symbols of combat success when that loss left intact and even underscored their functions as wardens of prisons.

Officers who were Knights of Malta had vested interests in resisting the decline in the number of slaves at the oars. Even in the eighteenth century Moslems and Christians enslaved each other as prisoners of war in the Mediterranean, and well after mid-century religion still justified, in some minds, the practice of putting infidels into the galleys as slaves. The Order of St. John was still making and selling them. Knights were officers in a status-ridden, tradition-conscious Order, and their religious connection gave them serious vows to discharge. Slaves at the oars were symbols of the past, but they were also living testimony to the service being given to the Church. By having such slaves at the oars of their galleys, Knights came close to discharging, pro forma, their obligation to serve the proselyting aims of their Order and Church.

But of course there were also officers with other motives for maintaining or increasing the contingent of slaves on the galleys. Some doubtless simply wanted to keep the galleys as much as possible like they were in earlier, more prestigious times. Other officers used slaves as servants.[14] When the number of slaves continually fell, it may have been difficult to make suitable choices. Thus some officers may have had personal reasons for seeking, as they did, "redistribution" of the slaves on hand, as well as for seeking the purchase of more.

Whatever their motives, the officers of the galley clung to the desire to have infidel slaves on the galleys until the last. In 1712 there were still well over 1,000 slaves on the galleys, divided between Marseilles and Toulon.[15] The number dwindled to under 200 by 1738, primarily as a result of restricted buying, the plague of Provence, and attrition. That year a plan was devised "to equalize the galleys in turcs," a scheme for redistributing the slaves on hand and purchasing more.[16] Few slaves were then being bought. Most of those acquired came from Malta, where the purchasing agent for the King's galleys from 1723 to 1749 was the

Bailiff d'Avernes de Boccage.[17] In the very last year of the separate existence of the Corps, agents were still purchasing slaves at Malta and Cartagena.[18] It was still being said that slaves were needed to give "tone" and strength to the rowing force. Even more, they were probably needed to give morale to the galley officers. The ministry of marine, for its part, was quite aware that the purchase of costly turcs offered no significant returns on investment, and could not be justified when ample numbers of able-bodied forçats were always on hand to man the oars of the few galleys the King was willing to order to sea. But some persons apparently believed that the satisfaction of certain officers, including d'Orléans, sufficiently repaid the expenditure.

The history of French galleys in the first half of the eighteenth century reveals a pervasive interplay of interests, some working to liquidate, others stubbornly seeking to conserve the Corps. Change was especially apparent in the inexorable progress toward a prison regime. By the end of the 1740's few could have supposed that the galley could ever again give significant service to the King in war. Yet as late as 1750 it was said that "when and if other powers still having some galleys [decide] to abandon entirely their use, as the Emperor is going to do at Leghorn, the question of suppressing the galleys will then, in all likelihood, be dealt with in France." To abandon entirely a weapon neighboring powers and princes still used was apparently considered unwise. It was widely admitted, however, that galleys had little use; they were maintained, one memoirist in France observed, "rather for their relation to the grandeur of the King than for the service they can render." [19]

But the conservationist forces were still determined, in 1750 and long afterward, to keep the galleys that remained, principally on the excuse that they were needed as long as any other powers had galleys. In accordance with those desires, new galleys were actually built: *La Bretonne* in 1749 and *L'Amazone* in 1750.[20] Some French galleys continued to be kept in seaworthy condition more than two decades after that, and though galleys no longer appeared on the official lists of the "vessels of the King" after 1773, even at that date there were still nine in the navy. There were five galleys at Toulon when the prison reformer John Howard visited there in 1786, and one French galley made a Mediterranean campaign as late as 1799.[21] Clearly, the galleys themselves long outlived the Corps of which they were part.

The Galley Corps itself disappeared in September 1748, less than four months after the death of the Chevalier d'Orléans. Thereupon, Minister of Marine Maurepas obtained an order uniting the galleys with the rest of the navy; the officers were transferred, on paper at least, to the sailing navy. Since the Chamber of Commerce at Marseilles expressed a strong desire (later regretted by some) to be rid of the galleys and men associated with them, eleven galleys were moved from the port, leaving only a pair of seaworthy and several crippled craft behind. Of the roughly 4,000 oarsmen at Marseilles, several thousand were transferred to Toulon, and about 1,000 were sent, via the Languedoc Canal and Bordeaux, to the naval base at Brest, where they were set to building a bagne, considered essential for housing in that climate. An additional bagne was ultimately established at Rochefort to accommodate the contingent of oarsmen there. But Brest was destined to become the principal port where oarsmen were worked and where their number by the end of the seventies exceeded the number at Toulon and Rochefort combined.[22]

Men condemned to the galleys after mid-century were no longer directed to Marseilles, and less than a third went to Toulon, to which the few remaining galleys had been moved. Instead, convicts were sent principally to Brest and Rochefort where the sailing navy was based. Neither of those ports possessed galleys at all. The Brittany, Paris, and Gascony chains of convicts no longer followed their old routes eastward and south to Marseilles; most convicts from Brittany and Paris went directly to Brest, those from Bordeaux and its environs went to Rochefort, and those from the center and south went to Toulon. Only the latter were ever likely to put their palms to the oars. Yet the term *galérien* continued to be used in courts of law and popular speech throughout the old regime, the Revolution, and the Empire, surviving as a synonym for convicts even after the Bourbon restoration of 1815.

Considered overall, the reunion of galleys and sailing vessels offered several important advantages. It was of course a step toward abandoning galleys. More important still, the dispersal of forçats offered a solution to the problem of high wages that the navy was paying at Brest and Toulon.[23] Howard observed, "Criminals will gladly work, when in prison, for one-fourth of what they would earn were they not in confinement."[24] That being the case, the arrival of some 1,000 forçats at Brest in 1749 was a disaster for the resident working-class population, committed to working in the arsenal. Similar effects were experienced at

Rochefort. But worse was in store because the numbers of forçats at the ports were destined to be largely increased.

In some other respects reunion had surprisingly little effect. Turcs continued to be bought. In 1749, when hundreds of forçats were being transferred from Marseilles, thirty-four Moslem slaves were purchased from merchants of Genoa, presumably for service on the galleys that were transferred to Toulon.[25] In addition, the French consul at Malta purchased eight slaves from Crete captured and sold on the Malta market by a Sardinian corsair, and in 1751 the consul at Malaga purchased eleven others, also from Crete.[26] These were destined to be among the last French purchases of galley slaves. Unfortunately, they had serious repercussions. News of the French purchase at Malta, reaching Crete, produced violent demonstrations against the French, said to have been instigated by friends and relatives of the men who had been bought. The local pasha was able to pacify the populace only by promising that ransom would be arranged, and in due course it was; some months later naval authorities at Toulon were ordered to free the slaves. Reaction to the purchase at Malaga was similarly forceful, and the slaves that had been acquired soon had to be freed.[27] Some years later the French ambassador at Constantinople was himself threatened by the Grand Vizier with imprisonment in the Seven Towers unless all the Sultan's subjects then on French galleys were released. In consequence, the frigate *La Chimère* carried thirty slaves from Toulon to Constantinople for release, and the Sultan indicated his great appreciation.[28] Afterwards a French memoirist pointed out that altercations with the Porte were certain to recur "unless purchases are restricted henceforth to barbaresques." [29]

But periodic international difficulties also discouraged purchases from North Africa. France and most other maritime powers had signed treaties of peace with the North African states which were surprisingly well adhered to compared with earlier treaties. North African supplies thus being eliminated, the legal market in slaves was exceedingly restricted. Any purchases attracted attention, and an illicit purchase was almost certain to be traced and to produce trouble, especially if the consuls were careless in purchasing. Perhaps none were more careless than the consul at Malta, a Knight whose crusading profession apparently led him to be unconcerned about the varieties of infidels in which he dealt; he made strangely obvious, noisy public purchases of the Sultan's subjects for French galleys at a time when such purchases were certain to produce friction between France and her Moslem political and trading connections.[30]

But the monarchy in France showed itself desirous of being at peace with Moslem potentates, both Ottoman and North African. The ministry seemed anxious not to give offense. When complaints were received from the Pasha of Tripoli in 1747 about the treatment received by his subjects on French galleys and comparable complaints came from the bey of Tunis in 1749, investigations were conducted. The intendant at Marseilles carefully explained that it was not true that slaves' funds were confiscated or that slaves were prevented from employing their funds for their own needs. Rather, the slaves could not be allowed to have large sums of money on their persons if they were to be prevented from putting such funds to uses "contrary to the interests of the King." He assured the bey that monies given by the slaves to their "papas," as they called their leaders, were likewise in safekeeping for them, and could be dispersed at will. In response to complaints about the rations provided for slaves, the intendant indicated that rations "were the same as they had always been," and "the quality of the victuals is now very good." He added that all sick slaves were treated at the hospital, and dead slaves were never deprived of shrouds, as was claimed. But the intendant did intimate that regulations issued in 1746 restricting testamentary privileges could understandably have produced some complaints.[31]

Legally, of course, the property of slaves who died was the property of the King by virtue of the fact that they were slaves. But until 1746, by custom, the King had "by grace" allowed the surviving slaves to share the product of the sale of personal property and effects of fellow slaves who died. But in 1746 there were objections to this established procedure. The few turcs remaining on the galleys at that date had given longer service on the average, were of greater average age, and were heirs more frequently than slaves in earlier years had been. They were thus heir to greater sums, since their collective wealth was becoming concentrated in successively fewer hands. Facing this problem, the ministry decreed in 1746 that His Majesty henceforth would allow only one-quarter of such effects to be divided and shared, though full testamentary powers could be exercised by slaves who became converts to Christianity. These changes gave rise to vigorous, sustained complaint and were apparently the major cause underlying intervention from the North African principalities.[32]

A comparable spirit was apparent in the navy's handling of another controversy, unimportant in itself perhaps, but indicative of the disposition of the ministry to recognize and protect the slaves' rights even when they were contested by French local interests in Marseilles and had distinctly religious overtones. It might also be noted in passing that Moslem slaves' rights were more extensive and better protected after the treaties. Thus, in 1750, the presence of the galleys at Toulon led their Moslem oarsmen to solicit a small plot where they could bury their dead; and when that ground was found to be too wet, another piece of ground was given instead, at Mourillon, close by, where the Moslems constructed "a cover" for their prayers, and the whole area was walled, at least partly at navy expense (1750). Orders were given that the Moslems must never be troubled in the practice of their religion in that place.[33]

Similar arrangements did not go so smoothly at Marseilles, where the échevins interfered in 1775 with the Moslems seeking to visit the long-established cemetery for slaves. The minister (Sartine) apparently heard of it from the Dey of Algiers, and wrote to Marseilles to know what was going on. The échevins responded with assertions that the "Musulmans" had abused their privilege and lost the right to exercise it. Sartine said that was impossible and told the officials that he was then writing the Dey to give assurances about the rights of visitation, as guaranteed by treaties: "Nor can there be any question of changing the location of this cemetery, still less of using land for that purpose within the confines of the arsenal walls." [34]

Considering all the difficulties entrained in purchasing and using slaves, the minister of marine must have looked with relief (1759) on proposals to substitute conscripts for turcs at galley oars.[35] It was said in 1776 that only three or four turcs remained, all of them old paupers who worked around the city and arsenal subsisting as they could, with no other place to go since they were converts to Christianity.

"A great number" of Protestants were aboard French galleys at mid-eighteenth century, according to the historian Brun.[36] Religionnaires were certainly more numerous than Moslems, though the next quarter century also saw the Protestants become less numerous and finally disappear from the scene. Similar circumstances produced concurrent numerical decline in the two religious groups. International treaties, the influence of foreign powers, and economic pressures generated by sea-borne trading interests obstructed the use of both infidels and heretics at eighteenth-century oars. Moreover, especially as regards the Protestants, an increasing number of enlightened men, Voltaire and others of the philosophes among them, criticized the protection or promotion of religion by judicial condemnations. For a variety of reasons, fewer were condemned to the galleys as religionnaires, and those who were condemned were more frequently released.

The total number of Protestants condemned to the galleys after 1748 is unknown. Many case histories have been gathered by French Protestant historians; they themselves are the first to admit the incompleteness of their researches and resulting lists. Among the cases researched by Gaston Tournier for the period after 1748 for which such details are known, nearly all were condemned to the galleys for illicit assembly, for having been married by a pastor of the R.P.R., or generally "for contravention of the edicts and declarations of His Majesty concerning matters of religion." The vast majority of the condemnations took place in the south of France, most in Languedoc, with a scattering at Grenoble and Bordeaux. In most cases where the nature of the punishment is known, a life term was imposed, with fewer than one-quarter being given less. Term condemnations for Protestants after 1748 were uncommon precisely because the rigor of the law and the burden of precedent left little room for anything less than life. Condemnations to terms short of life had technical importance for the individual concerned because they did not ordinarily involve civil death and the consequent loss of property. Some of those who received life terms were in fact released after serving as little as two years, though others served twenty-five or thirty years for illicit assembly and ultimately died in the galleys. In sum, condemnations to the galleys for religion still took place in considerable numbers even after mid-century.[37]

Well before mid-century, the laws against Protestants were widely recognized as being out of touch with the temper of the times. A very few officials — intendants such as Le Nain and de Saint-Priest of Languedoc, encouraged by that dangerous minister St.-Florentin — were responsible for many of the attempts at enforcement and actual condemnations to the galleys that took place. Popular opinion and many writers were "soft on Protestantism." The softening of policy came hardly at all in the old regime. But the divergence between the draconian rigor of the law and the relatively tolerant general state of public opinion was apparent in some of the judicial cases of the time. For example, a certain Jean Raymond was arrested in 1754 for attending Protestant services. Apparently no person in his town, Catholic or other, would publicly bear witness against him, but he was condemned to galères perpétuelles anyway. When his property was sold at public auction, the people of the town (Faugères), by common accord, allowed his wife to recover his belongings and property with a minimum bid. Influential persons sought to obtain Raymond's release, but St.-Florentin responded to one such petitioner saying that if Raymond were released "I myself will [personally] load him with chains." Raymond was finally released in 1767 after serving more than twelve years.[38] As late as 1753 a group of Lutherans from different villages of Alsace were arrested, imprisoned, and charged with attempting to emigrate from territory under French control; twelve of the men were sentenced to the galleys. But after forty-seven of the men, women, and children abjured their religion, Louis XV commuted the penalty of galleys, ordering that they be transported to the colonies instead. On 10 June 1753, therefore, this group of unfortunates left their prisons for Rochefort, the designated port of embarkation.[39]

In the two decades after 1748, however, official policy on the release of Protestants became more flexible. The navy itself was partly responsible, but many outside pressures helped. In the five years 1748–52, at least two hundred Protestants who were serving in the galleys were proposed by naval authorities for release, though by no means all were released.[40] A sensational blow was struck when the celebrated Jean Fabre was released, after serving only seven years of the life term he incurred in 1755 when he offered himself to the authorities as a substitute for his aged father, arrested for illicit religious assembly. At the end of 1762, there remained only thirty-three Protestants on the galleys of Toulon and Marseilles. For their liberty, the Duke of Bedford petitioned in vain to the "all-powerful St.-Florentin." Voltaire added his voice to the chorus of petitioners in 1764, with a project designed to startle by its fantasy, proposing payment of 90,000 livres as a "ransom" for the thirty Protestants who remained on the galleys; to "reassure" the authorities, said he, the Protestants thus released could be sent to Guiana. Not for another decade, after the intervention of many other powerful persons, were the last ones released. The last two were actually forgotten for a time, but were "rediscovered" and, after fifteen months of effort, officially released in 1775, at the ages of 58 and 72 years, each having served thirty years in the galleys.[41]

The statutes whose provisions put Protestants to the oar, though potentially as productive of oarsmen as ever, became relatively harmless in practice when the people and most of their governors rejected the religious policy inherited from the age of the Reformation, Richelieu, and Louis XIV. The third quarter of the eighteenth century saw a growing number of men in positions of authority in France declining to give sanction to the laws; they consented to undo some of their intended punitive effects, and connived at their evasion. But they did not, evidently could not, go so far as to make basic changes in that body of law. That was revolutionary work.[42] The gradual disappearance of Protestants and slaves from the galleys was a step toward toleration, and toward an end of the age when royal galleys served the Church as a multi-purpose tool for the incarceration, conversion, and repression of Protestants and infidels.

But the prison functions of the Galley Corps continued at the royal arsenals, as a service to the monarchy. The inmates of the bagnes at Brest, Rochefort, and Toulon grew more numerous, and each major naval base came to serve as a regional prison where transgressors of law were confined and worked. Collectively, the later-day galleys served as a national prison system for France and her dependencies. They also served an even broader function as an international prison. As early as 1737 the King of Poland asked permission to send his criminal subjects to serve on the galleys of the King of France.[43] In 1739 the Electress Palatine enjoyed the same permission, judging from the fact that one of her subjects, a Jew whose condemnation to death she commuted, was sent for service in the galleys of France.[44] Louis XV issued a decree during the Seven Years War condemning to his galleys civilian men in occupied territories of Germany (Hanover, for example) who attempted to join the forces of France's enemies.[45] There had always been an "international" flavor about French oarsmen, and this remained a characteristic of the institution even after the demise of the infidels, whose points of origin had always been the most far-flung. In 1787 the chains wending their way across France ordinarily included many offenders from Switzerland and some from the German states, who were received at Brest,

Rochefort, and Toulon under the terms of special agreements with the princes or governments of those states. Foreign offenders were customarily brought to the frontiers of France at the cost of their sovereign. The French minister of war ordered the intendants of the frontier provinces to allow their entry, and to arrange for their reception in the nearest prison where chains en route to navy arsenals touched.[46]

The basic methods of administration developed in the galleys and bagnes of Marseilles before 1748 remained the pattern afterward. The system had some virtues, and some defects. Lower officers were still described in the 1770's as "vile and mercenary" men, collectively "the horror of the oarsmen"; "nothing but the thought of gain leads them to embrace this profession, to promise to pay a fine for each forçat that escapes, to risk the possibility of being put to the chain in their place." That was unfriendly commentary; in more complimentary terms it was said that comites and argousins alike were schooled for years in their profession, that their occupation required them to live long periods with criminals, insane and dangerous men, that they get "to know their habits and their inclinations, their tricks and subterfuges, the ins and outs, and all the elasticity of the means they daily use to reach their ends."[47]

But the aim of all these men, apart from personal gain, was security; the prevention of escapes, not the reformation or rehabilitation of the men they held and worked, was their concern. Conforming to these aims, the system was traditional. One could hardly expect to find "enlightenment" or much "humanity" in prison administration in that period, given the generally appalling record of such administration during the nineteenth and into the twentieth century. Most of the standard monographs maintain — no doubt on the basis of selected contemporary authorities and especially Howard — that eighteenth-century prisons were abominable in England and on the continent, the most significant exceptions being found in certain model jails in Holland.[48]

In France, as elsewhere, the condition of prisons was generally bad in the eighteenth century, and often afterward as well, yet the bagnes at Brest, Toulon, and Rochefort, though they have been neglected by researchers, can certainly be said to have been exceptions to the rule, probably (by twentieth-century standards) the best of their time. These three establishments were different from their inception because the galleys were unlike the usual prisons. Security was always the first concern on galleys, but not the only major one. On oar-driven craft the physical condition of the prisoners was an important concern precisely because they were needed to work the oars. That distinguished galleys from almost all other prisons. And the dual purposes of security and the prisoners' health remained dominant features of the "system of the galleys" that prevailed at the bagnes of the ports.

Many small changes were made in administrative methods in the galleys even before mid–eighteenth century. For example, the chains were more carefully supervised than they had been in the days of Colbert and Seignelay, partly because regulations promulgated by them and their subordinates (notably Bégon) were actually being enforced, with some improvements. A commissaire and a barber-surgeon actually accompanied all major chains; the conductors were better paid; the convicts' rations were better and more abundant; more vehicles were provided for the weak and sick; and milder treatment was generally accorded. Notable indications of these improvements were made apparent by a letter of 1744, in which a provincial intendant complained that conductors were too lenient, an uncommon complaint a century earlier: "I am informed that when they are one day from Paris, they put strong, robust young men in those carts; last year they even obliged the mayor and échevins of Montreau to furnish triple the usual number of vehicles, in which they put all the convicts to the number of around 150 . . . I think it is essential to fix the number of horses and vehicles to be furnished to the conductor, for his postchaise, and a horse for the surgeon who accompanies the chain." [49] After arriving at the port, all convicts were allowed eight days' rest, with increased rations.

Some naval officials at the ports even began to show interest in the reformation of the prisoners held, considering them as human beings and not mere matériel. Thus when Louis XVI himself indicated interest in certain reforms, good groundwork was already prepared. In the 1780's Minister of Marine de Castries and Intendant Malouet at Toulon were notably receptive to the King's ideas, some of which they may have supplied. Among the administrative practices given special attention was the long-standing one of chaining prisoners in pairs for work. This method of mixing men was traditionally considered advantageous because: "It is certain that two forçats both condemned to life terms, have a common interest in breaking their chains and making [good] their escape. On the other hand, the man who will someday be free supports his punishment more patiently, and seeks to avoid making himself an accomplice to the escape of his comrade serving for life." [50] As a re-enforcement to this self-policing system, both men were held responsible if either escaped. Malouet claimed that this traditional system, using prisoners to thwart each other's escapes, was not notably effective. He saw little difference during his tenure in the propensities of lifers and term offenders to attempt escape. Malouet also had other criticisms of this security system, some of which he elaborated in great detail when the King indicated interest in and even enthusiasm for reform.

Louis XVI's interest in prison administration was perhaps partly a manifestation of his sentimentality or his predilection for good works and Christian charity, and he may also have been inclined to imitate the words and deeds of some other reigning princes — Frederick II, Joseph II, and Catherine II — at least in this matter. He could have known Mabillon's essay on prison administration. Perhaps he was moved by Beccaria's and Howard's recent books and the advice of de Castries and Malouet. Whatever the sources of inspiration, Malouet made Louis' objectives clear. Malouet (with a paraphrase of Beccaria) alluded in correspondence with Versailles to the "royal" interest in establishing "a just proportion between crimes and punishments." [51]

Whatever the sources of his inspiration, it was in consultation with naval advisers that the King decided to separate the prisoners into classes according to the seriousness of their offense. The aim was to limit, so far as possible, the associations of lesser offenders with hardened criminals. This remarkable objective of the King's and his subordinates', so "modern" and so seldom implemented even in the twentieth century, was opposed because adopting it would necessarily mean the end of the traditional system of security. If lifers and terms offenders were to be kept apart at all times, new security arrangements would have to be devised, and some administrators did not believe new ones could possibly be so effective as the old.

But the separation of offenders was apparently an objective that some naval officials, backed by the King, were convinced must be achieved. They deployed many surprising, enlightened, and "modern" arguments in its favor. Separation, they said, was an important step toward transforming the prison from a school for creating criminals into a correctional institution that would help men reform their own lives. One protagonist of this idea was Pierre Victor Malouet, later a deputy to the Estates General, who responded with enthusiasm and clear-sighted commentary when he learned from the minister that the King desired to establish separate treatment for prisoners of different sorts:

There is no doubt that the [traditional practice of pairing prisoners] . . . integrates three classes of men: criminals, deserters, and contrabanders. It imposes the same treatment on them all even though they are very different in basic character, [and also] in the consideration they merit, and in the real wrong they have done society. These unfortunates, being equally degraded in public eyes, [associating together] thereby acquire the same habits, the same sentiments and aversion for the public order of which they are all victims. Those who leave this school of misery and opprobrium to re-enter society carry with them all the vices of those they left behind in irons. Our laws, for lack of foresight, steer the prisoner designated for release to the road of crime, rather than to the road of legitimate industry. For after having been deprived for many years of the opportunity to employ their energy and time for private profit, these men are stigmatized with a brand of infamy that dispels [in others] trust and willingness to help at a time when they have new needs more pressing, sometimes, than those that led them into crime initially. The forces of public order have preserved every shortcoming of the laws instead of giving responsible, charitable care to these three classes of prisoners.[52]

Malouet went on to say that the system of mixing forçats, long deemed so necessary to security, often had the effect of putting side by side with a thief or murderer a man guilty of inability to pay his debts or desertion, neither of these crimes considered in the eighteenth century to be comparable to theft or murder. But, said Malouet, "this can be changed by conforming in all respects to the intentions of the King." He pointed out that the application of the theory should not be difficult; for example, the bagne at Toulon already consisted of several large halls, two of them suitably isolated: "one [hall] can be assigned to contrabanders and smugglers condemned to life imprisonment, another to those condemned to terms of years; the other two [can be used] for the criminals. The first two classes can be distinguished by a blue uniform, with the hair of the first being cut in a round style, the second with long hair; the criminals will retain a red uniform with shaven heads. . . . The same distinctions can be made in the work of the port: the most lucrative and the least difficult belong by right to the first two classes; while the fatigue duties will be reserved for the third."[53] Malouet disparaged the possibility that security problems might result when the traditional system of coupling criminals with lesser offenders was abandoned.

The minister responded that His Majesty had read Malouet's observations with great interest and had adopted most of the suggestions made.[54] Within a very few weeks, over the objections of Intendant Guillot at Brest,[55] these specific proposals for implementing reform were, with minor modifications, adopted by the central administration of the navy for use at all the port-prisons.

But that did not conclude the story. Louis XVI, de Castries, and Malouet himself soon learned that reforms require not only benevolence and decision but determined following through. Great was their surprise to learn that the forçats themselves, the intended beneficiaries of reforms, were shocked, embittered, and generally hostile to the changes. Malouet himself was the first to report the unfavorable reception:

I am obliged to inform you of the dissatisfaction of the first two classes. The uncoupling of these unfortunates has produced a sort of revolution in their society: such is the power of habit. Some miss their companions, others the room where they have friends and connections. Their complaints have been so vigorous that they have won over the lower officers, and even the officers of the administrative staff . . . [there are] many who adduce no other cause for regret . . . than the mutual confidence [men enjoyed] and the habit of carrying the same chain . . . these are gentle and true sentiments that one cannot help respecting even in men like these. . . . The King will be surprised that his benevolence has produced such an extraordinary sensation. . . . I am far from proposing, Monseigneur, abandonment of the arrangements made. On the contrary, I think . . . the favorable effects will soon be evident.[56]

Malouet expressed the view that if similar reactions came from the prisoners at the other ports (as they did), all these strange responses to intended benevolence would deserve "to be recorded in the moral history of man."

Another apparent effect of this new regime was an increase in escapes, as Guillot had foreseen. During the first thirty-two months of the new system of forçat coupling and separation at Toulon, 190 forçats escaped as compared with 149 during the period immediately preceding, both periods under Malouet's intendancy. At Brest, where Guillot consistently opposed the changes, the "new system" saw a much larger increase — from 474 in the earlier period to 801 in the first thirty-two months of the new (1 February 1783 to 30 September 1785). This increase was certainly evidence of deterioration in security, at least at Brest. Possibly the existence of war in the earlier period, with the normal intensification of surveillance that wartime conditions could entrain, might explain part of the differential at both ports. But all these figures seem high compared with the record for the early seventies, when the number of escapes from all three ports together totaled only 168 during three full calendar years 1772–74, according to one tabulation. In both decades, the total number of prisoners on hand remained fairly stable, ranging between 1,500 and 6,000, although nearly 12,000 new prisoners were brought to the arsenals in the period 1772–81; about equal numbers were held at Toulon and Brest (2,500 each) in the early 1770's, with the numbers at Toulon gradually declining to 1,600 and those at Brest increasing to about 3,200 in the eighties.[57]

At first sight, the new system appears to have severely damaged prison security. But the figures themselves pose significant questions. The total number of escapes indicated for the early seventies, for example, does not include men who were captured in attempts to escape or recaptured afterward. No available evidence indicates whether the figures for the eighties include or exclude the escapees who were retaken. Apart from the frailties of the figures, and assuming that they do indicate a deterioration in security, the deterioration was not necessarily a result of the controversial "new system." A wide range of factors could affect the number of escapes.

Even the presence of different administrators at different ports could be reflected in the figures. Malouet knew that an increase in the number would reflect unfavorably on the new system that was partly his brainchild. The forçats at Toulon under his administration may have enjoyed better working and living conditions (as Howard reported them) than did the forçats at Rochefort and Brest; fewer of them, according to the statistics, managed (or tried?) to escape.[58] On the other hand, Guillot opposed the changes from the outset, and escapes did increase remarkably under him. Recalling that intendants exercised a large measure of autonomous authority at their respective ports, each reporting to the minister the number of escapes at his port, the differences in the predisposition and reaction, and the differing roles of these men in the face of the innovations, could have been a decisive factor in producing differences in the statistics. Many factors were involved; the evidence now at hand makes it impossible to determine in what measure, if at all, the new system itself contributed to the deterioration of security. One other detail of the "enlightened" administration of the prisons at the ports should be noted. The navy concerned itself in the 1780's, surprisingly, with the economic problems that prisoners faced at the time of their release. To meet those needs Intendant Marchais of Rochefort recommended granting travel allowances of not less than two sous per league for the summer months. Such travel grants had strong support from Malouet, who thought that injustice was done when a man was returned penniless to society and thereby exposed, "at the very moment his chains are broken, to misery and the commission of new crimes." In the fall of 1784, Marshal de Castries accepted the principle of expanded aid to liberated forçats and authorized a generous grant of twelve livres to each liberated man having no resources of his own.[59] Such action not only implied concern for justice, but also an enlightened official interest in the prevention and cure of crime. That was a note not often sounded elsewhere in 1782, and almost never heard in the prison administration of the day in France.

John Howard believed that physical facilities contributed significantly, often decisively in forming the character of any prison situation. In fact, Howard's work has been criticized for placing too much stress on physical plant. He believed a prison must provide satisfactory working conditions, spacious rooms, workshops, and yards. The three large French naval arsenals met those requirements in relatively ample measure. At Toulon, the only one that he visited, briefly, Howard himself saw 1,600 prisoners still living aboard the old galleys. They were not crowded, he said, and "being swept twice every day, [the galleys] were clean and not offensive. The slaves also were kept clean, and their clothing was neat, even in that galley which is used for the aged and infirm."[60] The discipline, especially the use of chains, he thought severe. But he found the clothing ration and the diet to be more than adequate. Howard added that the prisoners at Toulon "had good brown bread, well baked, in loaves weighing a pound and three quarters. All had some little allowance of three sous every day for wine." On each galley he found that two canteens were maintained: one dispensed wine to those who worked "for the government, the other was for the sale of white bread, greens, etc."[61]

Granting that Howard may not have seen the arsenal at Toulon so closely as he would have liked, for his visit apparently was surreptitious, he was a careful observer, a sharp critic of jailors. On the one hand, he might have been disposed to spare Malouet some critticisms if, as seems probable, Malouet had helped to "arrange" the secret visit. On the other, Howard keenly felt the fact that he was not welcome in France. A patriotic Englishman, he was naturally unwelcome at most French naval bases, for war was very close. Moreover, Howard was often an outright francophobe. The trifling reservations he expressed about the condition of the Toulon prison galleys and the many complimentary things he said about the establishment generally therefore seem specially significant.

Howard insisted on the maxim that useful labor is the essence of sound prison discipline, that work itself exercises propitious rehabilitative influence. Certainly, the forçats at the three French naval arsenals were given ample work of many kinds. Yet they do not appear to have been overworked, given labor practices of the time. Within limits, a prisoner at Toulon (and other bases) was free to work as much or as little as he liked. There was also adequate religious exercise to meet Howard's ideal requirements. Apothecaries and barber-surgeons were provided, along with excellent hospital facilities. In short, French arsenals provided most of the essentials of good prison establishments and came very close to meeting the standards of John Howard, best-known prison authority of the time.

In only two essentials did the bagnes at French arsenals fall short of Howard's ideal — in the quality of prison guards and officers, and in the possibly insufficient security. Another prison reformer, William Eden (Lord Auckland) earlier had said, "jailors are in general a merciless race."[62] But at French ports, long-standing statutes and regulations protected prisoners against excesses of arbitrary conduct on the part of individual jailors. The give and take of the system of the galleys, its working arrangements, and the interplay of self-interest militated against excesses. The formal rules, coupled with self-interest, offered far more protection to prisoners than most other houses of detention of that day. The venal and self-interested conduct of many guards and some higher officers cannot be denied; such men certainly fell short of being the "good, honest, humane, sober men" that Howard said he thought jailors ought to be.[63] But the personnel at French arsenals were not free to be the arbitrary, independent agents that jailors were generally reputed to be. The guards and noncommissioned officers allowed some practices that Howard might have judged pernicious, but the worst types of abuses then common among jailors, extending even to the confiscation of food and clothing, had been officially proscribed by naval regulations ever since Colbert's day. The detail and thoroughness of those regulations went far beyond those the local or provincial contemporary jail or workhouse was apt to have. Much evidence suggests that the regulations of Colbert and Seignelay's time were being generally enforced by the 1780's, along with some improvements. One of the worst features of the system of the galleys had been the galleys themselves. Without them, the system was relatively efficient and even humane for the practice of the day. The methods of handling the prisoners themselves were calculated to preserve their physical health. Their exploitation was controlled by rules; the rules were deeply entrenched, policed by the self-interest of the jailors themselves, superintended by men attempting to effect reforms and apply ideals of the Enlightenment and serving the interests of prisoner rehabilitation, not merely the ancient objects of retribution and restraint. The prisons at Toulon, Brest, and Rochefort were part of the legacy of the galleys, and also bore the impress of the "Enlightenment."

Conclusions and Reflections

Navies and naval vessels have always been multipurpose tools, built to satisfy needs dictated by geographic situation, technology, and the particular policies of the society or government building them. Galleys necessarily had different uses for different powers at different times and were useful over a much longer period than any other major type of naval craft in the Mediterranean. Their versatility enabled them to serve the governors of different Mediterranean societies in extremely varied conditions for more than two thousand years. Even in the seventeenth century, galleys were still giving useful service to such widely divergent requirements as those of the Order of Saint John, the Papacy, the Ottoman Empire, the States of North Africa, the Venetian Republic, Spain, and France.

The fact that widespread use was still made of galleys in the seventeenth century was itself remarkable. Compared with the sailing warships then in use, galleys were not formidable. Galleys were outgunned by almost every other war craft. Added limitations stemmed from their shortness of range and inability to keep the sea in heavy weather. At first sight, these limitations would seem to have been damning to French oar-driven craft in a period when they could conceivably be called on to contend with elements of the navies of England, the Netherlands, and Spain, all of whom wielded sea power with fleets of sailing ships armed with scores of broadside guns.

In fact, however, French galleys were not intended to deal with sailing ships. The French Galley Corps was developed for use in the waters, especially the coastal waters, of the Mediterranean. The squadron built on the Atlantic seaboard in 1690 was destined for auxiliary use and coastal patrols, and scattered soon afterward, did nothing to modify the basic commitment of French galleys to the Mediterranean theater of affairs. No one expected galleys, no matter how numerous, to engage even a single ship of the line or frigate or any other well-gunned naval unit. The occasions when they did so with success were rare. Such improbable successes in isolated engagements should not be interpreted to mean that galleys were considered suited to such work. Yet neither the rarity of such engagements, nor the still greater rarity of battles pitting galleys against galleys in the seventeenth-century Mediterranean is a satisfactory basis for judging the overall usefulness of galleys.

Throughout the seventeenth century, many of the Mediterranean powers, including France, still used galleys to keep pirates away and to patrol their own and neighboring coasts. The very presence of galleys was found to be salutary. The larger powers also used them in collaboration with elements of their sailing navies, sometimes even with their armies. Some powers, such as Spain and the Order of Saint John, found that galleys satisfied their need for highly mobile craft to maintain their own or to interrupt enemy communications in the western Mediterranean, and to make prey of infidel Ottoman and North African commercial shipping and smaller corsairs.

Louis XIV himself probably conceived the value of his galleys at least partly in comparative and imitative terms. The geographic and strategic situation of France severely limited the potential combat usefulness of French galleys. But Louis XIV was predisposed to favor using them by the very fact that other powers had special reasons of their own to rely on them. Louis' pride and pursuit of his *gloire* led him to lavish energies on surpassing other princes and powers in all sorts of ways, and the building of galleys was one of them. His special rival was the King of Spain. If Spain had galleys, France must have them too. The campaigns conducted by French galleys against the Spanish in the western Mediterranean were considered useful by Louis with or without battles — hence, the fact that his galleys and the Spanish never fought during his reign did not damn the galley (or his galley officers!) in his eyes.

Louis wanted his galleys to demonstrate his superiority, if not by combat in other ways. They were symbols of his power. By their numbers and discipline, by appearances along the coasts, by touching not only major ports but also tiny ones, Louis' galleys left vivid impressions of his prestige and magnificence, and a residue of influence that could be useful to a king of France.

Such influence was magnified by the care lavished on French galleys and favor given to galley officers. Officers serving on galleys enjoyed interservice precedence, ranking above (or before) officers of the sailing navy. When the two divisions of the navy served together (as neither liked to do), galley officers, given equal rank, would take command. Louis paid the officers of his Galley Corps on a higher scale; hence they could enjoy a relatively sumptuous standard of living, as befitted knights and aristocrats who derived their precedence and primacy from the will of their king, and not from the power of the fighting craft they commanded. Care and money were lavished on the flag galleys. They carried the squadron and fleet commanders; hence they and their trappings, like the officers themselves, represented the prestige and authority of the King. Louis armed his oar-driven craft with the finest bronze ordnance. He insisted that the rowing force of his galleys include a significant component of "infidel" slaves, reputedly the elite of the oar; many of the slaves, being prisoners of war, served as symbols of Louis' superiority. He provided this Corps with an impressive base, acclaimed as the finest, most richly equipped galley base in all the Mediterranean, fit for the fleet of a powerful prince who had no peer in Christendom.

Significantly, Louis stationed his Galley Corps in a coastal city that had repeatedly resisted royal authority, and that he had reason to awe by surveillance, and perhaps punish with the presence, of such a base. He sanctioned expansion of the galley base beyond the limits judged either necessary or desirable by Colbert and many Marseillais, but the royal will was partly thwarted by surreptitious opposition from both. Yet Louis seemed determined that Marseilles would not be able to defy him with impunity, or ever forget the presence of royal power. He succeeded in that, for in his time and long afterward the Marseillais must have been reminded of their King, their duty to him, by the gangs of the

Conclusions and Reflections

King's oarsmen tramping the streets, the galley infantry holding parades and inspections in the town, the royal galleys tied up facing the city hall, the King's officers dancing on the public square, the signal guns of the Corps booming reminders over the harbor and town.

Louis' galleys were on a par with other objects of his munificence and had some similar purposes. Lavish, seemingly extravagant expenditures had pervasive public relations effects and enhanced authority. Spending for galleys, like that for Versailles and for gifts, pensions, and privileges, improved the obedience of men and conferred prestige and power in France and in Europe — in such measure that the very age itself came to be dominated by the reputation of Louis XIV and still carries his name. Acts of munificence served to demonstrate superiority and at the same time to increase Louis' power. Showmanship was part of Louis' leadership. At home and abroad, his splendid galleys magnified his prestige and authority and for that reason, without any other, would have been a source of satisfaction to Louis XIV.

But the usefulness of galleys went further. The interplay of Louis' interests, those of French clergy and nobility, and the equivocal role played by the pontiffs of Rome in those interests and relations were naturally reflected in the administration of the Galley Corps. In significant ways the Corps functioned as a sort of theater. On its stage French noblemen, Gallican clergy, and representatives of Rome came together, and not only revealed the nature of their attitudes toward royal authority and power, but at the same time gave the King opportunities to use them for his purposes. Such a theater of affairs was certain to attract a King who directed his own court almost as though it were a playhouse, took on roles himself, manipulated the actions and minds of men with remarkable finesse and attention to theatrical detail, especially to public relations effects.

Louis XIV had no greater preoccupation than his own authority, and he made this concern evident early in his reign at the very establishment of his Galley Corps. That Corps was developed and directed as a royal tool, owned by the Crown and based at a royal arsenal. Louis began with elements of the existing galley establishment. He eliminated foreign-built, foreign-owned, and private galleys, along with foreign officers and noncommissioned personnel — it was not to be a haven of mercenary hirelings, but a base for loyal officers, French servants of the Crown. Ultimately, even non-French chaplains had to go. Louis

301

nationalized the Corps just as he did his sailing navy and the army. Such a force would be more serviceable, responsive to his will, and dependable than the partly private, partly foreign-built, foreign-owned, and foreign-manned naval forces that the navy in France had hitherto been. Clearly, the organization given to the Galley Corps represented a major effort to expand royal control, to nationalize the armed forces of the realm with the object of re-enforcing the King's authority.

Louis desired to have his subjects, especially noblemen, primarily serve their King and France. He encouraged them to do so in many ways. Conversely, he discouraged them from working abroad, for example, in the service of foreign princes or governments. Emigration was discouraged, and Protestants (except pastors) were forbidden even to go abroad, except by permission. He sought to draw Knights of Malta back into the royal service. Whatever else they were, these measures manifested Gallican or "national" orientation and purposes that were evident in the composition of officers and crews aboard royal galleys.

After 1672 the galleys were commanded by French-born officers holding their commissions at the pleasure of the King. Significantly, Louis not only reserved all commissions for French noblemen, but gave special preference to aspirants who were French-born Knights in the papal Order of Saint John. Obviously, in commissioning such Knights, he did several things. He brought into the royal service experienced French-born officers. He gained added religiopolitical stature and gave more substance to his title "most Christian King." And the employment of Knights also illustrates Louis' striving for authority, and at the same time reveals significant facets of the conflict between his authority and that of Rome.

The monarchy in France and the Roman Catholic Church were close collaborators in many ways, but historically they were also competing powers, most vehemently competitive where control of the Church in France was at stake, where the obedience of Gallican clergy was involved, and when certain fundamental issues of foreign policy produced clashes of French and papal interests. Kings and popes were objects of divided loyalties in varying degrees at different times. Sometimes there was not only division but dangerous incompatibility. Without compromises, confrontation with Rome was unavoidable for kings of France. But Louis seemed to be unwilling to go very far in compromising with Rome, or at least with Innocent XI; he seemed at times to welcome confrontation, and aggravated it in many ways in the management of his Galley Corps as elsewhere.

Louis apparently believed it fruitful to introduce this clash of authority in a Corps that he commanded, where he controlled many of the variables and seemed reasonably sure to win. By offering commissions to Knights of Malta, Louis forced the authority issue. Every French-born Knight of Malta had to make a choice when, in effect, their King said, "Decide whether you will serve God and Christendom and the Church in the papal service or in mine."

Louis XIV must have realized that Knights accepting his commissions needed to be persuaded that they could give satisfactory service to God and Christendom and the Church (Gallican) while serving in his Corps. He did not want his repeated clashes with the Pontiff, whatever their seriousness, to obscure the fact that he had honest Catholic Christian beliefs, and also a certain serious commitment to campaigns against infidels, when they gave hurt to him or to his subjects. Louis must have thought the magnetism of his service was enhanced for French noblemen by his continual warfare with the infidel city-states of North Africa and the many expeditions he sent against them and the Turks to oblige them to respect French interests. And there was the further fact that at times Louis employed as many as 2,000 turcs (infidel slaves) at the oars of his galleys. They, by their presence, and the galleys, by their existence, were intended to symbolize his commitment to warfare with the infidel. The impressions they created may have helped to persuade some French-born Knights to enter his service and to accept his commissions. But it must have been disappointing to Louis that the vast majority of French Knights chose to stay at Malta, declining his proffered commissions, preferring instead to continue campaigning with the Order's own squadron.

Their doubts must have seemed confirmed by Louis' capitulations agreement with the Porte in 1673 and later agreements with North African states in the eighties and nineties, to mention only a few of the negative circumstances that piled up. Until the mid-eighties, it became increasingly difficult, from a religious point of view, for Knights to choose the royal service, though Louis tried by many means, continually, to encourage them to accept his commissions and likewise to convince the Catholic clergy in France and his subjects generally — that he was a good Gallican Christian prince. He wanted them all, when they faced the Gallican-ultramontane choice, to choose fidelity to him, to his service, and to "his" Gallican Church.

Yet sooner or later, Knights who chose Louis' Corps were certain to face further choices. Louis must have expected and intended that they would face dilemmas of conflicting loyalties. By the campaigns he ordered them to undertake and the expectations he had of them, he involved them inextricably in his fundamentally factious relations with foreign princes and powers, such as the Papacy and Spain. For he did, after all, consider the Papacy a foreign power. The choice between their services and his should be clear, and was not difficult if they had made the Gallican choice on entering the royal service. Hence, all Louis' Knights faced conflicting allegiances, and the commanding officers among them had, in addition, the responsibility of making choices in tactical and other situations where they demonstrated, with more or less precision at different times, but with a fair degree of clarity on the whole, the nature and degree of their choices and allegiances. Thus, Louis appears intentionally to have made them take roles in his contest with Rome, where loyalty and obedience, and the alternatives of serving Pope or King, Rome or France, of being ultramontane or Gallican, were the immediate issues at stake the basic Bourbon-Hapsburg struggle being always the backdrop of the choices made.

At a time when the structure and machinery of his government were still in process of fundamental change, and the extent of royal control was still uncertain, Louis naturally wanted the fullest possible measure of loyalty from his subjects. From his point of view, all Knights who accepted his commissions deserved commendation. He welcomed those entering his service, since they thereby showed a pleasing degree of preference for it and, implicitly, some degree of allegiance to him. They came much closer to fulfilling his ideal than their fellow Knights who remained at Malta in the service of their Grand Master and the Pope.

Yet obviously Knights who entered his service — being still bound by vows to their Order and Grand Master and to the First Superior of their Order, who was the Pontiff in Rome — were holding back some measure of the loyalty Louis sought. Louis' attitude about this was expressed clearly when he created the Order of Saint Louis in 1693. That Order was created for the explicit purpose of encouraging and rewarding zeal and loyalty in the service of the King. Louis designated himself as Grand Master of the Order of Saint Louis, and aspirants to his Order took an oath promising absolute obedience to the King of France. Significantly, the charter of his Order stated that membership in the extant orders of Saint Michael and of the Holy Ghost *was entirely compatible* with membership in the Order of Saint Louis. Between these two established French orders of knighthood and the Order of Saint Louis, no conflict of interest was involved. Conceivably, a man could be a member of all three. But the unmistakable implication was that membership in any other order of knighthood was a disqualification if vows taken for it could limit or obstruct the giving of the full measure of obedience and loyalty to the King required of men for admission to the Order of Saint Louis. No fully committed Knight of the Order of Saint John (of Malta) could qualify for the Cross of Saint Louis. The supreme degree of loyalty required by each made the orders of Malta and Saint Louis mutually exclusive.[1]

Many officers of the Galley Corps received the Cross of Saint Louis, but it seems extremely doubtful that any Knight of Malta in the royal service received the Cross of Saint Louis from Louis XIV or any other king without first having been absolved of their full obligation to the Grand Master of the Order of Malta. According to A.-C.-A. de Marsy, no Knight of Malta obtained the necessary absolution from his vows until the last quarter of the eighteenth century.[2] But perhaps we should remind ourselves that the Knights who refused even to enter the French service were, in the eyes of the King, a long step further from qualifying to receive this highest honor and reward.

The function of the Galley Corps as a theater of struggle between popes and kings was further highlighted by the problems entrained by the employment of infidels as galley slaves. Both infidel (nominally Moslem) and European (nominally Christian) governments in the Mediterranean enslaved captive infidels. Christians seem to have been alone in making a concerted and sustained effort to take all coreligionists out of slavery, alone in classifying infidels, and only infidels, as slaves. In Louis XIV's time the Papacy strongly supported the policy of enslaving Mediterranean infidels (Moslems, renegades, and certain others). Though some popes had earlier condemned the institution of slavery, especially where non-European and primitive or pagan native populations were involved, Moslems were different. The authorities of virtually all the Christian churches (*not only* the Roman Catholic) were disposed to put Moslems in a class with renegades, as being dangerous enemies of the Christian Faith, and consented to their enslavement. Christian governments, for example, commonly labeled the North African states as pirates or corsairs, and referred to them collectively as "Barbary." The virtual unanimity of the Christian sanction for this determination helped to perpetuate in the Western world the opprobrium in which such peoples as the North Africans and the Ottoman Turks were held. The Church of Rome preached crusades against these Mediterranean infidels as late as the 1680's. The infidel captives taken in such warfare, combatants or not, were held as prisoners taken in religious war and were commonly enslaved. Thousands were employed at the oars of the galleys of the Order of Saint John and of the papal galley fleet; the latter still held North African slaves when Napoleon Bonaparte invaded Italy, at the end of the eighteenth century. The Church of Rome thus set an example for other Christian princes and governments of the Mediterranean, and the West, and in doing so defined the religious limits of this slavery as a phase of the perennial "Christian" crusading warfare with the infidel powers of the Mediterranean. The enslavement of Moslem and renegade infidels may have been consistent with the spiritual objectives of Rome. Rome, in any case, supported such slavery, though some ecclesiastics and even some popes had reservations, ethical or spiritual, concerning it.

But certain secular governments of Mediterranean Europe, notably the Venetian and that of Louis XIV, viewed such slavery and the warfare that accompanied it with perspectives of their own. Their interests were predominantly secular. Louis considered himself a good Gallican Christian prince, the leading Catholic prince of Europe, and a crusader only where some combination of his own and Gallican Catholic interests were involved. Religion as such was seldom if ever the prime mover in his policies. Yet Louis, and other secular Mediterranean powers, acting individually as they normally did, had no choice but to live with the war; whether they liked it or not — and their long-term secular interests gave them little reason to like it — this essentially religious warfare was made the dominant factor in Mediterranean maritime affairs; war was imposed on them by the "crusader powers," and also by the so-called infidel powers, who were aware that the crusading interests derived their manpower and financing from the generality of Christendom; all the "Christian" maritime powers were therefore accomplices. The Christian powers at least tacitly accepted the papal policy of enslaving infidels.

Conclusions and Reflections

Louis, for his part, whether from conviction or out of public relations interest, showed himself to be willing to enslave the infidel, and over more than three decades seemed to take extraordinary pains to prove that he was determined to use infidel slaves at his galley oars. By being thus equipped in orthodox Roman Catholic Christian fashion, French galleys could perform a religiopolitical public relations role in Europe, to underscore the Christian crusading "commitment" of Louis XIV.

Of course Louis treated Mediterranean infidels, not only the slaves he held but the representatives of the infidel governments, with the high-handedness typically employed by Western Europeans in dealings with non-European and non-Christian peoples, treating them as primitive or uncivilized, misguided, and inferior, and accordingly in need of education or conversion to qualify for the benefits of full membership in the European community of Christian peoples and states. Western Christian self-confidence abounded in Louis, strengthened by more than the usual sense of superiority.

Louis might himself have been willing to agree that Mediterranean Islam was the principal, or at least a major enemy of the Faith, but religion did not provide the principal basis of his judgment in matters of state; still less was his Catholicism the basis of his foreign policy vis-à-vis the Mediterranean infidel states. Louis' seeming inconsistency or faithlessness in this gave his critics at home and abroad powerful weapons against him. At times doubt about his orthodoxy, even about the sincerity of his faith, seemed to weaken the very sources of his authority as a Christian prince, and seemed capable of creating doubts in some minds as to his suitability as head of the Gallican Church. Such doubts could be extremely dangerous, and threatening in that age of faith.

Yet Louis judged the Ottoman infidels to be potential and necessary allies for himself and his realm in contending with the east European Hapsburgs. Perversely, he even viewed the North African states of Algiers, Tunis, and Tripoli as potential allies for the struggle with the Spanish Hapsburgs and with the English and the Dutch. Peaceful ties with Mediterranean infidel states could contribute to French maritime prosperity too, even providing bases for French commercial predominance in the Mediterranean basin. These were the interests that led Louis to seek peace and trade treaties with the Mediterranean infidel powers. Thus, the fundamental character of some of his confrontations and clashes with the Papacy is clear. His troubles with the Papacy were not simply a superficial matter of insults or protocol alone, nor doctrine, but were basic problems deriving from the antithetical nature of some of his objectives and some of Rome's. In many respects, Louis and the Papacy had antithetical objectives and followed exactly opposite policies.

Progressively, as Louis obtained more or less durable peace and trade treaties, first from the Ottomans, later from the "Barbary" powers, he whittled down the number of infidel states whose subjects he could legitimately acquire and enslave at French galley oars. Undeniably, cooperative relations with infidel states, including profitable politico-economic ties, could more easily be maintained if neither party attacked the shipping nor enslaved the subjects of the other. But such ideal decencies were not easily attainable in the early modern Mediterranean. The confounding of piracy and corsairing, princely quarreling, swashbuckling adventuring, privateering, religious war, and warfare by secular governments with varied motives, created a milieu of savage struggle. G. N. Clark called it a melee. Whatever the name, that struggle was perpetuated by the interplay of ruthless greed, politicoeconomic self-interest, and religious zeal. The weaker princes and powers of Christian Europe had to live with that perennial war. So did the states of North Africa and the Ottoman Empire. Only the strongest, most determined leaders of the European great powers had any serious chance of obtaining significant unilateral improvement in their own situation in the Mediterranean. Even when peace treaties were obtained, by armed expeditions or other pressures, there was hardly reason to hope that peace could be maintained. Too many legitimate governments, too many merchants, and too many religious authorities followed policies grounded on the conviction that they stood to gain from war, and particularly from the perpetuation of that melee. Indeed, Louis' own peace offensive, if it can be dignified by that term, was not designed to end the warfare, but to enable France to benefit from its continuance.

Louis actually joined the Papacy in favoring the continuance of warfare with the infidel. He also ostentatiously supported the papal policy of enslaving captive infidels. Louis simply sought to minimize French participation and to control the use he made of galley slaves originating from infidel states with whose leaders he was seeking (or had made) treaties of peace. Hence hundreds of infidel slaves were released from

French galleys on Louis' own order or his officers' command during the actual negotiation of treaties, and afterward in accordance with treaty terms. It was understood, given the procedures by which France acquired slaves, that some infidels from treaty sources were bound to be acquired; such men were captured or purchased in unbreakable lots that included desirable men. Hundreds of slaves from treaty sources were thus acquired, but efforts were made regularly in France, in the eighties and nineties, to release them under treaty terms.

The fact that Louis willingly continued to use slaves, considering all the difficulties with infidel treaty states that were bound to ensue, and the further fact that he had thousands of surplus French forçats on hand for use at the oars, suggests that Louis wanted to give the appearance of conforming to the Christian orthodoxies in the matter of enslaving and keeping infidels. But it also seems clear that Louis intentionally chose, as far as his relations with the Papacy were concerned, to make clear the extent of his power as King in his realm and to make peace on his terms with infidel states. In short, Louis was firm on a collision course.

This was particularly evident in the confrontations that ensued from the conduct of Louis' program of selective slave acquisitions. In its early stages that program seemed to be testing the firmness and consistency of the papal policy opposing the use of Christians as slaves. Louis or the ministry of marine in his name acquired schismatic Russians and Greeks to be used in lieu of Mediterranean infidel slaves. Ample numbers were available (from the Constantinople market), but since they were Christians, their purchase was sure to rouse opposition, such as that expressed by the Inquisitor at Malta, who gave expositions of Church policy vigorously opposing their use. Whatever else these moves meant, they did have the effect of delineating clearly the Papacy's firm stand against the enslavement of Christians, and conversely, the powerful influence that the Papacy wielded as a supporter of infidel slavery among Mediterranean Christian peoples and states. For if the Papacy determined which men could *not* be enslaved, it implicitly determined also the types of men who, for religious reasons, *could* and *would* be enslaved if ever they came into the hands of the slavers.

The religious character of infidel slavery, and the determinative role of the Church in its promotion was further underscored when Louis brought shipments of slaves from West Africa for use on his galleys.

West African slaves were a potentially dangerous innovation from the standpoint of vested-interest groups, including some elements in the Roman Church itself and also many temporal slaving interests, desiring to continue the perennial Mediterranean campaigns against Ottoman and North African infidel states, presumably in defense of the Faith. These vested interests were threatened by the fact that unlimited quantities of West African slaves could be provided by the slaving companies of the Atlantic seaboard powers; if many such slaves were brought, they would restrict and might go far toward eliminating the market for indigenous Mediterranean infidel slaves, thus discouraging the campaigns of the corsairs and privateers in that sea, for whom marketable infidel slaves were lucrative prey.

But Louis did not push for the introduction and use of these West African substitute slaves, as he might have done had he really wanted to find substitutes, or had he wanted to take an important step toward ending the Mediterranean melee. The matter was dropped. The decision not to employ them, and not to bring any more, was apparently based on some dubious negative "evaluations" of their utility. A key man in that determination was Intendant Brodart. He decided, even before the West Africans were tried, that they were unsuited to the oar. Louis' minister of marine strongly and repeatedly encouraged the missionnaires to work hard to make Christian converts of the sample substitutes from West Africa, and they did so, with apparent success. Being then doubly disqualified for the oar, the remaining West Africans were shipped to the West Indies for sale. Thus the effort to tap the most promising conceivable source of slaves was summarily dropped by Louis after an obviously "mock" test of utility of the most superficial, false kind. In effect, Louis threatened the Mediterranean market in infidel slaves with possible extinction, but then he backed off, having demonstrated his power, and his restraint, thus showing his disposition to continue as a Christian king should, using infidel slaves on his galleys.

Louis also called on his colony of New France to play a role in his "search" for non-Moslem substitute slaves. The number of American Indians he enslaved was small. A few score, including some chiefs, were seized and sent to Marseilles for his galleys. Louis also had other reasons for starting that Indian war; the capture of a few slaves was a terribly inadequate excuse. Yet he was seeking slaves, he said. There is equal certainty about the negative effects of the Indian war on the mis·

sionary work hitherto carried on among the tribes of New France; that work and the very lives of the missionaries, and the prospects of the colony itself, were put in jeopardy.

The drama of the war and the seizure of North American Indians as slaves, whatever other meanings they held, did underscore lessons that Louis must have meant for both the Pope and his Apostolic Vicar in New France, François de Montmorency-Laval, Bishop of Quebec, who claimed that his jurisdiction derived directly from Rome and who promoted programs and policies contrary to the wishes of the King and representatives of the Crown.[3] Perhaps Laval did not understand his King, for he would not relieve him of duties or arrest him. Instead, Louis started a war that destroyed, predictably, much of the missionaries' work and some of their prospects of further success in effecting conversions, projects dear to Laval. By his seemingly ridiculous incidental seizure and enslavement of Indians for his galleys, Louis demonstrated that he was determined to exercise his authority as he pleased, regardless of cost. Implicitly at least, he was insisting that his interests and authority, even in faraway New France, must be given priority over all others, including those of Rome. A Bishop of Quebec, whatever his claims, must take orders from France, from secular authority, from his King. Shortly afterward (1688) Laval retired, and the surviving Indians were returned to New France, as was the royal Governor Frontenac. Even the highest purpose of the Church, the salvation of souls, Louis seemed to be saying, could be made to give way to the interests of the Gallican King of France. Louis showed that the achievement of the objectives of Rome would be thwarted unless they were achieved in cooperation with the secular power.

Louis' quarrel with the Papacy and Church concerned matters of discipline, jurisdiction, and policy, not doctrine. Far from having quarrel with Catholicism, Louis was confident that the Catholic religion alone could confer the power kings wanted and needed. That confidence was expressed in 1681 in letters prepared for the Kings of Cochin China and Siam, to whom Louis recommended French missionaries and the Catholic religion as "the highest, most noble, most holy and above all the [religion] best suited to enable Kings to reign absolutely over [their] peoples."[4] These praises for his faith, though probably penned by one of Louis' religious counsellors, seem nonetheless to mirror the essence of his own convictions. He had confidence in Catholicism; he saw his religion, his clergy, and the Gallican Church alike as tools to be grasped and used.

But to use them together and to the fullest advantage and effect, he was persuaded in the eighties that he had to take a long-prepared step, and to pay the high price that was sure to be entrained by the act, of revoking the Edict of Nantes. Unjustified, bigoted, and cruel in Protestant eyes, this revocation was a momentous culmination of Gallican policy that aimed, like many other acts in Louis XIV's own and the previous reign, to consolidate Church-State cooperation and power in France. The consequences were pervasive and long-lasting for France, and incidentally very important for the Galley Corps.

As an immediate result for the Corps, hundreds of Protestants were arrested and dispatched to Marseilles to serve on the galleys, both for purposes of punishment and to change, if possible, their minds on religious matters. Public worship or assembly by Protestants being forbidden on pain of condemnation to the oar, and pastors being ordered to leave the realm, on pain of galleys or worse punishment if they stayed and preached, there were many recruits. Thousands of Protestants fled, and when it was also forbidden for ordinary subjects to flee, or to help others to flee, more recruits resulted. The notorious dragonnades were used to force mass "conversions," and in some instances and provinces, as in the Cévennes, there was more than sporadic armed resistance. All this produced several thousand men now identifiable by name, and doubtless others now unknown, who were dispatched to serve as forçats for their faith.

Louis chose the Gallican course in the management of ecclesiastical affairs in his realm, but stopped short of separation from Rome; then, by ending toleration of Protestant worship, he "unified" Christian worship and strengthened both the Catholic Church and his own hand as Gallican King. Louis used his enormous power as chief of state in the service of his French Catholic clergy, to promote a cause dear to them, by forcing, insofar as possible, reunification and conversion of Protestants, thus increasing the numerical strength of the Catholic community in France. Criticisms were heard, of course, but they were drowned in the pervasive ground swell of approval and applause. Most of Louis' faithful subjects and clergy must have regarded the act of revocation as a manifestation of his zeal for the faith. Increased fidelity and obedience to him, subtle consequences not easily proved, must have radiated deeply into the thought and actions of good Catholics throughout the realm. For the remainder of Louis' life, the tentacles of royal controls in France were probably endowed with largely increased religiopolitical vigor and energy, stronger ecclesiastical muscles, and a degree of willingness to be obedient and loyal not seen before or afterward in early modern France.

Probably in the hope of making these effects more certain, Louis approached his long-standing antagonist in Rome, Pope Innocent XI by requesting, through his Ambassador, that the Holy Father make known his sentiments. In effect, Louis solicited praise from the Pope on his zealous service to the Church, though of course his underlying purpose in the revocation had gone far beyond and away from service to the Church. Louis, as an ally and protagonist of peace with infidels, needed and apparently relished all the compliments the Holy See could be induced to give. Innocent XI, harassed veteran of many encounters with Louis' impieties, whims, and disciplinary failures, had little choice but to comply with the request. Innocent sent his Apostolic benediction and his compliments to His Majesty:

None of the illustrious proofs that your Majesty has given of his natural piety is more dazzling than the zeal that led you to revoke all the laws [hitherto] rendered in favor of heretics in your realm, and to provide as you have for the propagation of the Catholic Faith, of which we learned from our dear son, the Duke d'Estrées, your ambassador to us. We believed it was our duty to write these letters to render an authentic and durable testimony of the eulogy that we give to the splendid religious sentiments that you have shown, and to congratulate you on the superfluity of immortal praises that you have added, by this latest action, to all those that have rendered your life so glorious up to now. The Catholic Church will not forget to record indelibly in its annals a work of devotion to the Church as great as yours, and will never cease to praise your name. But above all you must expect from divine grace the reward for such lofty resolution [as yours], and be persuaded that we pray continually and ardently for that divine goodness.[5]

Louis must have been pleased. He would probably have liked something more directly complimentary and enthusiastic; he could hardly miss the double meanings in some of the Holy Father's phraseology. Yet it was enough — his *gloire* was approved, and his power in France was strengthened. He may even have smiled at those double-edged allusions to the "superfluity of immortal praises" that he was said to have added

313

to his reputation, and to his "great work of devotion" to the Church. Both the Pope and Louis knew the extent of his indiscipline, and the distinctly limited extent of Louis' "devotion to the Church" and "lofty resolution." But apparently it was useful for both of them to have his name and "work of devotion" recorded "indelibly" in the annals of the Church, and to have the Church "never cease to praise" his name.

The statement of the Pontiff was as much (or more) than Louis might reasonably expect in the way of praise. He must have realized that. After all, he was defying the papal policy of warfare with the Mediterranean infidel. He was an ally of infidel powers, enslaver of Christians, destroyer of the good works of Christian missionaries in New France, on countless grounds a perennial problem for the Holy Father, often an outright opponent of the spirit, acts, and policies of Rome. But deftly used for propaganda purposes, the Pontiff's praises would go far toward creating the impression Louis said he wanted to create, that of a "perfect reconciliation between the Holy See and myself." [6] Louis may also have believed that the revocation would help his own salvation. Louis needed help in that department too. But in his own world, Louis needed to demonstrate his religious orthodoxy to other Catholic Christians, especially to his clergy, his nobility, his subjects born and to be born in France. He had done that. He needed the strength that Gallican orthodoxy could confer. He wanted and would welcome the fidelity that his Gallican clergy and pious Catholic Frenchmen everywhere could now willingly give to their King.

He needed such support in the middle eighties because his relative position as the leading European prince in the Catholic world had been rapidly deteriorating. His stature was imposing, but many other princes and powers considered him threatening. With papal sanction they had been giving much of their admiration to the Hapsburgs and even to Sobieski after the Turks were turned back from Vienna in 1683. It hardly helped for Louis to have sent that powerful punitive expedition to bombard Catholic Genoa, half destroying the splendid old city of St. George for helping the Hapsburgs and defying his will. Louis' own successful culmination of his campaign for peace with the infidel states of the Mediterranean, and the treaties he obtained, were distinctly unappreciated outside France. In some Christian circles they could even have been considered added evidence of Louis' wickedness. He already had a well-established, unsavory reputation as a confirmed ally of the

Conclusions and Reflections

Ottomans. General resistance to Louis' policies on political, personal, and dynastic grounds was on the way to becoming a duty of Christian princes; an alliance against him was being formed, seconded by the Pontiff, Christian zeal, and Hapsburg diplomacy. Conceivably, Louis' enemies might rally under a banner of righteousness to extinguish his wickedness. Louis was suffering in 1684–85 from that now classic malady, diplomatic isolation.

The revocation of the Edict of Nantes was Louis' miracle cure. Whatever the mix of complex motives for that act, the immediate effects were favorable for Louis. The revocation proved he was a crusader for the faith, a destroyer of heretics within his realm. It turned public eyes away from his quarrels with the Pope, masked his policy of peace and alliance with infidels, and brought to the fore instead his orthodox, pious policy of extirpating heresy. With this role as promoter of the faith, Louis dispelled the dissatisfaction of many pious Catholics over the division of Christianity and religio-political leadership in France. A semblance of Christian unity could be claimed to have been restored. Of course Louis incidentally stirred sectarian passions anew and revived the horrors of religious warfare. The revocation also generated strong, potentially reformist criticism in France and in Europe, perhaps helping in the long range to germinate the Enlightenment. But at the same time, Louis rallied the powerful Gallican party and clergy to himself and appeased Catholic conservatives generally. He muzzled, for a time, his domestic conservative critics and ultramontane enemies by donning the cloak of Gallican Catholic orthodoxy. His reputation among his critics, hitherto tending to the "godless and wicked," was now to be stabilized (for many generations), as "narrow and bigoted" (with almost equal falsity). At a blow, Louis confused and handicapped all Roman Catholic religious opposition to his policies. No act of his reign had greater influence in generating Protestant and liberal Catholic opposition. None contributed more to the obedience and loyalty he could command as a Gallican Catholic King; hence the revocation was a climactic Gallican contribution toward accomplishing some of Louis' highest purposes.

The long-standing duel with Spain, never a full-fledged combat enterprise for Louis' galleys, by the eighties and nineties became a series of campaigns to fly the flag, to get salutes, to demonstrate the magnificence and superiority of Louis' forces, if only by trying to navigate with

315

greater numbers of galleys for as many months each year as the Spanish did. Even these noncombat anti-Spanish operations became passé at the end of the century when France and Spain became allies. Louis XIV then reduced, at last, the size of his Mediterranean galley fleet, though only from forty galleys to thirty. At the same time, he sought to reassure younger officers about the future of the Corps, saying he expected to retire some of his older captains, but wanted to keep the officer corps essentially intact. Louis was encouraging noblemen, the Knights among them, to stay with this decadent division of his navy, and many did stay and thus served their King. Notwithstanding the reassuring words of their King, the Corps was dying even then, but the process was gradual. It was slowed by Louis while he lived; after his death in 1715, the decay was fought principally by the galley officers themselves and especially by Knights of Saint John, since they were the dominant officer group in the Corps.

In the history of the fighting capabilities of European galleys, a milestone was reached in the early eighteenth century when a large Tripolitan sailing vessel sank a flagship galley of the squadron of the Order of Saint John, inflicting the loss of some five hundred men. This loss, with others suffered by the Knights and other galley powers in that same period enabled Grand Master Perellos to persuade the Knights to place their principal reliance on the sailing ship (though they continued to use galleys). Thus, even the Knights, staunchest partisans of the Mediterranean galley, were finally recognizing the galley's dangerous weaknesses for naval operations. Significantly, the new sailing vessels the Order decided to use in consequence of its disastrous loss, were constructed in the French port of Toulon, with Louis' sanction, at a time when Moslem and renegade-manned privateers from North Africa were being refitted in those same ports of Provence, as they were permitted to do under the terms of Louis' treaties with the North African states. Louis preferred neutrality in the campaigns the Christian Knights waged against infidel North Africans. But he encouraged the continuance of religious war, by helping both sides.

In the eighteenth century, galleys epitomized reaction. Oars as propulsion power on major units of the navy had long since given way to sails. Galleys were obsolete, costly, and unnecessary even in Louis XIV's day and were bound to be looked upon with curiosity and contempt in a later age, especially in an age that placed its faith in reason, progress, and utility. The Corps had been created in Louis' reign by Colbert, and that alone was condemnation in many eighteenth-century eyes; absolute authority and fiscal, religious, and political oppression were associated with Colbert, Louis XIV, and galleys. The idea of galleys must have conjured up popular thoughts of arbitrary arrests, judicial condemnation, prisons, chains, police, bigotry, intolerance, oppressive privileges, and taxes. All the hates and horrors of the economically and socially oppressed were mixed and interwoven in the eighteenth-century reputation of the galley. The association was natural, perhaps inevitable in an age that was adopting as its own such ideals as tolerance, humanity, freedom, and equality. If the books and pamphlets of the enlightened eighteenth-century advocates of reason and reform make relatively little mention of the galleys, it was perhaps because the galleys had already, by 1748, undergone reform in France and most other European societies.

The system of detention developed for galleys was perhaps the most important legacy of the Corps. The system outlived the old regime, the Enlightenment, and the Revolution, though without receiving the recognition or even the description by reformers that it deserved. The foundations of that system had been developed gradually by generations of galley administrators, outside as well as inside France, long before Louis XIV established his Galley Corps in 1665. This groundwork — partly from the Order of Saint John but largely Italian, as the very vocabulary of galley management suggests — was adopted and improved upon in French galley administration by Colbert and Seignelay, aided by Bégon, with later improvements introduced by the administrators of the bagnes at Marseilles and Toulon after 1700. Other improvements, along correctional and even rehabilitative lines, were added in the 1770's and 1780's by Marshal de Castries and Malouet, with encouragement from Louis XVI himself.

The whole system was exceptional among penal systems of that age, since it reflected the interest of the navy in nurturing the physical well-being of men destined to serve the oars. The relative abundance of food and clothing reflected these purposes; the pay-or-starve system of most prisons of the time was singularly absent. The accumulated administrative know-how of generations of galley officials was the core of the system, incorporated and preserved in hundreds of decrees. Together they made the bagnes at French naval arsenals remarkable examples of prison management at the end of the old regime. The ideal standards and conditions conceived by the Englishman John Howard, the best-known prison reformer-propagandist of the time, were very nearly met in full at the prisons of Brest, Rochefort, and Toulon. John Howard did not know, or if he did know, neglected to advertize their excellence. Englishmen and Frenchmen did not browse freely in each other's naval arsenals in the 1780's. Howard, as he himself admitted, had only a superficial, secret visit at Toulon, which must have been the best of the three. But Howard's published work suggests he saw little more than the physical plant and something of its administration; he seems to have found Toulon to be practical and fully adequate.

Howard had no chance to see that the inmates at Toulon, and also at Brest and Rochefort, were handled in a fashion calculated to serve the interests of reform and rehabilitation, in the modern social welfare sense, and not simply the needs of security aimed at the prevention of escapes. Collectively, the prisons at the three French arsenals constituted what must have been the best administered, most enlightened major penal system of the time in Western Europe. Judged even by twentieth-century standards, the system had much to commend it, and the galériens held in those prisons were certainly among the most fortunate victims of the harsh judicial and fiscal systems of the time. But neither they nor their relatives and friends could appreciate the relative excellence of the system of detention at the ports. The reform writers of the eighteenth century, who had some basis for comparative judgment, did not visit naval arsenals, and did not see or describe the prisons themselves — Malouet was a rare exception, and he was swept up and out in the swift course of revolutionary events after 1789. Frenchmen thinking of galleys and galériens in the last days of the old regime and long afterward must have focused mainly on the judicial, fiscal, and police systems of Louis XIV's day that sent men to the galleys and kept them there; judgments about the injustices of an earlier period of the old regime helped to romanticize the galérien, and Victor Hugo immortalized him in *Les Misérables* as Jean Valjean.

Glossary

Glossary

The following translations and descriptions are intended to identify terms used in the French Galley Corps, but the terms themselves are neither exclusively maritime nor French. Some came from the language of the sea, others were adaptations of terms commonly used in other branches of French administration or in other European galley establishments long before the seventeenth century.

argousin. Police officer on the galleys, a watchman-guard, a noncommissioned functionary subordinate to the comite, charged with surveillance over the oarsmen; the argousins made rounds, inspected irons and chains, supervised the night sentinels, lit lanterns and navigation lamps at dusk, renewed supplies of wood and water aboard, and were assisted by sous-argousins and "trusty" aides.

argousin-major (or réal). Each squadron had an argousin-major who exercised authority over the argousins on all the galleys; as a sign of authority, he carried a special cane or stick.

bagne. Prison or prison compound; many Mediterranean port cities had one, particularly if their inhabitants engaged in slaving. At Marseilles after 1700, and at other ports later, the workhouse manufactory where workable invalids and many able-bodied forçats were housed, fed, and worked in conditions resembling those in some early modern factories.

banc. The five or more men who served the same oar, also the place where oarsmen rowed and slept; pieces of plank, rounded and padded with cowhide coverings to serve as a bench onto which they dropped in pulling their oar.

baraques. Dockside shanties or jerry-built structures housing the tiny stalls and workshops on the wharf where some oarsmen plied trades, and for which they paid rent.

bonnevoglie. Perhaps literally, a "good rower," but not judged to be such after 1670 in France; a man volunteering to serve as an oarsman, receiving remuneration, not subject to the chain and theoretically free (on French galleys) to quit the service at the expiration of his campaign or enlistment; were replaced by mariniers and forçats.

capitulations. Agreements, or the series of treaties signed between the Ottoman Imperial authority and certain European powers.

chaînes. Groups of men being escorted under guard from one prison to another or to the galleys. Normally, the men in a chain were manacled or linked to each other and to a central chain that was lengthened as the number of condamnés attached was increased. From Colbert's time onward, an effort was made to regulate the frequency with which the principal chains stopped at the major prisons along their varying routes.

comite. Noncommissioned officer charged with managing the rowing force and working the galley, assisted by two or more sous-comites; his post was toward the stern when under way, forward on the rambarde when entering a port; they wielded the whip.

commerce de galère. The give and take or interplay of interests (some might call it graft and corruption) aboard galleys.

commissaire des galères. Supervisory officials, ranking immediately after the intendant, sometimes with particular areas of responsibility: commissaire des classes, etc. (commissaire on a galley, see *écrivain*).

condottiere. Soldier, sailor, or nobleman (entrepreneur) following the profession of war, who voluntarily contracted to take or deliver service in the armed forces of any prince or power offering attractive remuneration.

currency. The livre was the basic unit (later the franc), of twenty sous, with twelve deniers to the sou, and three livres to the écu; of course equivalents differed from place to place and over time in France.

Congrégation de la Mission (Lazaristes; Vincentians; Prêtres de la Mission). A missionary order founded by St. Vincent de Paul. Vincent and his successors in the post of Superior General of the Congrégation were concurrently Chaplains General of the Galleys and Directors of Spiritual Affairs in the galley hospital at the base; most but not all galley chaplains were priests of the Congrégation; all chaplains were under the direction of the Superior of the Congrégation at Marseilles.

corbeaux. Forçats and other oarsmen assigned to assist with collecting and burying the bodies of victims of the plague at Marseilles, Aix, and Toulon during the great plague of Provence (1720–23).

droit d'échelle. On the galleys, a fee paid by oarsmen being unchained for work; a gangway or ladder fee, collected when an oarsmen left the galley.

échevin. Municipal magistrate, town elder.

Glossary

écrivain. Purser, performing clerical functions, sometimes called the commissaire on a galley.

enterprise. Method of accomplishing government work by using contractors, sometimes selected by competitive bidding. In any case, a reliance on private enterprise to do the work (cf. *régie*).

esclave, see *turc.*

Flûte. In this period, a sailing vessel designed to carry cargo, sometimes Dutch-built or designed along lines commonly identified as Dutch.

forçat. Convict or forced laborer. On the galleys, one of the King's subjects, or a subject of certain other Christian princes (e.g., Savoy, Monaco, and Wurtemburg at different times all supplied forçats for French oars).

galère de dépôt. A galley, usually old or unseaworthy, designated to remain in port, serving as a port of floating stockade, where newly arrived, invalid, or other unassigned men could be held.

galère sensille. Galley of ordinary size, as distinguished from the capitaine, réale, and grande réale, which were of larger size and served as flagships for detachments, squadrons, and the fleet, respectively.

galères perpétuelles. Condemnation to a life's term in the galleys.

galérien. Galley oarsman, whether freeman, forçat, or slave.

galleass. Vessel of medium or large size, most common in the sixteenth-century Mediterranean, using both oars and sails, with one or more gundecks and (unlike the galley) with broadside armament of heavy ordnance.

garde-magasin. Warehouse guard, watchman.

gens sans aveu. Historically perhaps, men (vassals) without a recognized overlord. As used by many early modern French police and judicial officers, a term roughly equivalent to the English *vagrants.*

guerre de course. Privateering war.

Huguenot. French Protestant (usually a Calvinist; occasionally also Lutherans or others), officially known as an R.P.R. or Religionnaire (see these terms).

infidel. An unbeliever; according to the *Catholic Encyclopedia,* a person ignorant of the true God (pagan), or one not recognizing Christ (Mohammedans and Jews).

intendant. Royal officer with large executive and judicial powers, particularly administrators of provinces or ports.

Knights of Malta, see *Order of Saint John.*

lettre de cachet. Sealed orders, emanating from the sovereign, usually relative to an individual, for arrest or imprisonment; their notoriety grew from their sometimes being issued in blank.

major des galères, see *argousin-major.*

manille. The wooden grip on the oar, designed to accommodate the hands of the oarsman and to facilitate the working of the oar.

marinier (matelot) de rame. French conscripts or sailors ordered to serve the oar, usually as auxiliary or relief oarsmen on campaign.

matelots de rambarde. Sailors, usually volunteers, sometimes conscripts serving only during campaigns. Employed to work the ship under sail and to man the rambarde (and guns) in the bow of the galley (see *rambarde*).

Maure, see *turc*.

Missionnaires. Priests or, on the galleys, chaplains of the Congrégation de la Mission. See also *Congrégation*.

munitionnaire. Contractor or merchant promising delivery of victuals and other supplies.

Officier de sel (or *grenier de sel*). Agent of the tax farmers collecting the salt tax (gabelle).

Order of Saint John (of Jerusalem, Rhodes, Malta; the Hospitalers). Known in early modern centuries as the Order of Malta and in contemporary literature and papers as La Religion. A military order of chivalry, arm of the Papacy and Church of Rome (the Pope being the "First Superior" of the Order) established at Malta for about three centuries after 1530. Nearly all the Knights were recruited from among the Catholic nobility of Europe, especially of France, Spain, and Italy, and vowed to serve Christendom — in effect, Roman Catholic Christendom — against the Infidel.

parlements. Assemblies (sometimes called courts) with provincial or regional jurisdictions, and with judicial authority of last resort in many types of cases.

passe-vogue. In rowing, the most rapid cadence.

pertuisanier. Halberdier, or guard armed with a pertuisane (halberd), and a regular member of the galley crew who maintained surveillance over the oarsmen, particularly at night and during work periods in the city. Also known as compagnons-gardiens after 1680.

prouyers. Youngsters of seven to thirteen years, often six per galley in the Colbert period, serving apprenticeships to become noncommissioned officers.

quarterol. Fourth oarsman on an oar; quinterol, fifth rower.

rambarde. A timbered, sometimes partly armored structure erected at or near the bow of a galley to provide some cover and protection for gun crews and oarsmen.

R.C.A.R. Abbreviation of the official phrase "Religion Catholique Apostolique et Romaine," or Roman Catholic Religion.

réale, grande réale. Names given to oversized galleys designed as flagships for squadrons or the fleet.

régie. Method of carrying on government work, using salaried officials of the State to manage or direct the operation instead of private enterprise (cf. *enterprise*).

La Religion. The Order of Saint John.

Religionnaire. A Protestant or adherent of the R.P.R.

Glossary

R.P.R. Abbreviation of "Religion Prétendue Reformée," the official designation used in France for Huguenots or Calvinists, or for Protestants generally.

sculpture des galères. Ornamentation, especially on the stern of the *réale* and other flag galleys.

Slave, see *turc.*

turc. Any Moslem slave, also a virtual synonym for *esclave.* In the Galley Corps of Louis XIV's time, the slaves were generally non-Christian oarsmen acquired by capture or purchase: Moslems, renegades, and non-Christians of other sorts, all of them commonly labeled *turcs.* They were North Africans primarily, men from the Balkans or Asia Minor secondarily; others came from west Africa, Africa south of the Sahara, even North America.

vogue-avant. Farthest inboard place on an oar.

Notes

Abbreviations of Major Archives

Aff Etr: Archives des Affaires Étrangères, Archives
Nationales or Quai d'Orsay (Paris)

BN: Bibliothèque Nationale (Paris)

BR: Archives Départmentales, Bouches-du-Rhône (Marseilles)

DCP: Archives de la Marine, Dépôt des Cartes et Plans (Paris)

Marine: Archives de la Marine (Paris)

Toulon: Archives de la Marine (Toulon)

Notes

The Uses of Galleys

1 The Musée du Désert, in the Cévennes not far from Nîmes, dedicated to the galèriens, or "forçats pour la foi." Thousands of their names are inscribed on its walls.

2 Albert Savine, *La Vie aux galères*, 5.

3 There seem to have been striking similarities between maritime enterprisers using galleys (the Duke de Centurion and the Duke de Tursis, for example) and the military enterprisers described by Fritz Redlich, *The German Military Enterpriser and His Work Force*; V. G. Kiernan, "Foreign Mercenaries and Absolute Monarchy." Neither the institution of maritime military entrepreneurship nor the forced labor establishments of various Mediterranean (and other) ports have been objects of the special study they deserve.

4 Maurice Lombard, "Arsenaux et bois de marine dans la Méditerranée musulmane (VIIᵉ–XIᵉ siècles)," 53–99; Frederic C. Lane, "Venetian Shipping during the Commercial Revolution," 18–22 and *passim*; Fernand Braudel, *La Méditerranée et le monde méditerranéen à l'époque de Philippe II*, I, 130–131, 277; II, 325–326. See Michel Devèze, *La Vie de la forêt française au XVIᵉ siècle* (Paris, 1961), 2 vols.; R. G. Albion, *Forests and Sea Power*, and P. W. Bamford, *Forests and French Sea Power*.

5 Alberto Tenenti, *Piracy and the Decline of Venice* (on the difficulties and costs involved in maintaining heavy ships, see chs. 5, 7); Lane, "Venetian Shipping," 18–21, on the lessening of the maritime power of Venice: "A basic reason for this failure [to keep up with other seagoing peoples] was the exhaustion of one of the most vital of her natural resources, ship timber" (p. 21). Significantly, it was reported to the French ministry of marine (1671) that a vessel destined for Tripoli had been captured with a cargo of timber including precut pieces for a galley, along with oars and some of the hardware (clouterie) (B⁴ 4 (Marine) fols. 278, 280).

6 Tenenti, *Piracy and the Decline of Venice*, Ch. 7. Cf. Carlo M. Cipolla, *Guns, Sails and Empires*, *passim*.

7 B⁶ 90 (Marine) fol. 3.

8 On the interrelated phenomena, maritime warfare, piracy, and privateering in

the early modern Mediterranean, the literature is large and growing. Braudel surveyed the sixteenth-century problem; Geoffrey Fisher's *Barbary Legend* and G. N. Clark's *War and Society in the Seventeenth Century* examine the seventeenth-century problem. Aspects of the general problem are also treated by S. Bono, *I corsari barbareschii* (Torino, 1964); Cipolla, *Guns, Sails and Empires*; Tenenti, *Piracy and the Decline of Venice*; Roger Coindreau, *Les Corsaires de Salé*; and Peter Earle, *Corsairs of Malta and Barbary*. Many of these works include references and bibliography. Histories of the Order of Saint John, of Mediterranean trade, of the Mediterranean navies and naval operations also throw light on phases of the melee. The confusion and instability characteristic of the Mediterranean in the earlier seventeenth century were largely overcome by the assertion of firm Western European (Christian) maritime predominance in the Mediterranean in the late seventeenth and early eighteenth centuries.

9 Louis Bergasse, *Histoire du commerce de Marseille*, IV, pt. 1, 84.

10 Mém et Doc (Aff Etr) Alger 12, fols. 120–123.

11 Bergasse, *Histoire du commerce*, IV, pt. 1, 84–85.

12 *Ibid.*

13 Paul Masson, "Les Galères de France, 1481–1781," 104.

14 Bergasse, *Histoire du commerce*, IV, pt. 1, 76–77. On the navy of the period, Charles de la Roncière, *Histoire de la marine française*, IV, and L.-A. Boiteaux, *Richelieu*, chs. 1, 2, 5, and *passim*.

15 Malthe 1 (Aff Etr) "Déclaration en faveur de l'Ordre de Malthe," 1634.

16 Antoine de Ruffi, *Histoire de la ville de Marseille*, II, 358–359; Charles de la Roncière, *Valbelle "Le Tigre"*, 20–25, and his *Histoire de la marine*, V, 32–38.

17 Cardinal Richelieu, *Testament politique*, 408–409.

18 *Ibid.*; cf. Edmond Esmonin, "Sur l'authenticité du *Testament politique*," 219–220. See also the original printing in the *Bulletin de la Société d'Histoire Moderne*, 1951–52, 14–20, including a discussion by R. Mousnier and V. L. Tapié.

19 Malthe 2 (Aff Etr) "Instruction pour Le Sieur Chevallier de Gout s'en allant de la part du roy à Toulon & en suit à Malthe," 18 Nov 1663.

20 A. Jal, *Abraham Duquesne et la marine de son temps*, I, 283, 290, 309, and *passim*.

21 Malthe 2 (Aff Etr) "Instruction," 18 Nov 1663.

22 Jean-Baptiste Colbert, *Lettres, instructions et mémoires*, III, pt. 1, 16.

23 Roncière, *Histoire de la marine*, V, 383.

Limitations of the Oar

1 B⁶ 85 (Marine) fol. 180.

2 B⁶ 87 (Marine) fols. 66–67, 70.

3 B⁶ 87 (Marine) fols. 66–70.

4 B⁶ 22 (Marine) fols. 227–228; B⁶ 23 (Marine) fol. 60.

5 B⁶ 87 (Marine) fols. 66–67, 495.

6 B¹ 523 (Aff Etr) Aubert to Pontchartrain, Genoa, 31 Dec 1697.

7 Colbert, *Lettres*, III, pt. 1, 221.

8 V. Brun, *Guerres maritimes de la France*, I, 58.

9 B⁶ 86 (Marine) fol. 71.

10 B⁶ 106 (Marine) fol. 737.

11 D¹ 18 (Marine) fol. 211.

12 B⁶ 115 (Marine) fol. 293.

13 B⁶ 85 (Marine) fol. 398.

14 B⁶ 115 (Marine) fol. 292.

15 Masson, "Les Galères de France," 88–100; B⁶ 87 (Marine) fol. 494.

16 DCP 49 (272) pièce 9, 1693.

17 *Ibid.*, 20ᵇⁱˢ.

18 B⁶ 82 (Marine) fol. 288.
19 B⁶ 87 (Marine) fol. 138.
20 Brun, *Guerres maritimes*, I, 221.
21 B⁶ 106 (Marine) fol. 737.
22 Brun, *Guerres maritimes*, I, 32.
23 Colbert, *Lettres*, III, pt. 1, 18–19.
24 B⁶ 87 (Marine) fol. 138.
25 B⁶ 22 (Marine) fols. 38, 56, 136, 164; B⁴ 12 (Marine) fols. 172–177.
26 B⁴ 18 (Marine) fol. 120.
27 DCP 49 (272) pièce 12, "Mémoire," Marseilles, 1 Jan 1693.
28 B⁶ 123 (Marine) fol. 124.
29 Colbert, *Lettres*, III, pt. 1, xlviii.
30 D¹ 18 (Marine) fol. 156.
31 B⁶ 89 (Marine) fol. 188.
32 B⁴ 18 (Marine) fol. 87.
33 DCP 49 (272) pièce 20ᵇ¹ˢ; B⁶ 89 (Marine) fols. 226–228. Barras de la Penne also emphasized the need to increase the firepower, urging heavier construction of the galleys themselves because, he said, speed was less important in galleys than it had earlier been (B⁴ 25 (Marine) fol. 225).
34 D¹ 18 (Marine) fols. 69–71. See also R. C. Anderson, *Oared Fighting Ships*, 79–81.
35 B⁶ 83 (Marine) fols. 186, 188; B¹ 513 (Marine) Compans to minister, Genoa, 11 Mar 1676.
36 DCP (Marine) "Instruction," signed Louis, Versailles, 1 Aug 1696.
37 B⁶ 83 (Marine) fols. 186, 188; other evidence of the superiority of selected Spanish fleet elements is found in B⁶ 84 (Marine) fol. 26; B⁶ 90 (Marine) fols. 15–16.
38 B⁶ 17 (Marine) fol. 263.
39 B⁶ 17 (Marine) "Instruction que Le Roy veut estre mise en mains du Sr Duc de Mortemart, Général des Galères," 25 Jy 1695.
40 DCP 3 (84) Louis XIV to Noailles, 26 Dec 1679.
41 DCP "Instruction," Louis XIV to Noailles, 14 Apr 1692.
42 DCP Louis XIV to Noailles, 1 Aug 1696.
43 D¹ 18 (Marine) fol. 167.
44 Concerning the possible influence of mercenary traditions and religious obligations in helping to produce unenterprising conduct on the part of some of Louis' galley officers, see P. W. Bamford, "Knights of Malta and the King of France," and pp. 302–304 herein on Louis' desire to be served by Knights of St. John.
45 On the Pailletrie action, see D¹ 18 (Marine) fol. 156; B⁶ 142 (Marine) "Mémoire," 1749; Roncière, *Histoire de la marine*, VI, 410–412. On the Langeron action, see Roncière, *Histoire de la marine*, VI, 456–458; Marteilhe, *Mémoires d'un protestant*, 94–104 *passim*.
46 DCP Mairobert MSS., 170; Roncière, *Histoire de la marine*, VI, 298.
47 DCP 3 (84) Recueil des ordres de Louis XIV, "Instruction," signed Louis, 16 Dec 1679.
48 *Ibid.*, 10 Je, 12 Oct 1680.
49 B⁴ 19 (Marine) fol. 83; DCP 49 (272) "Instruction," 7 Jy 1696.
50 DCP pièce 24 "Saluts," 1699.
51 Quoted in Roncière, *Histoire de la marine*, VI, 298.
52 DCP 3 (84) "Instruction," signed Louis, 1 Aug 1696.

The Base at Marseilles

1 Gaston Rambert, *Histoire du commerce de Marseille*, IV, pt. 2, 205.
2 BN (Nouv Acq Fr) 21306 fol. 432, Colbert to Arnoul, 17 Je 1666.
3 *Dictionnaire de biographie française*, III, 977–988; V, 1274.

4 Gaston Rambert, *Nicolas Arnoul: Intendant des Galères à Marseille, 1665–1674*, Ch. II and pp. 54ff.; see also his *Histoire du commerce de Marseille*, I, IV, pt. 2, and *passim*.

5 Rambert, *Nicolas Arnoul*, 70–95.

6 BN (Nouv Acq Fr) 21307 fols. 382–383, Colbert to Arnoul, 23 Feb 1688.

7 See evidence offered in Rambert, *Nicolas Arnoul*, 97–100, 125–128.

8 BN (Nouv Acq Fr) 21307 fols. 370, 382–384, 398, Colbert to Arnoul, 23 Feb 1668; Rambert, *Nicolas Arnoul*, II and 96–99. Arnoul's negotiations with the Bernardins initially moved them to cede a tract that the City was pressured into purchasing for use as part of the arsenal; in later purchases, however, Madame Arnoul was the buyer, pp. 41–44.

9 B⁶ 1 (Marine) fol. 133.

10 Quoted in Roncière, *Histoire de la marine*, V, 404.

11 Masson, "Les Galères de France," 194.

12 B⁶ 88 (Marine) fol. 208.

13 Cited in Masson, "Les Galères de France," 194. Translatable as "The great Louis built this base for unconquered fleets/ From here he gives his laws to conquered seas."

14 B⁶ 3 (Marine) fol. 21.

15 B⁶ 88 (Marine) fols. 232, 307–323 *passim*.

16 B⁶ 17 (Marine) fol. 229.

17 B⁶ 88 (Marine) fols. 236–237.

18 B⁶ 88 (Marine) fols. 234–235.

19 *Ibid.*

20 B⁶ 88 (Marine) fols. 233–234.

21 Rambert, *Histoire du commerce de Marseille*, IV, pt. 2, 414–417.

22 B⁶ 88 (Marine) fols. 236, 309.

23 B⁶ 88 (Marine) fol. 286, signed by fifteen officers and Intendant Montmort; fols. 207–237 contain extended discussions pro and con between architects and the administrators of the arsenal evaluating criticisms of the facilities.

24 Claude Farrère, *Histoire de la marine française*, 115, and his *Jean-Baptiste Colbert*, 8.

25 Quoted in René Mémain, *La Marine de guerre sous Louis XIV*, 968.

Building and Victualing the Galley Corps

1 B¹ 515 (Aff Etr) "Balance de la dépense," 1680. For the military condottiere of the period and the general background, ownership, composition, and management of military forces, primarily central European, see Fritz Redlich, *De Praeda Militari*; see also Kiernan, "Foreign Mercenaries and Absolute Monarchy," and Michael Roberts, "The Military Revolution."

2 On foreign constructions, see B⁶ 85 (Marine) fol. 303; Colbert, *Lettres*, III, pt. 1, 19–20n., 27.

3 The B⁶ series in the Archives de la Marine provides an infinity of detail concerning the construction of French galleys. That material was partially surveyed by Masson, "Les Galères de France," 201ff., and was very familiar to that excellent historian, A. Jal. See especially his *Glossaire nautique*.

4 See n. 3. For example, B⁶ 136 (Marine) "Longeurs et proportion de la mâture des Galères," 1725. On construction, equipment, and management of galleys in the period, see Jurien de la Gravière, *Les Derniers jours de la marine à rames*, 137–247, and Jal, *Glossaire nautique*. Some significant comparative analyses of the dimensions and qualities of French and Venetian galleys reported by Seignelay, *L'Italie en 1671*, 239–244. The general history of the subject by Anderson, *Oared Fighting Ships*, offers careful, detailed analysis on some themes, though little on French galleys.

5 B⁶ 19 (Marine) fols. 47–48; DCP 44 (272) pièce 23 illustrates some differences in the prestige associated with the command of galleys of various sizes and of different numbers of oarsmen.

6 Masson, "Les Galères de France," 209, cf. 201–202.

7 B⁶ 2 (Marine) fol. 153.

8 B⁶ 82 (Marine) fols. 143–148. See Masson, "Les Galères de France," 201–218, on the luxury aboard French galleys.

9 Roncière, *Histoire de la marine*, V, 383.

10 Masson, "Les Galères de France," 222–223.

11 B⁶ 123 (Marine) fol. 298; B⁶ 142 (Marine) "Mémoire concernant la construction des galères," 1749.

12 B⁶ 32 (Marine) fol. 91.

13 B⁶ 20 (Marine) fols. 64–65, 156.

14 B⁶ 85 (Marine) fol. 303. One estimate was about 14,000 livres by entreprise, and 28,000 by régie.

15 B⁶ 19 (Marine) fol. 143.

16 B⁶ 21 (Marine) fol. 67.

17 B⁶ 23 (Marine) fols. 229–234. He appointed an inspector to supervise constructions by régie, and ordered that efforts be made to reduce costs to levels achieved earlier by entreprise.

18 On the Chabert affair, see B⁶ 14 (Marine) fols. 136, 142, 155–156; B⁶ 21 (Marine) fol. 170; B⁶ 84 (Marine) fols. 18, 210–250. Chabert lesson outlines or plans; B⁶ 85 (Marine) fol. 47.

19 B⁶ 2 (Marine) fols. 154, 157.

20 B⁶ 9 (Marine) fol. 96.

21 Bibliothèque Municipale de la Ville de Marseille, ms. 49.034; B⁶ 9 (Marine) fol. 96; B⁶ 19 (Marine) fols. 179–180; B⁶ 25 (Marine) fols. 7–8; B⁶ 24 (Marine) fol. 137.

22 B⁶ 116 (Marine) fols. 154–155, 163.

23 A² XVI (Marine) p. 123.

24 B⁶ 22 (Marine) fol. 183.

25 The desire for such rapid construction was probably much intensified, if not actually rooted in knowledge that the Venetians had accomplished such feats. The whole affair points up the highly competitive spirit which characterized French maritime effort and, at the same time, underscores the considerable extent of borrowings of technical knowledge and method from the Venetians and the Order of Saint John for the organization and management of the French Galley Corps. Seignelay himself, soon to be minister, visited Venice and, though disliking its government, prepared long memoranda on its arsenal and related matters, partially printed in *L'Italie en 1671*, 228–265. On Venetian galley constructions in general, see Frederic C. Lane, *Venetian Ships and Shipbuilders of the Renaissance*; many of Lane's articles are listed and a selection of them is reprinted in his *Venice and History*.

26 Colbert, *Lettres*, III, pt. 1, 299.

27 B⁶ 83 (Marine) fols. 32–35 "Relation d'une galère bâtie à Marseille dans vingt-quatre heures en l'année 1678." See also B⁶ 10 (Marine) fols. 174–175, where a later construction "trial" is described.

28 Colbert, *Lettres*, III, pt. 1, 19.

29 *Ibid.*, 279.

30 *Ibid.*, pt. 2, 39.

31 B⁶ 9 (Marine) fol. 83.

32 B⁶ 11 (Marine) fol. 144.

33 B⁶ 78 (Marine) fol. 152.

34 B⁶ 2 (Marine) fol. 148; Colbert, *Lettres*, III, pt. 1, 298.

35 Colbert, *Lettres*, III, pt. 1, 57.

36 B⁶ 88 (Marine) fol. 209.

37 B⁶ 25 (Marine) fol. 83; cf. fols. 332, 341–342, 347.

38 BN (Fonds Fr) 6171, fol. 154.

39 Colbert, *Lettres*, III, pt. 1, 502.

40 B⁶ 13 (Marine) fol. 20.

41 B⁶ 16 (Marine) fol. 189.

42 B⁶ 13 (Marine) fols. 20, 47.

43 B⁶ 83 (Marine) fol. 47.

44 B⁶ 10 (Marine) fols. 35, 40–41.

45 B⁶ 10 (Marine) fol. 150.

46 Bamford, *Forests and French Sea Power*, 75, 87.

47 B⁶ 24 (Marine) fols. 301–303, primarily intended for use as *bordages*, etc.

48 Albion, *Forests and Sea Power*, 388–391.

49 On the Messina expedition and the problem of worms, see B⁶ 9 (Marine) fols. 44, 65, 111–113, 119, 152–153, 157–158, 203.

50 B⁶ 19 (Marine) fols. 179–180.

51 B⁶ 13 (Marine) fol. 20; B⁶ 83 (Marine) fol. 47. Officials at the École des Eaux et Forêts at Nancy suggest, in correspondence, that it is extremely unlikely that such chemical action could produce such rot; probably the author of these remarks didn't consider it possible either, and was simply disparaging certain fellow officers.

52 B⁶ 3 (Marine) fol. 20; B⁶ 83 (Marine) fol. 47.

53 B⁶ 83 (Marine) fol. 47.

54 BN (Nouv Acq Fr) 21307 fols. 383–384.

55 *Ibid.*

56 B⁶ 20 (Marine) fol. 11. For the weights and measures involved, see Raymond Collier and Joseph Billioud, *Histoire du commerce de Marseille*, III, 302–305.

57 B⁶ 19 (Marine) fol. 71–72.

58 B⁶ 83 (Marine) fol. 168.

59 B⁶ 8 (Marine) fol. 114.

60 B⁶ 7 (Marine) fol. 98; B⁶ 8 (Marine) fol. 137.

61 B⁶ 10 (Marine) fol. 163ᵇⁱˢ (1–3), fols. 172–173.

62 B⁶ 13 (Marine) fol. 46.

63 B⁶ 13 (Marine) fol. 21.

64 B⁶ 8 (Marine) fols. 16–18.

65 B⁶ 8 (Marine) fols. 16–18, 28, 32, and *passim*.

66 B⁶ 9 (Marine) fols. 30, 32.

67 B⁶ 8 (Marine) fols. 13, 89, 115.

68 B⁶ 13 (Marine) fols. 21, 46; B⁶ 16 (Marine) fols. 81–82.

69 B⁶ 19 (Marine) fol. 30.

70 Jal, *Duquesne*, I, 283, 290, 309, and *passim*.

71 1L 124 (Toulon) p. 37.

Officers and the Crown

1 B¹ Malthe 1 (Aff Etr) fols. 373–374, 1650; fol. 420, 1658.

2 B⁶ 12 (Marine) fol. 104; B⁶ 13 (Marine) fols. 32, 190; B⁶ 16 (Marine) fol. 154.

3 Ernest Lavisse, "Sur les galères du roi," 227. See also Masson, "Les Galères de France," 240–241.

4 Marquis de Ternes (Jean d'Espincha), quoted in Masson, "Les Galères de France," 230, 319.

5 Marquis de Centurion, "Gentilhomme Genois," and a maritime mercenary of the problem sort (Colbert, *Lettres*, III, pt. 1, 171–172, 201; B⁶ 1 (Marine) fols. 184–196 "Traité" with Centurion, 3 Nov 1669; B⁶ 4 (Marine) fol. 39).

6 Masson, "Les Galères de France," 232–233.

7 BN (Nouv Acq Fr) 21307 fol. 395 (Arnoul papers).

8 *Ibid.*

9 Abbé René de Vertot, *Histoire des Chevaliers Hospitaliers de Saint Jean*, V, 301.

10 D¹ 18 (Marine) fol. 162 "Chevalier Barras de la Penne."

11 Chevalier Luc de Boyer d'Argens, *Réflexions politiques sur l'état et les devoirs des Chevaliers de Malthe.*

12 *Ibid.*, 115–117.

13 Colbert, *Lettres*, III, pt. 1, 143.

14 B⁶ 4 (Marine) fols. 14, 66.

15 B⁶ 12 (Marine) fol. 42.

16 Colbert, *Lettres*, III, pt. 1, 143.

17 B⁶ 12 (Marine) fol. 36.

18 B⁶ 4 (Marine) fols. 51–52 "Noms des galères du roy," with names of captains, 26 Apr 1672.

19 B⁶ 8 (Marine) fols. 1–2 list of squadron commanders and captains ordered to campaign in 1674, with names of their commands, 4 Jan 1674.

20 B⁶ 8 (Marine) fol. 72 "Lettre du roi," 27 Je 1676.

21 B⁶ 12 (Marine) fols. 32–35 list of officers assigned to thirty galleys, 28 Jan 1680.

22 BN (Nouv Acq Fr) 21381 fols. 17–21 "Liste géneralles des officiers de galères," Jan 1692. DCP 49 (272) "Extrait . . . sur les 25 galères commandées par M. Bailly de Noailles, 24 Jy 1694. For some discussion of lack of confidence or willingness to engage Roman Catholic belligerents, see Bamford, "The Knights of Malta and the King of France" (where the importance of the Knights is emphasized, and the services of non-Knights are perhaps too little stressed), and P. Auphan, *La Marine dans l'histoire de France*, 43–45. The writer was informed that a work being prepared by M. Perrichet will throw light on the officers' role in the Corps.

23 Roncière, *Valbelle*, 96.

24 *Ibid.*, 73–75, 80.

25 B⁶ 77 (Marine) fols. 287–288.

26 A³ 12 (Marine) p. 65.

27 B⁶ 5 (Marine) fols. 201–202.

28 C⁷ 194 (Marine) "M. de Manse."

29 Masson, "Les Galères de France," 227–231.

30 Roland Mousnier, *La Vénalité des offices sous Henri IV et Louis XIII*, is the basic work on the problem.

31 DCP Recueil des ordres, congés.

32 B⁶ 3 (Marine) fol. 218; A³ 12 (Marine) fol. 119.

33 B⁶ 19 (Marine) fols. 172, 188–189, 225–226.

34 B⁶ 9 (Marine) fol. 165.

35 B⁶ 9 (Marine) fols. 53–54.

36 B⁶ 13 (Marine) fol. 221. Galleys had distinct military characteristics, and experience in the army was considered to be excellent preparation for officer status aboard, even for commanding, a galley. For example, Charles-François de Vintimille, Count du Luc, having commanded Louis' troops and having lost an arm on the battlefield, was considered qualified by experience (and proved loyalty) to command in the Galley Corps, at various times a single galley, a squadron of galleys, and the infanterie des galères in an amphibious operation (Teignmouth, 1690). He subsequently became Commandeur de St. Louis, Ambassador to Swiss Cantons, and then Ambassador to Vienna (C¹ 160–161 (Marine) "du luc"). P. Anselme and Augustin Dechaisse, *Histoire généalogique et chronologique de la maison royale de France*, II, "Charles-François de Vintimille."

37 B⁶ 13 (Marine) fol. 220.

38 B⁶ 13 (Marine) fol. 220.

39 B⁶ 88 (Marine) fol. 342.

40 B⁶ 19 (Marine) fol. 133.

41 B⁶ 24 (Marine) fols. 206–207.
42 DCP "Recueil des ordres," 16 Sept 1693.
43 B⁶ 12 (Marine) fol. 9.
44 B⁶ 9 (Marine) fols. 115–116, 172; C⁷ (Marine) "de Foresta."
45 B⁶ 12 (Marine) fol. 232; B⁶ 19 (Marine) fols. 245, 255.
46 B⁶ 10 (Marine) fol. 87.
47 B⁶ 25 (Marine) fol. 295.
48 B⁶ 9 (Marine) fol. 49.
49 B⁶ 25 (Marine) fols. 368, 389.
50 B⁶ 87 (Marine) fols. 424–425.
51 IL, 119 (Toulon) "Ordre du roi," 8 Jan 1685, p. 1; BN (Nouv Acq Fr) 21381 Arnoul Papers, 9 Je 1689.
52 B⁶ 98 (Marine) fol. 414.
53 BR (Fonds Cor) XIV E 824, "Ordonnance," 14 Feb 1686.
54 *Ibid.*, XIV E 827, "Ordonnance," 2 Jan 1717, art. 45.
55 *Ibid.*, XIV E 824, "Ordonnances," 8 Jan 1686, 9 May 1689.
56 *Ibid.*; 1L 119 (Toulon) pp. 93–95.
57 B⁶ 6 (Marine) fols. 43–44; 1L 119 (Toulon) "Ordonnance," 16 Feb 1682.
58 B⁶ 19 (Marine) fol. 229; B⁶ 6 (Marine) fol. 139.

Chaplains, Lower Officers, and Freeman Crew

1 Gaston Tournier, *Les Galères de France et les galériens protestants des XVIIᵉ et XVIIIᵉ siècles*, I, 34, 101ff.
2 *Ibid.*, 34.
3 Pierre Coste, *La Congrégation de la Mission dite de Saint-Lazare*, 129ff.
4 *Ibid.*, 133.
5 BN (Colbert papers, Mélange) 84, fols. 268–270.
6 B⁶ 24 (Marine) fols. 64, 72.
7 Colbert, *Lettres*, III, pt. 2, 112.
8 *Ibid.*, 123–124. See also Tournier, *Les Galères de France*, I, 120ff.
9 B⁶ 13 (Marine) fols. 201–202.
10 A³ 12 (Marine) fol. 121.
11 DCP "Recueil des ordres," 11 Nov 1685, signed Bégon. A³ 12 (Marine) fol. 139.
12 DCP "Recueil des ordres," 11 Nov 1685.
13 B⁶ 19 (Marine) fol. 217; BN (Nouv Acq Fr) 21381 printed Ordonnance du Roi, 23 Oct 1687, signed Bégon.
14 B⁶ 27 (Marine) fols. 425, 459–460.
15 B⁶ 28 (Marine) fol. 183. As early as 1687 the Congrégation de la Mission was proposing establishment of a seminary for chaplains and seeking help from Bégon to do so. (B⁶ 19 (Marine) fol. 35) Such a seminary, obviously, could supply additional chaplains and provide more uniform training for them, and also bring the priests already in the service to conform to new standards.
16 Tournier, *Les Galères de France*, I, 120–195.
17 *Ibid.*, 30, 94–95.
18 *Ibid.*, 95.
19 *Ibid.*, 101.
20 *Ibid.*
21 Charles de Bombelles, Chevalier de Saint Louis, 1694. Ludovic de Colleville and François Saint-Christo, *Les Ordres du Roi*, 173.
22 Jean Bion, *Relation des tourments qu'on fait souffrir aux Protestants qui sont sur les galères de Fance*, i–xxvi.
23 B⁶ 12 (Marine) fol. 65.

24 B⁶ 12 (Marine) fols. 85, 105, 139, 170.

25 B⁶ 13 (Marine) fols. 62–63, 84.

26 B⁶ 13 (Marine) fol. 156.

27 B⁶ 19 (Marine) fol. 123.

28 B⁶ 19 (Marine) fol. 2.

29 B⁶ 11 (Marine) fol. 273.

30 B⁶ 85 (Marine) fol. 449.

31 B⁶ 125 (Marine) fol. 168.

32 B⁶ 11 (Marine) fol. 273.

33 B⁶ 13 (Marine) fol. 19.

34 D.C.P. *"Recueil des ordres,"* 11 Nov 1685.

35 BN (Nouv Acq Fr) 21381 fol. 296, 23 Oct 1687. But see René Mordacq's treatment of a perhaps more representative surgeon, whose career René Mordacq reconstructed using a selection of letters and papers in private hands, in "Maître Antoine Moulinneuf, chirurgien des galères du roi," 249.

36 B⁶ 24 (Marine) fol. 269.

37 Roncière, *Histoire de la marine,* V, 372.

38 Tournier, *Les Galères de France,* I, 35.

39 *Ibid.*

40 Colbert, *Lettres,* III, pt. 1, 218n.

41 Roncière, *Histoire de la marine,* V, 372; Jal, *Duquesne,* I, 483.

42 Quoted in Tournier, *Les Galères de France,* I, 29.

43 A³ 12 (Marine) p. 179.

44 Tournier, *Les Galères de France,* I, 95.

45 Roncière, *Valbelle,* 44–45.

46 B⁶ 33 (Marine) fol. 182.

47 Colbert, *Lettres,* III, pt. 1, 305n.

48 B⁶ 98 (Marine) fol. 418.

49 B⁴ 4 (Marine) fol. 379; Gaston Rambert, *Histoire du commerce de Marseille,* IV, 394–396.

50 B⁶ 82 (Marine) fol. 11.

51 B⁶ 95 (Marine) fols. 194ff., 261ff.

52 B⁶ 93 (Marine) fol. 350.

53 B⁶ 82 (Marine) fol. 11; B⁶ 93 (Marine) fol. 350.

54 BR (Fonds Cor) XIV E 824 "Convention," 12 Je 1688.

55 *Ibid.*

56 B⁶ 6 (Marine) fol. 138.

57 B⁶ 12 (Marine) fols. 282–283; B⁶ 87 (Marine) fols. 476–482; Masson, "Les Galères de France," 250–251.

58 B⁶ 87 (Marine) fol. 476.

59 B⁶ 20 (Marine) fol. 62.

60

	Sailing Ships	Galleys
Soldat	10 livres	9 livres
Caporal	15	10
Sergent	21	15

B⁶ 90 (Marine) fols. 319–331; B⁶ 6 (Marine) fols. 43–44. Soldiers in 1706 were receiving 6 livres a month for sea duty, 9 livres ashore, the former apparently including full rations from the King (Masson, "Les Galères de France," 250).

61 B⁶ 90 (Marine) fols. 423–424.

62 B⁶ 89 (Marine) fol. 221.

63 B⁶ 89 (Marine) fol. 542.

64 B⁶ 11 (Marine) fols. 256–257.

65 B⁶ 13 (Marine) fol. 240.

66 B⁶ 84 (Marine) fol. 422 (1683); BR (Fonds Cor) XIV E 824 "Ordonnance," 9 Jan 1686; B⁶ 87 (Marine) fols. 476–482; A³ (Marine) p. 208.

67 B⁶ 20 (Marine) fols. 159–160.

68 B⁶ 2 (Marine) fol. 148. The deductions for uniforms were discussed above.

69 B⁶ 13 (Marine) fols. 223, 240.

70 B⁶ 87 (Marine) fol. 476.

71 A³ 12 (Marine) fol. 208.

72 B⁶ 78 (Marine) fol. 417.

73 B⁶ 78 (Marine) fols. 45, 417–422.

74 Colbert, *Lettres*, III, pt. 1, 218n; B⁶ 2 (Marine) fol. 13; B⁶ 109 (Marine) fol. 445.

75 B⁶ 78 (Marine) fols. 320–331; B⁶ 80 (Marine) fol. 227; Jal, *Glossaire nautique*, "Marinier de rame," 979.

76 On maritime conscription generally, see Eugene L. Asher, *The Resistance to the Maritime Classes*, and René Mémain, *Matelots et soldats des vaisseaux du roi*.

77 B⁶ 80 (Marine) fols. 227–229; Jal, *Glossaire nautique*, "Marinier de rame," 979.

78 B⁶ 109 (Marine) fol. 443.

79 B⁶ 78 (Marine) fol. 395.

80 B⁶ 109 (Marine) fol. 447.

81 B⁶ 86 (Marine) fol. 47.

82 A³ 13 (Marine) pp. 9, 57.

The Procurement of Slaves

1 B¹ 373 (Aff Etr) Nointel to minister, 19 August 1670; B⁶ 137 (Marine) "État de la chiourme des galères du roy," 1673.

2 A considerable literature treats the history of the institution of slavery in the Americas, particularly in the South, and in Western society generally; for a survey of the field and literature, see David Brion Davis, *The Problem of Slavery in Western Culture*. Considerable attention has also been given to the slave trade, particularly to its transatlantic phases (for a survey, see Philip D. Curtin, *The Dimensions of the African Slave Trade*). Neither Davis nor Curtin is concerned with Mediterranean slavery in early modern times. No general history of Mediterranean slavery seems to exist; even the nature and extent of the problem is in many respects a confusing one in the early modern period. A start can be made with Charles Verlinden's closing section in *L'esclavage dans l'Europe médiévale* and with the general bibliographical surveys by Jean Sauvaget, *Introduction to the History of the Muslim East*; Ch.-André Julien, *Histoire de l'Afrique du Nord*, and the *Cambridge Modern Histories*. Histories of the Mediterranean naval establishments, privateering and piracy, trade, religion, and international law also touch upon slavery.

3 Hugo Grotius, *The Rights of War and Peace*, titles IV, V, VI (IX in the original), 346.

4 Thus, some Spanish, presumably Roman Catholic prisoners of war were put to the oar on French galleys in the later 1670's, but as an exceptional act of retribution on Louis' part. His apparent intention was that the Spaniards were to be treated as forçats rather than as slaves and that they would be released after he obtained satisfaction from the King of Spain; the survivors were, in fact, released.

5 For example, see R. W. Southern, *Western Views of Islam in the Middle Ages*, 43–44, 57, and *passim* (especially his discussion of Bacon, Wycliffe, John of Segovia, and Nicolas of Cusa).

6 John W. Bohnstedt, "The Infidel Scourge of God" (abstract of his Ph.D. thesis, University of Minnesota). On Luther, see Southern, *Western Views of Islam*, 104–107.

7 Elizabeth Schermerhorn, *Malta of the Knights*, 231.

8 *Ibid.*

9 *The Catholic Encyclopedia*, XV, "Urban VIII," 219. In 1462, Pius II declared that slavery was "a great crime"; in 1537, Paul III forbade the enslavement of the Indians; then Urban VIII and later Benedict XIV issued edicts forbidding it (*ibid.*, XIV, "Slavery").

10 Schermerhorn, *Malta of the Knights*, 231–232.

11 England also owned and maintained two galleys of her own for a brief period in the 1670's, based in Italy (Sir Julian Corbett, *England in the Mediterranean, 1603–1713*, II, 363–365).

12 Clark, *War and Society*, chs. 1, 5.

13 B⁶ 135 (Marine) fol. 227; B⁶ 78 (Marine), fol. 133.

14 Colbert, *Lettres*, III, pt. 1, 27–28.

15 O (Toulon) 106ᵇⁱˢ *passim*.

16 B⁶ 78 (Marine) fols. 172, 414.

17 Colbert, *Lettres*, III, pt. 1; B⁶ 78 (Marine) fols. 172, 176–178, 180.

18 Brun, *Guerres maritimes*, I, 79. The expedition was probably connected with the Balkan slave purchasing schemes then afoot.

19 *Ibid.*, 182–183.

20 B¹ 696 (Aff Etr) Cotolendy to minister, Leghorn, 10 Dec 1677 and 14 Jan 1678.

21 B¹ 696 (Aff Etr) Cotolendy to minister, Leghorn, 11 Mar 1678; Corbett, *England in the Mediterranean*, II, 386–387.

22 B¹ 517 (Aff Etr) Aubert to minister, Genoa, 17 Dec 1681; B⁶ 14 (Marine) ministei to Aubert, St. Germain, 18 Jan and 9 Feb 1682; B¹ 301 (Aff Etr) Robert Paris to min ister, Cagliari, 12 Mar 1682.

23 Vertot, *Histoire des Chevaliers*, VI, 429–455.

24 B¹ 814 (Aff Etr) Chevalier de Gout, letters of 11, 18 Mar and 24, 29 Apr 1644.

25 The Order apparently had few slaves to sell in the period immediately follow ing the loss of Crete (1669), but the shortage must have been alleviated by the 1,200 infidel prisoners of war reported to have been taken by the Knights in 1673. It was reported at the end of the first quarter of the eighteenth century that La Religion had "more than six thousand slaves" on hand and was "surchargé."

26 B⁶ 79 (Marine) fols. 309–310.

27 B⁶ 5 (Marine) fols. 160, 212.

28 B¹ 814 (Aff Etr) Bailly d'Escrainville to minister, 12 Dec 1692, 9 Nov 1697. D'Escrainville was given the generalship of the galleys of the Order in 1697.

29 Cotolendy was described by Cardinal d'Estrées as "very active and very intelli gent" (J. Cordey, ed., *Correspondance de Louis-Victor de Rochechouart*, I, 3n.).

30 A³ (Marine) "Ordonnance" 15 Feb 1678; Colbert, *Lettres*, III, pt. 2, 84n.; the ordonnance was renewed 30 Je 1686.

31 B¹ 695 (Aff Etr) Cotolendy to minister, Leghorn, 2 Mar 1674; Corbett *England in the Mediterranean*, II, 363–365.

32 B⁶ 14 (Marine) fol. 62.

33 B¹ 696 (Aff Etr) Cotolendy to minister, Leghorn, 10 Dec 1677, 10 Mar 1679. See also B¹ 1158 (Aff Etr) Le Blond to minister, Venice, 12 Apr 1687.

34 B⁶ 78 (Marine) fols. 112–113; B¹ 700 (Aff Etr) Cotolendy to minister, Leghorn, 1 Mar 1692.

35 O (Toulon) 106ᵇⁱˢ offers an excellent month-by-month illustration of the func tioning of the transportation system for getting slaves from northern Italy to Mar seilles, including transport by the galleys themselves from time to time.

36 The edict of prohibition sought to facilitate customs collections at Marseilles by crushing direct traffic between northern Italy and Lyons. Bⁱⁱⁱ 235 (Aff Etr) "Mémoire touchant le commerce des navires françois de Levant en Italie" with Le Bret letters of 13 and 18 Feb 1688. B¹ 699 (Aff Etr) Cotolendy to minister, 22 Nov 1690; one group of 123 slaves were on hand for more than three months.

37 B¹ 699 (Aff Etr) Cotolendy to minister, 14 Jy 1690.

38 B⁶ 14 (Marine) fols. 62, 68–70, 97.

39 B¹ 698 (Aff Etr) Cotolendy letters for the last four months of 1686; G. B. Depping, *Correspondance administrative sous le règne de Louis XIV*, III, 658–659. On releases, see pp. 260–265 below.

40 Colbert, *Lettres*, III, pt. 1, 188.

41 *Ibid.*, 187; Depping, *Correspondance administrative*, II, 912, 921–22.

42 Colbert, *Lettres*, III, pt. 1, 503.

43 B¹ 814 (Aff Etr) Piancourt to minister, Malta, 8 Je 1674.

44 *Ibid.*; B⁶ 6 (Marine) fol. 102. For evidence that the person involved was young Seignelay, see Piancourt's letter of 20 Sept 1674.

45 B¹ 814 (Aff Etr) Piancourt to minister, 13 Nov 1674.

46 B⁶ 9 (Marine) fols. 157–158.

47 B⁶ 10 (Marine) fol. 24.

48 B⁶ 10 (Marine) fols. 182, 194; B⁶ 11 (Marine) fols. 30–31, 47–48.

49 B¹ 814 (Aff Etr) Tincourt to minister, 19 May and 3 Je 1680.

50 *Ibid.*

51 Colbert, *Lettres*, III, pt. 1, 57n., revealing Colbert's early views on the nature and condition of the "guinee" natives; his later interest focused on "Cap Vert."

52 A considerable number of blacks were present in France during the period, most of them servants or craftsmen. (J. Mathorez, *Les Étrangers en France sous l'ancien régime*, I, 392).

53 B⁶ 91 (Marine) fols. 102–103.

54 B⁶ 9 (Marine) fol. 232.

55 Masson, "Les Galères de France," 266.

56 B⁰ 10 (Marine) quoting letter of the minister to Brodart, 29 Jan 1678; see also 13 Mar 1678.

57 B⁶ 10 (Marine) fol. 164.

58 B⁶ 11 (Marine) fols. 90, 145.

59 B⁶ 14 (Marine) fol. 257; B⁶ vols. 11, 12, and 13 *passim*, correspondence connected with deliveries, care, and health of the blacks. See also Mathorez, *Étrangers*, I, 397.

60 B⁶ 12 (Marine) fol. 252.

61 Colbert, *Lettres*, III, pt. 2, 154–155.

62 B⁶ 11 (Marine) fols. 102–103.

63 B⁶ 11 (Marine) Colbert to Brodart, 15 Sept 1679.

64 B⁶ 12 (Marine) fols. 281–282.

65 B⁶ 13 (Marine) fols. 176, 180.

66 B⁶ 80 (Marine) "État des rations," 1671.

67 B⁶ 90 (Marine) fols. 198–199.

68 B⁶ 13 (Marine) fols. 34, 172.

69 B⁶ 14 (Marine) fol. 249.

70 B⁰ 14 (Marine) fol. 257.

71 *Ibid.*

72 About this time Monsieur Mariage was discharged (B⁶ 15 (Marine) fol. 20).

73 B⁶ 17 (Marine) fol. 438. For a few further details on the effort to employ black slaves, see P. W. Bamford, "Slaves for the Galleys of France, 1665–1700" (an earlier version of this section).

74 1L 124 (Toulon) p. 294.

75 O (Toulon) 106ᵇⁱˢ "Registre des Esclaves." Those identified as blacks were numbers 3, 15, 22, 23, 43, 77, 86, 96, 167, 287, 288, 356, 371, 401, 444, 550, 569, 1084, 1110, 1127, 1223 (all of whom arrived *before* the 1679 shipments, and most of whom continued to serve long *afterward*).

76 DCP 49 (272) pièce 14 "Mémoire sur l'état des chiourmes," c. 1690.

77 Treaties or conventions were signed with Algiers in 1681, 1684, 1689; Tripoli in 1683, 1685, 1693; and Tunis in 1685; similar arrangements had earlier been made

with Salé (Gaston Zeller, *La Méditerranée et ses problèmes aux XVIe et XVIIe siècles*, no. iv, 189–194; B⁶ 14 (Marine) fols. 91–92).

78 Zeller, *La Méditerranée*, no. iv, 190.

79 B⁶ 14 (Marine) fols. 91–92.

80 *Ibid.*

81 Plantet, *Correspondance des Deys d'Alger*, I, 97, 99.

82 *Ibid.*, 100.

83 *Ibid.*, 117n., cf. 111n.

84 Zeller, *La Méditerranée*, no. iv, 191–194; B⁶ 20 (Marine) fols. 74–77.

85 *Ibid.*, 194. See also O (Toulon) 106ᵇⁱˢ "Registre des esclaves."

86 M. Girouard, "L'Expédition du Marquis de Denonville," 94.

87 *Ibid.*, 94–95.

88 G. M. Wrong, *The Rise and Fall of New France*, II, 504.

89 B⁶ 19 (Marine) fol. 247.

90 B⁶ 20 (Marine) fols. 3–4; Girouard, "L'Expédition," 93.

91 B⁶ 20 (Marine) fol. 165.

92 Girouard, "L'Expédition," 93.

93 Chevalier de Beugy, "Journal of the Expedition of the Marquis de Denonville against the Iroquois: 1687."

94 Girouard, "L'Expédition," 93.

95 Quoted in Henri Lorin, *Le Comte de Frontenac* (Paris, 1895), 269.

96 *Ibid.*, 369–370; B⁶ 21 (Marine) fols. 38, 44; Girouard, "L'Expédition," 89.

97 B¹ 1158 (Aff Etr) Le Blond to minister, Venice, 8 Jan 1683; B¹ 814 (Aff Etr) Escrainville to minister, Malta, 6 Mar 1685. On the sack of Arta, Malta, 10 Jy 1685, "their troops took great booty before ours could arrive."

98 B¹ 1158 (Aff Etr) de la Haye to minister, Venice, 29 Dec 1685 and Jan 1686; response of 16 Mar to mémoire of 3 Jan 1686.

99 B¹ 1158 (Aff Etr) Le Blond to minister, Venice, 1 Je 1686.

100 Depping, *Correspondance administrative*, II, 951.

101 B⁶ 19 (Marine) fols. 215–216.

102 B¹ 814 (Aff Etr) Tincourt to minister, Malta, 6 May 1680.

103 B¹ 696 (Aff Etr) Cotolendy to Seignelay, Leghorn, 10 Dec 1683.

104 B¹ 1158 (Aff Etr) Le Blond to minister, Venice, 7 Je 1687.

105 B⁶ 16 (Marine) fols. 117, 144.

106 B⁶ 19 (Marine) fol. 37.

107 B⁶ 19 (Marine) fols. 106–108, 146.

108 B⁶ 19 (Marine) fol. 87.

109 Depping, *Correspondance administrative*, II, 949–950.

110 B¹ 814 (Aff Etr) Escrainville to minister, Malta, 16 Dec 1687. See also B⁶ 19 (Marine) fol. 167; B⁶ 20 (Marine) fol. 41.

111 B¹ 1158 (Aff Etr) Le Blond to minister, Venice, 25 Oct 1687; B⁶ 21 (Marine) fol. 2.

112 Depping, *Correspondance administrative*, II, 951–952.

113 B¹ 521 (Aff Etr) Aubert to Pontchartrain, Genoa, 10 Jan 1691.

114 B⁶ 20 (Marine) fol. 116.

115 B⁶ 19 (Marine) fol. 180, 193.

116 B⁶ 19 (Marine) fols. 106–108.

117 B⁶ 19 (Marine) fols. 160, 200ff.

118 B⁶ 19 (Marine) fols. 158, 160.

119 B⁶ 19 (Marine); B⁶ 20 (Marine) fols. 7–38; B¹ 1158 (Marine), especially Le Blond to minister, 25 Oct, 1 Nov 1687, and de la Haye to minister, 3 Jan 1688.

120 Arpad Karolyi's *Buda és Pest visszavivása 1686-ban* (The Recapture of Buda and Pest in 1686) (2nd ed., rev. by I. Wellmann; 1936) mentions sales of prisoners of war; the majority of one batch of some 6,000 Turkish prisoners (soldiers, civilians, women, children) were offered for sale at very low prices at the Corn Market in Vienna.

Sandor A. Takács in a short essay ("Hungarian Slaves on Italian Galleys" in his book *A magyar mult tarlójáról* (Gleanings from the Hungarian Past) (Budapest, 1926)) "mentions that 'immense numbers of Turkish prisoners taken in the war of liberation were sold to various slave traders, and that the Court Chamber and the War Council in Vienna offered Turkish soldiers for sale at the price of 25 to 30 Florins. . . .' Takács worked on material found in Vienna." For the information in this note, I am indebted to Mme. A. Varkonyi, historian and chief of research at the Hungarian Academy of Historical Sciences, Budapest, and to the International Conference of Economic History at the University of Indiana, Bloomington, for making our meeting possible.

121 B⁶ 24 (Marine) fols. 110, 114, 128, 138 (see n. 116 above).

122 B⁶ 25 (Marine) fol. 387. Undesirable Bosnians could presumably be sold, able-bodied turcs retained.

123 B⁶ 123 (Marine) fol. 168.

124 This fitting phrase from Michael Ott, "Innocent XI," in *The Catholic Encyclopedia*, VIII, 22.

Condemnations to the Oar

1 F. A. Isambert et al., eds., *Recueil général des anciennes lois françaises* (hereafter cited as *Recueil général*), XXI, Déclaration, 4 Mar 1724; *Lettres patentes adressées au Parlement de Rouen, au sujet de la marque des condamnés au galères* (Rouen, 1750).

2 Marcel Marion, *Dictionnaire des institutions françaises au XVIIᵉ et XVIIIᵉ siècles*, 252.

3 *Ibid.*, 252. See also comment by Pierre Clement in his introduction to Colbert, *Lettres*, III, pt. 1, 1.

4 On the interplay of the powers of Crown and parlements, principally before 1661, see A. Lloyd Moote, "The French Crown versus Its Judicial and Financial Officials, 1615–1683."

5 Depping, *Correspondance administrative*, II, 878.

6 Colbert, *Lettres*, III, pt. 1, 389.

7 B¹ 814 (Aff Etr) letters of 16, 24 Apr 1664; Colbert, *Lettres*, III, pt. 1, 8, 12–13, 147, 155; Depping, *Correspondance administrative*, II, 897–899; Louis André, *Michel Le Tellier*, 107–111.

8 O 97 (Toulon) "Registre des forçats," with marginal notes from the two dozen–odd entries for Boulonnais, scattered through numbers 383–466.

9 René Memain, *Matelots et soldats*; Asher, *Resistance*.

10 Ordonnance of 29 Aug 1669, cited by Brun, *Guerres maritimes*, I, 46.

11 Depping, *Correspondance administrative*, II, 927.

12 B⁶ 115 (Marine) fols. 101–102; A³ 12 (Marine) "Ordonnance," 4 Dec 1686, p. 127; Isambert, *Recueil général*, XIX, 465.

13 B³ 85 (Marine) fol. 253.

14 B⁶ 115 (Marine) fols. 101–102; D⁵ 2 (Marine) "Matricule ou rolle général des Forçats," 1739.

15 Isambert, *Recueil général*, XXI, 127; B⁶ 125 (Marine) fols. 209–210.

16 B⁶ 142 (Marine) Comte d'Estrées to minister, 2 Je 1749.

17 Colbert, *Lettres*, III, pt. 1, 1.

18 D⁵ 2 (Marine) "Matricule," 1739.

19 BN (Nouv Acq Fr) 21303, Arnoul papers; B⁶ 5 (Marine) fols. 148, 163–165; B⁶ 10 (Marine) fols. 111–113; François de Vaux de Foletier, *Les Tsiganes*, 145ff. and ch. 12 *passim*.

20 François de Vaux de Foletier, "La Déclaration de 1682 contre les Bohémiens," 2–10 *passim*.

21 Depping, *Correspondance administrative*, II, 910.

22 B⁶ 78 (Marine) fol. 109, listing relevant regulations.

23 According to Georges D'Avenel, *Richelieu et la monarchie absolue* (Paris, 1895), III, 183.

24 A³ 12 (Marine) p. 63; B⁶ 2 (Marine) fol. 36; Depping, *Correspondance administrative*, II, 931.

25 A³ 12 (Marine) fols. 51, 71; B⁶ 14 (Marine) fol. 12; Colbert, *Lettres*, III, pt. I, 502n.; Charles Woolsey Cole, *Colbert and a Century of French Mercantilism*, II, 473.

26 BN (Nouv Acq Fr) 21307 fol. 332, Colbert to Arnoul, 13 Jan 1668.

27 Bamford, "Procurement of Oarsmen," 39, 40.

28 Tournier, *Les Galères de France*, I, 65.

29 *Ibid.*; Bamford, "Procurement of Oarsmen," 36n.

30 O 97 (Toulon) "Registre de forçats," lists 479 as arriving in 1684.

31 Tournier, *Les Galères de France*, I, 63.

32 *Ibid.*, I, 63–65, 68; vols. II and III *passim*.

33 B⁶ 2 (Marine) fol. 166.

34 Tournier, *Les Galères de France*, I, 136–137.

35 *Ibid.*, 60–63.

36 *Ibid.*, 129, 135.

37 Marion, *Dictionnaire des institutions*, 247–250 (*sel* and *gabelle*), 524–525 (*tabac*). On the two monopolies, see George T. Matthews, *The Royal General Farms*, 88–130.

38 Marion, *Dictionnaire des institutions*, 250.

39 Colbert, *Lettres*, III, pt. 2, 100; B⁶ 10 (Marine) fol. 160.

40 B⁶ 10 (Marine) fol. 153.

41 Marion, *Dictionnaire des institutions*, 457.

42 B⁶ 27 (Marine) fol. 11.

43 B⁶ 115 (Marine) fol. 366.

44 B⁶ 85 (Marine) fol. 473.

45 Colbert, *Lettres*, III, pt. 1, 188.

46 B⁶ 17 (Marine) fols. 16–17, 56, 129.

47 Wilhelm Oechsli, *History of Switzerland, 1499–1914*, 225.

48 B³ 333 (Marine) fols. 499–500; B⁶ 124 (Marine) fols. 241–242.

49 B³ 410 (Marine) fols. 403ff.; B³ 411 (Marine) fols. 52–54; B³ 419 (Marine) fols. 269ff.

50 *Correspondance et dépêches de Henri d'Escoubleau de Sourdis* (Paris, 1839), I, 527–528. Richelieu approved releases of prisoners of war, on the condition that a substitute or ransom payment be provided.

51 B⁶ 1 (Marine) fol. 30 "Lettre du roi," 26 Je 1659.

52 B⁶ 21 (Marine) fol. 204.

53 B⁶ 23 (Marine) fol. 333.

54 Colbert, *Lettres*, III, pt. 1, 280.

55 *Ibid.*, 390n.

56 B¹ 1 (Marine) fol. 393.

57 B⁶ 10 (Marine) fol. 160.

58 Colbert, *Lettres*, III, pt. 2, 62n.

59 B⁴ 15 (Marine) fol. 471.

60 Quoted by Lavisse, "Sur les galères du roi," 245.

61 B⁶ 86 (Marine) fols. 109–125 *passim*.

62 B⁶ 21 (Marine) fols. 56–57.

63 Depping, *Correspondance administrative*, II, 955.

64 John Howard, *The State of the Prisons* and *An Account of the Principal Lazarettos in Europe*.

65 B⁶ 27 (Marine) fol. 10.

66 B⁶ 85 (Marine) fol. 295.

67 B⁶ 85 (Marine) fol. 473.

68 B⁶ 85 (Marine) fol. 475.

69 B⁶ 109 (Marine) fols. 16–17; B⁶ 115 (Marine) fols. 366–387 *passim.*

70 Depping, *Correspondance administrative*, II, 935.

71 O (Toulon) "Registre général," 9 Je 1685 to 24 Dec 1686 *passim.*

72 B⁶ 82 (Marine) fol. 162.

73 According to Lavisse they weighed about 150 livres (165 lbs.); the reforming intendant Bégon recommended a maximum of 40 kilos. In practice, weights must have varied widely, with different conductors dealing with different suppliers for their chains. The poor quality of the iron available must have raised "safe" minimums considerably.

74 B⁶ 82 (Marine) fol. 169.

75 B⁶ 85 (Marine) fol. 205, citing an instance where one conductor used only four guards for a chain of 49 men.

76 Bibliothèque de la Marine (Paris) MS. 104.

77 B⁶ 85 (Marine) fol. 296.

78 B⁶ 85 (Marine) fol. 296.

79 B⁶ 85 (Marine) fol. 299.

80 1O 570 (Toulon) "Instruction," 14 Mar 1701.

81 B⁵ 1 (Marine) "Mémoire sur les chiourmes," 7 Sept 1787.

82 Marteilhe, *Mémoires d'un protestant*, 172–173.

83 B⁶ 20 (Marine) fol. 184.

84 A³ 12 (Marine) "Règlement pour la conduite des chaînes," 18 Feb 1686. Full text in Bibliothèque de la Marine (Paris), MS. 7.

85 B⁶ 82 (Marine) fol. 169.

86 Lavisse, "Sur les galères du roi," 248.

87 Bibliothèque de la Marine (Paris), MS. 7.

88 O (Toulon), "Registres des forçats," Paris chain arriving Marseilles, 10 Nov 1697, and chains arriving 3 May and 11 Nov 1698.

89 O 570 (Toulon), "Instruction" for Sieur Parnault, 14 Mar 1701.

90 B⁶ 105 (Marine) fols. 320–321.

91 B⁶ 21 (Marine) fol. 3.

92 B⁶ 21 (Marine) fol. 3.

93 B³ 484 (Marine) fols. 275, 277.

94 Depping, *Correspondance administrative*, II, 885.

95 B⁶ 77 (Marine) fol. 342.

96 Depping, *Correspondance administrative*, II, 936.

97 B⁶ 15 (Marine) fol. 16.

98 B⁶ 15 (Marine) fol. 32.

99 Depping, *Correspondance administrative*, II, 942.

100 C⁷ 181 (Marine) dossiers on the conductors known as Le Prince, Desmarais.

101 B⁶ 105 (Marine) fol. 320.

102 B⁶ 105 (Marine) fol. 320.

103 B⁶ 108 (Marine) fol. 18.

104 B⁶ 85 (Marine) fol. 294.

105 O (Toulon), "Registres des forçats," rolls of chains arriving 1746–49; B⁶ 130 (Marine) fol. 247; B⁶ 133 (Marine) fol. 194; and *passim*; B⁶ 134 (Marine) fols. 237, 246, 313; B³ 484 (Marine) fols. 275, 277.

Life Aboard

1 B⁶ 88 (Marine) fol. 271; B⁶ 105 (Marine) fol. 320.

2 Marteilhe, *Mémoires*, 76.

3 *Ibid.*, 76–77.
4 B⁶ 82 (Marine) fol. 26; B⁶ 85 (Marine) fol. 552.
5 A³ 12 (Marine) fols. 173, 175.
6 B⁶ 78 (Marine) fol. 402.
7 B⁶ 77 (Marine) fol. 388.
8 B⁶ 22 (Marine) fols. 200–206, 228–229, 288.
9 B⁶ 80 (Marine) "État des rations," 10 Mar 1671.
10 Colbert, *Lettres*, III, pt. 1, 114.
11 B⁶ 82 (Marine) fols. 11–12.
12 Colbert, *Lettres*, III, pt. 1, 244.
13 *Ibid.*, 244n.
14 A³ 12 (Marine) p. 175.
15 B⁶ 134 (Marine) fols. 107–108.
16 Colbert, *Lettres*, III, pt. 1, 572–573.
17 B⁶ 87 (Marine) fol. 436.
18 B³ 484 (Marine) fol. 19.
19 B⁴ 15 (Marine) fol. 463.
20 A³ 12 (Marine) p. 149, "Ordonnance," 16 Je 1686.
21 B⁶ 83 (Marine) "Ordonnance," 27 Sept 1678.
22 B⁶ 32 (Marine) fol. 460.
23 B⁶ 89 (Marine) fol. 229.
24 B⁶ 90 (Marine) fol. 218 "Mémoire sur les chiourmes des galères, et les moyens de les maintenir en bon état," by Chevalier de Breteuil, 29 Mar 1695.
25 *Ibid.*, letter of transmittal from Breteuil, 30 Mar 1695.
26 *Ibid.*
27 *Ibid.*
28 *Ibid.*
29 B⁶ 33 (Marine) fols. 182–183.
30 Masson, "Les Galères de France," quoting Barras, 71.
31 Marteilhe, *Mémoires*, 234.
32 *Ibid.*
33 A³ 12 (Marine) fols. 149, 161, 173.
34 B⁶ 83 (Marine) fol. 451.
35 Depping, *Correspondance administrative*, II, 911.
36 B⁶ 135 (Marine) "Mémoire instructif sur la police de chiourme," Toulon, 24 May 1751.
37 B⁶ 21 (Marine) fol. 87.
38 B⁶ 115 (Marine) Barras de la Penne to minister, 14 Apr 1723.
39 B⁶ 115 (Marine) fols. 151–152.
40 B⁶ 115 (Marine) fols. 15–19, 345.
41 B⁶ 115 (Marine) fols. 15–19. Claude Poclet was an engraver, "very well-known in his trade" (fol. 345).
42 Jacques L. Godechot, *Institutions de la France sous la Révolution*, 69.
43 A³ 12 (Marine) pp. 89, 113; B⁶ 85 (Marine) fols. 215, 238; Colbert, *Lettres*, III, pt. 1, 215.
44 Masson, "Les Galères de France," 136–137.
45 B⁶ 77 (Marine) fols. 231–238 "Lettres patentes par lesquelles le roy establit un hôpital en la ville de Marseille pour les pauvres forçats malades qui sont dans ses galères," Fontainebleau, Jy 1646.
46 A³ 12 (Marine) p. 59.
47 Colbert, *Lettres*, III, pt. 2, 13.
48 B⁶ 85 (Marine) fol. 57.
49 B⁶ 84 (Marine) fol. 455.
50 B⁶ 23 (Marine) fols. 315, 399.

51 B⁰ 85 (Marine) fol. 57; B⁰ 89 (Marine) fol. 219.

52 B⁰ 89 (Marine) fol. 231.

53 B⁰ 78 (Marine) fol. 317.

54 Colbert, *Lettres*, III, pt. 1, 280.

55 *Ibid*., pt. 2, 183n.

56 B⁶ 85 (Marine) fol. 57; B⁶ 109 (Marine) fol. 544.

57 B⁴ 15 (Marine) fol. 507.

58 B⁰ 85 (Marine) fols. 497–499. See also Yvonne Bezard, *Fonctionnaires maritimes et coloniaux sous Louis XIV*, 71–72.

59 Masson, "Les Galères de France," 195.

60 B⁶ 82 (Marine) fols. 32–34.

61 *Ibid*.

62 B⁶ 85 (Marine) fols. 54–57.

63 Colbert, *Lettres*, III, pt. I, 280.

64 B⁶ 142 (Marine) "Mémoire sur la correspondance par lettres des forçats," 21 Sept 1751.

65 A³ 12 (Marine) p. 251 cites ordonnance, 11 Apr 1696.

66 B⁶ 116 (Marine) fol. 274.

67 B⁶ 115 (Marine) fols. 151–152.

68 Marteilhe, *Mémoires*, 77.

69 B⁶ 79 (Marine) fol. 204.

70 B⁶ 135 (Marine) fol. 177.

71 B⁶ 106 (Marine) fol. 57.

72 B⁶ 32 (Marine) fols. 267–268 "Instructions au Marquis de Fornille," 27 May 1699.

73 B⁴ 3 (Marine) fol. 321.

74 B⁶ 78 (Marine) fols. 401–402.

75 Depping, *Correspondance administrative*, II, 886.

Life Ashore

1 B¹ 49 (Marine) fol. 71; B⁶ 33 (Marine) fol. 352.

2 B⁶ 87 (Marine) fol. 425.

3 *Ibid*., fols. 425–426; B⁶ 116 (Marine) fols. 242–244.

4 B⁶ 125 (Marine) *passim*.

5 Jal, *Glossaire nautique*, "Prouyers," p. 1232.

6 A³ 12 (Marine) p. 177; B⁶ 109 (Marine) fol. 357.

7 B⁶ 109 (Marine) fols. 357, 428ff., 434–435.

8 A³ 13 (Marine) p. 149.

9 B⁶ 89 (Marine) fol. 232.

10 B⁶ 96 (Marine) fols. 256–260 "Règlements pour la sûreté des forçats et turcs qui seront donnez à l'avenir aux maîtres des Boutiques," 3 Jy 1702.

11 B⁶ 77 (Marine) fol. 313.

12 Masson, "Les galères de France," 130–131.

13 B⁶ 134 (Marine) fol. 62.

14 A³ 12 (Marine) p. 247.

15 B⁶ 100 (Marine) fols. 221–222.

16 B⁶ 134 (Marine) fols. 114, 145.

17 A³ 12 (Marine) pp. 77, 113, 225.

18 A³ 12 (Marine) pp. 277, 345, 365; A³ 13 (Marine) pp. 63–65.

19 Masson, "Les Galères de France," 305.

20 *Ibid*., 186.

21 Colbert, *Lettres*, III, pt. 1, 57.

22 B⁶ 17 (Marine) fol. 35.

23 A³ 12 (Marine) p. 241; B⁶ 78 (Marine) fols. 164, 175–176; B⁶ 87 (Marine) fol. 425; B⁶ 89 (Marine) fols. 232ff.

24 Brun, *Guerres maritimes*, I, 164–165, 178–179.

25 B⁶ 89 (Marine) fol. 545.

26 B⁶ 21 (Marine) fols. 190–191, 205.

27 B⁶ 24 (Marine) fols. 48, 152–153.

28 A³ 12 (Marine) p. 230.

29 A³ 12 (Marine) p. 273.

30 Brun, *Guerres maritimes*, I, 164–165.

31 *Ibid.*, 178–179.

32 *Ibid.*, 165, 264.

33 Colbert, *Lettres*, III, pt. 1, 101.

34 *Ibid.*, 101, 147, 200.

35 B⁶ 84 (Marine) fol. 455.

36 B⁶ 89 (Marine) fol. 219.

37 B⁶ 90 (Marine) fol. 390.

38 Masson, "Les Galères de France," 292–293.

39 B⁶ 96 (Marine) fol. 392.

40 B⁶ 97 (Marine) fols. 390–391.

41 B⁶ 97 (Marine) fols. 352–353.

42 B⁶ 97 (Marine) fols. 357–363.

43 B⁶ 97 (Marine) fol. 357.

44 Contract of 1700, art. 32.

45 B⁶ 97 (Marine) fols. 357–363 *passim*.

46 B⁶ 101 (Marine) fols. 100–101 "Mémoire sur ce que les forçats et turcs du Bagne payent," 29 Jy 1708.

47 B⁶ 97 (Marine) fol. 363; B⁶ 100 (Marine) fol. 316, with ordonnance of 10 Nov 1707 concerning card money in the bagne.

48 B⁶ 35 (Marine) fol. 170; B⁶ 142 (Marine) "Mémoire sur le payement que l'on fait aux forçats des ouvrages," Aug 1721.

49 B⁶ 142 (Marine) "Mémoire sur le payement."

50 B⁶ 101 (Marine) fols. 100–101.

51 B⁶ 96 (Marine) fols. 165–166.

52 B⁶ 97 (Marine) fols. 352–354.

53 B⁶ 108 (Marine) fols. 121–164 *passim*; A³ 12 (Marine) pp. 389, 395.

54 B⁶ 96 (Marine) fol. 392.

55 B⁶ 96 (Marine) fol. 391; B⁶ 34 (Marine) fol. 173.

56 B⁶ 142 (Marine) "Mémoire sur le payement," Aug 1732.

57 *Ibid.*

58 Masson, "Les Galères de France," 294.

59 B¹ 26 (Marine) fol. 139; B¹ 36 (Marine) fols. 28–30.

60 B¹ 49 (Marine) fols. 158–162, 176. For the general history of the plague, see Paul Gaffarel and M¹ˢ de Duranty, *La Peste de 1720 à Marseille et en France.*

61 B⁶ 113 (Marine) fols. 318–319; B¹ 49 (Marine) fol. 182.

62 B¹ 49 (Marine) fol. 188; B⁶ 113 (Marine) fols. 325–326.

63 B⁶ 113 (Marine) fols. 325–326.

64 B¹ 56 (Marine) fol. 188.

65 B¹ 49 (Marine) fol. 222.

66 B¹ 49 (Marine) fol. 189.

67 B¹ 49 (Marine) fols. 205, 213.

68 D¹ 18 (Marine) fols. 138–139.

69 B⁶ 113 (Marine) fols. 334–335 "Extrait des registres des délibérations de la ville de Marseille," 6 Sept 1720; B¹ 49 (Marine) fols. 211–213.

70 B⁶ 113 (Marine) fols. 334–335.

71 B¹ 49 (Marine) fol. 287; B¹ 56 (Marine) fol. 189.
72 B⁶ 113 (Marine) fols. 178, 180, 186.
73 On slave-forçat service during the plague, see also p. 260 below.
74 B⁶ 116 (Marine) fol. 343.

Releases and Escapes

1 B⁶ 130 (Marine) fol. 484.
2 Colbert, *Lettres*, III, pt. 1, 542; A³ 12 (Marine) p. 89.
3 B⁶ 26 (Marine) fols. 79–80, 87.
4 Colbert, *Lettres*, III, pt. 1, 388.
5 *Ibid.*
6 *Ibid.*, pt. 2, 62–63.
7 *Ibid.*, 135.
8 B⁶ 87 (Marine) fols. 413–422 *passim*.
9 B⁶ 87 (Marine) fols. 413–414.
10 B⁶ 23 (Marine) fols. 344–345.
11 For discussion of some of the techniques, see B⁶ 10 (Marine) fols. 33, 174, 184; B⁶ 11 (Marine) fols. 256–258, 276.
12 B⁶ 82 (Marine) fol. 21.
13 B⁶ 84 (Marine) fol. 455.
14 B⁶ 85 (Marine) fol. 494.
15 B⁶ 77 (Marine) fol. 212.
16 B⁶ 17 (Marine) fol. 438.
17 B⁶ 17 (Marine) fol. 449.
18 Depping, *Correspondance administrative*, II, 948–949.
19 B⁶ 19 (Marine) fols. 99–100.
20 B⁶ 85 (Marine) fols. 385–386.
21 B⁶ 21 (Marine) fol. 20; B⁶ 22 (Marine) fols. 260–261.
22 B⁶ 90 (Marine) fol. 390.
23 B⁶ 88 (Marine) fols. 324–325.
24 B⁶ 89 (Marine) fol. 219.
25 B⁶ 109 (Marine) fol. 375.
26 B⁶ 105 (Marine) fols. 346–348.
27 B⁶ 33 (Marine) fols. 215–216; Depping, *Correspondance administrative*, II, 942–943.
28 Philippe Mieg, "Mulhouse et les galériens huguenots au début du XVIIIᵉ siècle," 8.
29 Tournier, *Les Galères de France*, I, 198.
30 B⁶ 106 (Marine) fol. 440; Mieg, "Mulhouse et les galériens," 9.
31 Mieg, "Mulhouse et les galériens," 10–13.
32 Tournier, *Les Galères de France*, I, 193.
33 B¹ 1 (Marine) fol. 393; B⁶ 109 (Marine) fol. 418.
34 B¹ 20 (Marine) fols. 138–139.
35 B⁶ 32 (Marine) fol. 31.
36 A³ 13 (Marine) p. 99 "Ordonnance," 18 Jan 1723.
37 Masson, "Les Galères de France," 310; Lavisse, "Sur les galères du roi," 233.
38 Colbert, *Lettres*, III, pt. 1, 419, 504.
39 *Ibid.*, 525.
40 *Ibid.*, pt. 2, 38.
41 *Ibid.*, 62–63, 135.
42 B⁶ 17 (Marine) fols. 165–168.
43 B⁶ 21 (Marine) fol. 2.

44 B⁶ 24 (Marine) fols. 66–68.

45 B⁶ 23 (Marine) "Liste de huit turcs," 5 Jan 1691. For later instances, see Brun, *Guerres maritimes*, I, 279; Masson, "Les Galères de France," 450–451.

46 B¹ 56 (Marine) fols. 1, 83.

47 B⁶ (Marine) fol. 86.

48 Evidently a few isolated individuals managed to do reasonably well in these circumstances. One extant document, dated 1694, suggests that the King ordered the release of a certain turc who conducted commerce on the galleys "by which a number of forçats subsist" (B⁶ 26 (Marine) fols. 13, 17).

49 B¹ 12 (Marine) fol. 97.

50 B⁶ 115 (Marine) fols. 63–64, 98–99, 119–120, 187.

51 Colbert, *Lettres*, III, pt. 2, 38.

52 B⁶ 141 (Marine) "Ordonnance de M. de la Guette," 2 Mar (no year).

53 B⁶ 80 (Marine) fols. 37, 40; Masson, "Les Galères de France," 407–408.

54 B⁶ 81 (Marine) fol. 48.

55 B⁶ 82 (Marine) fol. 9.

56 *Ibid.*, 9, 17–18.

57 B⁶ 8 (Marine) fol. 52.

58 *Ibid.*, 119–120.

59 B⁶ 82 (Marine) fol. 18.

60 A³ 12 (Marine) p. 115; B⁶ 85 (Marine) fol. 262; B⁶ 87 (Marine) fols. 429–430.

61 B⁶ 89 (Marine) fols. 232–233; B⁶ 87 (Marine) fols. 427–428.

62 A³ (Marine) p. 33; B⁶ 106 (Marine) fols. 80–90; B⁶ 109 (Marine) fols. 394–395. In subsequent years the fine was again raised to 600 livres.

63 B⁶ 96 (Marine) fols. 256–260 "Règlements pour la sûreté des forçats et turcs."

64 B³ 483 (Marine) M. de Sinely to minister, 3 and 31 Dec 1749; B⁵ 1 (Marine) "Mémoire sur les chiourmes," 7 Sept 1787.

65 B⁶ 106 (Marine) fol. 88; BN (Nouv Acq Fr) 21383 fol. 293 Arnoul papers, "Extrait de l'état des evasions des forçats et turcs" (1682–1707).

The Transition to Prisons

1 DCP Recueil des ordres, Louis XIV to Bailly de Noailles, signed Louis, 2 Mar 1701.

2 B⁶ 105 (Marine) fol. 397.

3 A³ 13 (Marine) pp. 22, 41, 43, 299; Masson, "Les Galères de France," 388ff.

4 Born in 1702 to Marie-Louise-Victoire Le Bel de la Boissière de Sery (later Countess d'Argenton), legitimated 1706, admitted to the Order of Saint John by special papal dispensation (1716), elected Grand Prior of France in that Order (1719) (Masson, "Les Galères de France," 361–365).

5 Masson, "Les Galères de France," 365–367; C⁷ 268 (Marine) dossier de Rance.

6 B⁶ 39 (Marine) fols. 34, 88–91; BN (Nouv Acq Fr) 21383 Arnoul papers, fol. 224.

7 See pp. 184–186 above.

8 B¹ 25 (Marine) fols. 75–76, 198.

9 A³ 13 (Marine) p. 141; B⁶ 116 (Marine) fols. 342–346; B⁶ 123 (Marine) fols. 23, 299–301.

10 Masson, "Les Galères de France," 411ff., 423–424.

11 EE 155 Archives Municipales (Marseilles) "Role des officiers et equipages . . . pour le payement et l'exemption de capitation," 1701.

12 XIV E 827 BR (Fonds Cor) "Ordre," signed Barras de la Penne, 23 Jy 1728.

13 Masson, "Les Galères de France," 445, 452.

14 Brun, *Guerres maritimes*, I, 345.

15 B⁶ 105 (Marine) fol. 358.

16 B⁶ 123 (Marine) fol. 168.

17 Masson, "Les Galères de France," 400–401.

18 B⁶ 134 (Marine) fols. 73–74, 82, 301.

19 B⁶ 142 (Marine) "Observations sur un mémoire concernant les galères," Mar 1750, marginal reponses.

20 B⁵ 1 (Marine) "Mémoire sur les chiourmes" by M. le Boucher, 7 Sept 1787; Masson, "Les Galères de France," 450.

21 Masson, "Les Galères de France," 457–458, 461–462; Howard, *Lazarettos*, 54.

22 B³ (Marine) vols. 481–484 *passim* "Réunion des galères"; B⁵ 1 (Marine) "Mémoire sur les chiourmes," 7 Sept 1787; B⁶ 135 (Marine) fol. 209; Masson, "Les Galères de France," 439–461; Brun, *Guerres maritimes*, I, 337–339. These changes were lamented by friends of the galleys, one of whom warned that the dispersal of oarsmen was "certain to lead to the loss of at least part of the galleys" (B⁶ 142 (Marine) "Mémoire sur les galères," 11 Jan 1750).

23 B⁶ 142 (Marine) "Mémoire sur les galères," 15 Jan 1750.

24 Howard, *Lazarettos*, 54.

25 Brun, *Guerres maritimes*, I, 343.

26 B⁶ 135 (Marine) fols. 227–228; Brun, *Guerres maritimes*, I, 343.

27 B⁶ 135 (Marine) fols. 227–228.

28 B⁶ 135 (Marine) fol. 227; Masson, "Les Galères de France," 450.

29 B⁶ 139 (Marine) fol. 227.

30 B⁶ 134 (Marine) fols. 73–74, 82, 301; Masson, "Les Galères de France," 400–401.

31 B³ 484 (Marine) fols. 289–291, 293.

32 B³ 484 (Marine) fols. 289–291; B³ 12 (Marine) p. 357; Bibliothèque de la Marine (Paris), MSS 7, 8 Nov 1746. But it was said that the turcs had "never been better treated than they are on the galleys today."

33 B³ 495 (Marine) fol. 69; Brun, *Guerres maritimes*, I, 345.

34 G 51 Archives de la Chambre de Commerce (Marseilles) Sartine to Echevins, 16 Feb.

35 B⁶ 135 (Marine) fols. 228–229.

36 Brun, *Guerres maritimes*, I, 342.

37 Tournier, *Les Galères de France*, III, 241–273. Tournier here lists Protestants condemned to serve the oars in the eighteenth century.

38 *Ibid.*, I, 207; III, 261–262.

39 B³ 519 (Marine) fols. 46–47.

40 B⁴ 135 (Marine) fols. 14–15, 142–144, 223–225 (with lists of the names of persons involved).

41 Tournier, *Les Galères de France*, I, 207–214; III, 216–217.

42 But see Geoffrey Adams on the struggle for toleration, "A Temperate Crusade," especially 83–85, and its negligible pre-Revolutionary successes.

43 B³ 383 (Marine) fols. 499–500.

44 B⁶ 124 (Marine) fols. 241–242.

45 A³ 33 Archives de Guerre, pièce 123 "Ordonnance," 15 Jan 1758. I am indebted to Lee Kennett for this reference.

46 B⁵ 1 (Marine) "Mémoire sur les chiourmes," 7 Sept 1787.

47 B³ 595 (Marine) fols. 119–121.

48 Howard, *Lazarettos*. But see Thorsten Sellin, *Pioneering in Penology*, dealing with aspects of the eighteenth century, as well as with evidence of the long-term influence of the Dutch in Europe and elsewhere (esp. ch. 12). This and Sellin's other works deal with phases of European, including German, Italian, French, and early American prison history.

49 B³ 437 (Marine) fols. 536–537.

50 B⁵ 1 (Marine) Malouet to minister, Toulon, 15 Dec 1782. Cf. the views of Guillot at Brest (D⁵ 1 (Marine) Guillot to minister, 18 Dec 1782).

51 B⁵ 1 (Marine) Malouet to minister, Toulon, 15 Dec 1782. Beccaria's work already

had widespread influence (Elio Monachesi, "Pioneers in Criminology," and Coleman Phillipson, *Three Criminal Law Reformers*, 83–106). The earlier essay by Mabillon was apparently unknown (Thorsten Sellin, "Dom Jean Mabillon," 123–124, 141).

52 B⁵ 1 (Marine) Malouet to minister, Toulon, 15 Dec 1782; Brun, *Guerres maritimes*, II, 84–85.

53 B⁵ 1 (Marine) Malouet to minister, Toulon, 15 Dec 1782; and Brun, *Guerres maritimes*, II, 84–85; B⁵ 1 (Marine) "Mémoire sur les chiourmes," 1787.

54 Brun, *Guerres maritimes*, II, 85.

55 D⁵ 1 (Marine) Guillot to minister, Brest, 18 Dec 1782.

56 D⁵ 1 (Marine) Malouet to minister, Toulon, 7 Jan 1783; Brun, *Guerres maritimes*, II, 86.

57 B⁵ 1 (Marine) "Mémoire sur les chiourmes," 1787; D⁵ 1 (Marine) "États," 1774–87, and "Chiourmes," 1783.

58 Brun, *Guerres maritimes*, II, 87n.

59 D⁵ 1 (Marine) Marchais to minister, Rochefort, 7 Jan 1783; Brun, *Guerres maritimes*, II, 87–88.

60 Howard, *Lazarettos*, 54.

61 *Ibid.*

62 Max Grünhut, *Penal Reform*.

63 Walter C. Reckless, *Criminal Behavior*, commenting on Howard.

Conclusions and Reflections

1 "Édit du roy portant création & institution d'une ordre militaire sous le titre de Saint Louis," Versailles, 10 Apr 1693 *passim*; Colleville and Saint Christo, *Les Ordres du Roi, passim*.

2 A.-C.-A. de Marsy, "L'Ordre de Malte dans la marine de France en 1790," 2.

3 *The Catholic Encyclopedia*, IX, "Laval, François de Montmorency," 45–46.

4 Edmond Esmonin, "L'Anti-cléricalisme sous Louis XIV," 373–374. Esmonin contends Louis was weakened by the rising tide of criticism, at least in some respects (pp. 372–379), but I find that in the same post-revocation period, Louis appears to have enjoyed generally increased authority. The nature of the impact of the revocation on royal power needs further study.

5 Charles Gerin, "Innocent XI et la révocation de l'Édit de Nantes," 426.

6 E. Michaud, *Louis XIV et Innocent XI*, IV, 497–498. Cf. Jean Meuvret's evidence, which seems to confirm this reconciliation policy, "Les Aspects politiques de la liquidation du conflit Gallican."

Bibliography

Bibliography

Manuscript Sources

Manuscript materials relating to the history of French galleys can be found in the archives and libraries of all the countries of Western, Central, and Mediterranean Europe. This dispersion is a natural consequence of the fact that the men who served aboard French galleys — officers, crewmen, and oarsmen alike — came from widely scattered parts of Europe. The very materials with which French galleys were constructed came from regions almost equally scattered. No one could consult all the relevant documents; certainly, I make no claim to have been able to use all of them, or even all the collections touching the subject inside France itself. But the principal manuscript collections, the Archives Nationales, Archives de la Marine, and Bibliothèque Nationale, have been used extensively. They hold rich and concentrated series of relevant papers.

Archives Nationales (Paris)

Most of the data for this study have been drawn from the Dépôt du Service Historique de la Marine at the Archives Nationales.

Papers in the collection relating to the Marine des Galères are concentrated in the B^6 series. The series is made up of two types of records: out-letters (seventy-six registers, cited as B^6 1 to B^6 76) covering the period 1669–1748, and in-letters (fifty-eight letterbooks, numbered B^6 77 to B^6 134) for the period 1665–1748. As the notes suggest, particular attention has been given to this correspondence for the period 1665–1695 (registers B^6 1 to B^6 25 and letterbooks B^6 77 to B^6 90).

The B^1, B^2, and B^3 series in the general service files of the sailing navy (registers and letterbooks) include scattered references to galleys, easily located with the published inventory for Series B: *Inventaire des Archives de la Marine: série B, service général* (Paris, 1885–1913, 7 vols. — others in manuscript).

Some use was made of the B^4 series (campaigns) and of subseries B^5 (*armements*).

The C series (personnel) provided the few dossiers of officers and other individuals consulted; the D series (*matériel*) includes *constructions navales,* and also data on galley oarsmen in D⁵ 1 to D⁵ 8 (*chiourmes, matricules, signalements,* and related documents).

Administrative regulations, ministerial and royal decrees relating to galleys are found in the A² and A³ series ("Recueil d'ordonnances sur les galères"), volumes A² XVI and A³ XII–XIII being the "Sommaire du Recueil" and "Tables," respectively.

Archives de la Marine, Dépôt des Cartes et Plans (Paris)

The Dépôt des Cartes et Plans also offers a scattering of documents of special value for this study, particularly the "Recueil des ordres," sailing instructions, campaign plans, and related letters and papers for the Marine des Galéres, 49 (272) pièces 9, 12, 14, 20, and 23 relative to campaigns in the last three decades of the seventeenth century.

Archives des Affaires Etrangères (Archives Nationales; Quai d'Orsay)

The consular correspondence at the Archives Nationales (B¹ series Aff Etr) was helpful on the Mediterranean trade in slaves. The documents cited are clustered in the correspondence with Leghorn and Malta, with a few others in the series for Venice and Genoa. At the Quai d'Orsay, the series Mémoires et Documents (Mem et Doc) Algiers (vol. 12), and Malta (vols. 1 and 2).

Bibliothèque Nationale (Paris)

Nouvelles Acquisitions Françaises (Nouv Acq Fr); the Arnoul Collection, 21306, 21307, 21381, 21383, and 6171; the *Mélanges* Colbert, vol. 84; and a few pieces in the general collection, Fonds Fr.

Archives de la Marine (Toulon)

1L 119, 1L 124 and documents of the O series. The O series comprises a "Registre général des turcs" (vol. 106ᵇ¹ˢ) and various "Matricules des forçats" at Marseilles (vols. 108–125). These records were developed and used at Marseilles in managing the rowing force and bagnes of the Corps, and were moved to Toulon after the Corps was dismantled around mid-eighteenth century.

The documents bound together to compose the "Registre général des forçats" constitute a list of men who were condemned to serve on the galleys, their names and some other data about most of them being recorded when they arrived at Marseilles, with later modifications and additions in many instances. Some numerical use was made of a small part of this material (see p. 145), but the data invite, and will elsewhere receive, more intensive treatment than would be consistent with the general nature of this study.

Archives at Marseilles

The Archives Départementales du Bouches-du-Rhône includes XIV E 822, 824, 827 (Fonds Coriolis), comprising ordres and ordonnances, and a mémoire by the Bailiff de Forbin.

The Archives de la Ville de Marseille contains Series EE (Marine) 127, 155, 162.

Bibliography

Books

Albion, Robert G. *Forests and Sea Power*. Cambridge, Mass.: Harvard University Press, 1926.

Anderson, R. C. *Naval Wars in the Levant, 1559–1853*. Princeton: Princeton University Press, 1952.

————. *Oared Fighting Ships: From Classical Times to the Coming of Steam*. London: Percival Marshall, 1962.

André, Louis. *Michel Le Tellier et Louvois*. Paris: A Colin, 1942.

Anselme, P., and Augustin Dechaisse. *Histoire généalogique et chronologique de la maison royale de France*. 3rd ed. Paris, 1726.

d'Argens, Luc de Boyer. *Réflexions politiques sur l'état et les devoirs des Chevaliers de Malthe*. The Hague, 1739.

Asher, Eugene L. *The Resistance to the Maritime Classes*. Berkeley & Los Angeles: University of California Press, 1960.

Auphan, Gabriel Paul. *La Marine dans l'histoire de France*. Paris: Plon, 1955.

Bamford, Paul W. *Forests and French Sea Power, 1660–1789*. Toronto: University of Toronto Press, 1956.

Beccaria, Cesare de. *On Crimes and Punishments*, trans. by Henry Paolucci. Indianapolis: Bobbs-Merrill, 1964.

Bergasse, Louis. *Histoire du commerce de Marseille, 1599–1660*. Paris: Plon, 1954.

Bezard, Yvonne. *Fonctionnaires maritimes et coloniaux sous Louis XIV: Les Bégon*. Paris: Plon, 1932.

Bion, Jean-François. *Relation des tourments qu'on fait souffrir aux protestants qui sont sur les galères de France*, ed. by O. Douen. Amsterdam, 1709; reprinted 1881; Geneva: Droz, 1966 (this ed. with a biographical introduction on Bion by Pierre Conlon).

Boiteaux, L.-A. *Richelieu: Grand maître de la navigation et du commerce de France*. Paris: Ozanne, 1955.

Braudel, Fernand. *La Méditerranée et le monde méditerranéen à l'époque de Philippe II*. 2nd ed. 2 vols. Paris: Colin, 1966.

Brun, V. *Guerres maritimes de la France: Port de Toulon, ses armements, son administration depuis son origine jusqu'à nos jours*. 2 vols. Paris, 1861.

Cambridge Economic History of Europe, ed. by E. E. Rich and C. H. Wilson. Cambridge: University Press, 1941–   .

The Catholic Encyclopedia, ed. by Herbermann, Pace, et al. New York: Appleton, 1912–14.

Cipolla, Carlo M. *Guns, Sails and Empires*. New York: Minerva Press, 1965.

Clark, G. N. *War and Society in the Seventeenth Century*. Cambridge: University Press, 1958.

Coindreau, Roger. *Les Corsaires de Salé*. Paris: Société d'Editions Geographiques, Maritimes, et Coloniales, 1948.

Colbert, Jean-Baptiste. *Lettres, instructions et mémoires*, ed. by Pierre Clément. 8 vols. Paris, 1861–82.

Cole, Charles Woolsey. *Colbert and a Century of French Mercantilism*. 2 vols. New York: Columbia University Press, 1939.

Colleville, Ludovic de, and François Saint-Christo. *Les Ordres du Roi*. Paris, 1924.

Collier, Raymond, and Joseph Billioud. *Histoire du commerce de Marseille*, ed. by G. Rambert. Paris: Plon, 1951.

Corbett, Sir Julian S. *England in the Mediterranean, 1603–1713*. 2 vols. London: Longmans, 1917.

Cordey, J., ed. *Correspondance de Louis-Victor de Rochechouart, Comte de Vivonne*. Paris: Champion, 1911.

357

Coste, Pierre. *La Congrégation de la Mission dite de Saint-Lazare.* Paris: Lecoffre-Gabalda, 1927.

Curtin, Philip D. *The Dimensions of the African Slave Trade: A Census.* Madison: University of Wisconsin Press, 1969.

Davis, David Brion. *The Problem of Slavery in Western Culture.* Ithaca: Cornell University Press, 1966.

Debien, Gabriel. *Le Peuplement des Antilles françaises au XVIIe siècle: Les engagés partis de La Rochelle, 1683–1715.* Cairo: Port-au-Prince, 1942.

Depping, G. B. *Correspondance administrative sous le règne de Louis XIV.* 4 vols. Paris, 1850–55.

Dictionnaire de biographie française, ed. by J. Balteau, M. Barroux, M. Prevost, et al. Paris: Librairie Letouzey, 1933– .

Earle, Peter. *Corsairs of Malta and Barbary.* London: Sidgwick & Jackson, 1970.

Engel, Claire-Éliane. *L'Ordre de Malte en Méditerranée, 1530–1798.* Monaco: Editions du Rocher, 1957.

Farrère, Claude. *Histoire de la marine française.* Paris: Flammarion, 1934.

———. *Jean-Baptiste Colbert.* Paris: Grasset, 1954.

Fisher, Sir Godfrey. *Barbary Legend: War, Trade and Piracy in North Africa, 1415–1830.* Oxford: Clarendon Press, 1957.

Gaffarel, Paul, and M^{1s} de Duranty. *La Peste de 1720 à Marseille et en France.* Paris: Perrin, 1911.

Godechot, Jacques L. *Les Institutions de la France sous la Révolution et l'Empire.* Paris: Presses Universitaires de France, 1951.

de la Gravière, Jurien. *Les Derniers jours de la marine à rames.* Paris, 1885.

Grotius, Hugo. *The Rights of War and Peace,* trans. by A. M. Campbell. New York: Oxford University Press, 1901.

Hazard, Paul. *The European Mind, 1680–1715.* Cleveland & New York: World, 1963.

Howard, John. *An Account of the Principal Lazarettos in Europe.* London, 1791.

———. *The State of the Prisons.* London, 1777.

Isambert, F. A., Decrusy, and A. J. L. Jourdan, eds. *Recueil général des anciennes lois françaises depuis l'an 420 jusqu'à la Révolution de 1789.* 29 vols. Paris, 1821–33.

Jal, A. *Abraham Duquesne et la marine de son temps.* 2 vols. Paris, 1873.

———. *Glossaire nautique.* Paris, 1848.

Julien, Ch.-André. *Histoire de l'Afrique du Nord, Tunisie, Algérie, Maroc.* 2 vols. Paris: Payot, 1951–52.

Lane, Frederic C. *Venetian Ships and Shipbuilders of the Age of the Renaissance.* Baltimore: Johns Hopkins Press, 1934.

———. *Venice and History.* Baltimore: Johns Hopkins Press, 1966.

Lavedan, Henri. *Monsieur Vincent: Aumônier des galères.* Paris: Plon, 1928.

Lewis, Archibald R. *Naval Power and Trade in the Mediterranean.* Princeton: Princeton University Press, 1951.

Marion, Marcel. *Dictionnaire des institutions françaises au XVIIe et XVIIIe siècles.* 2nd ed. Paris: Editions Picard, 1968.

Marteilhe, Jean. *Mémoires d'un protestant: Jean Marteilhe de Bergerac,* ed. by Gaston Tournier. Cévennes: Musée du Désert, 1949.

Masson, Paul. *Histoire du commerce français dans le Levant au XVIIe siècle.* Paris, 1897.

Mathorez, J. *Les Étrangers en France sous l'ancien régime.* 2 vols. Paris: Champion, 1919, 1921.

Matthews, George T. *The Royal General Farms in Eighteenth Century France.* New York: Columbia University Press, 1958.

Mémain, René. *La Marine de guerre sous Louis XIV.* Paris: Hachette, 1937.

———. *Matelots et soldats des vaisseaux du roi.* Paris: Hachette, 1937.

Michaud, E. *Louis XIV et Innocent XI.* 4 vols. Paris, 1883.

Bibliography

Mirot, Albert. *Manuel de géographie historique de la France.* 2nd ed. 2 vols. Paris: Picard, 1950.

Mollat, Michel, ed. *Le Navire et l'économie maritime du moyen âge au XVIIIe siècle.* Paris, s.e.v.p.e.n., 1958.

Mousnier, Roland. *La Vénalité des offices sous Henri IV et Louis XIII.* Rouen, 1946.

Oechsli, Wilhelm. *History of Switzerland, 1499–1914.* Cambridge: University Press, 1922.

Orcibal, Jean. *Louis XIV contre Innocent XI.* Paris: Bibliothèque de la Société Ecclesiastique de la France, 1949.

Paris, Robert. *Histoire du commerce de Marseille: Le Levant, 1660–1789.* Paris: Plon 1957.

Phillipson, Coleman. *Three Criminal Law Reformers.* London: Dent; New York: Dutton, 1923.

Plantet, Eugene, ed. *Correspondance des Deys d'Alger avec la Cour de France, 1579–1833.* 2 vols. Paris, 1889.

Rambert, Gaston. *Histoire du commerce de Marseille: 1660 à 1789.* Paris: Plon, 1954.

———. *Nicolas Arnoul: Intendant des Galères à Marseille, 1665–1674.* Marseilles: Editions de Provincia, 1931.

Reckless, Walter C. *Criminal Behavior.* New York: Appleton, 1940.

Redlich, Fritz. *De praeda militari: Looting and Booty, 1500–1815.* Wiesbaden: F. Steiner, 1956.

———. *The German Military Enterpriser and His Work Force.* 2 vols. Wiesbaden: F. Steiner, 1964–65.

Richelieu, Cardinal (Armand-Jean du Plessis). *Testament politique,* ed. by Louis André. Paris: R. Laffont, 1947.

de la Roncière, Charles. *Histoire de la marine française.* 6 vols. Paris: Plon, 1899–1932.

———. *Valbelle "Le Tigre": Marin de Louis XIV.* Paris: Grasset, 1935.

Rothkrug, Lionel. *Opposition to Louis XIV.* Princeton: Princeton University Press, 1965.

Ruffi, Antoine de. *Histoire de la ville de Marseille.* 2nd ed. 2 vols. Marseilles, 1696.

Sauvaget, Jean. *Introduction to the History of the Muslim East: A Bibliographical Guide,* rev. by C. Cahen. Berkeley & Los Angeles: University of California Press, 1965.

Savine, Albert. *La Vie aux galères: Souvenirs d'un prisonnier.* Paris: Louis Michaud, 1909.

Schermerhorn, Elizabeth W. *Malta of the Knights.* New York: Houghton, 1933.

Seignelay, Marquis de, Jean-Baptiste Colbert. *L'Italie en 1671: Relation d'un voyage du Marquis de Seignelay,* ed. by Pierre Clément, Paris, 1867.

Sellin, Thorsten. *Pioneering in Penology: The Amsterdam Houses of Correction in the Sixteenth and Seventeenth Centuries.* Philadelphia: University of Pennsylvania Press, 1944.

Sourdis, Henri d'Escoubleau de. *Correspondance de Henri d'Escoubleau de Sourdis.* 3 vols. Edited by E. Sué. Paris, 1839.

Southern, R. W. *Western Views of Islam in the Middle Ages.* Cambridge, Mass.: Harvard University Press, 1962.

Tenenti, Alberto. *Piracy and the Decline of Venice, 1580–1615.* Berkeley & Los Angeles: University of California Press, 1967.

Tournier, Gaston. *Les Galères de France et les galériens protestants des XVIIe et XVIIIe siècles.* 3 vols. Cévennes: Musée du Désert, 1943–49.

Vaux de Foletier, François de. *Les Tsiganes dans l'ancienne France.* Paris: Société d'Editions Geographiques et Touristiques, 1961.

Verlinden, Charles. *L'Esclavage dans l'Europe médiévale.* Brussels: De Tempel, 1955– .

Vertot, Abbé René Aubert de. *Histoire des Chevaliers Hospitaliers de Jean de Jerusalem.* 7 vols. Paris, 1761.

Wolf, John B. *The Emergence of the Great Powers, 1685–1715.* New York: Harper, 1951.

––––––. *Louis XIV.* New York: Norton, 1968.

Wrong, G. M. *The Rise and Fall of New France.* 2 vols. New York: Macmillan, 1928.

Zeller, Gaston. *La Méditerranée et ses problèmes aux XVIᵉ et XVIIᵉ siècles.* Paris: Centre de Documentation Universitaire, n.d.

Articles

Adams, Geoffrey. "A Temperate Crusade: The Philosophe Campaign for Protestant Toleration," in H. T. Parker and R. Herr, eds., *Ideas in History* (Essays for Louis Gottschalk), pp. 65–85. Durham, N.C., 1965.

Alezais, H. "L'Héritage de Pierre Mirmand, médecin réal des galères," offprint from Mémoires de l'Academie de Marseille.

Bamford, P. W. "Knights of Malta and the King of France, 1665–1700," *French Historical Studies,* III (1964), 429–453.

––––––. "The Procurement of Oarsmen for French Galleys, 1660–1748," *American Historical Review,* LXV (1959), 31–48.

––––––. "Slaves for the Galleys of France, 1665–1700," in John Parker, ed., *Merchants and Scholars,* pp. 173–191. Minneapolis, 1965.

Beugy, Chevalier de. "Journal of the Expedition of the Marquis de Denonville against the Iroquois: 1687," *Rochester Historical Society Publication,* IX (1930), 3–56.

Billioud, J. "Les Bois des Hautes-Alpes," *Bulletin de la Société des Études des Hautes-Alpes,* LII (1960), 106–112.

Bohnstedt, John W. "The Infidel Scourge of God: The Turkish Menace as Seen by German Pamphleteers of the Reformation Era," *Transactions of the American Philosophical Society,* LVIII (1968), pt. 9.

Esmonin, Edmond. "L'Anti-cléricalisme sous Louis XIV," *Études sur la France des XVIIᵉ et XVIIIᵉ siècles,* pp. 367–379. Paris: Presses Universitaires de France, 1964.

––––––. "Sur l'Authenticité du *Testament politique*," *Études sur la France des XVIIᵉ et XVIIIᵉ siècles,* pp. 219–232. Paris: Presses Universitaires de France, 1964.

Forget, M. "Une Quadruple exécution pour sacrilège à Marseille en 1693," *Mélanges Busquet: Questions d'Histoire de Provence, XIᵉᵐᵉ–XIXᵉᵐᵉ siècles,* pp. 240–243. Vaison-la-Romaine, 1956.

Gerin, Charles. "Innocent XI et la révocation de l'Édit de Nantes," *Revue des Questions Historiques,* XXIV (1878).

Giesey, Ralph E. "Juristic Basis of Dynastic Right to the French Throne," *Transactions of the American Philosophical Society,* LI, 1961, pt. 5.

Girouard, M. "L'Expédition du Marquis de Denonville," *Proceedings and Transactions of the Royal Society of Canada,* 1899, 2nd ser., V.

Kiernan, V. G. "Foreign Mercenaries and Absolute Monarchy," Trevor Aston, ed., *Crisis in Europe, 1560–1660,* pp. 117–140. New York, 1965.

Lane, Frederic C. "Venetian Shipping during the Commercial Revolution," in his *Venice and History,* pp. 3–24. Baltimore: Johns Hopkins Press, 1966.

Lavisse, Ernest. "Sur les galères du roi," *Revue de Paris,* IV (1897), 225–262.

Lombard, Maurice. "Arsenaux et bois de marine dans la Méditerranée musulmane VIIᵉ–XIᵉ siècles," in Michel Mollat, ed., *Le Navire et l'économie maritime du moyen âge au XVIIIᵉ siècle,* pp. 53–99, 100–106. Paris, 1958.

Marsy, A.-C.-A. de. "L'Ordre de Malte dans la marine de France en 1790," extrait de *La Revue héraldique,* pp. 1–7. Angers, 1874.

Masson, Paul. "Les Galères de France, 1481–1781: Marseille, port de guerre," *Annales de la Faculté de Lettres d'Aix,* XX (1937–38), 1–4, 7–479.

Bibliography

Meuvret, Jean. "Les Aspects politiques de la liquidation du conflit gallican," *Revue d'Histoire de l'Église de France*, XXXIII (1947), 257–270.

Mieg, Philippe. "Mulhouse et les galériens huguenots au début du XVIIIᵉ siècle," *Bulletin du Musée historique de Mulhouse*, XLIX (1929).

Monachesi, Elio. "Pioneers in Criminology: IX. Cesare Beccaria (1738–1794)," *The Journal of Criminal Law, Criminology and Police Science*, XLVI (1955), 439–449.

Moote, A. Lloyd. "The French Crown versus Its Judicial and Financial Officials, 1615–1683," *Journal of Modern History*, XXXIV (1962), 146–160.

Mordacq, René. "Maître Antoine Moulinneuf, chirurgien des galères du roi," *Revue d'histoire économique et sociale*, XLVII (1969), 249–259.

Pagès, Georges. "Note sur le recrutement et la libération des galériens sous Louis XIV au début du ministère de Colbert," *Revue d'histoire moderne et contemporaine*, XI (1908–1909), 35–53.

———. "La Paix de Religion et l'Édit de Nantes," *Revue d'histoire moderne*, XI (1936), 393–413.

Roberts, Michael. "The Military Revolution, 1560–1660," in his *Essays in Swedish History*, pp. 195–225. Minneapolis, 1967.

Sellin, Thorsten. "Correction in Historical Perspective," *Law and Contemporary Problems*, XXIII (1958), 585–593.

———. "Dom Jean Mabillon: A Prison Reformer of the Seventeenth Century," *Annales Internationales de Criminologie*, VI (1967), 123–143.

———. "A Look at Prison History," *Federal Probation*, 1967.

———. "Penal Servitude: Origin and Survival," *Proceedings of the American Philosophical Society*, CIX (1965), 277–281.

Vaux de Foletier, François de. "La Déclaration de 1682 contre les Bohémiens: Son Application en Languedoc," *Études Tsiganes*, III, 1957, No. 1, 2–10.

Index

Index

Adriatic ports, as slave markets, 146
Adriatic Sea, 15
Aegean Sea, 15
Africa, proposed importation of slaves from, 156
d'Aiguillon, Duchesse, endows hospital, 214
Aix-en-Provence: 193; plague at, 247
Alcohol, *see* Wine
Aleppo, plague reported at, 245
Alexandria, slaves from, 144
Algiers: important slave source, 143, 263; treaties with, 160, 161, 162, 285; relations with France, 163, 307; envoy to France given gift of turcs, 263–264. *See also* Infidels; Turcs; War, privateering
Almería (Spain), site of galley loss, 36
Alps, and Spanish communications, 42
Alsace, Lutherans arrested and imprisoned, 287
L'Amazonne, 281
Ambreville, pickpocket, 210
America, 11. *See also* New France; West Indies
American Indians: significance as galley slaves, 163, 164, 165–166, 310–311; war on French, 165; survivors returned to New France, 165

Anchors, oarsmen employed manufacturing, 231
Angers, prison conditions at, 190
Anne, Queen Mother of France, provides galley, 18
Antoine Court Collection (Geneva), 219
Architects, of galley arsenal, 54, 58, 61, 63, 54
d'Argens, Chevalier Luc de Boyer, quoted on responsibilities of Knights, 98–99
Argousin réal, 129–130
Argousins: character, 126, 321; salary and perquisites, 129; criticisms of, 208, 212; "abandon" some oarsmen, 229; as guards in bagne, 238, 241–242; and escapes, 266, 268, 268–270
Arles, canal dredged by oarsmen, 232
Armada, Spanish, 16
Armor: on rambarde, 32; proposed for new galley, 40, 41
Armorers, employ oarsmen, 229
Armory: impressive, 60; criticized by Colbert, 61
Army: officers of in Galley Corps, 97; oarsmen as troops in, 258–259, 275
Arnoul, Nicolas, intendant of galleys: general administration, 54, 56, 57, 72, 76, 79, 87, 88, 216, 218, 221, 332*n*; criticism of, 57–58, 61, 63, 87–88, 216,

218, 332*n*; recruitment and management of oarsmen, 147, 152, 180, 203–204, 211, 212, 221, 261–262, 267–268
Arsenal: qualities, 60–61; "old" and "new", 61; criticized by officials, 62, 63, 332*n*; oarsmen work in, 231
Arta, reported sacked by Venetian army, 167
Atlantic seaboard, galleys on, 12, 41, 46
"Atrocious" crimes, preclude release from galleys, 251, 252
Aubert, consul at Genoa, slaves purchased by, 150, 169
Austria, reported supplier of slaves to Mediterranean galley powers, 167–168, 169–170
d'Avernes de Boccage, Bailiff, French slave buyer at Malta, 280–281
Avignon, 191–193

Bagne: economic function in galley management, 234–235; for invalids, 235–237, 275; and interest of the King, 237–240, 243, 245; advantages of entrepreneurs, 238–239; organization of production, 239, 242–245; life of workers in, 239–245 *passim*; at Brest and Rochefort, 282, 289, 292; at Toulon, 292, 317; of all ports, 293–297, 317–318 *passim. See also* Prisons, galleys as
Balearic Islands, Spanish base, 36, 40
Balkans, provide slaves, 142, 144, 167, 170–171
Ball, held by officers, 278–279
Baltic, 11, 12
Banc, comite's own, 220–221
Banditry, Mediterranean, *see* War, privateering
"Baptiste Fedeli," 168
Baraques: 130, 276; women in, 231; bagne and, 237
Barbary, corsairs of, 23
Barbary States, 14, 29, 308
Barber-surgeon: sidelines, 123–124; post and duties, 123–125, 213; with major chains, 290
Barcelona, 34
Barras de la Penne: 34; on galley speed, 39; on combats with Spain, 45; crowded conditions, 208; theft aboard, 210; refuses to allow discretionary bastonnades, 212; on officer's dances, 278–279; importance of firepower, 331*n*

Barrel makers, 130
Bastille, "greatest horror of old regime," 11
Bastonnade, types of, 211, 212
Bayona, Marquis de, commander of Spanish squadron, 44
Beachy Head, 52
Beauvais, Bishop of, intervenes for officer, 105
Beccaria, 291
Bedford, Duke of, petitions for release of Protestants, 287
Beggars, to the galleys, 180
Bégon, Michel, intendant of galleys: 54, 61; proposed use of mariniers, 112; moderation in punishments, 121, 127; on invalids, 122–123, 255; issues rules for conductors, 194, 195, 199; work judged, 290, 317
Benediction, over newly built galley, 77
Bernardins, waterfront properties of at Marseilles, 57
Besançon, parlement of, 190
Bethomas, Chevalier and Commander, 34, 39, 40
Bibliothèque Protestante (Paris), 219
Bion, Jean-François, Chaplain, became Protestant, 121
Biscay, Bay of: Spanish privateers on, 40; weather of, 203
Bishop of Marseilles: and galley base, 57; penalizes chaplains, 119; victim of forçat pickpocket, 210
Black Sea, source of timber, 14
Blacks (*noirs*), listed in register of slaves, 340*n*
Blacks, West African: project for using on galleys as slaves, 154–160; and M. Mariage, 156; spiritual condition, 156–157; physical condition, 158–160; assessment of "experiment," 159, 309–310
Blacksmiths, employ oarsmen, 229
Blasphemy, galley penalty for, 179
Blond, Consul de France, *see* Le Blond
Bombelles, Charles de, Major of the Galleys: rigorous policy, 121; calculates costs, 235; Chevalier de Saint Louis (*1694*), 336*n*
Bonaparte, Napoleon, and papal slaves, 306
Bonneau, Louis, Christianized turc, 217
Bonnevoglies, 127, 131, 135–136
Bordeaux: galley wrecked on banks below, 37; chain, approximate route

of, 191–192, 198, 282; Protestants condemned at, 286
Bosnia, source of slaves, 170, 171
Boulanger, "Sieur": superior at Marseilles, 118; policies, 118–120. *See also* Chaplains; Congrégation de la Mission
Boulonnais, condemned to galleys, 177–178
Bounties, for enlistments, 131
Bourbons, dynasty, 272
Bourges, smugglers wait in prisons, 186
Branding: with *GAL*, 173; with *V*, 173; with *fleur-de-lis* on each cheek, 178
Brazil: 12; Indians not to be enslaved, 140
Bread, two-month supply on galley, 35
Brest: 53, 270; bagne at, 288, 289, 290, 318
Breteuil, Chevalier and Captain, criticizes noncommissioned officers, 208
La Bretonne, 281
Brittany, chain from, 188, 191–192, 197, 282
Brodart, Jean Baptiste, intendant of the galleys: and West African slave imports, 52, 155, 310; Colbert connections, 54, 60, 92, 93; and one-day galley construction, 76–77; corruption of administration, 89–93, 124, 129, 149, 268; warned not to buy Greeks or Russians, 153, 154; on victuals, 204, 206; on mortality and releases, 253, 255; quarrels with hospital staff, 216–217
Buccari (Imperial Istria), slaves sought at, 168
Budapest, French slave buyer at, 168
Building trades, oarsmen employed in, 230
Bullion, Spanish galleys transport, 43
Burgundy: source of oak, 68; parlement of, 190
Button makers, employ oarsmen, 226, 229

Cadiz, 49
Cairo, slaves from, 144
Canada, *see* New France
Candia, *see* Crete
Cannon: bronze versus iron, 31; jettisoned in heavy weather, 33; caliber and characteristics, 70, 71, 83
Canteens, on galleys at Toulon, 295. *See also* Taverns
Capitane, 71–72

Capitulations agreement, 99, 147–148, 303
Captains of galleys: 101–112 *passim*; recruiting subordinates, 109–110, 131, 132, 133–136; compete for oarsmen, 201; table allowances, 278. *See also* Officers
Capuchins: convent at Marseilles, 57, 61, 63; as chaplains in plague, 247
Card money, in bagne, 241–242
Cardinale, 18
Cardinals, carried aboard galleys, 277
Caribbean, Spanish galleys in, 12
Carpenters, 77, 130, 229
Cartagena, slaves purchased at, 281
Cartography, state of knowledge criticized, 36, 37, 38
Carts, for sick and invalids of chains, 194–195, 199
de Castries, Charles, Marshal and minister of marine: enlightened ideas, 290–291, 293; grants to men released without funds, 295; on rehabilitation, 317
Catalonia, 34, 35
Catherine II, Empress of Russia, 291
Cattle, used in victualing, 88
Caulkers, in galley constructions, 77, 130
Cayenne, Bégon proposes sending invalids to, 257
Central America, 12
de Centurion, Marquis (and Duke), Genoese mercenary, 41, 69, 329n
Cette: 232; as port and refuge for galleys, 34, 35, 38
Cévennes: armed resistance in, 312; Musée du Desert in, 329n
Chaban, Noé, Christianized Tunisian turc, 264
Chabert clan, constructors of galleys, 40, 41, 73–74, 75, 76, 81
Chains: routes of, 27, 189, 191–199 *passim*, 282; management of, 186, 190, 193–199; revolt on, 196–197; improved condition of, 290. *See also* Conductors; Prisons, civil
Châlons-sur-Saône, 191, 193, 198
Chamber of Commerce, Marseilles, seeks removal of Galley Corps, 282
Champigny, Intendant, trickery toward Indians, 164
Chancelier, M. le, 198
Channel, English, controlled by French, 41

Chaplains, of galleys: religio-political role, 28–29; praised and criticized, 114–115, 117–118; nationality of, 117, 301; complain about Superior, 118–119; Bishop of Marseilles and, 120, 121; and Vincent de Paul, 213; establish "École de Vertu," 228; in plague, 247; school for, 336n. *See also* Congrégation de la Mission; Vincent de Paul

Charles II, King of Spain, 49, 272

Charles (Pierre) et Cie, general contractor: 89, 236, 238; bagne contract of opposed, 237

Charts, French coastal, criticized 36, 37, 38

Château d'If: 34, 221, 222; as prison, 118

Chaulnes, Duke de, 33

Cheese, Gruyère or Hollande, in victualing, 88

La Chimère, returns slaves to Constantinople, 283

Chios, slaves from, 167

Chivalry, orders of, *see* Order of the Hospital of Saint John of Jerusalem; Order of Saint Louis

Choisy, Abbé, quoted on J. B. Colbert, 64

Christendom: French galleys and defense of, 29, 30; and religious slavery, 138, 139–143, 171, 264–265, 284–285, 305–307, 308–310

Church of Rome, *see* Papacy

Città Vecchia, 223

Clark, G. N., 308

Clergy, Gallican, accords and friction with King and Pope, 4, 9. *See also* Louis XIV; Papacy

Clothing: ration of to forçats, 201–202; manufactured in bagne, 242; distinctive to prevent escapes, 266

Coast of France, charted from Rochefort to Dunkirk, 37

Cochin China, 311–312

Colbert(s), Jean-Baptiste, father and son (Marquis de Seignelay): general administration of, 13, 39, 54, 64–65, 67, 69, 74, 79–80, 87, 89–93, 128–129, 181, 190, 207–208, 215–218, 227–228, 235, 317; and slaves, 23, 24, 143, 147, 156, 167, 203–204, 252, 253, 254, 261–262; and nobility, 33, 84, 85, 97, 112; on interplay of merchant-royal interests, 57–58, 59, 61, 62, 63, 67, 87–

88, 104, 112; and intendants, 57–58, 60, 61, 87, 89–93, 109, 112, 124; posthumous criticism of, 62, 63, 64, 66, 85; and Chaberts, 73, 74–76; on bonnevoglies, 127, 135–136; and forçats, 174, 175, 176, 179, 181, 187, 188, 189, 198; and oarsmen generally, 222, 223, 254; and later prison administration, 290, 296–297. *See also* Louis XIV; Minister of marine

Colonies: use of galleys in, 12. *See also* New France; West Indies

Comites: reputation and role of, 125, 126, 128, 200–201, 202; favoritism of, 220, 221, 229; ruthlessness of, 211–212, 226; and tavern of galley, 128–129, 207–208, 240–241; perspective on, 125, 227–228

Commerce de galère, 129–131, 225

Commissaires: accompanying chains, 290; in bagne, 240, 242–243

Communications, technology of, influence on administration, 65–67

Communications, Spanish, in Mediterranean, 42–45

Compagnie du Cap Nègre, 263

Condemnations, to galleys, 174–178 *passim*

Condottiere, Mediterranean maritime, 14, 18, 41, 69, 102–103

Conductors, of chains: management of, 190–199 *passim*, 290; character of, 191. *See also* Chains

Congrégation de la Mission: and galleys, 3, 114–121 *passim*, 336n; seek converts, 120–121, 151–152, 156, 157, 336n; and hospital administration, 213–218 *passim*, 260, 264. *See also* Chaplains; Vincent de Paul

Conscription, maritime, 136, 178

Conseil de Marine, sends invalids to West Indies, 260

Constantinople, slave market of, 144, 152

Construction, of galleys, 68–86 *passim*

Converts, to Christianity, 120–121, 151–152, 156–157, 216–217, 264, 285, 310–311

Convicts, *see* Forçats

Copper, for galley constructions, 68

Coral, polishing of, 226

Corbeaux, oarsmen as in plague of Provence, 245–248, 260

Corps des Galères, *see* Galley Corps

Corsica: base for Spain, 19, 33; incorrectly shown on French charts, 38; held by Genoese, 36

Corunna, 49

Cotolendy, François, French consul at Leghorn and buyer of slaves, 148–150, 169, 170

Cotoner, Nicolas, Grand Master of the Order of St. John, 23, 146, 153

Counterfeiters, galley penalty for, 181

Coursier (chaser), 70

Coursier (gangway between bancs), as gauntlet, 211

Court-martial: of comite, 211–212; of petitioner Claude Leger Poclet, 213

Creissel, collusion of with Brodart, 90–91

Crete, campaign for, 23, 97, 102, 135, 147, 223, 283

Crimes: "atrocious" prevents release, 251–252. See also Punishments

Criminals, see Forçats

Croatia, Governor of, in Order of Saint John, 167

Cross of Saint Louis, denied Knights of Malta, 305

Crown, authority of, and condemnations, 176

Crusading, Christian maritime, 5–8, 17, 19, 29–30, 102, 140–141, 306. See also Crete; Order of the Hospital of St. John

Cruvelier, contracts to deliver Greeks, 153, 154

Cutlers, employ oarsmen, 229

Cyprus, slaves from, 144

Dalmatia, source of slaves, 170

Dames de la Charité, help prisoners, 187

Dauphiné, 191, 272

Dautan, André, associate of Pierre Charles, 238

Death (legal), result of condemnation for life, 251

Denonville, Marquis de, and American Indians, 164–165

Deserters: from conscription, 136; from army, 178–179, 190, 275

Dicasse, Raymond, held in Morocco as slave, 264

Dietrichstein, Prince of, at Austrian Court, approached for slaves, 168

Dijon: charity to inmates of prison, 187; public prosecutor quoted, 190, 191

Dissenters, attitudes on infidels, 140

Djielli expedition, 23

Docks, many oarsmen employed at, 232

Doctors, see Barber-surgeon

Domaine du Marquisat, Arnoul properties, 59

Droit d'echelle, 130, 322

du Luc, Count, Charles-François de Vintimille, military distinction of, 335n

Dunkirk, 37, 40, 201

Duquesne, Admiral Abraham, ordered to exact salutes, 49

Durance River: timber rafted on, 68; crewmen used as guards along, 274

Dutch: encouraged to war with infidels, 6; provide naval aid, 20; warship taken, 46; defeat at Beachy Head, 52; as source of slaves, 141, 144; seek release of Protestants, 259–260

Dyers, employ oarsmen, 229

Échevins, of Marseilles: and "Plan Formiguier," 56, 58; relations with Corps, 56–57, 58, 246–248; and officers' dances, 278; and infidels, 285

Éclatante: sent to Toulon, 234; and plague of Provence, 247

École de Vertu, conducted by chaplains, 228

École des Eaux et Forêts (Nancy), opinion on chemistry of timber rot, 334n

École navale, Order of Malta as, 23, 25, 26, 98, 228

Eden, William (Lord Auckland), quoted on jailors, 296

Edict of Nantes, revocation of, 10–11, 112, 115, 137, 182–184, 286, 312–315

Egypt, plague reported in, 245

"Egyptians" (gypsies), and galleys, 180. See also Vagabonds

English: 11; frigate captured, 46; decline to salute, 48; defeat at Beachy Head, 52; in slave trade, 141, 144, 146, 148, 149; squadron burns Spanish galleys at St. Tropez, 187; and Huguenots, 219, 259–260

English Channel, privateers of, 40

Engravers, oarsmen work as, 220, 226, 345n

Enlightenment, religious slavery in, 143

Enterprise, contracts for construction by, 62, 73, 74

Escapes, responsibility and penalties for, 126, 189, 265–271 *passim*, 289, 293–294

d'Escrainville, Chevalier, French consul at Malta and supplier of slaves, 148
Estates General, Malouet deputy to, 292
d'Estrées, César, Cardinal du titre and Duke of Leon, French ambassador to Rome, 313
d'Estrées, Victor Marie, Marshal, on bribery, 258
Exile see Releases; West Indies

Fabre, Jean, Protestant, released, 287
Falsehood (involving oaths), galley penalty for, 179
Faugères, home of Jean Raymond, 287
Filth, as possible cause of rot, 83–84
Fire, danger of in arsenal, 63, 278
Firemen, oarsmen serve as, 245
Firewood, supplied for cooking, 88
Flags, carried on galleys, 68, 71. See also Salutes
Flogging: of Protestants, 121; various types of, 211–212
Florence, Grand Duke of, slaves sent to, 167–168
Flota system, of Spain, 43
Food, see Rations; Victuals and Supplies
Forbin, Bailiff of, Lieutenant-Général des Galères, 19
Forçats: compete with free laborers, 14, 230, 233–234; compared with slaves, 142–143; French and Spanish, 187–188; desirable physique of, 188, 189, 190; on chains, 193–194, 195, 196–199, 290; rations for, 193–194, 201–207, 276; communications censored, 218–219; as teachers, 227–228; in plague of Provence, 246–248; resist being transported, 257. See also Chains; Oarsmen; Protestants
Forest, Chevalier de, on campaign, 217
Forest resources, of Mediterranean basin, 14, 329n
Forfait, French engineer, estimates speed of galleys, 39
Forgery, galley punishment for, 179
Fort Frontenac, fish and game supplied to, 164
Fort St. Jean (Marseilles): 54; as prison, 118
Forville, Marquis de, campaign of, 222
Fougon, kitchen on galley, 210
Founders, employ oarsmen, 229
Fournisseur général, see Munitionnaires
Franche-Comté, source of oak, 68
Frederick II, King of Prussia, 291

Freeman, and forçat labor, 14, 233–234
Frionnet, promised liberty for thirty turcs, 253
Frontenac, Governor General, 165, 311
Furriers, employ oarsmen, 229

Gabelle, see Salt monopoly
Gahiette, 50
La Galante, 124
Galérien: persistence of the term, 282. See also Forçats; Oarsmen; Protestants
Galleasses, at Lepanto, 16
Galley Corps: establishment at Marseilles, 3, 4, 13, 22, 52–53, 317; administration of, 6, 25–26, 87–93, 126–127, 289–295, 317–318; officers of, 25–26, 45, 95–113 passim, 273–274, 279–280, 303–305; development of, 52, 68–69, 78, 116, 273; expenditures for, 93–94, 300, 301; procurement of oarsmen, 138–199 passim; transition to prisons, 273, 274, 277, 279–281, 316–318; integrated into Navy, 281–282
Galleys: utility of, 10–30 passim, 273, 299–300, 316; characteristics of, 12–25 passim; operational limitations of, 31–51 passim, 298–300
— French: prison functions of, 11, 25–27, 115, 173, 266, 273, 274, 276–297 passim; expenditures for, 46–47, 93–94, 300, 301; base at Marseilles, 52–67 passim; constructions, 68–78; variable durability, 79–85
— Spanish: 10, 16, 33, 300; characteristics and function of, 41–44, 167, 187, 299, 311n
Gallican Church, see Louis XIV
Gardane, M. de, 212
Gardeners, oarsmen employed as, 230
Gardes-magasin, responsibility of, 89–90
Garonne River, 191
Gascony chain, 282. See also Chains
Genoa: 16, 17, 33, 35, 41, 171; naval battle near (1638), 21; construction of galleys at, 80; as slave market for French buyers, 146, 148, 149, 150, 169, 170, 283; bombarded by Louis' fleet, 314
Gens sans aveu, 180, 181, 323
German princes, use of French galleys as prison, 187
Gibraltar, 277
"Gigery" (Djielli) expedition, 23
"de Gout," Chevalier, sent to Malta, 146

Index

Government contracting: 72, 74; advantages and risks, 236–243 *passim*
Grain, for victualing, 88
Grand Master, *see* Cotoner; Order of the Hospital of Saint John
Grand Vizier, Ottoman, 283
Gratzen, French slave buyer at, 168
Greeks: and Ottoman shipping, 140, 153; as slaves, 152, 153–154
Grenoble: condemnations at to oar, 176, 286; chains from, 192
Grotius, Hugo, on religion and slavery, 138–139
Guards: aboard galleys, 130, 210, 267–268; on chains, 191–192, 193, 194; ashore, 225–226, 231
Guerre de course, *see* War, privateering
de la Guette, Chevalier: at Malta, 22, 146; on transporting invalids, 256; security measures of, 266, 267
Guiana, 287
Guilds, use of forçat labor, 229–230
Guillot, intendant at Brest, objects to innovations, 293–294
Guinea, slaves from, *see* Blacks, West African
de Guise, Duke, puts down corsairs, 18
Guns, *see* Cannon
"Guyenne" chains, *see* Chains
Gypsies, harassment of, 180–181

Hanover, civilians threatened with galleys, 288
Hapsburgs: and Bourbons, 42, 304, 314, 315; and Ottomans, 141, 142, 166
L'Hardie, 227
Hatters, oarsmen as, 226
de la Haye, French ambassador at Venice, 167
de la Haye, French ambassador at the Porte, 152
Health, of oarsmen, 26, 289–290
Heemskerk, Dutch Ambassador, 259
Hemp, for cordage, 68
Henry IV, and galley hospital, 214
Herbert, Arthur, English Admiral, 146
d'Héricourt, Intendant: on chain, 197; on forçat labor, 230; on bagne, 244
L'Heureuse, 107
Hogs, used in victualing, 88
Holland: 69; Huguenots and, 219, 259; model jails of, 289
Holy Ghost, Order of, 305
Holy League, organized by Papacy, 166, 167

Holy Trinity, Church of the, saluted, 50
Hospital, for forçats and slaves: 62, 114, 199; Vincent de Paul tradition in, 213; staff and administration of, 214–218; mortality in, 122–124, 246–247, 251; escapes from, 266
Household servants, oarsmen employed as, 230
Howard, John, describes conditions on French galleys, 281, 289, 291, 294, 295–296, 318
Hubac clan, constructors of galleys, 73–74
Hugo, Victor, 318
Huguenots: and the notoriety of galleys, 11, 12, 29, 219; excluded from navy, 96; and revocation of Edict of Nantes, 112, 115, 137, 182–184, 286, 312–315; research on by descendents, 114–121, 286. *See also* Protestants
Hungary, slaves from, 166, 170
Hurons, *see* American Indians
d'Hyères, îles, 39, 223

Imprisonment, cost of, 27
India, 12
Indians, *see* American Indians
Infidels (unbelievers from Christian standpoint): enslavement of, 11, 29, 139–143, 150, 260–263, 283, 284–285, 306–307, 308–310; as source of debate between Louis XIV and the Papacy, 305–307, 308–311 *passim*. *See also* Louis XIV; North African states
Innocent XI: and Louis XIV, 302; reacts to revocation of Edict of Nantes, 313–314, 315. *See also* Louis XIV
Inquisitor, at Malta, 153–154
Intendants of galleys: responsibilities of, 54–55, 89, 93; and Colberts, 57–58, 60, 61, 87, 89–93, 109, 112, 124. *See also* Arnoul; Bégon; Brodart; Malouet; Montmort
Invalids: shipped to West Indies, 178, 183, 184, 255–257, 260, 262; in chains, 185, 186, 188, 199; numbers of, 186, 228, 255–256, 257–258; employed as hospital, 215; and bagne, 235–237, 257–258, 275; as corbeaux, 246; releases of, 250, 252, 253; characteristics and status of, 252–253
Invincible, smallest oversize galley, 71
Ionian Islands, plague at, 245
Iron: cannon, 31; as matériel, 68; in chains, 344n

Iroquois, *see* American Indians

Istria, 168

Italians, on Spanish galleys, 41

Italy: 14, 16, 34, 35, 36; coast of little known, 38; French galleys ordered to, 49, 222, 277

Jailors, and security problems, 189, 268–269

Jails, *see* Prisons

Jesuits, 163–166 *passim*, 310–311

Jews: and Ottoman shipping, 140; enslaved at Arta, 167; sent to French galleys, 288

Joly, Superior Général of the Congrégation de la Mission, 119

Joseph II, Holy Roman Emperor, 291

Judicial system, differential treatment in, 181

Knights (Hospitalers), *see* Order of the Hospital of St. John

Knitting, by oarsmen, 226

Labor, free and forced compete, 13, 14, 230, 233–234

Lacemakers, oarsmen work as, 226

Lachine, massacre at, 165

Langeron, Chevalier: captures English frigate, 46; reports punishment of Poclet, 212–213

Languedoc: 18, 191, 274; few havens for galleys, 37; traversed by oarsmen, 282; Protestants condemned in, 286

La Rochefoucauld, Louis de Roye de, supporter of galleys, 274

La Rochelle: 156; campaigns at, 20

Launderers, in bagne, 241

Laval, Bishop of Canada, *see* Montmorency-Laval

Lead, in galley construction, 68

Le Blond, French consul at Venice, difficulties in procuring slaves, 167–168, 169

Le Febvre, Pastor Isaac, failure to doff cap to Blessed Sacrament, 121

Leghorn: 13, 35, 167; bagne at, 13, 235; French intelligence reports from, 41; as source of slaves, 146, 148–149, 162, 170

Le Havre: 39; base against privateers, 40

Le Nain, Intendant of Languedoc, 286

Lepanto, Battle of (*1571*): 12; significance in the history of galleys, 16

Le Tellier, Michel, and Louvois, father-son team, 64, 65, 175

Le Vacher, Père, Apostolic Vicar of Barbary and French consul, 263

Lifers, *see* Forçats

Linen trade, employs oarsmen, 229

Lisbon, slave market at, 146

Locksmiths, employ oarsmen, 229

Loire River, 191

"Lorance, Sieur," Superior of the Congrégation, 118

Lorraine, Duke of, and siege of Vienna, 166

Lorraine, princes of use French galleys as prisons, 187

Louis XIII, King of France: 18, 20; and galley hospital, 214. *See also* Richelieu

Louis XIV, King of France:

— character of his reign: authority, 4, 5, 301–302, 313; concern with reputation, 5, 8, 47, 300, 313; policies with multiple aims, 9, 64–67, 85; administration, 64–67, 85; economic policies, 85, 93–94; before revocation of Edict of Nantes, 314

— crusading by: for Faith, 5, 6, 7, 8, 143; serves both Church and State, 28, 29, 166, 303–304, 306, 307, 311

— galleys of: 103; tool of authority, 4, 5, 106, 113, 115, 301–302; symbol of superiority, 8, 54, 93–94; reasons for building, 13–30 *passim*; criticisms of galley officers, 43, 44, 45, 46; expansion, 47, 54, 63–64, 78, 93–94; "nationalizes" Corps, 68–69, 301–302; expenditure, 93–94

— and Gallican Church: religious policies, 28, 29, 312; good Gallican Christian prince, 303–304, 306, 307

— and infidels: policy of peace with, 6, 163, 172, 263, 308; treaties with, 150, 160–163 *passim*, 172, 263, 283, 284, 303, 308, 240n; quarrels over with Rome, 15, 151; pose as Catholic zealot, 143, 151, 152, 172

— and Knights of Saint John: 4, 5, 26, 95, 96, 101; demands loyalty, 4–5, 98, 148, 302–305; employs as galley and squadron commanders, 97, 98, 148; seeks as junior officers, 99, 100

— and the Papacy: relations with, 4–5, 6, 7, 30, 97, 246, 305–315; and crusading warfare, 5–8, 9, 102, 143, 308, 316; and infidel slaves, 151–152, 172; insistence on primacy of royal authority, 166, 311

— and Protestants: ends religious toleration, 10, 11, 12, 29, 182–184; revocation of the Edict of Nantes, 10–11, 112, 115, 137, 182–184, 286, 312–315; excludes Huguenot officers from navy, 96; opposes releases for, 236, 252, 260; persecution of improves papal relations, 314–315

Louis XV, King of France, retains Galley Corps, 273

Louis XVI, King of France, enlightened ideas and reforms, 290, 291, 293, 317

Louis, Order of Saint, *see* Order of Saint Louis

Louvigny, Sieur de, secret mission to Venice, 168

Louvois, Marquis de (Michel Le Tellier), and father, 64, 65, 175

Lustucru, War of, 177–178

Lutherans, of Alsace, condemned to galleys, 287

Lyons, 196

Lyons, Gulf of, 33, 34, 37

Mabillon, essay on prison administration, 291

Magasin général, 236

Magistrates, oppose Colbert, 175–176

Main de pain, 205

Major of the galleys, value of post, 130

Majorca: 19; slave market at, 146

Malaga, 283

Malouet, Pierre-Victor, intendant at Marseilles: thought on correction and rehabilitation, 290–295, 317; surprise at opposition, 293; in Revolution, 318

Malta, *see* Order of the Hospital of St. John

Manille, function described, 221

Mantin, vice admiral, squadron of, 18

Marchais, intendant at Rochefort, recommends travel allowances to prisoners, 295

Mariage, Monsieur: teaches West Africans French, 156; maltreats blacks for gain, 156, 158, 159

Mariniers de rame, recruitment of, 111, 131, 135, 136, 324

Maritime conscription, 136

Marseilles: 27, 37, 38, 39, 189, 190, 191, 192, 193, 199, 201, 203; free and forced labor compete in, 13, 14, 233–234; relations with Galley Corps, 13, 18,

19, 55–64, 179, 245–248, 268, 270, 282, 285; merchants of, 18, 19, 88, 129, 270; galley base at, 42, 53, 54, 55–64, 84, 282; échevins of, 56–57, 58, 129, 220–221, 278, 285; development of, 66, 67; recruitment in 110; plague at, 179, 245–246, 246–248; bagne of, 229, 245; dredging of port, 232

Marseilles, weights and measures of, 90, 91

Marsy, A.-C.-A. de, 305

Marteilhe, Jean, Protestant galérien: treatment of, 194, 229; arrives at galley base (Dunkirk), 201–202

Mass, in hospital, 216

Masts, galley, 68, 70

Maulevrier Count de, 227

Maurepas, Jean-Frédéric, minister of marine, 282

Mazarin, Cardinal, 54, 102

Measures and scales, oarsmen manufacture, 229

Meat, in victualing, 88

Médecin-général, 122–124

Medicine chest, contents and abuses, 123

Mediterranean: 8, 39, 191; preference for galleys in, 12–30 *passim*; privateering in, 17, 19, 23, 40, 140–142, 329–330n; galley navigation in, 34, 36, 37, 38, 42, 281; Spanish communications in, 42–45; "French lake," 47; slavery in, 138, 141–142; research problems of, 306, 338n

Melos, supplies slaves, 162

Mercenaries: 68, 69; maritime and military compared, 329n

Messina, expedition to, 32, 33, 82–83, 90, 137

Metalworkers, oarsmen as, 231

Metz, 190

Miermand, Dr., surgeon-general of the galleys: character, 122; clashes with religious, 122; treatment of the sick, 122, 123; supported by minister, 122–124; administration of, 123, 215

Milhan, Jean-Baptiste, banker of Marseilles, 238

Minister of marine: authority of, 119, 124, 124–125; and slaves, 155–156, 157; and oarsmen, 204, 206, 241, 246. *See also* Colbert(s); Galley Corps

Mirabeau, Bailiff de, defends galleys, 279

Miromesnil, M. de, 190

Misérables, Les, 318
Missionaries, *see* American Indians
Mohacs (*1687*), Austrian victory in Hungary, 166
Monaco, forçats from, 187, 193
Montmorency-Laval, Bishop of Quebec, claims jurisdiction direct from Rome, 166, 311
Montmort, Jean-Louis Habert, Sieur de, intendant of galleys: 123; ignores officers' abuses, 109; harsh administration of, 120–121, 127, 171; recommends wine for oarsmen, 206
Montreau, échevins of, 290
Morea, source of slaves, 170
Morocco: source of slaves, 144; emissary visits Marseilles, 161; Frenchman slave in, 264
"Mort à l'hôpital," in register, 251
Mortar ships, 163
Mortemart, Louis de Rochechouart, Duke of, 34, 45
Moslems, rights of after treaties, 285. *See also* Infidels; North African states; Ottoman Empire
Moulins, prisons of, 186, 189
Mourillon, Moslem worship and burials at, 285
Munitionnaires, problems and profits of, 88, 89, 90, 91
Musée du Desert, in the Cévennes, 219, 329*n*
Muster rolls, 110–112
Mutiny, 126, 212–213, 257

Nailers, in construction of galley, 77
Nantes, Edict of, revocation, 10–11, 112, 115, 137, 182–184, 286, 312–315
Naples: 41, 148, 149; slave market at, 146
Narbrough, Admiral John, sells captives at Leghorn, 146
Naval warfare, Order of Saint John as school of, 23, 25, 26, 98, 228
Navy, French: power struggle with Marseilles, 55–64; methods and problems of administration, 87–94, 128–131. *See also* Colberts
Necker, Jacques, financier and minister, on gabelle, 185
Negropont, slaves sought at, 168
Netherlands, 11, 42. *See also* Dutch
New France: 256; as source of slaves, 163, 164–165; missionary work in, 164–166, 310–311

Nîmes, 192
Nimwegen, Treaty of, 188
Noailles, Bailiff Jacques de: de facto commander of galleys, 34, 103, 107, 171; seeks larger rations, 170–171; on revolt, 257
Noailles, Cardinal de, Archbishop of Paris, 183–184
Nobility (Second Estate): commands aboard galleys, 3, 95, 96–97, 110–112; as Knights of St. John, 7, 97–98; and Colberts, 23, 84, 85, 97, 112; of Provence, 82, 95, 100–101; Huguenot, 96. *See also* Officers; Order of the Hospital of Saint John
North African states: 4; expeditions to, 8, 36, 96, 163, 277; enslavement of subjects of, 11, 29, 139–143, 150, 260–263, 283, 284–285, 306–307, 308–310; timber resources of, 14, 329*n*; and privateers, 17, 19, 149; use of galleys by, 22, 298; treaties with, 150, 160–163 *passim*, 172, 263, 283, 284, 303, 308, 340*n*
North American Indians, *see* American Indians
North Sea, weather of, 203
Norway, masts and spars from, 68

Oars: of beech and elm, 68, 70; characteristics and dimensions, 69, 70; use of, 70, 220–221, 250
Oarsmen: varied condition and treatment, 10, 11, 12, 126–127, 223; and free labor, 13, 14, 230, 233–234; mortality among, 32, 124, 213, 222–224; at the oars, 33, 39, 44, 202, 209, 220–221, 250; correspondence of, 120, 218–219; invalid, 124, 215, 218, 223, 259–260; relations with comite, 125, 126, 128, 200–202, 207–208, 211–212, 220–221, 226–229, 240–241; revolts of, 126, 212–213, 257; bonnevoglies as, 131, 135–136; rations of, 193–194, 202, 203–207, 276; crowded conditions among, 208–210; work of ashore, 211, 225, 226–227, 229–230, 231–232, 245–248, 276–277, 282; numbers of, 214, 230, 275, 294–295; as teachers, 227; relations with women, 231; earnings of, 248–249; as soldiers, 258–259, 275. *See also* Bagne; Forçats; Releases; Turcs
Officers, commissioned: from nobility, 3, 95, 96–97, 110–112; Knights as, 4–5, 95–101, 148, 302–305; double role of,

25, 26, 28, 126, 279–280; criticisms by, 36, 37, 38, 63, 215, 237, 253–254, 279; criticisms of, 36, 43, 44, 45, 101, 104–113 *passim*, 131, 133–135; responsibilities of, 44, 45, 46, 107, 110, 212; interservice rivalry among, 53, 105–106; and life of a galley, 84, 85, 86; and Colbert, 84–86, 97, 101, 112; salaries and perquisites of, 85, 93, 104, 110–112, 131, 209–210, 278, 300; recruiting by, 109–110, 131, 132, 133–136; views about slaves, 148, 155, 201, 279, 280; retirement of, 316

Officers, noncommissioned: 289; and oarsmen's health, 26–27; types of, 121–130

Oil, for victualing, 88

Order of the Holy Ghost, 305

Order of the Hospital of St. John of Jerusalem (Knights of Malta): 224; model galley management of, 6, 18, 23, 25–26, 32, 98, 228, 235, 266; obligations of, 6–7, 25–26, 68, 97–99, 302–305; aristocratic character of, 7, 97–98; relations of with French, 20, 23, 25–26, 98, 183–184, 228; war of upon infidel, 23, 97, 138, 140–141, 147; slave market of, 44, 138, 146–147, 153, 162, 168–169, 261, 280–281, 283, 339*n*; use of galleys by, 273, 298, 299, 316. *See also* Papacy

— in French service: 4, 5, 95–97, 99, 101; as commanders, 97, 98, 148; as junior officers, 99, 100; serving two masters, 4–5, 98, 148, 302–305; views about slaves, 148, 155, 279, 280; disqualified for Order of St. Louis, 305

Order of Saint Louis (royal): founding of, 304–305; incompatible with Order of St. John, 305

Order of Saint Michael, 305

Ordnance: 31; cost of, 14–15. *See also* Cannon

d'Orléans, Chevalier Jean Philippe, General of the Galleys, influence in preserving Corps, 273–274, 279, 281–282

Ortières, Étienne Gravier d', investigates hospital, 218

Ostend, 46

Ottoman Empire: 4, 277, 298; timber resources of, 14; Christians war with, 23, 29–30, 97, 166; subjects of enslaved, 142, 143, 150, 261, 283, 341*n*, 342*n*; shipping of, 153; as French allies, 307, 308, 315; object of friction between Louis and Papacy, 305–311 *passim. See also* Turcs

Pailleterie, Charles Davy, Chevalier de la, 46

Palatine, Her Electoral Highness, sends forçats to France, 187, 288

Palermo, 277

La Palme, Marteilhe assigned to, 201

Papacy: and Knights of St. John, 4–5, 98, 140, 148, 302–305; encourages maritime crusading, 5–8, 17, 19, 29–30, 140–141, 306; use of galleys by, 12, 138, 273, 298; campaign of for Crete, 23, 97, 102, 135, 147, 228, 283; opinions of on slavery, 29, 138–140, 146, 148, 151, 153–154, 171–172, 305–307, 309, 339*n*

— relations of with Louis XIV: 4–7, 30, 97, 305–315 *passim*; and crusading warfare, 5–8, 9, 143, 308, 316; and infidel slaves, 151–152, 172; aid in plague, 246

Papermakers, employ oarsmen, 229

Paraguay, 140

Paris: bankers of, 88; vagabonds arrested in, 260. *See also* Chains

Parlements: and royal power, 182; furnish clothing for forçats, 190, 191

Passe-vogue, 39, 324

Patronne, large galley, 71

Patrols, galleys for, 35

Paul, Chevalier and commander, 102

Pavia, 21

"Pay or strip" system, in prisons, 26

Peace with infidels, an object of friction between Louis and Papacy, 4–7, 305–315

Peddlers, in bagne, 241

Pellissery, surgeon general, severity of, 171

Penal System, *see* Prisons

Perellos, Grand Master of the Order of St. John, and sailing vessels, 273, 316

Perjury, galley penalty for, 179

Perpignan, 192

Persecution, religious, *see* Protestants; Huguenots; Infidels; Turcs

Pertuisaniers (guards), 225–226, 231, 324

Peter the Great, Tsar of Russia, galleys of, 12

Petitions, by forçats, 212, 213, 219–220

Petty officers: 237; schools for, 227–228

Pewterers, employ oarsmen, 229

Philip of Anjou, grandson of Louis XIV, 272

Philippines, Spanish galleys in, 12

Philosophes, critical of religious persecution, 286

Piancourt, Chevalier de, French consul at Malta, buys slaves, 148, 152, 153

Pilles, M. de, commander of squadron: 246; defends the galley, 279

Pilots, recruited for Atlantic squadron, 37; 130

Pinmakers, employ oarsmen, 229

Piracy, Mediterranean, see War, privateering

Pirano (Piram), 170

Plague, of Provence: 245–248; deaths among oarsmen, 179, 246–248, 280; oarsmen as corbeaux in, 246–248, 260

"Plan Formiguier," for development of Marseilles, 56, 58

Poclet, Claude Leger: 345n; execution for petition, 213, 220

Poitou, intendant of, reports convicts on hand, 189

Poland, King of, sends forçats to French galleys, 187, 288

Poles, released, 154

Pontchartrain, Louis de, minister of marine: 63; and galley constructions, 74, 80; on prisons, 190

Popes, of Rome, see Papacy

Port de Bouc: as base, 54; dredging at, 232

Port Mahon, 33

Port-Vendres, 38

Porters, oarsmen as, 77, 230

Portland, 146

Portrait painters, oarsmen as, 226

Portuguese: 20; on French galleys, 187–188

Poussel, Sieur, contracts to provide turcs, 144

Precedence, at sea, see Salutes

Prisons, civil: 174; function of, 26, 27; conditions in, 26, 186–187, 189, 190; at Soissons, 186–187; at Poitou, 189; escapes from, 189

Prisons, galleys as: conditions and treatment in, 10–12, 26–28, 126–127, 223, 249, 289–293, 295–297, 318–319; galley officers as wardens, 25–28, 126, 279–280; compared with contemporary prisons, 26–27, 249, 318; rations in, 27, 193–194, 201–207, 249, 276; releases from, 27, 250–265 passim, 275–276, 295; punishments in, 27–28, 120–

121, 126–127, 173–174, 177–178, 210–213, 220, 231, 252, 266, 275; work in (with rehabilitative effects), 27–28, 211, 225–232, 245–249, 276–277, 282; escapes from, 126, 189, 265–271 passim, 289, 290–291, 293–294; numbers held in, 214, 230, 275, 294–295; censorship in, 218–219; bagne as part of, 234–245 passim, 275, 282, 289, 293–297, 317–318; prison function gradually becomes dominant, 276–297 passim

Prisoners of war: English, 25; Spanish and Portuguese, 187–188, 338n. See also Turcs

Privateering, see War, privateering

Protestants: condemned to galleys, 10–11, 28, 29, 182–183, 184, 286, 312; and the revocation of Edict of Nantes, 10–11, 112, 115, 182–184, 286, 312–315; rigorous treatment of, 11, 29, 120–121, 126, 183–184; releases of, 236, 250, 252, 259–260, 275, 276; Tournier historian of, 114–121 passim, 125, 286. See also Huguenots

Prouyers, 227–228

Provence: 18, 22, 88, 191, 274, 315; forest resources of, 68, 81–82, 84; nobility of, 82, 95, 100–101; plague in, 179, 245–248, 286. See also Marseilles; Toulon

Prussia, seek release of religionnaires, 259–260

Puget, Pierre, sculptor, 24

Punishments: 27, 179, 188–189; of Protestants, 120–121, 126; by flogging, 121, 211–212; severity of, 126–127, 210–213, 220; by death, 136, 178, 179, 252, 275; by branding, 173–174; mutilating and corporal, 173–174, 177–178, 231, 266. See also Prisons, galleys as

Purses, forbidden aboard, 210–11

Pyrenees, source of beech and elm, 68

Quarantine, for plague, 245

Quay de la Ville, 62

Raab, 168

Ragusa, 168

Rambarde, 32, 33

Rance, Le Bouillier de, Chevalier, commandant of galley base, 246, 274

Rations: wine in, 35, 88, 206–207; in chains, 193–194; aboard galleys, 203–204; quantity and quality of, 203–204,

205–206, 218; en baraque, 276–277.
See also Victuals and supplies
Raymond, Jean, 287
Razilly, Chevalier Isaac de, commander
of Brittany squadron, 19
Réale (flagship): 24, 75, 212–213; size
and characteristics of, 71, 72; as hulk,
124, 200
Recollets, among American Indians, 164
Redemptorist Orders, role in releases,
263, 264
Regency, 260, 276
Régie, construction by, 72, 74
La Reine, 18
Releases, from galleys: 27; of Protestants,
236, 250, 252, 259–260, 275, 276; of
invalids, 250, 252, 253; prerequisites
for, 251–252; problems of, 251–252,
295; and financial condition, 252, 253,
254, 262, 295; of turcs, 260–261, 264–
265; regular, 275, 276, 295
Religion, and differences in treatment
of oarsmen, 10, 11, 12, 29, 120–121,
126, 138–141, 183–184, 280, 286. *See
also* Papacy; Protestants; Turcs
Religion, La (Order of Malta), *see* Order
of the Hospital of St. John
Religion Prétendue Reformée (R.P.R.),
official designation of Protestant religion, 29. *See also* Huguenots; Protestants
Renegades, 3, 11, 144
Rennes, prison at, 189
Reunion, a step toward abandoning
galleys, 281–282
Revocation of the Edict of Nantes, 10–
11, 112, 115, 137, 182–184, 286, 312–
315
Revolts: by oarsmen, 126, 212–213, 257;
on chains, 196–197
Rewards, 266
Rhine River, 42
Rhodes, 144, 147
Rhône River, 37, 274; timber rafted on,
14, 68; chains on, 191, 193
Rice, in victualing, 88
Richelieu, Cardinal: 26, 187; counsels
construction of galleys, 18–23 *passim*;
service to Crown and Church, 19, 20
Rive Neuve, 62
Roannes, Count de Lieutenant General
of the Galleys: 274; on treatment of
oarsmen 189, 206, 212, 220; oppose
releasing turcs, 265
Rochechouart, Louis Victor de, Count
(later Duke) de Vivonne, General of

the Galleys: 89, 103, 157; on victuals,
205–206; and oarsmen, 223, 267
Rochefort: 37, 39, 53, 270, 318; con-
structions at, 232, 255; bagne at, 282–
283, 288, 289–290
Roches, Chevalier de, sent to Malta, 18
Rome, 33
Rome, Sieur de, commissaire des galères,
73
Rosas, Spanish garrison at, 38
Rouen, 191
Roussillon, 35
Rowing force, *see* Oarsmen
Roye, Marquis de, 274
Rozel, Commissaire, quoted, 197, 243,
259
R.P.R., *see* Huguenots; Protestants
Russian Christians, as possible oarsmen,
152, 153, 154
Ryswick, Treaty of, 259

Saddlers, employ oarsmen, 229
Sailing navy: 13, 16, 35, 46, 274–275;
rivalry of officers with galleys, 53, 105–
106. *See also* Toulon
Sailmakers, oarsmen as, 231, 242
Sailors: duties of, 111; quarters aboard,
208, 210; as day-laborers, 234
Saint-Aignan, Duke de, 277
Saint-Christophe (St. Kitts), 256
Saint-Croix, 256
Saint-Esprit, Order of, 305
St.-Florentin, minister of marine, policy
of toward Protestants, 286, 287
Saint John, Order of, *see* Order of the
Hospital of Saint John
Saint Louis, Order of, *see* Order of St.
Louis
St.-Martin, 256
Saint Michael, Order of, 305
St. Nicolas, Citadel of, at Marseilles, 54
Saint-Priest, intendant at Languedoc,
286
Saint Tropez, 187
Salé: as source of slaves, 143, 144; priva-
teers of, 277
Salgas, Baron de, harsh treatment of
on galleys, 183–184
Salis, Sieur Chevalier de, seeks to buy
slaves, 168, 169, 170
Salonica, plague at, 245
Salt monopoly: enforcement of, 181, 184,
185–187, 188, 189, 276; releases of
smugglers, 275
Salutes, at sea: types of, 48–50; cam-
paigns for, 277, 315

Sandals and shoes, provided oarsmen, 223

Sardinia: 146, 224; as Spanish base, 19, 36; for victualing, 88

Sault, Count of, 73

Saumur, prison of, 190

Savoy: 17; as source of oarsmen, 147, 187; and Maltese corsairs, 152, 153

Sawyers, in construction of galleys, 77

School: of naval warfare, galleys of St. John as, 23, 25, 26, 98, 228; for trades, 27, 225–232; for galley construction, 74–75, 232–233; for petty officers, 227–228; for chaplains, 336n

Sculptors: decorate galleys, 24; oarsmen as, 229

Sea worms, as occasional problem, 82–83

Seaworthiness, of galleys, 31, 32, 33

Seignelay, Marquis de, see Colbert(s)

Seine River, 191

Self-policing (pairing), in security system, 290–291, 291–293

Senegal Company, 154, 155, 156

Separation system: need for, 291–293; criticized, 291–293, 293–294

Servants, turcs as, 230

Sète, see Cette

Seven Towers, 283

Ship of the line, 13, 15, 46

Ship timber, see Timber

Shipwrights: schools for, 74–75, 232–233; master, 77

Shoemakers, oarsmen as, 226, 229, 242

Siam, 311

Sicily: 33, 49–50; as Spanish base, 33, 41; slave market of, 146

Silk workers, employ oarsmen, 229

Simian, Nicolas, receiver general of Provence, 238

Sixtus V, Pope, 140

Slavery, Mediterranean: of infidels, 138, 139–143, 284–285, 305–307, 308–310; of Christians, 139–140, 171, 264–265, 309, 339n; varied forms of 141–142; as research problem, 338n

Slaves: West African, 29, 154–160, 309–310; American Indian, 29, 163–166, 310–311. See also Turcs

Smugglers of salt, galley penalty for, 181, 184, 185–187, 188, 189, 276

Smyrna: 144; plague at, 245

Sobieski, John III, King of Poland, raises siege of Vienna, 166, 314

Soissons, prisons of, 186

Soldiers: 130, 247, 278–279; recruitment of, 109–111, 131, 132; exploited by officers, 131, 133–135; drills of, 133; on board, 209–210, 267–268; invalids as, 258–259, 275

Soldiers, Ottoman, enslaved, 142, 167, 341–342n

Sourdis, 187

Spain: 49, 167; use of galleys by, 8, 10, 16, 20–22, 33, 41, 42–45, 222, 299–300; communications of, 16, 20–22, 33, 42–45, 222; relations of with France, 16, 20–22, 41, 48, 187–188, 272–273, 277, 299–300, 315; at La Rochelle, 20

Spanish Succession, War of: 243; effect of on Galley Corps, 272–273, 274; oarsmen serve in, 258–259, 275

Stockings, made in bagne, 242

Stevedores, oarsmen as, 230

Strasbourg, intendant at, on conductors, 199

Strikebreakers, oarsmen as, 233–235

Sultan, see Ottoman Empire

Superior General, see Congrégation de la Mission

Surgeon General, 122–124

Switzerland: 11, 219; reaction in to revocation, 187; convicts sent to French galleys, 288

Tabarka, expedition to, 277

Tailors, oarsmen as, 226

Tangier, bagne at, 235

Taragona, Battle of (1641), 21

Taverns: aboard galleys, 27, 128–129, 207–208; comite as tavern keeper, 128–129, 207–208, 240–241; in bagne, 240–241

Teachers, oarsmen as, 227–228

Teignmouth, 41

Tents: of galleys, 203, 209–210; manufactured in bagne, 242

Ternes, Marquis de, squadron commander: 96; on conductors, 191

Tessé, Marshal de: 222; on Galley Corps, 273

Testament politique (Richelieu), 21, 22

Theft: galley penalty for, 179, 210; aboard galleys, 210

Thirty Years War, 187

Timber, shipbuilding: sources of supply, 14, 68, 73, 81–82, 84, 329n; importance of seasoning, 78, 79, 80–82, 86; softwood in, 82

Tincourt, Chevalier de, French consul at Malta, as slave buyer, 148, 154, 167

Tobacco, on galleys, 27

Tobacco monopoly, enforcement of, 184–185, 185–186, 189, 276

Tolerance, religious, see Edict of Nantes

Toulon: 19, 53, 82, 203; oarsmen at, 13, 230, 234, 280, 282, 287, 288; as galley base, 42, 53, 84, 222, 283; as base of sailing navy, 53, 274–275; plague at, 247–248; galleys as prisons at, 270, 289–290, 292–293, 318; bagne at, 288

Toulouse, 191

Tour de Saint-Bernard (Paris), 268

Tournier, Gaston, Protestant historian: criticisms by, 114–121 passim; research on condemnations, 286

Tours, prison of, 190

Transatlantic voyages, by galleys, 35

Transportation, see West Indies

Treaties of peace and trade, with North African states: 150, 160–163 passim, 172, 263, 283, 284, 303, 308, 340n; difficulties of enforcing, 161, 162, 163

Trieste (Pirano), 169–170

Trinitarians, see Redemptorists

Tripoli: 316; as source of slaves, 143, 144; treaties with, 160, 163, 284, 307; bombarded, 277; imports timber, 329n

Tunis: campaigns against, 36, 277; as source of slaves, 143, 144, 261–262; treaties with, 160, 163, 284

Turcs: 5, 29, 44; treatment of, 11, 211; elite of the oar, 142–143, 220, 232, 279–280; symbolism of, 142–143, 232, 279–280, 283–284; Christianized, 154, 264–265; numbers of, 171–172, 279–281, 285, 286; rights of, 184–185, 285; employment of, 215, 216–217, 230, 232–233, 349n; communications of censored, 218–219; in plague, 246–248; releases of, 260–261, 349n. See also Infidels; Oarsmen

Turin, 193

Turks, see Ottoman Empire

Tursis, Duke de, 41, 329n

Tuscany, Duke of, slaves of, 146, 148, 171

Tyrrhenian Sea, 15

Unemployment, 234

United Kingdom, see English

United Provinces, see Dutch

Urban VIII, Pope, prohibits slavery, 140

Utrecht, Treaty of, 259

Vagabonds: galley penalty for, 180; arrested in Paris and sent to West Indies, 260

"Vaguans des Landes" (of Gascony), to the oar, 181

Valbelle, Jean-Baptiste de, as an officer, 101–102, 127

Valjean, Jean (fictional character), 318

Varkonyi, Mme A., 342n

Vauban, Sébastien Le Prestre, marquis de, 61

Vaucresson, M. de, 265

Vegetables, for victualing, 88

Velasco, Don Roderigo de, Spanish commander, 21

Velleron, Marquis de, 105

Venality, subversive of royal power, 103–104

Venereal disease, 216, 231

Venetian Republic: and galleys, 12, 16, 17, 79, 153, 298, 333n; and timber, 14, 79, 329n; and privateers, 140–141; as source of slaves, 166–167, 168, 306

Versailles: small galleys at, 24; expenditure for, 258

Vertot, Abbé de, quoted, 98, 146

Vervins, prison at, 186

Vessels and galleys, compared as to cost, 46–47

Vialet, Montmort's secretary, 120

Victuals and supplies: 35, 129; listed, 88; difficulties with, 90, 91; quality of, 205–206, 218. See also Rations

Vienna, 168

Vienne, 196

La Vigilante, "revolt" aboard, 257

Viking routes, 35

Villefranche: 17, 39; forçats at, 187

Vincent de Paul, Saint, chaplain general of the galleys: 3, 114, 116; legacy of, 213, 246

Vincheguerre, Jacques de, Knight of Malta, 18

Vinegar, for victualing, 88

Vintimille, Charles-François de, Count du Luc, 335n

Viviers, Guillaume Clement de, squadron commander, criticizes fraudulent releases, 253–254

Vivonne, Duke de, see Rochechouart, Louis Victor

Voltaire: quoted, 27–28; critic of religious persecution, 286, 287

Wages: forced and free compared, 231, 233–235, 282; in plague, 247

379

War, privateering (in Mediterranean): 23, 329–330n; multiple motive of, 17, 141–142; and pirates, 19; English, 40; recalled to Malta, 140–141. *See also* Crusading

Weather: and navigation by galleys, 15, 32, 33, 34, 46; winter on chains, 198–199; winter aboard, 203, 210

Weights and Measures, different systems of, 90, 91

West Africans, *see* Blacks, West African

West Indies: inhabitants of not to be enslaved, 140; oarsmen deported to, 177, 260, 275; unfit and invalid sent to, 183, 184, 188, 255–256, 256–257, 260, 262; converts sent to, 251, 287

Wharves, criticized, 62

Wheelwrights, employ oarsmen, 229

Wigmakers, oarsmen as, 226

Wine: on galleys, 27, 128–129, 207–208; in victualing, 35, 88, 129; controls on, 206–208; in bagne, 240–241

Women, consorting with oarsmen, 231

Wood carving, oarsmen work at, 226

Wool combers, employ oarsmen, 229

Work, rehabilitative, *see* Oarsmen; Prisons, galleys as

Worms and dry rot, in galleys, 82–83, 84

Zaandam, shipyards at, 69

Zara, 168